PHILOSOPHICAL
DICTIONARY

PHILOSOPHICAL DICTIONARY

VOLTAIRE

EDITED AND WITH AN INTRODUCTION BY
JOHN R. IVERSON

BARNES & NOBLE
NEW YORK

THE BARNES & NOBLE
LIBRARY OF ESSENTIAL READING

Introduction and Suggested Reading
© 2006 by Barnes & Noble, Inc.

Originally published in 1764

This 2006 edition published by Barnes & Noble, Inc.

Barnes & Noble, Inc.
122 Fifth Avenue
New York, NY 10011

ISBN: 978-0-7607-7176-1

Printed and bound in the United States of America

3 5 7 9 10 8 6 4

Contents

INTRODUCTION

ON JULY 1, 1766, IN THE FRENCH TOWN OF ABBEVILLE, THE chevalier de La Barre, age nineteen, was ceremonially tortured, beheaded, and burned, his ashes scattered to the winds. In the eighteenth century, his actions — failing to doff his hat in the presence of the Holy Host and singing impious songs — were not normally punished by death. But this young blasphemer was also guilty of owning a book that had been banned immediately upon publication in 1764, and his execution was in part an act of retaliation by the members of the Parisian *Parlement* against its author. This book, which was burned along with La Barre's body, was Voltaire's *Philosophical Dictionary*, one of the most emblematic works of the French Enlightenment. Caustic, witty, and bold, the work was accused by French authorities of undermining the foundations of civil society by rashly applying human reason to matters long considered sacred. The two small volumes of the *Philosophical Dictionary* did not claim to present a complete or systematic exposition of philosophical ideas. Rather, the articles they contained chipped away at the archaic institutional structures of Old Regime France and the power of the Catholic Church, denouncing the absurdities of traditional dogma and profoundly questioning the existing social and religious order.

In 1764, when the *Philosophical Dictionary* appeared, Voltaire was an enfeebled seventy-year-old hypochondriac living in virtual exile, far from the French capital. But he was also an extremely prolific writer universally recognized as the leader of the Enlightenment. Based in his château near the Swiss border, he dedicated the last twenty years of his life to an epic struggle, attacking hypocrisy and championing the free exercise of critical reason. In 1759, his *Candide*, a scandalous philosophical tale, articulated a lesson of constructive engagement in the world by brilliantly satirizing the philosophy of "optimism" and its passive acceptance of evil and human suffering. In 1763, the *Treatise on Tolerance* powerfully rejected religious fanaticism and promoted the idea that freedom of conscience was a philosophical and political necessity. In 1764, finally, building on the success of his previous works, Voltaire launched his most aggressive attack against superstition and religious prejudice, the *Philosophical Dictionary*. Like *Candide* and the *Treatise on Tolerance*, this work used innovative literary techniques to reshape contemporary debates. The result was the third great masterwork from this most fertile period of Voltaire's life. At the time of his death in 1778, he was hailed as the figurehead of an age that prided itself on its dedication to the idea of progress and the spirit of rational inquiry.

As a younger man, Voltaire had pursued more conventional kinds of success by writing in the most esteemed literary genres. Born in 1694 to a wealthy Parisian family, his given name was François Marie Arouet. He received a humanistic education at Louis-le-Grand, the most prestigious school in France, run by the Jesuits. In this setting, he studied the classics and regularly completed rhetorical exercises including poetic and dramatic composition. In 1718, his version of the Oedipus story—the first of some forty theatrical works he produced—earned him accolades as the next great French tragedian. Also at this time he adopted the name he would use throughout the rest of his life—Voltaire. Soon thereafter, he published the *Henriade*, an epic poem based on France's sixteenth-century Religious Wars and King Henry IV's ascension to the throne. By 1745, Voltaire's fame as a writer, reinforced by social connections at the court of Louis XV in Versailles, earned him membership in the French Academy, the title of Royal Historiographer, and an honorary position as Gentleman of the Royal Chamber. At the same time, however, while Voltaire was generally admired for the diversity of his talents, his constant challenges to authority were widely recognized. At age twenty-two, in the first of many encounters with censorship and police repression, he was exiled from Paris on suspicion of composing satirical poetry targeting the Regent Philippe d'Orleans. He also took great interest in radical new philosophical ideas. After a period of exile in England where many of these ideas originated, he published a series of religious, political, and literary essays, the *Letters Concerning the English Nation* (1734), and an introduction to Newtonian physics (1738) that helped revolutionize scientific thinking in France. Even in his seemingly more conventional works, Voltaire worked to promote controversial notions like religious tolerance. The tragedies *Zaïre* (1732) and *Alzire* (1736) dramatized the cruelty he associated with prejudice and narrow parochialism.

In 1736, Voltaire's brilliant reputation brought him into contact with another of the period's most remarkable individuals, the crown prince of Prussia, later known as Frederick the Great. An aspiring poet and fervent admirer of the Enlightenment, the young prince wrote to Voltaire as a disciple eager to receive advice from the greatest writer of the day. When Frederick assumed the throne in 1740, he urged Voltaire to accept a position in his court at Potsdam where several radical writers had already taken refuge. In 1750, frustrated by his experience at Versailles and mourning the death of his longtime lover, the marquise Du Châtelet, Voltaire finally yielded to Frederick's invitation. Although the *philosophe* abandoned Potsdam in 1753, after a falling-out with the "Philosopher King," it was on Prussian soil that the *Philosophical Dictionary* first took shape.

At Frederick's court, Voltaire found some of the boldest thinkers of his day. Dinners at the palace of Sans-Souci were typically animated by irreverent discussion of philosophical and religious questions. According to Voltaire's secretary, Collini, one of these discussions gave birth to the idea of a "philosophical dictionary," a collective enterprise that would attack the Judeo-Christian tradition. Indeed, Voltaire's correspondence reflects the rapid evolution of this concept. The *philosophe* immediately sent to his royal patron articles dealing with religious subjects that would later reappear in the *Philosophical Dictionary*—"Atheist," "Baptism," etc. Voltaire's departure from Prussia effectively put an end to the project as it was originally conceived, since it was clearly intended to be a collaborative undertaking developed under Frederick's direction. But the seed of the work had been planted, waiting only for a time when Voltaire would enjoy sufficient personal freedom to give full rein to his ideas.

Voltaire eventually took up residence near Geneva in 1755. His arrival there coincided with the heroic era of the French Enlightenment, the years marked by the movement's most ambitious publications. Chief among these was the *Encyclopedia*, directed by Diderot and d'Alembert, with the collaboration of Montesquieu, Rousseau, and d'Holbach, among others. This massive work aspired to integrate all current knowledge in the arts, sciences, and literature. Its seventeen volumes of text and eleven volumes of images highlighted the Enlightenment's spirit of philosophical and technical progress. Published in Paris, however, and therefore subject to royal oversight, the *Encyclopedia* ran afoul of civil and religious authorities. In 1752 and again in 1759, official decrees interrupted the publication of the *Encyclopedia*, reflecting the constant threat of censorship that hung over all French works.

Partly as a response to the difficulties encountered by the *Encyclopedia*, Voltaire modified his writing strategies in order to evade censorship. He particularly advocated short works, claiming that cheap, portable books were the most effective means of communicating with a broader audience. Often, as with *Candide*, Voltaire hid behind a thin veil of anonymity and refused to acknowledge authorship of works that were quickly suppressed by censors in France. In other cases, he signed his works openly and used massive epistolary campaigns to generate public support for his ideas. In 1762, when religious fanaticism resulted in the torture and execution of Jean Calas, a Protestant merchant falsely convicted of murdering his own son, Voltaire used both techniques as he worked to obtain a revised judgment. In 1765, these efforts were finally rewarded when a decree from Versailles reestablished Calas' innocence.

Using diverse strategies, Voltaire thus assailed with increasing frequency the intolerance and hypocrisy he observed around him, imperiously calling for destruction of *l'Infâme*. (The term might be rendered in English as "The Unspeakable," "The Vile," or "Infamy.") It was in this spirit that he resurrected the idea of a philosophical dictionary. With respect to the earlier formulation of this project, two important things had changed. Voltaire now felt an even greater sense of urgency, brought on by repressive measures in France that jeopardized the progress of the preceding decades. The Calas affair, in particular, had served as a bloody reminder that religious fanaticism was alive and well, capable of eliminating its victims in the most horrifying manner. In addition, Voltaire had achieved a degree of personal independence that enabled him to act more boldly than in 1752. His isolation on the Swiss border and his immense fortune gave him a certain feeling of invulnerability. His "dictionary of heresies," as he now called it, was, therefore, no longer designed simply for the amusement of a liberal-minded monarch. As it evolved during the early 1760s, the work targeted a wide European public.

In the *Philosophical Dictionary*, Voltaire capitalized on a recent publishing trend. During the 1750s and 1760s, dictionaries abounded on the shelves of French booksellers. The tremendous vogue of alphabetical works responded to the period's fondness for the orderly classification of knowledge. This phenomenon was also the product of a burgeoning trade in printed matter that made books an increasingly common part of life for reasonably well-to-do members of European society. Among the available titles, dozens of specialized dictionaries dealing with topics ranging from language to horsemanship led one critic to call this the "century of the dictionary." Some of these were voluminous works of erudition, presenting knowledge in an easily accessible form. Others assumed the dimensions of a "pocket" volume, providing a succinct overview of a particular subject and allowing readers to peruse articles as their whims might dictate. In the *Philosophical Dictionary*, Voltaire adopted the second of these two models. The work's original title — *Portable Philosophical Dictionary* — amply demonstrates this filiation, as does the author's preface: "Individuals of all conditions will find something both instructive and amusing. This book does not require continuous reading; but at whatever page it is opened, it will furnish matter for reflection." For eighteenth-century readers, the general form of Voltaire's dictionary was thus quite familiar. Indeed, some may have been acquainted with an earlier work bearing exactly the same title, published in 1751.

Familiarity with the "pocket dictionary" format would not, however, have prepared eighteenth-century readers for the *Philosophical Dictionary*'s polemical verve and rhetorical pyrotechnics. From the opening of the article "Abbé" — which quotes a popular eighteenth-century song —, to the conclusion of the article "Virtue" — where the author responds to critics of the Emperor Antoninus by wishing for other "such knaves" —, Voltaire constantly surprises his reader. Occasionally, as in the article

"Enthusiasm," he begins in conventional fashion, providing a definition. More frequently, he seeks to intrigue and provoke, beginning with a query ("Metamorphosis"), an enigma ("Fanaticism"), or a response to an imaginary interlocutor ("Limits of the human mind"). He frames some of the articles as found documents ("Civil and ecclesiastical laws"), others as short stories ("Glory") or dialogues ("Papism"), and others still as historical inquests ("Salomon"). His tone ranges from serious ("Atheism") to gay ("Job"), from respectful ("Julian the Philosopher") to indignant ("Torture"). He uses irony, sarcasm, enumerations, maxims, and quotations to engage the reader, creating an eminently readable work that bears little resemblance to what we today expect from a "dictionary."

The explanation for this astonishing variety of textual procedures resides in the fact that Voltaire's "dictionary" is anything but a collection of objective definitions. On the contrary, it is a keenly polemical work, designed to refute, persuade, and convince. To this end, the text seeks to create a sort of complicity, forcing the reader to draw larger conclusions from Voltaire's examples and arguments. As the preface explains, "The most useful books are those to which the readers themselves contribute half; they elaborate on the thoughts that are presented to them in embryonic form; they correct that which seems defective to them, and they strengthen by their reflections that which to them seems weak." To the modern reader, the *Philosophical Dictionary* sometimes proves disconcerting, particularly because of its constant attacks on Jews and Judaism, and its emphatic use of insignificant, albeit humorous, details and absurd anecdotes taken from the Bible ("On Ezekiel") or hagiographic literature ("Martyr"). But, as Voltaire's preface suggests, these details are not supposed to constitute, in themselves, a substantive critique of the Judeo-Christian tradition. Rather, they lead the reader to extrapolate and to ask whether any religion (or any religious

institution, like the Catholic Church) that includes such foolishness in its teachings deserves the adherence of rational
beings. The response Voltaire seeks from his reader is, of
course, one that rejects religious orthodoxy and prejudice in
order to embrace more essential principles, like reason and
philosophical moderation. Accordingly, the articles dealing
with specific texts and points of dogma are reinforced by others that confront larger ideas and challenge us to cultivate the
better angels of our nature, that is, those qualities that can
improve life on earth for all, regardless of differences in creed
or custom. This aspect of the *Philosophical Dictionary* emerges
gradually, as some articles destroy preconceptions and others
equip the reader with new analytical tools. Thus, despite the
fragmentation of the alphabetical form, the work ultimately
communicates a powerful message of justice and tolerance. In
tandem with the infectious corrosiveness of Voltaire's wit, this
positive content grants the *Dictionary* an eloquence that still
speaks today.

Voltaire's readers proved to be adept interpreters of the
Philosophical Dictionary. In particular, those in positions of
privilege—those most threatened by its relentless jibes—
quickly condemned it as a work of dangerous impiety. The
censor's report submitted to the Magnificent Council of
Geneva in June 1764 insightfully indicated that the haphaz-
ard order of the alphabetical articles actually *increased* their
critical impact by dissolving the overarching coherence of
Christian theology. It also spoke pertinently of Voltaire's ability
to desacralize religious matters and thus undermine the moral
underpinnings of civil society. In thus emphasizing the destruc-
tive force of the *Philosophical Dictionary*, the report to the
Genevan Council anticipated numerous other hostile assess-
ments. (As an example, the Appendix contains excerpts from
the *Anti-Philosophical Dictionary* by Louis Mayeul Chaudon.)

After Voltaire's death in 1778, the two-volume work from the 1760s disappeared as later editors indiscriminately combined its articles with hundreds of other short texts. Nevertheless, the original *Philosophical Dictionary* continued to shape attitudes towards Voltaire. Throughout the nineteenth century, particularly when relations between Church and State turned sour, both admirers and critics of Voltaire focused on the negative power of his anti-religious writings. Defenders of religion demonized the *philosophe* and his sardonic smile, while freethinkers lionized him as a brilliant iconoclast. Nevertheless, the affirmative humanism of Voltaire's struggles was not lost on readers like the great novelist and poet, Victor Hugo. In a speech commemorating Voltaire's death in 1878, Hugo drew an intentionally provocative parallel, "Jesus wept; Voltaire smiled." His point was not that Voltaire was a new Messiah; rather, he presented both figures as champions of humanity who made the lives of their fellow human beings better. While Jesus, according to Hugo, accomplished this by showing compassion and by helping the downtrodden, Voltaire achieved similar results by using the mocking power of his pen to correct the inequities of the age in which he lived. Indeed, still today, this idea of the engaged intellectual is the strongest portion of the Voltairean legacy.

John R. Iverson is Assistant Professor of French language and literature at Whitman College in Walla Walla, Washington. His research interests center on Voltaire and the notion of glory and emulation in eighteenth-century France.

NOTES ON THE TEXT

TWO PARTICULAR FEATURES OF THE PHILOSOPHICAL DICTIONARY deserve special mention. As part of his efforts to cloud questions of authorial responsibility, Voltaire added fictitious attributions to certain articles. Some of these names refer to real (though dead) eighteenth-century writers, while others thinly mask his own identity (the author of "Job," for example, is listed as "an invalid at the waters of Aix-la-Chapelle"). Also notable are the notes Voltaire added to the text. (In the present edition, Voltaire's notes are configured as footnotes. Additional endnotes have been added as an aid to the modern reader.) Though not numerous, these notes provided him with an important means of channeling the attentions of his readers, providing the key to coded names (as in "The Japanese Catechism") or responding to critics of earlier editions of the *Dictionary*. Indeed, between 1764 and 1769, Voltaire issued six successive states of the work, as he gradually increased the number of articles from 73 to 118.

For modern scholarly purposes, the Voltaire Foundation's recent critical edition, completed under the direction of Christiane Mervaud, is now the authoritative reference (*Les Oeuvres completes de Voltaire* vols. 35-36 [Oxford, 1994]). For this English language edition, the basic translation was taken from the 1901 E. R. DuMont edition of *The Works of Voltaire*, edited and supplemented as needed to correspond to the text of the 1769 edition. For their help in preparing the text, my heartfelt thanks go to Katie Firman, Sarah Hurlburt, and Nicole Schaub.

PHILOSOPHICAL DICTIONARY

PRÉFACE / PREFACE[1]

THERE HAVE ALREADY BEEN FIVE EDITIONS OF THIS *DICTIONARY*, but all are incomplete and disfigured; we were unable to oversee any of them. Finally we offer this one, which will prove superior to the others in terms of correctness, organization, and the number of articles. We have drawn them all from the best authors in Europe, and we have had no scruples in sometimes copying a page from a familiar book when this page seemed necessary to our collection. There are complete articles from individuals who are still living, including several learned pastors. These passages have long been well known to the learned community, like *Apocalypse, Christianity, Messiah, Moses, Miracles*, etc. But in the article *Miracles* we have added an entire page by the famous doctor Middleton, librarian in Cambridge.

There are also several passages by the learned Bishop of Gloucester, Warburton. The manuscripts of M. Dumarsais have been very useful to us; but we rejected unanimously all that seemed to favor Epicureanism. The tenet of Providence is so sacred, and so necessary to the happiness of the human race, that no honest man should lead readers to doubt a truth that can do no harm in any case and can always produce great good.

We do not view this tenet of universal Providence as a system of thought but rather as a thing that is evident to all reasonable minds. On the other hand, diverse systems regarding the nature of the soul, grace, or metaphysical opinions, which create divisions between different faiths, can be subjected to examination. Since they have been under discussion for seventeen hundred years, it is clear that they are not at all characterized by certainty. These are enigmas that each individual can resolve according to the penchant of his thoughts.

The article *Genesis* comes from a very clever man who enjoys the favor and confidence of a great prince; we ask his pardon for having shortened this text. The limitations we imposed on this work did not allow us to print it in its entirety; it would have filled nearly half of one volume.

Regarding purely literary questions, the sources we have used will be easily recognized. We have tried to combine the useful with the agreeable, and we have no other role and no merit in this work except with respect to the selection of the passages included. Individuals of all conditions will find something both instructive and amusing. This book does not require continuous reading; but at whatever page it is opened, it will furnish matter for reflection. The most useful books are those to which the readers themselves contribute half; they elaborate on the thoughts that are presented to them in embryonic form; they correct that which seems defective to them, and they strengthen by their reflections that which to them seems weak.

In fact, this book should really be read only by enlightened individuals; ordinary men are not made for such knowledge; philosophy will never be open to them. Those who say that there are truths that must be hidden from the people need not be alarmed. The common people do not read; they work six days each week and on the seventh go drinking. In a word, philosophical works are made only for philosophers, and every honest man should try to be a philosopher, without priding himself on being one.

We conclude by offering our most humble apologies to the distinguished individuals who graced us with several new articles, since we were unable to use them as we had hoped; they arrived too late. We are all the more touched by their generosity and their admirable zeal.

ABBÉ / ABBÉ

WHERE ARE YOU GOING, MONSIEUR L'ABBÉ? ETC. [2] ARE YOU AWARE that the word *abbé* signifies *father*? If you become one, you render a service to the state; you doubtless perform the best work that a man can perform; you give birth to a thinking being. In this action there is something divine.

But if you are only *Monsieur l'Abbé* because you have had your head shaved, wear a small collar and a short cloak, and are waiting for a fat benefice, you do not deserve the name of *abbé*.

The ancient monks gave this name to the superior whom they elected. The *abbé* was their spiritual father. What different things the same words signify at different times! The spiritual *abbé* was once a poor man at the head of others equally poor. But the poor spiritual fathers have since acquired incomes of two hundred or four hundred thousand pounds, and there are poor spiritual fathers in Germany who have regiments of guards.

A poor man, making a vow of poverty and, in consequence, becoming a sovereign? It has been said, and it must be repeated a thousand times, this is intolerable! The laws exclaim against such an abuse, religion is indignant at it, and the true poor, who lack food and clothing, appeal to heaven on *Monsieur l'Abbé's* doorstep.

But I hear the *abbés* of Italy, Germany, Flanders, and Burgundy ask: "Why shouldn't we accumulate wealth and honors? Why shouldn't we become princes? The bishops, who were originally poor, are like us; they have enriched and elevated themselves; one of them has become superior even to kings; let us imitate them as far as we are able."

Gentlemen, you are right. Invade the land; it belongs to him whose strength or skill obtains possession of it. You have made ample use of times of ignorance, superstition, and infatuation, to strip us of our inheritances and trample us under your feet, that you might get fat from the substance of the unfortunate. Tremble for fear that the day of reason will arrive!

ABRAHAM / **ABRAHAM**

ABRAHAM is one of those names that was famous in Asia Minor and Arabia, as Thaut was among the Egyptians, the first Zoroaster in Persia, Hercules in Greece, Orpheus in Thrace, Odin among the northern nations, and so many others, known more by their notoriety than by any authentic history. I speak here of profane history only; as for that of the Jews, our masters and our enemies, whom we at once detest and believe, their history having evidently been written by the Holy Ghost, we have for it all the respect it deserves. We will address here only the Arabs. They boast of having descended from Abraham through Ishmael, believing that this patriarch built Mecca and died there. The fact is that the race of Ishmael has been infinitely more favored by God than has that of Jacob. Both races, it is true, have produced robbers; but the Arabian robbers have been prodigiously superior to the Jewish ones. The descendants of Jacob conquered only a very small country, which they have lost, whereas the descendants of Ishmael conquered parts of Asia, Europe, and Africa, established an empire more extensive than that of the Romans, and drove the Jews from their caverns, which they called The Promised Land.

Judging of things only by examples found in our modern histories, it would be difficult to believe that Abraham was the father of two nations so vastly different. We are told that he was born in Chaldaea, and that he was the son of a poor potter, who earned his bread by making small earthen idols. It is hardly likely that this son of a potter should have passed through impracticable deserts and founded the city of Mecca, at a distance of four hundred leagues, under a tropical sun. If he was a conqueror, he doubtless cast his eyes on the fine country of Assyria. If he was no more than a poor man, as he has been depicted, he did not found kingdoms abroad.

The Book of Genesis relates that he was seventy-five years old when he went out of the land of Haran after the death of his father, Terah the potter. But the same book also tells us that Terah, having begotten Abraham at the age of seventy years, lived to that of two hundred and five; and that Abraham left Haran only after the death of his father. By this count, it is clear from the Book of Genesis itself that Abraham was one hundred and thirty-five years old when he left Mesopotamia. He went from a reputedly idolatrous country to another idolatrous country named Sichem, in Palestine. Why did he go there? Why did he leave the fertile banks of the Euphrates for a spot as remote, barren, and stony as Sichem? The Chaldaean language must have been quite different from the one in Sichem. It was not a place of trade, and Sichem was more than a hundred leagues from Chaldaea, and deserts lay between. But God wanted him to make this journey; he wanted to show him the land his descendants would occupy several centuries later. The human mind has difficulty understanding the reasons for such a journey.

Scarcely had he arrived in the little mountainous country of Sichem, when famine compelled him to leave it. He went into Egypt with his wife Sarah, to seek subsistence. The distance from Sichem to Memphis is two hundred leagues. Is it natural that a man should go so far to beg for wheat in a country where he did not understand the language? Truly these were strange journeys, undertaken at the age of nearly a hundred and forty years!

He brought with him to Memphis his wife, Sarah, who was extremely young, and almost an infant when compared with him; for she was only sixty-five. As she was very beautiful, he resolved to turn her beauty to account. "Say that you are my sister that it may go well with me because of you." He should rather have said to her, "Say that you are my *daughter.*" The king fell in love with the young Sarah, and gave the pretended brother an abundance of sheep, oxen, he-asses, she-asses, camels, men-servants, and maid-servants; which proves that Egypt was then powerful and well-regulated, and consequently an ancient king-dom, and that brothers who came and offered their sisters to the kings of Memphis received magnificent rewards.

The young Sarah was ninety years old when God promised her that Abraham, who was then a hundred and sixty, would get her pregnant within the year.

Abraham, who was fond of traveling, went into the horrible desert of Kadesh with his pregnant wife, ever young and ever pretty. A king of this desert could not fail to fall in love with Sarah, like the king of Egypt. The father of the faithful told the same lie as in Egypt, making his wife pass for his sister, which brought him more sheep, oxen, men-servants, and maid-servants. It might be said that this Abraham became rich principally on account of his wife. Commentators have written a prodigious number of volumes to justify Abraham's conduct, and to explain away the errors in chronology. We must therefore refer the reader to these commentaries. They are all composed by men with dis-cerning and acute minds, excellent metaphysicians, devoid of prejudice and by no means pedants.

For the rest, this name Bram, or Abram, was famous in India and in Persia. Several of the learned even assert that he was the same legislator whom the Greeks called Zoroaster. Others say that he was the Brahma of the Indians, which has not been proven. But it appears very reasonable to many scholars that this Abraham was Chaldaean or Persian. Later, the Jews boasted of having descended from him, just as the Franks descend from Hector, and the Bretons from Tubal. It cannot be denied that the Jewish nation were a very modern horde; that they did not establish themselves on the borders of Phoenicia until very late; that they were surrounded by ancient peoples, whose language they adopted, receiving from them even the name Israel, which is Chaldaean, according to the testimony of the Jew Philon. We know that they took the names of the angels from the Babylonians, and that they called God by the names Eloi or Eloa, Adonaï, Jehovah, or Hiao, after the Phoenicians.

It is probable that they knew the name of Abraham or Ibrahim only through the Babylonians; for the ancient religion of all the countries from the Euphrates to the Oxus was called Kish Ibrahim or Milat Ibrahim. This is confirmed for us by all the research made on the spot by the learned Hyde.

The Jews, then, treated ancient history and legend as their used clothing vendors treat old coats—they turn them inside out and sell them for new at as high a price as possible.

It is a singular example of human stupidity that we have so long considered the Jews as a nation that taught all others, while their historian Josephus himself confesses the contrary.

It is difficult to penetrate the shadows of antiquity; but it is evident that all the kingdoms of Asia were in a very flourishing state before the wandering horde of Arabs, called Jews, had a small spot of earth to call their own, before they had a town, laws, or even a fixed religion. When, therefore, we see an ancient rite or an ancient opinion established in Egypt or Asia, and also among the Jews, it is quite natural to conclude that this small, newly formed, ignorant, stupid people, deprived of all arts, copied, as well as they were able, the ancient, flourishing, and industrious nation.

It is on the basis of this principle that we must judge Judea, Biscay, Cornwall, Bergamo, the land of Harlequin, etc. Most certainly triumphant Rome did not in anything imitate Biscay, Cornwall, or Bergamo; and he who would say that the Jews taught anything to the Greeks must be either very ignorant or a great knave.

(article taken from M. Fréret)[3]

ADAM / **ADAM**

THE pious Madame Bourignon was sure that Adam was a hermaphrodite, like the first men of the divine Plato. God had revealed this great secret to her; but since I have not had the same revelation, I shall say nothing of the matter. The Jewish rabbis have read Adam's books; they know the names of his preceptor and his second wife; but since I have not read our first parent's books, I shall remain silent on these points. Some empty and very learned minds are quite astonished when they read the *Veidam* of the ancient Brahmins, to find that the first man was created in India, and called Adimo, which means "the begetter," and his wife, Procriti, meaning "life." They say the sect of the Brahmins is incontestably more ancient than that of the Jews; that it was not until very late that the Jews could write in the Canaanite language, since it was not until very late that they established themselves in the small country of Canaan. They say the Indians were always inventors and the Jews always imitators; the Indians always ingenious and the Jews always backwards. They say it is difficult to believe that Adam, who was fair and had hair on his head, was father to the Negroes, who are black as ink and have black wool in the place of hair. What, indeed, do they *not* say? As for me, I say nothing; I leave these matters to the

Reverend Father Berruyer of the Society of Jesus. He is the most perfect Innocent I have ever known. His book was burned as the work of a man who wished to make the Bible an object of ridicule; but I am quite sure he had no such wicked end in view.

(taken from a letter by the chevalier de R**)

ÂME / SOUL

IT would be a fine thing to see one's soul. *Know thyself* is an excellent precept; but it belongs only to God to put it into practice. Who but He can know His own essence?

We call *soul* that which animates. Owing to our limited intelligence, we know scarcely anything more of the matter. Three-fourths of mankind go no further, and give themselves no concern about the thinking being; the other fourth seek it; no one has found it, or ever will find it.

Poor pedant! You see a plant that vegetates, and you say, *vegetation*, or perhaps *vegetative soul*. You remark that bodies have and communicate motion, and you say, *force*; you see your hunting dog learn his craft from you, and you exclaim, *instinct, sensitive soul*! You have complex ideas, and you exclaim, *spirit*!

But pray, what do you understand by these words? This flower vegetates; but is there any real being called *vegetation*? This body pushes along another, but does it possess within itself a distinct being called *force*? Your dog brings you a partridge, but is there a being called *instinct*? Would you not laugh, if a quibbler—even if he were Alexander's preceptor—were to say to you: "All animals live; therefore there is in them a being, a substantial form, which is life?"

If a tulip could speak and were to tell thee: "I and my vegetation are two beings evidently joined together," wouldn't you laugh at the tulip?

Let us first see what you know with certainty: that you walk with your feet; that you digest with your stomach; that you feel with your whole body; and that you think with your head. Let us see if your reason alone can have given you light enough by which to conclude, without supernatural aid, that you have a soul.

The first philosophers, whether Chaldaeans or Egyptians, said: "There must be something within us that produces our thoughts; that something must be very subtle; it is a breath; it is fire; it is an ether; it is a quintessence; it is a slender likeness; it is an entelechy; it is a number; it is a harmony." Lastly, according to the divine Plato, it is a compound of the *same* and the *other*; it is atoms that think in us, said Epicurus, following Democrites. But, my friend, how does an atom think? Admit that you know nothing of the matter.

The opinion that one ought to adopt is, doubtless, that the soul is an immaterial being. But certainly you cannot grasp what an immaterial being is? No, answer the learned; but we know that its nature is to think. And how do you know this? We know it, because it thinks. Oh, learned ones! I am much afraid that you are as ignorant as Epicurus! The nature of a stone is to fall, because it does fall; but I ask you, what makes it fall?

We know, they continue, that a stone has no soul. Granted; I believe it as well as you. We know that an affirmative and a negative are not divisible, are not parts of matter. I am of your opinion. But matter, otherwise unknown to us, possesses qualities that are not material, that are not divisible; it has gravitation towards a center, which God has given it; and this gravitation has no parts; it is not divisible. The moving force of bodies is not a being composed of parts. In like manner the vegetation of organized bodies, their life, their instinct, are not beings apart, divisible beings; you can no more cut in two the vegetation of a rose, the life of a horse, the instinct of a dog, than you can cut in two a sensation, an affirmation, a negation. Therefore your fine argument, drawn from the indivisibility of thought, proves nothing at all.

What, then, do you call your *soul?* What idea do you have of it? You cannot by yourselves, without revelation, affirm the existence within you of anything other than an ability to feel and think that escapes your understanding.

Now tell me honestly, is this ability to feel and think the same as that which causes you to digest and to walk? You admit that it is not; for in vain might your understanding say to your stomach—*digest*; it will not, if it be sick. In vain might your immaterial being order your feet to walk; they will not stir, if they have the gout.

The Greeks clearly perceived that thought has frequently nothing to do with the play of our organs; they posited the existence of an animal soul for these organs, and for the thoughts a finer, subtler soul—a *nous.*

But we find that this soul of thought has, on a thousand occasions, the ascendancy over the animal soul. The thinking soul commands the hands to take, and they take. It does not tell the heart to beat, the blood to flow, the chyle to form; all this is done without it. Here then are two souls much intertwined, and neither fully in charge of the house.

Now, this first animal soul certainly does not exist; it is nothing more than the movement of our organs. Take heed, O man! lest you have no more proof but your weak reason that the other soul exists. You can know only by faith; you are born, you eat, you think, you wake, you sleep, without knowing how. God has given you the faculty of thinking, as He has given you all the rest; and if He had not come at the time appointed by His providence to teach you that you have an immaterial and immortal soul, you would have no proof of it whatever.

Let us examine the fine systems that philosophy has constructed around these souls.

One says that the soul of man is part of the substance of God Himself; another that it is part of the great whole; a third that it is created from all eternity; a fourth that it is made, rather than created. Others assure us that God makes souls gradually as they are needed, and that they arrive at the moment of copulation. They are lodged in the seminal animalcules, cries one. No, says another, they take up their abode in the Fallopian tubes. A third comes and says: You are all wrong; the soul waits for six weeks, until the fetus is formed, and then it takes possession of the pineal gland; but if it finds a false conception, it returns and waits for a better opportunity. The latest opinion is that its dwelling is in the corpus callosum; this is the position assigned to it by La Peyronie. Only the first surgeon to the king of France can dispose in this way of the lodging of the soul. Yet the corpus callosum did not enjoy the same success in this world as the surgeon.

St. Thomas in his seventy-fifth question and following, says that the soul is a form subsisting per se, that it is all in all, that its essence differs from its power; that there are three *vegetative* souls, viz., the *nutritive,* the *argumentative,* and the *generative;* that the memory of spiritual things is spiritual, and the memory of corporeal things is corporeal; that the rational soul is a form *immaterial in its operations,* and *material in its being.* St. Thomas wrote two thousand pages, of similar force and clarity; and he is the guiding spirit of scholasticism.

Nor have there been fewer systems concocted about the way in which this soul will feel when it has laid aside the body with which it felt previously; how it will hear without ears, smell without a nose, and touch without hands; what body it will afterwards adopt, whether that which it had at two years old or at eighty; how the *I,* the identity of the same person, will subsist; how the soul of a man who has become an imbecile at the age of fifteen, and dying as an imbecile at the age of seventy, will resume the thread of the ideas which he had at the age of puberty; by what contrivance a soul, the leg of whose body shall be cut off in Europe, and one of its arms lost in America, will recover this leg and arm, which, having been transformed into vegetables, will have passed into the blood of some other animal. We would never come to the end, if we were to seek to give an account of all the extravagances this poor human soul has imagined about itself.

It is very curious that, in the laws of God's people, not a word is said of the spirituality and immortality of the soul; nothing in the Decalogue, nothing in Leviticus or in Deuteronomy.

It is quite certain, it is indubitable, that Moses nowhere proposes to the Jews pains and rewards in another life; that he never mentions to them the immortality of their souls; that he never gives them hopes of heaven, nor threatens them with hell; all is temporal.

He told them, before his death, in Deuteronomy: "When you have had children and children's children and become complacent in the land, you will soon utterly perish from the land, and only a few of you will be left among the nations."

"I am a jealous God, punishing children for the iniquity of parents, to the third and fourth generation."

"Honor your father and your mother so that your days may be long."

"You will have bread forever without lack."

"If you obey, you will have the early rain and the later rain, grain, oil, wine, grass for your livestock, and you will eat your fill, and drink to your thirst."

"Put these words in your hearts, in your hands, between your eyes, write them on your doorposts, so that your days may multiply."

"Do what I command you, neither add to it nor take away from it."

"If a prophet appears among you and promises you prodigious things, if his prediction is true, and if his portents take place, and if he says to you, 'Let us follow other gods. . .' kill him immediately, and let all the nation strike with you."

"When the Lord has delivered nations to you, slay them all without sparing a single man, and have pity on none."

"You shall not eat impure animals, like the eagle, the griffin, the centaur, etc."

"You shall not eat animals that chew the cud and whose hoof is uncleft, like the camel, the hare, the porcupine, etc."

"By observing all the commandments, blessed shall you be in the city and in the field; blessed shall be the fruit of your womb, of your ground, and of your livestock. . . ."

"If you will not observe all the commandments and ceremonies, cursed shall you be in the city and in the field. . . you will experience famine, poverty, you will die from misery, cold, poverty, fever; you will have scurvy, the itch, boils. . . you will have ulcers on your knees and the fat part of your legs."

"Strangers will lend to you at interest, but you will not lend to them. . . because you will not have served the Lord."

"And you will eat the fruit of your womb, the flesh of your own sons and daughters, etc."

It is obvious that in all these promises and in all these threats everything is purely temporal, and there is not a word about the immortality of the soul or of a future life.

Many illustrious commentators have thought that Moses was perfectly acquainted with these two great dogmas; and they prove it by the words of Jacob, who, believing that his son had been devoured by wild beasts, said in his grief: *I will descend with my son into the grave*—in infernum—*into hell*; that is, *I will die, since my son is dead.*

They further prove it by passages in Isaiah and Ezekiel; but the Hebrews, to whom Moses spoke, could not have read either Ezekiel or Isaiah, who did not come until several centuries later.

It is quite useless to dispute about the private opinions of Moses. The fact is that in his public laws he never spoke of a life to come; that he limited all rewards and punishments to the present time. If he knew of a future life, why did he not expressly set forth that dogma? And if he did not know of it, what were the object and extent of his mission? These questions are raised by many notable persons. They respond that the master of Moses, and of all men, reserved for Himself the right of expounding to the Jews, at His own time, a doctrine that they were not in a condition to understand when they were in the desert.

If Moses had announced the immortality of the soul, a great school among the Jews would not have constantly combated it subsequently. The great school of the Sadducees would not have been authorized in the State; the Sadducees would not have filled the highest offices, nor would pontiffs have been chosen from their body.

It appears that it was not until after the founding of Alexandria that the Jews were divided into three sects—the Pharisees, the Sadducees, and the Essenes. The historian Josephus, who was a Pharisee, informs us in the thirteenth book of his *Antiquities* that the Pharisees believed in metempsychosis. The Sadducees believed that the soul perished with the body. The Essenes, says Josephus, held that souls were immortal; according to them souls descended in an aerial form into the body, from the highest region of the air, carried there by a violent attraction; and after death, those which had belonged to the good dwelt beyond the ocean in a country where there was neither heat nor cold, nor wind, nor rain; the souls of the wicked went into a climate of an opposite description. Such was the theology of the Jews.

He who alone was to instruct all men came and condemned these three sects; but without Him we could never have known anything of our soul; for the philosophers never had any determinate idea of it; and Moses—the only true lawgiver in the world before our own—Moses, who talked with God face to face, left men in the most profound ignorance on this great point. It is, then, only for seventeen hundred years that there has been any certainty of the soul's existence and immortality.

Cicero had only doubts; his grandson and granddaughter might have learned the truth from the first Galileans who came to Rome.

But before that time, and since then, in all the rest of the earth where the apostles did not penetrate, each individual must have said to his soul: What are you? Where do you come from? What do you do? Where do you go? You are I know not what, thinking and feeling. And were you to feel and think for a hundred thousand million years, you would never know any more by your own light, without the assistance of God.

O man! God has given you understanding so that you may behave well, and not so that you might penetrate into the essence of the things He created.

So thought Locke; and before Locke, Gassendi; and before Gassendi, a multitude of sages; but we have bachelors who know everything those great men didn't.

Some cruel enemies of reason have dared to rise up against these truths, acknowledged by all the wise. They have carried their dishonesty and impudence so far as to accuse the authors of this work with having affirmed that the soul is composed of matter. You well know, persecutors of innocence, that we have said quite the contrary. You must have read these very words against Epicurus, Democritus, and Lucretius: *My friend, how does an atom think? Admit that you know nothing of the matter.* It is evident that you are calumniators.

No one knows what that being is, which is called *spirit*, to which you give this material name, signifying *wind.* All the first fathers of the Church believed the soul to be corporeal. It is impossible for us limited beings to know whether our intelligence is substance or faculty: we cannot thoroughly know either the extended being, or the thinking being, or the mechanism of thought.

We exclaim to you, along with the respectable Gassendi and Locke, that we know nothing by ourselves of the secrets of the Creator. And are you gods, who know everything? We repeat to you, that you cannot know the nature and destination of the soul except by revelation. And is this revelation not sufficient for you? You must surely be enemies of this revelation that we call for, since you persecute those who expect everything from it and believe only in it.

We defer wholly, we say, to the word of God; and you, enemies of reason and of God, you who blaspheme against both, you treat the humble doubt and humble submission of the philosopher just as the wolf in Aesop's fables treated the lamb. You say to him: *You said ill of me last year; I must suck your blood.* Philosophy takes no revenge; she smiles in peace at your vain endeavors; she slowly enlightens the men whom you seek to render as stupid as yourselves.

AMITIÉ / FRIENDSHIP

FRIENDSHIP is the marriage of the soul; it is a tacit contract between two affectionate and virtuous persons. I say affectionate, for a monk or a hermit may well be devoid of meanness, yet he lives without knowing friendship. I say virtuous, for the wicked only have accomplices; the voluptuous, companions; the selfish, associates; politicians assemble factions; the generality of idle men have connections; princes, courtiers. Virtuous men alone possess friends. Cethegus was the accomplice of Catiline, and Maecenas the courtier of Octavius; but Cicero was the friend of Atticus.

What does this contract between two tender, honest minds entail? Its obligations are stronger or weaker according to their degree of affection and the number of services rendered, etc.

The enthusiasm of friendship was stronger among the Greeks and Arabs than among us. The tales that these people imagined on the subject of friendship are admirable; we have none to compare to them. We are rather dry and reserved in everything.

Friendship was a point of religion and legislation among the Greeks. The Thebans had a regiment of lovers. Fine regiment! Some have taken it for a regiment of sodomites. They are deceived; that would be taking an accessory characteristic for the primary one. Friendship was prescribed by Greek law and religion. Pederasty was unfortunately tolerated by custom; but shameful abuses should not be imputed to the law. We will speak of this again.[4]

AMOUR / LOVE

AMOR omnibus idem.[5] We must return to the physical realm here; it is the natural fabric upon which the imagination has embroidered. Do you wish to form an idea of love? Look at the sparrows in your garden; behold your doves; contemplate the bull when introduced to the heifer; look at that powerful and spirited horse, which two of your grooms are conducting to the mare that quietly awaits him and is evidently pleased at his approach; observe the flashing of his eyes, notice the strength and loudness of his neighing, the bounding, the curveting, the ears erect, the mouth opening with convulsive gasping, the distended nostrils, the breath of fire, the raised and waving mane, and the impetuous movement with which he rushes towards the object that nature has destined for him. Do not, however, be jealous; but reflect on the advantages of the human species; we receive ample compensation in love for all those advantages that nature has conferred on mere animals—strength, beauty, lightness, and rapidity.

There are even some classes of animals totally unacquainted with sexual pleasure. Scaly fishes are destitute of this enjoyment. The female deposits her millions of eggs on the slime of the waters, and the male passes over them and renders them fertile with his seed, never bothering about the female to whom they belong.

The greater part of those animals that copulate feel the enjoyment only with a single sense; and once this appetite is satisfied, the whole is over. No animal, besides you, is acquainted with embraces; your whole body is sensitive; your lips particularly experience a delight that never wearies and that is exclusively the lot of your species; finally, you can surrender yourself at any moment to the endearments of love, while animals possess only limited periods. If you reflect on these high preeminences, you will readily join in the Earl of Rochester's remark that love would impel a whole nation of atheists to worship the Divinity.

As men possess the talent of perfecting whatever nature has bestowed upon them, they have accordingly perfected the gift of love. Cleanliness, personal attention, by making the skin more delicate, increase the pleasure of touch, and care for one's health renders the organs of voluptuousness more sensitive.

All the other sentiments enter afterwards into that of love, like metals that amalgamate with gold; friendship and esteem readily fly to its support; and talents both of body and of mind are new and strengthening bonds.

> *Nam facit ipsa suis interdum femina factis,*
> *Morigerisque modis, et munde corpore culto,*
> *Ut facile insuescat te secum degere vitam.*
> —LUCRETIUS, iv, 1280

Self-love, above all, strengthens these ties. Men pride themselves in the choice they have made; and numerous illusions enhance this work, of which the foundation is so firmly laid by nature.

Such are the advantages that you hold above the animals. But, if you enjoy so many delights unknown to them, how many vexations, also, from which they are free! The most dreadful thing for you is that nature has poisoned, in three-quarters of the world, the pleasures of love and the sources of life with a terrible disease, to which man alone is subject and which infects only his reproductive organs.

Nor is it with this pestilence as with various other maladies, which are the natural consequences of excess. It was not introduced into the world by debauchery. The Phrynes and Laises, the Floras and Messalinas, were never attacked by it. It originated in islands where humankind dwelt together in innocence, and has thence been spread throughout the Old World.

If nature could in any instance be accused of despising her own work, thwarting her own plan, and counteracting her own views, it would be in this case. Can this, then, be the best of all possible worlds? What! If Caesar, Antony, and Octavius never had this disease, was it not possible to prevent Francis the First from dying of it? No, it is said; things were so ordered all for the best; I am disposed to believe it; but it is unfortunate for those to whom Rabelais dedicated his book.[6]

AMOUR NOMMÉ SOCRATIQUE / LOVE CALLED SOCRATIC

How is it that a vice that would destroy the human race if it were generalized, an infamous crime against nature, could nevertheless be so natural? It seems to be the ultimate degree of meditated corruption, and yet it is the normal lot of those who have not even had time to become corrupt. It enters into young hearts that have no knowledge of ambition, fraud, or the thirst for riches; it is blind youth, just emerging from childhood that throws itself into this disorder in accordance with a poorly understood instinct.

The attraction of the two sexes for each other appears early on; but whatever may have been said about African and South Asian women, this attraction is generally much stronger in men than in women; this is a law established by nature for all animals. It is always the male who attacks the female.

Young males of our species, raised together, feeling this force that nature has begun to unleash in them, and finding no natural object for their instinct, fall back on their fellows. With his fresh complexion, the brilliance of his coloring, and the softness of his eyes, a young boy often resembles a pretty girl for two or three years. If he is loved, it is because nature is fooled; the fair sex is honored by this attachment to that which possesses the same beauties, and when maturity makes this resemblance fade, the error ceases.

Citraque juventamam
Aetatos breve ver et primos carpere flores.

It is well known that this error of nature is much more common in temperate climates than in the icy north, because the blood runs hotter there, and opportunities are more frequent. Thus, that which seems to be only a weakness in young Alcibiades is a disgusting abomination in a Dutch sailor and in a Muscovite camp cook.

I cannot tolerate that some assert the Greeks authorized this license. Solon the legislator is cited because he said in two lines of bad poetry:

Tu chériras un beau garçon,
Tant qu'il n'aura barbe au menton.
You will cherish a handsome young man,
As long as he has no beard on his chin.

But in good faith, was Solon writing as legislator when he penned these two ridiculous lines? He was then young, and when the debauchee had become wise, he did not include such an infamy among the laws of his republic. It is as if Théodore de Bèze were accused of preaching pederasty in his church because, in his youth, he composed verse for young Candide, informing him:

Amplector hunc et illam.
I embrace the one and the other.

Similar abuse has been made of Plutarch, who in his ram-blings in the Dialogue of Love has one of his interlocutors explain that women are not worthy of true love; but another interlocutor defends the cause of women, as is fitting. Montesquieu was quite mistaken.

It is as certain as our knowledge of antiquity can be that Socratic love was not an infamous type of passion. It is the word "love" that has deceived the world. Those called the lovers of a young man were precisely such as among us are called the min-ions of our princes; like the honorable youths attached to the education of a child of distinction, partaking of the same studies and the same military exercises; a warlike and sacred custom, which was perverted, like nocturnal feasts and orgies.

The company of lovers instituted by Laius was an invincible troop of young warriors, bound by oath each to preserve the life of any other at the expense of his own. Ancient discipline never exhibited anything more admirable.

Sextus Empiricus and others have boldly affirmed that ped-erasty was recommended by the laws of Persia. Let them cite the text of such a law; let them exhibit the code of the Persians; and if they can find such a thing, still I would disbelieve it, and I will maintain that the thing was not true, because it is impossible. No, it is not in human nature to make a law that contradicts and outrages nature itself, a law that would annihilate humankind, if it were literally observed. How many persons have mistaken shameful practices, when merely tolerated, for the laws of a country! Sextus Empiricus, who doubted everything, should have doubted this piece of jurisprudence. If he lived in our time and witnessed two or three young Jesuits abusing a few students, would he be justified in the assertion that such practices are authorized by the orders of Ignatius Loyola?

The love of boys was so common in Rome that there was no attempt to punish this nonsense in which almost everyone was fully involved. Octavius Augustus, that murderer, debauchee, and coward, who dared to exile Ovid, thought it right that Virgil should sing the charms of Alexis and that Horace, his other poetical favorite, should compose little odes for Ligurinus. Yet the ancient *Lex Scantinia*, which forbade pederasty, always existed. The emperor Philip put it into force and drove away from Rome the boys who made a profession of it. To conclude, I firmly believe that no civilized nation has ever existed that made formal laws contrary to morals.*7

AMOUR-PROPRE / SELF-LOVE

A beggar of the suburbs of Madrid was boldly asking alms. Someone passing by said to him: *Are you not ashamed to carry on this infamous trade, when you can work? Sir,* replied the mendicant, *I ask you for money, not for advice,* and turned his back on him with Castilian dignity. This gentleman was a haughty beggar; his vanity was wounded by very little: he asked alms for love of himself and would not suffer the reprimand because of a still greater love of himself.

---

* Messieurs the . . . should be required to present to the police each year a child of their making. The abbé Desfontaines was on the verge of being cooked on the Place de Grève; protectors saved him. A victim was needed; Deschauffours was cooked in his stead. This is excessive; *est modus in rebus*: punishments should be proportionate to crimes. What would Caesar, Alcibiades, the king of Bithynia Nicomedes, the king of France Henry III, and so many others, have said? When Deschauffours was burned, the *Establishments of Saint Louis* were invoked, set into French in the fifteenth century. *Anyone suspected of . . . shall be led before the bishop and, if it is proved, shall be burned, and all his belongings shall belong to the baron, etc.* But *Saint Louis* does not say what should be done to the baron, if the baron is suspected of . . . *Saint Louis* is referring to heretics, who were called by no other name at the time. An ambiguous statement led to the burning in Paris of Deschauffors, the gentleman from Lorraine. Despréaux was justified in writing a satire against ambiguous statements, which have caused more evil than we realize.

A missionary, traveling in India, met a fakir loaded with chains, naked as an ape, lying on his stomach, and lashing himself for the sins of his countrymen, the Indians, who gave him some coins of the country. *What a renouncement of himself!* said one of the spectators. *Renouncement of myself!* said the fakir, *learn that I only lash myself in this world so that I can serve you the same in the next, when you will be the horses and I the rider.*

Those who have said that love of ourselves is the basis of all our sentiments and actions are justified, in India, in Spain, and throughout the entire inhabitable planet; and just as no one has written to prove to men that they have a face, there is no need to prove to them that they possess self-love. This self-love is the instrument of our preservation; it is like an instrument for the perpetuation of humankind; it is necessary, it is dear to us, it gives us pleasure, and we must conceal it.

ANGE / ANGEL

ANGEL, in Greek, is envoy. The reader will hardly be the wiser for being told that the Persians had their *peris*, the Hebrews their *malakim*, and the Greeks their *demonoi*.

But it is perhaps better worth knowing that one of the first of man's ideas has always been to place intermediate beings between the Divinity and us; such were those demons, those genii, invented in the ages of antiquity. Man always made the gods after his own image; princes were seen to communicate their orders by messengers; therefore, the Divinity had also his couriers. Mercury and Iris were couriers or messengers.

The Hebrews, the only people under the conduct of the Divinity Himself, did not at first give names to the angels whom God deigned to send them; they borrowed the names given them by the Chaldaeans when the Jewish nation was captive in Babylon; Michael and Gabriel are named for the first time by Daniel, a slave among those people. The Jew Tobit, who lived at Ninevah, met the angel Raphael, who traveled with his son to assist him in recovering the money due to him from the Jew Gabaël.

In the Jewish laws, that is, in Leviticus and Deuteronomy, not the least mention is made of the existence of the angels—much less of the worship of them. Neither did the Sadducees believe in the angels.

But in the Jewish histories, they are much spoken of. The angels were corporeal; they had wings at their backs, as the Gentiles imagined that Mercury had at his heels; sometimes they concealed their wings under their clothing. How could they be without bodies, since they all ate and drank, and the inhabitants of Sodom wanted to commit the sin of pederasty with the angels who went to Lot's house?

The ancient Jewish tradition, according to Ben Maimon, recognizes ten degrees, ten orders of angels: 1. The *chaios ecodesh*, pure, holy. 2. The *ofamin*, swift. 3. The *oralim*, strong. 4. The *chasmalim*, flames. 5. The *seraphim*, sparks. 6. The *malakim*, angels, messengers, deputies. 7. The *elohim*, gods or judges. 8. The *ben elohim*, children of the gods. 9. The *cherubim*, images. 10. The *ychim*, animated.

The story of the fall of the angels is not to be found in the books of Moses. The first testimony respecting it is that of the prophet Isaiah, who, apostrophizing the king of Babylon, exclaims, "Where is now the exacter of tributes? The pines and the cedars rejoice in his fall. How did you fall from heaven, O Hellel, star of the morning?" The word Hellel was rendered by the Latin word Lucifer; and afterwards, in an allegorical sense, the name of Lucifer was given to the prince of the angels who made war in heaven; and finally this word, signifying Phosphorus and Aurora, became the name of the devil.

The Christian religion is founded on the fall of the angels. Those who revolted were precipitated from the spheres they inhabited into hell, in the center of the earth, and became devils. A devil, in the form of a serpent, tempted Eve, and damned humankind. Jesus came to redeem humankind and to triumph over the devil, who tempts us still. Yet this fundamental tradition is to be found nowhere but in the apocryphal book of Enoch; and there it is in a form quite different from that of the received tradition.

St. Augustine, in his 109th letter, does not hesitate to give slender and agile bodies to the good and bad angels. Pope Gregory II reduced to nine choirs—to nine hierarchies or orders—the ten choirs of angels acknowledged by the Jews. These were the seraphim, the cherubim, the thrones, the dominations, the virtues, the powers, the principalities, the archangels and finally the angels, who give names to the eight other hierarchies.

The Jews had in their temple two cherubs, each with two heads—the one that of an ox, the other that of an eagle with six wings. We paint them now in the form of a flying head, with two small wings below the ears. We paint the angels and archangels in the form of young men, with two wings at the back. As for the thrones and dominations, no one has yet thought of painting them.

St. Thomas, in question 108, article 2, says that the thrones are as near to God as the cherubim and the seraphim, because it is upon them that God sits. Scot has counted a thousand million angels. The ancient mythology of the good and bad genii, having passed from the East to Greece and Rome, consecrated this opinion, by accepting the idea that for each individual there is a good and an evil angel, one who assists while the other torments him, from his birth to his death; but it is not yet known whether these good and bad angels are continually passing from one to another, or are relieved by others. On this point, consult St. Thomas's *Summa*.

It is not known precisely where the angels dwell—whether in the air, in the void, or in the planets. It has not been God's pleasure that we should be informed of their abode.

ANTHROPOPHAGES / CANNIBALS

WE have spoken of love. It is hard to pass from people *kissing* to people *eating* one another. It is, however, only too true that there have been cannibals. We found them in America; they are, perhaps, still to be found; and the Cyclops was not the only individual in antiquity who sometimes fed on human flesh. Juvenal relates that among the Egyptians—that wise people, so renowned for their laws, those pious worshippers of crocodiles and onions—the Tentyrites ate one of their enemies who had fallen into their hands. He does not tell this tale on hearsay; the crime was committed almost before his eyes; he was then in Egypt, and not far from Tentyra. On this occasion he quotes the Gascons and the Saguntines, who formerly fed on the flesh of their countrymen.

In 1725 four savages were brought from the Mississippi to Fontainebleau; I had the honor of conversing with them.[8] There was among them a lady of the country, whom I asked if she had eaten men; she answered, with great simplicity, that she had. I appeared somewhat scandalized; on which she excused herself by saying that it was better to eat one's dead enemy than to leave him to be devoured by wild beasts, and that the conquerors deserved to have their preference. We kill our neighbors in regular or irregular battles; and, for the most vile compensation, provide meals for the crows and the worms. There is the horror; there is the crime. What does it matter, when a man is dead, whether he is eaten by a soldier or by a dog and a crow?

We have more respect for the dead than for the living. It would be better to respect both the one and the other. The so-called civilized nations have done right in not putting their vanquished enemies on the spit; for if we were allowed to eat our neighbors, we should soon eat our countrymen, which would be rather unfortunate for the social virtues. But civilized nations have not always been so; they were all for a long time savage; and, in the infinite number of revolutions this globe has undergone, humankind has been sometimes numerous and sometimes scarce. It has been with human beings as it now is with elephants, lions, or tigers, the race of which has very much decreased. In times when a country was but thinly inhabited by men, they had few arts; they were hunters. The custom of eating what they had killed easily led them to treat their enemies like their stags and their boars. It was superstition that caused human victims to be immolated; it was necessity that caused them to be eaten.

Which is the greater crime—to assemble piously together to plunge a knife into the heart of a girl adorned with fillets, in honor of the Divinity, or to eat a worthless man who has been killed in self-defense?

Yet we have many more instances of girls and boys sacrificed than of girls and boys eaten. Almost all the nations of which we know anything have sacrificed boys and girls. The Jews immolated them. This was called *the Anathema;* it was a real sacrifice; and in Leviticus 27:29, it is ordained that the living souls so designated shall not be spared; but it is not in any manner prescribed that they shall be eaten; this is only threatened. And Moses, as we have seen, tells the Jews that unless they observe his ceremonies they will not only have the itch, but the mothers will eat their children. It is true that in the time of Ezekiel the Jews must have had the custom of eating human flesh; for, in his thirty-ninth chapter, he foretells to them that God will cause them to eat not only the horses of their enemies, but moreover the horsemen and the rest of the warriors. This is indisputable. And, indeed, why should the Jews not have been cannibals? It was the only thing lacking to make the people of God the most abominable people on earth.

I have read among the anecdotes from the history of England during Cromwell's time that a woman who kept a tallow chandler's shop in Dublin sold excellent candles, made of the fat of

Englishmen. After some time one of her customers complained that the candles were not so good. "Alas," said the woman, "it is because we are short of Englishmen this month." I ask which were the most guilty—those who assassinated the English, or the poor woman who made candles of their fat?

ANTITRINITAIRES / ANTI-TRINITARIANS

To know their sentiments, it suffices to say that they maintain that nothing is more contrary to right reason than what is taught among Christians concerning the Trinity of persons in one sole divine essence, of whom the second is begotten by the first, and the third proceeds from the other two.

That this unintelligible doctrine is not to be found in any part of the Scriptures.

That no passage can be produced which authorizes it; or to which, without in any wise departing from the spirit of the text, a sense cannot be given more clearly, more naturally, or in greater conformity with common notions and with primitive and immutable truths.

That to maintain, as the orthodox do, that in the divine essence there are several distinct *persons*, and that the Eternal is not the only true God, but that the Son and the Holy Ghost must be joined with Him, is to introduce into the Church of Christ a most gross and dangerous error, since this openly favors polytheism.

That a contradiction is implied in saying that there is but one God, and that, nevertheless, there are three *persons*, each of which is truly God.

That this distinction, of *one* in *essence*, and *three* in *person*, was never in the Scriptures.

That it is manifestly false, since it is certain that there are no fewer essences than persons, nor persons than essences.

That the three persons of the Trinity are either three different substances, or accidents of the divine essence, or the essence itself without distinction.

That, in the first case, there are three Gods.

That, in the second, God is composed of accidents; accidents are worshiped and metamorphosed into persons.

That, in the third, without grounds and to no purpose, an indivisible subject is divided, and that which within itself has no distinction is made into *three*.

That if it be said that the three personalities are neither different substances in the divine essence, nor accidents of that essence, it will be difficult to persuade ourselves that they are anything at all.

That it must not be believed that the most rigid and decided Trinitarians have themselves any clear idea of the way in which the three *hypostases* subsist in God, without dividing His substance, and consequently without multiplying it.

That St. Augustine himself, after advancing on this subject a thousand thoughts equally impenetrable and false, was forced to confess that nothing intelligible could be said about the matter.

They then repeat the passage by this father, which is, indeed, a very singular one: "When," says he, "it is asked what are *the three*, human language is insufficient, and terms are lacking to express them. *Three persons*, has, however, been said—not for the purpose of expressing anything, but in order to say something and not remain mute. *Dictum est tres personae, non ut aliquid diceretur, sed ne taceretur.*"—De Trinitate v, 9.

That modern theologians have done no better in clearing up this matter.

That, when they are asked what they understand by the word *person*, they explain themselves only by saying that it is a certain incomprehensible distinction by which are distinguished in one nature only, a Father, a Son, and a Holy Ghost.

That the explanation which they give of the terms *begetting* and *proceeding*, is no more satisfactory, since it reduces itself to saying that these terms indicate certain incomprehensible relations existing among the three *persons* of the Trinity.

That it may be gathered from this that the state of the question between them and the orthodox consists of knowing whether there are in God three distinctions, of which no one has any definite idea, and among which there are certain relations of which no one has any more idea.

From all this they conclude that it would be wiser to abide by the testimony of the apostles, who never spoke of the Trinity, and to banish from religion forever all terms that are not in the scriptures, like *trinity, person, essence, hypostasis, hypostatic* and *personal union, incarnation, generation, proceeding*, and many others of the same kind, which being absolutely devoid of meaning, since they are represented by no real existence in nature, can excite in he understanding none but false, vague, obscure, and incomplete notions.

(taken from the article *Unitarians* in the *Encyclopédie*, written by the abbé Bragelogne.)[9]

To this article let us add what Dom Calmet says in his dissertation on the following passage of the Epistle of John the Evangelist: "There are three that bear witness in earth: the spirit, the water, and the blood; and these three are one. There are three that bear record in heaven, the Father, the Word, and the Holy Ghost; and these three are one." Dom Calmet acknowledges that these two verses are not in any ancient bible; indeed, it would be very strange if St. John had spoken of the Trinity in a letter, and said not a word about it in his Gospel. We find no trace of this dogma, either in the canonical or in the apocryphal gospels. All these reasons and many others might excuse the anti-Trinitarians, if the councils had not made decisions. But as the heretics pay no regard to councils, we know not what measures to take to confound them.

APIS / APIS

WAS the ox Apis worshipped at Memphis as a god, as a symbol, or as an ox? It is likely that the fanatics regarded him as a god, the wise as merely a symbol, and that the more stupid part of the people worshipped the ox. Did Cambyses do right in killing this ox with his own hand when he had conquered Egypt? Why not? He was showing the imbeciles that their god might be put on the spit without nature arming herself to avenge the sacrilege. The Egyptians have been much extolled. I have not heard of a more miserable people. There must always have been in their character, and in their government, some radical vice which constantly made vile slaves of them. I will grant that in times almost unknown they conquered the earth; but in historical times they have been subjugated by all who have chosen to take the trouble— by the Assyrians, by the Greeks, by the Romans, by the Arabs, by the Mamelukes, by the Turks, by all, in short—but our crusaders, who were even more ill-advised than the Egyptians were cowardly. It was the Mameluke militia that beat the French. There are, perhaps, only two tolerable things in this nation; the first is that those who worshipped an ox never sought to compel those who adored an ape to change religions; the second, that they have always hatched chickens in ovens.

We are told of their pyramids; but these are the monuments of an enslaved people. The whole nation must have been set to work on them, or those unsightly masses could never have been raised. And for what use were they? To preserve in a small chamber the mummy of some prince, or governor, or intendant, which his soul was to reanimate at the end of a thousand years.

But if they looked forward to this resurrection of the body, why did they take out the brains before embalming them? Were the Egyptians to be resuscitated without brains?

APOCALYPSE / **APOCALYPSE**

JUSTIN the Martyr, who wrote around the year 270 of the Christian era, was the first who spoke of the Apocalypse; he attributes it to the apostle John the Evangelist, in his dialogue with Tryphon. That Jew asks him if he does not believe that Jerusalem is one day to be re-established. Justin answers that he believes it, as all Christians do, who think correctly. "There was among us," he says, "a certain person named John, one of the twelve apostles of Jesus; he foretold that the faithful shall spend a thousand years in Jerusalem."

The belief in this reign of a thousand years was long prevalent among the Christians. This period was also in great credit among the Gentiles. The souls of the Egyptians returned to their bodies at the end of a thousand years; and, according to Virgil, souls in purgatory were exorcised for the same space of time—*et mille per annos*. The New Jerusalem of a thousand years was to have twelve gates, in memory of the twelve apostles; its form was to be square; its length, breadth, and height were each to be twelve thousand *stadii*—*i.e.*, five hundred leagues, so that the houses were to be five hundred leagues high. It would be rather disagreeable to live in the upper story; but we find all this in the twenty-first chapter of the Apocalypse.

If Justin was the first who attributed the Apocalypse to St. John, some individuals have rejected his testimony; because in the same dialogue with the Jew Tryphon he says that, according to the relation of the apostles, Jesus Christ, when he went into the Jordan, made the water of this river boil, which, however, is not to be found in any writing of the apostles.

The same St. Justin confidently cites the oracles of Sibyls; he moreover pretends that he had seen the remains of the small cells in which the seventy-two interpreters were confined in the Egyptian pharos, in Herod's time. The testimony of a man who had had the misfortune to see these places seems to indicate that he ought to have been confined there himself.

St. Irenaeus, who comes afterwards, and who also believed in the reign of a thousand years, tells us that he learned from an old man that St. John wrote the Apocalypse. But St. Irenaeus is reproached with having written that there should be but four gospels, because there are but four quarters of the world, and four cardinal points, and Ezekiel saw only four animals. He calls this way of reasoning a proof. It must be confessed that Irenaeus's method of proof is quite worthy of Justin's power of vision.

Clement of Alexandria, in his *Electa*, mentions only an Apocalypse of St. Peter, to which great importance was attached. Tertullian, a great partisan of the thousand years' reign, not only assures us that St. John foretold this resurrection and reign of a thousand years in the city of Jerusalem, but also asserts that this Jerusalem was already beginning to form itself in the air, where it had been seen by all the Christians of Palestine, and even by the Pagans, at the latter end of the night, for forty nights successively; but, unfortunately, the city always disappeared as soon as it was daylight.

Origen, in his preface to St. John's Gospel, and in his homilies, quotes the oracles of the Apocalypse, but he likewise quotes the oracles of Sibyls. And St. Dionysius of Alexandria, who wrote toward the middle of the third century, says, in one of his fragments preserved by Eusebius, that nearly all the doctors rejected the Apocalypse as a book devoid of reason, and that this book was composed, not by St. John, but by a certain Cerinthus, who made use of a great name to give more weight to his reveries.

The Council of Laodicea, held in 360, did not reckon the Apocalypse among the canonical books. It is very singular that Laodicea, one of the churches to which the Apocalypse was addressed, should have rejected a treasure designed for itself, and that the bishop of Ephesus, who attended the council, should also have rejected this book of St. John, who was buried at Ephesus.

It was visible to all eyes that St. John was continually turning about in his grave, causing a constant rising and falling of the earth. Yet the same persons who were sure that St. John was not quite dead were also sure that he had not written the Apocalypse. But those who were for the thousand years' reign were unshaken in their opinion. Sulpicius Severus, in his *Sacred History*, book 9, treats as mad and impious those who did not accept the Apocalypse. At length, after numerous oppositions between various councils, the opinion of Sulpicius Severus prevailed. The matter having been thus cleared up, the Church came to the decision that the Apocalypse is incontestably St. John's. Thus, there can be no questions.

Every Christian communion has applied to itself the prophecies contained in this book. The English have found in it the revolutions of Great Britain; the Lutherans, the troubles of Germany; the French reformers, the reign of Charles IX, and the regency of Catherine de Medici, and they are all equally right. Bossuet and Newton have both commented on the Apocalypse, yet, in the end, the eloquent declamations of the one, and the sublime discoveries of the other, have done them greater honor than their commentaries.

ARIUS / ARIUS

HERE is an incomprehensible question, which, for more than sixteen hundred years, has furnished exercise for curiosity, sophistic subtlety, animosity, the spirit of cabal, the fury of dominion, the rage of persecution, blind and sanguinary fanaticism, barbarous credulity, which has produced more horrors than the ambition of princes, and which has occasioned a great many. Is Jesus the Word? If He is the Word, did He emanate from God in time or before time? If He emanated from God, is He coeternal and consubstantial with Him, or is He of a similar substance? Is He distinct from Him, or is He not? Is He made or begotten? Can He beget in his turn? Has He paternity, or productive virtue without paternity? Is the Holy Ghost made, or begotten, or produced, or proceeding from the Father, or proceeding from the Son, or proceeding from both? Can He beget, can He produce? Is His hypostasis consubstantial with the hypostasis of the Father and the Son? And how is it that, having the same nature, the same essence as the Father and the Son, He cannot do the same things done by these persons who are Himself?

Assuredly, I can understand nothing of these matters; no one has ever understood a thing about them; and this is why people have slaughtered one another.

The Christians sophisticated, nitpicked, hated, and excommunicated one another for the sake of some of these dogmas inaccessible to human intellect before the time of Arius and Athanasius. The Egyptian Greeks were clever people; they would split a hair into four, but on this occasion they split it only into three. Alexandros, Bishop of Alexandria, thought proper to preach that God, being necessarily individual—single—a monad in the strictest sense of the word, this monad is triune.

The priest Arios or Arious, whom we call Arius, was quite scandalized by Alexandros's monad, and explained the thing in quite a different way. He nitpicked in part like the priest Sabellius, who had nitpicked like the Phrygian Praxeas, who was a great nitpicker. Alexandros quickly assembled a small council of those of his own opinion, and excommunicated his priest. Eusebius, bishop of Nicomedia, took the side of Arius. Thus the whole Church was in a flame.

The Emperor Constantine was a villain, I confess it; a parricide, who had smothered his wife in a bath, cut his son's throat, assassinated his father-in-law, his brother-in-law, and his nephew, I cannot deny it; a man puffed up with pride and immersed in pleasure, granted; a detestable tyrant, like his children, *transeat*; but he was a man of sense. He would not have obtained the empire, and subdued all his rivals, had he not reasoned justly.

When he saw the flames of civil war lighted among the scholastic brains, he sent the celebrated Bishop Osius with dissuasive letters to the two belligerent parties. "You are great fools," he expressly tells them in this letter, "to quarrel about things which you do not understand. It is unworthy of the gravity of your ministry to make so much noise about so trifling a matter."

By "so trifling a matter," Constantine meant not what regards the Divinity, but the incomprehensible manner in which they were striving to explain the nature of the Divinity. The Arabian patriarch, who wrote the history of the Church of Alexandria, makes Osius, on presenting the emperor's letter, speak in the following words:

"My brethren, Christianity is just beginning to enjoy the blessings of peace, and you would plunge it into eternal discord. The emperor is all too justified in telling you that *you quarrel about a very trifling matter*. Certainly, had the object of the dispute been essential, Jesus Christ, whom we all acknowledge as our legislator, would have mentioned it. God would not have sent His Son on earth, to return without teaching us our catechism. Whatever He did not expressly tell us is the work of men, and error is their portion. Jesus has commanded you to love one another, and you begin by hating one another and stirring up discord in the empire. Pride alone has given birth to these disputes, and Jesus, your Master, commanded you to be humble. Not one among you can know whether Jesus is made or begotten. And in what does His nature concern you, provided your own is to be just and reasonable? What has the vain science of words to do with the morality that should guide your actions? You cloud our doctrines with mysteries—you, who ought to strengthen religion by your virtues. Would you leave the Christian religion a mass of sophistry? Did Christ come for this? Cease to dispute, adore, humble yourselves, edify one another, clothe the naked, feed the hungry, and pacify the quarrels of families, instead of giving scandal to the whole empire by your dissensions."

But Osius was talking to an obstinate audience. The Council of Nicea was assembled, and the Roman Empire was torn by a spiritual civil war. This war brought on others and mutual persecution has continued from age to age, unto this day.

ATHÉE, ATHÉISME / ATHEIST, ATHEISM

FIRST SECTION

FORMERLY, whoever possessed a secret in any art was in danger of passing for a sorcerer; every new sect was charged with murdering infants in its mysteries; and every philosopher who departed from the jargon of the schools was accused of atheism by knaves and fanatics, and condemned by blockheads.

Anaxagoras dares to assert that the sun is not driven by Apollo, mounted in a chariot and four; he is condemned as an atheist and compelled to flee.

Aristotle is accused of atheism by a priest, and not being powerful enough to punish his accuser, he retires to Chalcis. But the death of Socrates is the most odious blot on the page of Greek history.

Aristophanes—he whom commentators admire because he was a Greek, forgetting that Socrates was also a Greek—Aristophanes was the first who accustomed the Athenians to regard Socrates as an atheist.

This comic poet, who is neither comic nor poetical, would not, among us, have been permitted to exhibit his farces at the fair of St. Lawrence. He appears to me to be much lower and more despicable than Plutarch represents him. This is what the wise Plutarch says of this buffoon: "The language of Aristophanes bespeaks his miserable quackery; it is made up of the lowest and most disgusting puns; he is not even funny for the common people; and to men of judgment and honor he is intolerable; his arrogance is unacceptable, and all good men detest his malignity."

This, then, is the joker whom Madame Dacier, an admirer of Socrates, ventures to admire! Such was the man who, indirectly, prepared the poison by which infamous judges put to death the most virtuous man in Greece.

The tanners, cobblers, and seamstresses of Athens applauded a farce in which Socrates was represented lifted in the air in a basket, announcing that there was no God, and boasting of having stolen a cloak while he was teaching philosophy. A whole people, whose ill-advised government sanctioned such infamous licenses, well deserved what happened to them—to become slaves to the Romans, and, subsequently, to the Turks.

Let us traverse the ages between the Roman commonwealth and our own times. The Romans, much wiser than the Greeks, never persecuted a philosopher for his opinions. Not so the barbarous nations that succeeded the Roman Empire. No sooner did the Emperor Frederick II begin to quarrel with the popes, than he was accused of being an atheist and of being the author of the book *The Three Impostors*, conjointly with his chancellor De Vineis.

Our high-chancellor, Michel de l'Hôpital, declares his opposition to persecution? He is immediately charged with atheism. *Homo doctus, sed vetus atheus* (*Commentarium rerum Gallicarum*, L. 28). There was a Jesuit, as much beneath Aristophanes as Aristophanes is beneath Homer—a wretch, whose name has become ridiculous even among fanatics—the Jesuit Garasse, in a word, who found atheists everywhere. He bestows the name upon all who are the objects of his virulence. He calls Théodore de Bèze an atheist. It was he, too, who led the public into error concerning Vanini.

The unfortunate end of Vanini does not excite our pity and indignation like that of Socrates, because Vanini was only a foreign pedant, without merit; however, Vanini was not, as was pretended, an atheist; he was quite the contrary.[10]

He was a poor Neapolitan priest, a theologian and preacher by trade, an outrageous disputer on quiddities and universals, *et utrum chimera bombinans in vacuo possit comedere secundas intentiones.* But there was nothing in him tending to atheism. His notion of God is that of the soundest and most approved theology: "God is the beginning and the end, the father of both, without need of either, eternal without time, in no one place, yet present everywhere. To him there is neither past nor future; he is within and without everything; he has created all, and governs all; he is immutable, infinite without parts; his power is his will, etc."

Vanini prided himself on reviving Plato's fine idea, adopted by Averroës, that God had created a chain of beings from the smallest to the greatest, the last link of which was attached to his eternal throne; an idea more sublime than true, one must admit, but as distant from atheism as being is from nothingness.

He traveled to seek his fortune and to dispute; but, unfortunately, disputation leads not to fortune; a man makes himself as many irreconcilable enemies as he finds men of learning or of pedantry to argue against. Vanini's ill-fortune had no other source. His heat and rudeness in disputation procured him the hatred of some theologians; and having quarreled with a certain Francon or Franconi, this Franconi, the friend of his enemies, did not fail to charge him with being an atheist and teaching atheism.

This Francon or Franconi, aided by some witnesses, had the barbarity, when confronted with the accused, to maintain what he had advanced. Vanini, on the stand, being asked what he thought of the existence of a God, answered that he, with the Church, adored a God in three persons. Taking a straw from the ground, "This," said he "is sufficient to prove that there is a Creator." He then delivered a very fine discourse on vegetation and motion, and the necessity of a Supreme Being, without whom there could be neither motion nor vegetation.

The president Grammont, who was then at Toulouse, repeats this discourse in his history of France, now so little known; and the same Grammont, through some unaccountable prejudice, asserts that Vanini said all this "through vanity, or through fear, rather than from inward conviction."

On what could this atrocious, rash judgment of the president be founded? It is evident, from Vanini's answer that he ought to be acquitted of the charge of atheism. But what followed? This unfortunate foreign priest also dabbled in medicine. There was found in his house a large live toad, which he kept in a vessel of water; he was forthwith accused of being a sorcerer. It was maintained that this toad was the god he worshiped. An impious meaning was attributed to several passages of his books, a thing which is both common and easy, by taking objections for answers, giving some bad sense to a loose phrase, and perverting an innocent expression. At last, the faction that oppressed him forced from his judges the sentence condemning him to die.

In order to justify this execution it was necessary to charge the unfortunate man with the most enormous of crimes. The gray friar—the *very* gray friar—Mersenne, was so besotted as to publish that Vanini had set out from Naples, with twelve of his apostles, to convert the whole world to atheism. What a pitiful tale! How should a poor priest have twelve men in his pay? How should he persuade twelve Neapolitans to travel at great expense, in order to spread this abominable and revolting doctrine at the peril of their lives? Would a king himself have it in his power to pay twelve preachers of atheism? No one before

Father Mersenne had advanced so enormous an absurdity. But after him it was repeated; the journals and historical dictionaries were infected with it, and the world, which loves the extraordinary, has believed the fable without examination.

Even Bayle, in his miscellaneous thoughts (*Pensées Diverses*), speaks of Vanini as an atheist. He cites his example in support of his paradox that "a society of atheists might exist." He assures us that Vanini was a man of very regular morals and that he was a martyr to his philosophical opinions. On both these points he is equally mistaken. The priest Vanini informs us in his "Dialogues," written in imitation of Erasmus, that he had a mistress named Isabel. He was as free in his writings as in his conduct; but he was not an atheist.

A century after his death, the learned Lacroze, and he who took the name of Philaletes, endeavored to justify him. But, as no one cares anything about the memory of an unfortunate Neapolitan who was a bad writer, scarcely anyone has read these apologies.

The Jesuit Hardouin, more learned and no less rash than Garasse, in his book entitled *Athei Detecti,* charges Descartes, Arnauld, Pascal, and Malebranche with atheism. Happily, they did not meet the same fate as Vanini.

From these facts, I move on to the moral question, discussed by Bayle, "Whether a society of atheists can exist." Here let us first observe the enormous self-contradictions of men in disputation. Those who have been most violent in opposing the opinion of Bayle, those who have denied with the greatest virulence the possibility of a society of atheists, are the very men who have since maintained with equal ardor that atheism is the religion of the Chinese government.

They have most assuredly been mistaken concerning the government of China; they had only to read the edicts of the emperors of that vast country, and they would have seen that those edicts are sermons, in which a Supreme Being—governing, avenging, and rewarding—is continually mentioned.

But, at the same time, they are no less deceived respecting the impossibility of a society of atheists; nor can I conceive how Bayle could forget a striking example that might have rendered his cause victorious.

In what does the apparent impossibility of a society of atheists consist? In this: It is judged that men without some restraint could not live together; that laws have no power against secret crimes; and that it is necessary to have an avenging God who punishes, in this world or in the next, evil-doers who escape human justice.

The laws of Moses, it is true, did not teach the doctrine of a life to come, did not threaten with chastisements after death, nor even teach the primitive Jews the immortality of the soul; but the Jews, far from being atheists, far from believing that they could elude divine vengeance, were the most religious of men. They believed not only in the existence of an eternal God, but that He was always present among them; they trembled lest they should be punished in themselves, their wives, their children, their posterity to the fourth generation. This was a very powerful check.

But among the Gentiles various sects had no such check; the Skeptics doubted everything; the Academics suspended their judgment on everything; the Epicureans were persuaded that the Divinity could not meddle in human affairs, and in their hearts admitted no Divinity. They were convinced that the soul is not a substance, but a faculty that is born and perishes with the body; consequently, they had no restraint but that of morality and honor. The Roman senators and knights were in reality atheists; for the gods did not really exist for men who neither feared nor hoped anything from them. The Roman senate, then, in the time of Caesar and Cicero, was in fact an assembly of atheists.

That great orator, in his oration for Cluentius, says to the whole assembled senate: "What does he lose by death? We reject all the silly fables about the infernal regions. What, then, has death taken from him? Nothing but the susceptibility of sorrow."

Does not Caesar, wishing to save the life of his friend Catiline, threatened by the same Cicero, object that to put a criminal to death is not to punish him—that death is nothing—that it is but the termination of our ills—a moment rather fortunate than calamitous? Did not Cicero and the whole senate yield to this reasoning? The conquerors and legislators of all the known world then, evidently, formed a society of men who feared nothing from the gods, but were real atheists.

Bayle next examines whether idolatry is more dangerous than atheism, whether it is a greater crime not to believe in the Divinity than to have unworthy notions of it. In this he thinks like Plutarch; he believes it is better to have no opinion than a bad opinion; but, without offence to Plutarch, it was clearly infinitely better that the Greeks should fear Ceres, Neptune, and Jupiter than that they should fear nothing at all. It is clear that the sanctity of oaths is necessary; and that those are more to be trusted who think a false oath will be punished, than those who think they may take a false oath with impunity. It cannot be doubted that, in an organized society, it is infinitely more useful to have a religion (even a bad one) rather than no religion at all.

It appears then that Bayle should rather have examined whether atheism or fanaticism is the most dangerous. Fanaticism is certainly a thousand times the most to be dreaded; for atheism inspires no sanguinary passion, but fanaticism does; atheism does not oppose crime, but fanaticism prompts to its commission. Let us suppose, with the author of the *Commentarium Rerum Gallicarum,* that the High-Chancellor de l'Hôpital was an atheist; he made only wise laws; he recommended only moderation and concord. The massacres of St. Bartholomew were committed by fanatics. Hobbes passed for an atheist; yet he led a life of innocence and quiet, while the fanatics of his time deluged England, Scotland, and Ireland with blood. Spinoza was not only an atheist, he also taught atheism; but assuredly he had no part in the judicial assassination of Barneveldt; nor was it he who tore in pieces the two brothers De Witt and ate them off the grill.

Atheists are, for the most part, men of learning, bold but bewildered, who reason ill and, unable to comprehend creation, the origin of evil, and other difficulties, have recourse to the hypothesis of the eternity of things and of necessity.

The ambitious and the voluptuous have but little time to reason and to adopt defective systems; they have other occupations than that of comparing Lucretius with Socrates. This is how things are among us.

It was otherwise with the Roman senate, which was composed almost entirely of theoretical and practical atheists, that is, believing neither in Providence nor in a future state; this senate was an assembly of philosophers, men of pleasure, and ambitious men, who were all very dangerous, and who ruined the commonwealth. Under the emperors, Epicureanism prevailed. The atheists of the senate had been factious in the times of Sulla and of Caesar; in those of Augustus and Tiberius, they were atheistic slaves.

I should not wish to cross paths with an atheistic prince, who might find it in his interest to have me pounded in a mortar; I am quite sure that I should be so pounded. Were I a sovereign, I would not wish to deal with atheistic courtiers, whose interest it was to poison me; I should be under the necessity of taking an antidote every day. It is then absolutely necessary for princes and for the common people that the idea of a Supreme Being—creating, governing, rewarding, and punishing—be profoundly engraved in their minds.

There are nations of atheists, says Bayle in his "Thoughts on Comets." The Kaffirs, the Hottentots, and many other small populations, have no god; they neither affirm nor deny that there is one; they have never heard of Him; tell them that there is one, and they will easily believe it; tell them that all is done by the nature of things, and they will believe you just the same. To pretend that they are atheists would be like saying they are anti-Cartesians. They are neither for Descartes nor against him; they are true children; a child is neither atheist nor deist; he is nothing.

From all this, what conclusion is to be drawn? That atheism is a most pernicious monster in those who govern; that it is the same in the men of their cabinet, even if they live innocent lives, since they have access to those in power; that, although less to be dreaded than fanaticism, it is almost always fatal to virtue. And especially, let it be added, that there are fewer atheists now than ever, since philosophers have become persuaded that there is no vegetative being without a germ, no germ without a design, etc., and that the corn in our fields does not spring from rottenness.

Unphilosophical geometers have rejected final causes, but true philosophers admit them; and, as it has elsewhere been observed, a catechist announces God to children, and Newton demonstrates Him to the wise.

Second Section

If there be atheists, who are we to blame? Who but the mercenary tyrants of our souls, who, while disgusting us with their knavery, oblige some weak spirits to deny the God whom these monsters dishonor? How often have the bloodsuckers of the common folk pushed the citizens so far that they revolt against the king! (See *Fraude* / Fraud)

Men who have become fat on our substance, cry out to us: "Be persuaded that an ass spoke; believe that a fish swallowed a man and threw him up three days after, safe and sound, on the shore; doubt not that the God of the universe ordered a Jewish prophet to eat excrement (Ezekiel), and another to buy two prostitutes and have bastards by them (Hosea)." Such are the words put into the mouth of the God of purity and truth! Believe a hundred things either visibly abominable or mathematically impossible, otherwise the God of Mercy will burn you in hell-fire, not only for millions of billions of centuries, but for all eternity, whether you have a body or not.

These inconceivable absurdities are revolting to rash and weak minds, as well as to firm and wise ones. They say: "Our teachers represent God to us as the most demented and barbarous of all beings; therefore, there is no God." But they ought to say, "Our teachers attribute to God their own absurdities and furors, therefore God is the reverse of how they describe Him; thus He is as wise and good as they say He is foolish and wicked." Thus do the wise reason. But, if a fanatic hears them, he denounces them to a magistrate—a sort of priest's officer, and this officer has them burned alive, thinking that he is therein imitating and avenging the Divine Majesty he insults.

BABEL / **BABEL**

VANITY has always raised stately monuments. It was through vanity that men built the lofty tower of Babel. "Let us go and raise a tower, the summit of which shall touch the skies and render our name famous before we are scattered upon the face of the earth." The enterprise was undertaken in the time of a patriarch named Phaleg, who counted the good man Noah for his fifth ancestor. It can be seen that architecture and all the arts that accompany it had made great progress in five generations. St. Jerome, he who saw fauns and satyrs, did not see the tower of Babel any more than I have, but he assures us that it was twenty thousand feet high. This is a trifle. The ancient book, *Jacult*, written by one of the most learned Jews, proves the height to be eighty-one thousand Jewish feet, and everyone knows that the Jewish foot was nearly as long as the Greek. These dimensions are still more likely than those given by Jerome. This tower remains, but it is no longer quite so high. Several quite reliable travelers have seen it. I, who have not seen it, will talk as little of it as of my grandfather Adam, with whom I never had the honor of conversing. But consult the reverend father Calmet; he is a man with a fine mind and a profound philosopher; he will explain the thing to you. I do not know why it is said, in Genesis, that Babel signifies confusion, for ba means father in the eastern languages, and *bel* signifies God. Babel means the city of God, the holy city. But it is incontestable that Babel means confusion, possibly because the architects were confounded after having raised their work to eighty-one thousand feet, perhaps because the languages were then confounded, as it is clear that from that time forward the Germans no longer understood the Chinese, although, according to the learned Bochart, it is clear that Chinese is originally the same language as High German.

Baptême / Baptism

Baptism, a Greek word, meaning immersion. Humankind, which has always been guided by the senses, easily imagined that a thing that cleansed the body would also cleanse the soul. There were great vats in the subterranean regions of the Egyptian temples for the priests and the initiates. From time immemorial the Indians purified themselves in the waters of the Ganges, and this ceremony is still very much in fashion. It was conveyed to the Hebrews; all foreigners who embraced Judaic law and who refused circumcision, and particularly the women who were not subjected to this operation, except in Ethiopia, were baptized. It was a regeneration; it gave a new soul, as in Egypt. See, on this point, Epiphanius, Maimonides, and the Gemara.

John baptized in the Jordan, and he even baptized Jesus, who never baptized anyone, but who deigned to consecrate this ancient custom. Every sign is indifferent in itself, and God attaches his grace to any sign he pleases to choose. Baptism soon became the chief rite, the principal seal of Christianity. However, the first fifteen bishops of Jerusalem were all circumcised; it is not certain they were baptized.

In the first ages of Christianity this sacrament was often abused; nothing was more common than to postpone the receiving of baptism until the last agony. The example of the Emperor Constantine is a very strong proof of this. Here is how he reasoned. Baptism purifies everything; I can, therefore, kill my wife, my son, and all my relatives, after which I will have myself baptized, and I will go to heaven, as in fact he did not fail to do. This example was dangerous; little by little the custom of deferring the use of the sacred bath until the hour of death was abolished.

The Greeks always retained baptism by immersion. The Latins, around the close of the eighth century, having extended their religion into Gaul and Germany and seeing that immersion could be fatal to infants in cold countries, substituted simple aspersion and thus drew upon themselves frequent anathemas from the Greek Church.

St. Cyprian, bishop of Carthage, was asked if those were really baptized who had only had their bodies sprinkled all over. He answers, in his seventy-sixth letter, that several churches did not believe the sprinkled to be Christians; that, for his own part, he believes that they are Christians, but that they have infinitely less grace than those who have been thrice dipped, according to custom.

A person was initiated among the Christians as soon as he was dipped; until then he was only a catechumen. To be initiated it was necessary to have sponsors, called *god parents,* to answer to the Church for the fidelity of the new Christians and that the mysteries should not be divulged. Hence it was that in the first ages the Gentiles had, in general, as little knowledge of the Christian mysteries as the Christians had of the mysteries of Isis and the Eleusinian Ceres.

Cyril of Alexandria, in his writing against the Emperor Julian, expresses himself thus: "I would speak of baptism but that I fear my words would reach those who are not initiated."

In the second century infants began to be baptized; it was natural that the Christians should desire that their children, who would have been damned without this sacrament, be provided with it. It was at length concluded that they must receive it at the end of eight days, because that was the period at which, among the Jews, they were circumcised. In the Greek Church this is still the custom. However, in the third century, the habit of being baptized only at the moment of death prevailed.

Those who died in the first week were damned, according to the most rigorous fathers of the Church. But Peter Chrysologos, in the fifth century, imagined limbo, a sort of mitigated hell, or properly, the border, the outskirt of hell, whither all infants dying without baptism go and where the patriarchs remained until the time of Jesus Christ's descent into hell. So that the opinion that Jesus Christ descended into limbo, and not into hell, has since then prevailed.

It was disputed whether a Christian in the deserts of Arabia might be baptized with sand; this was answered in the negative. It was asked if rosewater might be used; it was decided that pure water would be necessary but that muddy water might be used. It is easy to see that all this discipline depended on the discretion of the first pastors who established it.

Notions of Rigid Unitarians Concerning Baptism

"It is evident to whosoever is willing to reason without prejudice that baptism is neither a mark of grace conferred nor a seal of alliance, but simply a mark of profession.

That baptism is not necessary, either by necessity of precept or by necessity of means.

That it was not instituted by Christ and that a Christian may omit it without his suffering any inconvenience therefrom.

That baptism should be administered neither to children, nor to adults, nor, in general, to any individual whatsoever.

That baptism may have been customary in the early infancy of Christianity for those who abandoned paganism in order to make their profession of faith public and give an authentic mark of it, but that now it is absolutely useless and altogether indifferent."

(taken from the *Encyclopedic Dictionary,* article "Unitarians.")

Important Addition

The Emperor Julian, the philosopher, in his immortal satire on the Caesars, puts these words into the mouth of Constantius, son of Constantine: "Whosoever feels himself guilty of rape, murder, plunder, sacrilege, and every most abominable crime, as soon as I have washed him with this water, he shall be clean and pure."

It was, indeed, this fatal doctrine that led all the Christian emperors and all the great men of the empire to defer their baptism until death. They thought they had found the secret of living criminal and dying virtuous.

(taken from M. Boulanger)[11]

Further Addition

What a strange idea drawn from the wash—that a pot of water should cleanse all crimes! Today, all children are baptized because an idea no less absurd supposes them all criminal; they are all saved until they have the use of reason and the power to become guilty! Cut their throats, then, as quickly as possible, to insure their entrance into paradise. This is so just a consequence that there was once a devout sect that went about poisoning and killing all newly baptized infants. These devout persons reasoned with perfect correctness, saying: "We do these little innocents the greatest possible good; we prevent them from being wicked and unhappy in this life, and we give them life eternal."

(by Monsieur l'abbé Nicaise.)

BEAU, BEAUTÉ / BEAUTIFUL, BEAUTY

ASK a toad what is beauty—the great beauty, the *To Kalon*? He will answer that it is the female with two great round eyes coming out of her little head, her large flat mouth, her yellow belly, and brown back. Ask a Negro of Guinea; beauty is to him a black, oily skin, sunken eyes, and a flat nose.

Ask the devil; he will tell you that the beautiful consists in a pair of horns, four claws, and a tail. Then consult the philosophers; they will answer you with jargon; they must have something that corresponds to the archetype of the essence of the beautiful—to the *To Kalon*.

I was once seated near a philosopher while watching a tragedy. "How beautiful!" he said. "What is beautiful about it?" I asked. "It is," said he, "that the author has attained his goal." The next day he took his medicine, which did him some good. "It has attained its goal," I said to him; "that is a beautiful medicine." He understood that it cannot be said that a medicine is beautiful, and that to apply to anything the epithet beautiful it must cause admiration and pleasure. He admitted that the tragedy had inspired him with these two sentiments, and that that was the *To Kalon*, the beautiful.

We took a journey to England. The same play was performed, and, although perfectly translated, it made all the spectators yawn. "Oh, oh!" he said, "the *To Kalon* is not the same for the English as for the French." He concluded after many reflections that "the beautiful" is often merely relative, as that which is decent in Japan is indecent in Rome; and that which is fashionable in Paris is not so in Peking; and he was thereby spared the trouble of composing a long treatise on the beautiful.

Bêtes / Animals

What a pity and what a poverty of mind to assert that animals are machines deprived of knowledge and sentiment, that carry out all their operations in the same manner, learn nothing, never improve, etc.

What! this bird, who makes its nest in a semicircle when he attaches it to a wall, a quarter circle when it is in a corner, and in a circle on a tree—this bird does everything in the same manner? The hunting dog that you have disciplined for three months, does he not know more at the end of this time than he did before these lessons? Does the canary, to which you teach a tune, repeat it instantly? Do you not employ a considerable time in teaching it? Have you not seen that he sometimes makes mistakes and that he corrects himself?

Is it because I speak to you that you judge I have sentiment, memory, and ideas? Well, suppose I do not speak to you; you see me enter my room with an afflicted air, I worriedly seek a paper, I open the desk in which I recall having locked it away, and I find it and read it with joy. You judge that I have felt the sentiment of affliction and of joy; that I have memory and knowledge.

Extend the same judgment to the dog who has lost his master, who has sought him everywhere with grievous cries, and who enters the house agitated and restless, goes upstairs and down, from room to room, and at last finds in the reading room the master whom he loves, and testifies his joy by the gentleness of his cries, by his leaps, and his caresses.

Some barbarians seize this dog that so prodigiously excels man in friendship; they nail him to a table and dissect him live to show the mesenteric veins. You discover in him the same organs of sentiment that are in yourself. Answer me, machinist, has nature arranged all the springs of sentiment in this animal so that he should not feel? Does he have nerves so that he will be incapable of suffering? Do not assume this impertinent contradiction in nature.

But the scholastic masters ask, what is the soul of animals? I do not understand this question. A tree has the faculty of absorbing in its fibers the circulating sap, of opening the buds of its leaves and fruits. Will you ask me what is the soul of this tree? It has received these gifts. The animal has received those of sentiment, memory, and a certain number of ideas. Who has bestowed these gifts; who has given all these faculties? He who makes the grass of the fields to grow, and who makes the earth gravitate towards the sun.

The souls of animals are *substantial forms,* said Aristotle; and after Aristotle, the Arabian school; and after the Arabian school, the Angelical school; and after the Angelical school, the Sorbonne; and after the Sorbonne, no one else.

The souls of animals are material, exclaim other philosophers. These have been no more successful than the former. They are in vain asked what a material soul is. They must agree that it is matter that has sensation; but who has given it this sensation? It is a material soul, that is to say, it is composed of a matter that gives sensation to matter. They cannot get out of this circle.

Listen to one kind of animals reasoning about others; their soul is a spiritual being that dies with the body; but what proof have you of it? What idea do you have of this spiritual being, which, in truth, has sentiment, memory, and its share of ideas and combinations, but which will never be capable of knowing the things a six-year-old child knows? On what ground do you imagine that this being, which is not corporeal, perishes with the body? The greatest asses are those who have suggested that this soul is neither body nor spirit—an excellent system! We can only understand by spirit something unknown, which is not body. Thus the system of these gentlemen amounts to this, that the soul of animals is a substance that is neither body, nor something that is not body.

Where can so many contradictory errors come from? From the habit men have always had of examining what a thing is before they know whether it exists. The flap or the valve of a bellows is called the "soul" of the bellows. What is this soul? It is a name I have given to this valve that falls, lets the air in, raises itself, and forces it through a pipe when I move the bellows.

There is not, then, a soul distinct from the machine. But who moves the bellows of animals? I have already told you: he who moves the stars. The philosopher who said, *"Deus est anima brutorum,"*—God is the soul of the brutes—was right; but he should have gone much further.

Bien. Souverain Bien / Good. The Sovereign Good

Antiquity had great discussions about the sovereign good. It might as well have been asked: What is the sovereign blue, or the sovereign ragout, or the sovereign walk, or the sovereign reading, etc.?

Everyone places his good where he can, and has as much of it as he can, each in his own way.

> *Quid dem? quid non dem? renuis tu quod jubet alter.*
> *Castor gaudet equis, ovo prognatus eodem*
> *Pugnis.*

The greatest good is that which delights us so powerfully as to render us totally incapable of feeling anything else; as the greatest evil is that which goes so far as to deprive us of all feeling. These are the two extremes of human nature, and these moments are short.

Neither extreme delight nor extreme torture can last a whole life. The sovereign good and the sovereign evil are nothing more than chimeras.

We all know the beautiful fable of Crantor. He introduces upon the stage at the Olympic Games, Wealth, Pleasure, Health, and Virtue. Each claims the prize apple. Wealth says, I am the sovereign good, for with me all goods are purchased. Pleasure says, the apple belongs to me, for it is only on my account that wealth is desired. Health asserts that without her there can be no pleasure, and wealth is useless. Finally, Virtue states that she is superior to the other three, because, although possessed of gold, pleasures, and health, a man may make himself quite miserable by misconduct. The apple was conferred on Virtue.

The fable is very ingenious; it would be still more so if it resolved the absurd question of the sovereign good. Virtue is not a good; it is a duty. It is of a different nature; of a superior order. It has nothing to do with painful or with agreeable sensations. A virtuous man, laboring under stone and gout, without aid, without friends, deprived of basic necessities, persecuted, and chained down to the floor by a voluptuous tyrant in good health, is very wretched; and his insolent persecutor, caressing a new mistress on his bed of purple, is very happy. Say, if you please, that the persecuted sage is preferable to the insolent persecutor; say that you admire the one and detest the other; but confess that the sage in chains is seething. If he does not himself admit it, he is deceiving you; he is a charlatan.

Tout Est Bien / All Is Well

It made a great commotion in the scholastic world, and even among people who think when Leibniz, paraphrasing Plato, elaborated his theory of the best of all possible worlds and imagined that all was for the best.[12] From the northern reaches of Germany, he affirmed that God could make only one world. Plato had at least allowed God the liberty of making five worlds, based on the idea that there are five regular solids in geometry, the tetrahedron, or three-sided pyramid with a regular base; the cube, the hexahedron, the dodecahedron, and the icosahedron. But since our world is not formed like any of Plato's five solids, he ought to have allowed God a sixth possibility.

Let us put aside Plato. Leibniz, who was assuredly a better geometer than he and a more profound metaphysician, thus did the human race the service of showing that we ought to be very happy and that God could do no more for us—that He had of necessity chosen among all the various possibilities the very best, without contradiction.

What will become of original sin? he was asked. It will become what it can, replied Leibniz and his friends. But in public he wrote that original sin necessarily participated in the best of all possible worlds.

What! to be chased from a delicious place, where we might have lived forever, only for the eating of an apple? What! to produce in misery wretched children, who will suffer everything, and who will produce others to suffer after them? What! to experience all maladies, feel all vexations, die in the midst of grief, and by way of recompense to burn for all eternity—is this lot the best possible? It certainly is not too *good* for us, and in what manner can it be good for God?

Leibniz felt that nothing could be said to these objections, but nevertheless made great books, in which he did not even understand himself.

Lucullus, in good health, partaking of a good dinner with his friends and his mistress in the hall of Apollo, may jocosely deny the existence of evil; but let him put his head out of the window and he will behold wretches; let him be seized with a fever, and he will be one himself.

I do not like to quote; it is ordinarily a thorny process. What precedes and what follows the passage quoted is too frequently neglected; and thus a thousand objections may arise. I must, notwithstanding, quote Lactantius, one of the fathers of the Church, who, in the thirteenth chapter on the anger of God, makes Epicurus speak as follows: "God can either take away evil from the world and will not; or being willing to do so, cannot; or He neither can nor will; or, lastly, He is both able and willing. If He is willing to remove evil and cannot, then this is impotence, which is contrary to the nature of God. If He can, but will not remove it, then this is cruelty, which is no less contrary to His nature; if He is neither able nor willing, this is both cruelty and impotence; lastly, if both able and willing to annihilate evil (which is the only one of these options that befits God), where does evil on earth come from?"

The argument is weighty, and Lactantius replies to it very poorly by saying that God wills evil, but has given us wisdom to secure the good. It must be confessed that this answer is very weak in comparison with the objection; for it implies that God could bestow wisdom only by allowing evil; and then again, our wisdom is pretty paltry!

The origin of evil has always been an abyss, the depth of which no one has been able to sound. It was this difficulty that reduced so many ancient philosophers and legislators to resort to two principles—the one good, the other wicked.

Typhon was the evil principle among the Egyptians, Arimanes among the Persians. The Manicheans, as you know, adopted this theology; but since these people had never spoken either with the good or the bad principle, we don't have to take their word for it.

Among the absurdities abounding in this world, and which may be placed among the number of our ills, it is not the least which presumes the existence of two all-powerful beings, fighting to determine which shall prevail most in this world, and making a treaty like the two physicians in Moliére: "Allow me the emetic, and I grant to you the lancet."

As early as the first century of the Church, Basilides contended, following the Platonists, that God gave the making of our world to His lowliest angels, and these, being inexpert, constructed it as we find it. This theological fable is invalidated by the overwhelming objection that it is not in the nature of a deity all-powerful and all-wise to entrust the construction of a world to incompetent architects.

Simon, who felt the force of this objection, obviates it by saying that the angel who presided over the workmen is damned for having done his business so slovenly, but the roasting of this angel does not cure us.

The adventure of Pandora among the Greeks scarcely meets the objection better. The box in which every evil is enclosed, and at the bottom of which remains Hope, is indeed a charming allegory; but this Pandora was made by Vulcan, only to avenge himself on Prometheus, who had made a man with mud.

The Indians have succeeded no better. God, having created man, gave him a drug that would ensure him permanent health of body. The man loaded his ass with the drug, and the ass being thirsty, the serpent directed him to a fountain, and while the ass was drinking, took the drug for himself.

The Syrians pretended that man and woman having been created in the fourth heaven, they resolved to eat a cake in lieu of ambrosia, their natural food. Ambrosia was exhaled by the pores; but after eating cake, they were obliged to relieve themselves in the usual manner. The man and the woman asked an angel to direct them to a water closet. Behold, said the angel, that small planet which is almost of no size at all; it is situated about sixty million leagues from this place, and is the privy of the universe—go there as quickly as you can. The man and woman went there, and they were left there; and it is since that time that our world has been as it is now.

The Syrians will eternally be asked why God allowed man to eat the cake, and why, as a result, we have inherited such a crowd of formidable ills?

To avoid boredom, I quickly pass from this fourth heaven to Lord Bolingbroke. This writer, who doubtless was a great genius, gave to the celebrated Pope the plan for his "all for the best," as it is found word for word in the posthumous works of Lord Bolingbroke, and previously inserted by Lord Shaftesbury in his "Characteristics."[13] Read in Shaftesbury the chapter on the Moralists, you will find the following words:

"Much may be replied to these complaints of the defects of nature—How did it emerge so powerless and defective from the hands of a perfect Being?—But I deny that it is defective . . . its beauty results from contrasts, and universal concord springs out of a perpetual conflict. . . . . It is necessary that each being be sacrificed to others—vegetables to animals, and animals to the earth . . . and the laws of the central power of gravitation, which give to the celestial bodies their weight and motion, are not to be disrupted for the sake of a pitiful animal, who, protected as he is by the same laws, will soon be reduced to dust."

Bolingbroke, Shaftesbury, and Pope, their working artisan, resolve the general question no better than the rest. Their "all for the best" says no more than that all is governed by immutable laws; and who did not know that? You learn nothing when you notice, like little children, that flies are created to be eaten by spiders, spiders by swallows, swallows by hawks, hawks by eagles, eagles by men, men by one another, to afford food for worms; and at last, at the rate of about a thousand to one, to be the prey of devils.

There is a constant and regular order established among animals of all kinds—there is order everywhere. When a stone is formed in my bladder, the mechanical process is admirable; sandy particles pass by small degrees into my blood; they are filtered by the kidneys; and passing the urethra, deposit themselves in my bladder; where, uniting in accordance with a fine Newtonian attraction, a stone is formed, which gradually increases, and I suffer pains a thousand times worse than death by the finest arrangement in the world. A surgeon, having perfected the art invented by Tubal-Cain, thrusts into me a sharp instrument; and cutting into the perineum, seizes the stone with his pincers, which breaks during these endeavors, by the necessary laws of mechanics; and owing to the same mechanism, I die in frightful torments. All this is "for the best," being the evident result of unalterable physical principles; I am in agreement; I knew it as well as you.

If we were insensitive, there would be nothing to say against this system of physics; but this is not the point. We ask if there are not physical evils, and where they originate. There is no absolute evil, says Pope in his fourth epistle on all is good; *or if there are particular evils, they compose a general good.*

It is a singular general good that is composed of the stone and the gout—of all sorts of crime and sufferings, and of death and damnation.

The fall of man is the bandage we apply to all these particular maladies of body and soul, which you call "the general health;" but Shaftesbury and Bolingbroke don't give a fig for original sin. Pope says nothing about it; but it is clear that their system saps the foundations of the Christian religion, and explains nothing at all.

In the meantime, this system has recently been approved by many theologians, who willingly embrace contradictions. So be it; we ought to leave to each the consolation of reasoning in his own way upon the deluge of ills that overwhelm us. It is only fair to allow incurable patients to eat what they please. It has even been maintained that this system is comforting. "God," says Pope, "beholds, with an equal eye, a hero perish or a sparrow fall; the destruction of an atom, or the ruin of a thousand planets; the forming of a bubble or of a world."

This, I must confess, is an odd consolation. Do you not find great comfort in the declaration of Lord Shaftesbury, who asserts, "that God will not derange His general system for so miserable an animal as man?" It must be confessed at least that this pitiful creature has a right to cry out humbly, and to endeavor, while bemoaning himself, to understand why these eternal laws do not take into account the good of every individual.

This system of "all for the best" represents the Author of Nature as a powerful and malevolent monarch, who cares not for the destruction of four or five hundred thousand men, nor for the others who spend their days in penury and tears, provided He succeeds in His designs.

Therefore, far from being consolatory, this doctrine of the best of all possible worlds is a hopeless one for the philosophers who embrace it. The question of good and evil remains an irremediable chaos for those who seek to fathom it in good faith. It is a mere mental sport for the disputants; they are captives who play with their chains. As to the unthinking common people, they resemble fish transported from a river to a holding pond; they have no suspicion that they are to be eaten during Lent. Likewise, by ourselves, we know nothing of the causes of our destiny.

Let us place at the end of nearly every chapter of metaphysics the two letters used by Roman judges when they did not understand a pleading. *N. L. non liquet.* This is not clear.

BORNES DE L'ESPRIT HUMAIN / LIMITS OF THE HUMAN MIND

THEY are everywhere, poor pedant. Do you wish to know how your arm and your foot obey your will, and why your liver does not obey? Do you seek how thoughts form in your feeble brain and this child in the uterus of your wife? I will give you time to respond. What is matter? Your fellows have written ten thousand volumes on this question; they have identified some qualities of this substance—children are just as aware of them as you and I. But this substance, what is it fundamentally? And what is this thing you have named *spirit,* based on the Latin word meaning *breath,* since it was impossible to do any better, given that you have no real idea of it?

Look at this kernel of wheat that I sow in the ground, and tell me how it springs up to produce a stem holding grain. Inform me how the same ground produces an apple at the top of this tree and a chestnut on the one next to it. I could make up for you a whole compendium of questions to which you could only reply with these four words: *I have no idea.*

And yet you have acquired diplomas, and you wear a mantle and a square hat, and you are called master. And this haughty imbecile, holder of a petty office, in a small town, thinks he has acquired the right to judge and condemn things he doesn't understand.

Montaigne's motto was, "What do I know?" and yours is, "What don't I know?"[14]

CARACTÈRE / CHARACTER

FROM the Greek word signifying *impression, engraving*. It is what nature has engraved in us: Can we change it? Good question. If I have a crooked nose and cat's eyes, I can hide them behind a mask. Can I do anything more to the character that nature has given me? A man born violent and passionate presents himself before Francis I, King of France, to complain of a trespass. The countenance of the prince, the respectful behavior of the courtiers, the very place he is in, make a powerful impression upon this man. He automatically casts down his eyes, his rude voice is softened, he presents his petition with humility, you would think him as mild (at that moment at least) as the courtiers, among whom he is quite disconcerted. But if Francis I knows anything of physiognomy, he will easily discover in his eyes, though downcast, glistening with a sullen fire, in the tense muscles of his face, in his fast-closed lips, that this man is not so mild as he is forced to appear. The same man follows him to Pavia, is taken prisoner along with him and thrown into the same dungeon at Madrid. The majesty of Francis I no longer makes the same impression on him; he becomes familiar with the object of his reverence. One day, pulling off the king's boots, and happening to do so clumsily, the king, soured by misfortune, grows angry, on which our man sends his majesty to the devil and throws his boots out the window.

Sixtus V was by nature petulant, obstinate, haughty, impetuous, vindictive, arrogant. This character, however, appears to be softened by the trials of his novitiate. Does he begin to acquire some influence in his order? He flies into a passion against a guard and beats him with his fists. Is he an inquisitor in Venice? He exercises his office with insolence. He becomes cardinal, he is possessed *della rabbia papale;* this rage triumphs over his natural propensities; he buries his person and his character in obscurity and counterfeits humility and infirmity. He is elected pope, and this event restores to the mechanism that politics had checked all the force of its long-restrained energy; he is the proudest and most despotic of sovereigns.

Naturam expellas furca, tamen ipsa redibit.
Although expelled, nature will still return.

Religion and morality curb the strength of the natural disposition, but they cannot destroy it. The drunkard in a cloister, reduced to a quarter of a pint of cider with each meal will never more get drunk, but he will always be fond of wine.

Age weakens the character; it is like an old tree that produces only a few degenerate fruits, but always of the same nature; it is covered with knots and moss and becomes worm-eaten, but is ever the same, whether oak or pear tree. If we could change our character we could give ourselves one and become the master of nature. Can we give ourselves anything? Don't we receive everything? Try to animate the indolent man with sustained activity, or to freeze with apathy the boiling blood of the impetuous, or to inspire a taste for music and poetry into him who has neither taste nor ears: you will succeed no better than if you attempted to give sight to one born blind. We perfect, we soften, we conceal what nature has placed in us, but we place nothing there ourselves.

An agriculturist is told: "You have too many fish in this pond; they will not thrive. There are too many cattle in your meadows; grass will run short, they will grow lean." After this exhortation pikes come and eat half of this man's carp, and wolves half of his sheep, and the rest fatten. Will he applaud his wise economy? This peasant is you; one of your passions has devoured the rest, and you think you have triumphed over yourself. Don't almost all of us resemble the old general of ninety, who, having found some young officers behaving in a rather disorderly manner with some young women, said to them in anger: "Gentlemen, is this the example that I provide for you?"

CARÊME / LENT

QUESTIONS ABOUT LENT

DID the first who were advised to fast put themselves on this diet by order of a physician, because of indigestion?

The lack of appetite we feel in grief—was it the primary origin of the fast-days prescribed in melancholy religions?

Did the Jews take the custom of fasting from the Egyptians, all of whose rites they imitated, including flagellation and the scapegoat?

Why did Jesus fast for forty days in the desert, where He was tempted by the devil—by the "Chathbull?" St. Matthew remarks that after this fast *He was hungry*; He was therefore not hungry during this fast.

Why, in days of abstinence, does the Roman Church consider it a crime to eat terrestrial animals, and a good work to be served sole and salmon? The rich Papist who has had five hundred francs' worth of fish on his table will be saved, and the poor wretch dying with hunger, who has eaten four pennies' worth of salt pork, will be damned.

Why must we ask the bishop's permission to eat eggs? If a king ordered his people never to eat eggs, would he not be thought the most ridiculous of tyrants? What strange aversion do bishops have for omelets!

Can we believe that among Papists there have been tribunals imbecile, dull, and barbarous enough to condemn to death poor citizens, who had committed no other crime than that of having eaten horseflesh during Lent? The fact is all too true; I have in my hands a sentence of this kind. What renders it still stranger is that the judges who passed such sentences believed themselves superior to the Iroquois.

Foolish and cruel priests! To whom do you prescribe Lent? Is it to the rich? They take good care not to observe it. Is it to the poor? They keep Lent all year. The unhappy peasant scarcely ever eats meat and has no means to buy fish. Fools that you are, when will you correct your absurd laws?

CATÉCHISME CHINOIS / THE CHINESE CATECHISM

or Dialogue between Cu-su, *a Disciple of Confucius, and Prince* Kou, *Son of the King of Lou, Tributary to the Chinese Emperor, Gnenvan, 417 Years before our Common Era*

Translated into Latin by Father Fouquet, formerly a Jesuit. The Manuscript is in the Vatican Library, Number 42759.[15]

Kou. What is meant when I am told to worship heaven? (Chang-ti)

Cu-su. Not the material heaven, which we see; for this heaven is nothing but the air, and the air is composed of every kind of earthly exhalation. What a folly it would be to worship vapors.

Kou. I would not be much surprised by it, however. Men, in my opinion, have committed even greater follies.

Cu-su. Very true; but you, being born to rule over others, you must be wise.

Kou. There are whole nations who worship heaven and the planets.

Cu-su. The planets are only so many earths, like ours. The moon, for instance, might do as well to worship our sand and dirt, as we do in prostrating ourselves before the dirt and sand of the moon.

Kou. What is meant when one says, *heaven and earth; ascend to heaven; be deserving of heaven?*

Cu-su. These are silly statements. (See article *Ciel* / Heaven) There is no such thing as heaven. Every planet is surrounded by its atmosphere like a shell, and rolls in space around its sun. Every sun is the center of several planets, which are continually going their rounds. There is neither high nor low, up nor down. You can sense that, should the inhabitants of the moon talk of ascending to earth, of making one's self deserving of the earth, it would be talking madly. We are little wiser in talking of deserving heaven. We might as well say, a man must make himself deserving of the air-deserving of the constellation of the dragon—deserving of space.

Kou. I believe I understand you. We are to worship only the God who created heaven and earth.

Cu-su. No doubt; we must only adore God. But in saying that he made heaven and earth, however devout our meaning may be, we speak poorly. For if, by heaven, we mean the prodigious space in which God kindled so many suns and set so many worlds in motion, it is much more ridiculous to say, "heaven and earth," than it is to say, "the mountains and a grain of sand." Our globe is infinitely less than a grain of sand, in comparison to those millions of ten thousands of millions of worlds, among which we disappear. All that we can do is to join our feeble voice to that of the innumerable beings, who, throughout the expansive abyss, pay homage to God.

Kou. It was, then, a great imposition to tell us that Fo came down among us from the fourth heaven, assuming the form of a white elephant.

Cu-su. These are tales, which the bonzes tell to old women and children. The Eternal Author of all things is alone to be worshiped.

Kou. But how can one being make the other beings?

CU-SU. You see that star. It is fifteen hundred thousand millions of *Lis* from our globe, and emits rays which, on your eyes, form two angles equal at the top; and they form the same angles on the eyes of all animals. Is this not manifest design? Is this not an admirable law? And is it not the workman who makes the work? And, who frames laws if not a legislator? Therefore, there is an eternal Artist, an eternal Legislator.

KOU. But who made this Artist, and what is he like?

CU-SU. My dear Prince, as I was yesterday afternoon walking near the magnificent palace, so lately built by the king, your father, I overheard two crickets. One said to the other, "What an imposing edifice." "Yes," said the other; "and as proud as I am, I admit that he who has made this prodigy must be more powerful than crickets; but I have no idea of that being. I see that he must exist, but I do not know what he is."

KOU. You are a cricket of infinitely more knowledge than I; but what I particularly like in you is that you don't pretend to know things you really do not understand.

SECOND DIALOGUE

CU-SU. You allow, then, that there is an Almighty Being, self-existent, supreme Creator and Maker of all nature.

KOU. Yes; but if he be self-existent, he is unlimited; consequently, he is everywhere? He exists throughout all matter and in every part of me?

CU-SU. Why not?

KOU. I should then be a part of the Deity.

CU-SU. Perhaps that may not be the consequence. This piece of glass is thoroughly penetrated by light; yet, is it light itself? It is mere sand, and nothing more. Unquestionably, everything is in God; that, by which everything is animated, must be everywhere. God is not like the emperor of China, who dwells in his palace, and sends his orders by *koloas*. As existing, he must necessarily fill the whole of space, and all his works; and since he is in you, this is a continual monition never to do anything that would make you blush in his presence.

Kou. But what must a person do in order to dare consider oneself without repugnance and shame in the presence of the Supreme Being?

Cu-su. Be just.

Kou. And what further?

Cu-su. Be just.

Kou. But Loakium's sect says, "There is no such thing as just or unjust, vice or virtue."

Cu-su. And does Loakium's sect say, "There is no such thing as health or sickness?"

Kou. No, to be sure; what egregious nonsense that would be!

Cu-su. To think there is neither health nor sickness of the soul, virtue nor vice, is as egregious an error, and much more mischievous. They, who have advanced that everything is the same, are monsters. Is it the same, to carefully bring up a son, or, at his birth, to dash him against the stones? To relieve a mother, or to plunge a dagger into her heart?

Kou. You make me shiver! I detest Loakium's sect. But there are so many nuances of *just* and *unjust*! One is often at a loss. Who can be said to know precisely what is forbidden, and what is allowed? Who can safely set the limits separating good and evil? What rule will you give me to distinguish them?

Cu-su. Those of Confucius, my master: *"Live as you would like to have lived, when you are dying; treat your neighbor as you want him to treat you."*

Kou. Those maxims, I own, should be humankind's standing law. But when I die what will it matter if I have lived a good life? What will I gain? When that clock is destroyed, will it be happy for having struck the hours regularly?

Cu-su. That clock is without thought or feeling, and incapable of remorse, which you feel sharply when you have feelings of guilt.

Kou. But what if, by frequent crimes, I succeed in no longer feeling remorse?

Cu-su. Then it will be time to suffocate you; and you can be sure that since men do not like to be oppressed, there will be someone who will prevent you from committing other crimes.

Kou. At that rate, God, who is in them, after allowing me to be wicked, would allow them likewise to be so?

Cu-su. God has endowed you with reason; neither you nor they are to make a wrong use of it. Not only will you be unhappy in this life, but who told you that you won't meet the same fate in another?

Kou. And who told you there is another life?

Cu-su. The very doubt should make you behave as if there were.

Kou. But if I am sure there is no such thing?

Cu-su. I defy you to prove it.

Third Dialogue

Kou. You are pushing me Cu-su. My being rewarded or punished after death, requires that something, which feels and thinks in me, must continue to subsist after me. Now, as no part in me had any thought or sense before my birth, why should it possess them after my death? What can this incomprehensible part of me be? Will the humming of that bee continue when the bee no long exists? Will the vegetation of this plant subsist when the plant is plucked up by the roots? Isn't *vegetation* a word used to designate the inexplicable way in which the Supreme Being ordained that plants imbibe the juices of the earth? In the same way, *soul* is a word invented to express faintly and obscurely the mechanism of human life. All animals move, and this ability to move, is called active force; but there is no distinct being that is this force. We have passions, memory, and reason; but these passions, this memory, and this reason, are surely not separate things; they are not beings existing within us; they are not diminutive persons having an individual existence; they are generic words, concocted to define our ideas. Thus the soul itself, which signifies our memory, our reason, our passions, is only a word. What causes movement in nature? It is God. Who makes all plants grow? It is God. What causes motion in animals? It is God. What makes thought in man? It is God.

If the human soul (See article *Âme* / Soul) were a diminutive person, enclosed within our body, who directed its movements and ideas, wouldn't that betray, in the eternal maker of the world, an impotence and an artifice quite unworthy of him? He would thus not have been capable of making automatons having the gift of motion and thought in themselves. You taught me Greek, you made me read Homer; I find Vulcan to be a divine smith, when he makes golden tripods that walk by themselves to the council of the gods; but had this same Vulcan concealed within those tripods one of his boys, to make them move without being perceived, I would consider him a bungling cheat.

There are obscure dreamers who have been charmed by the idea of having the planets rolled along by genii who push them ceaselessly; but God was not reduced to such a paltry shift. In a word, why put two springs to a work when one will do? You will not dare deny that God has the power to animate that little known substance called matter, why then would he make use of another agent to animate it?

Furthermore, what would that soul be, which you are pleased to give to our body? Where did it come from? When? Must the Creator of the universe be continually observing the couplings of men and women, attentively noting the moment when a seed leaves the body of a man and enters the body of a woman, and then quickly sending a soul for this seed? And if this seed dies, what will this soul become? It will thus have been created to no purpose, or it will await another occasion.

This, I admit, is really a strange employment for the Sovereign of the world, and not only must He pay continual attention to the copulation of the human species, but must do the same with all animals whatever; for, like us, they all have memory, ideas, and passions; and, if a soul is necessary for the formation of these sentiments, this memory these ideas, these passions, God must work perpetually to forge souls for elephants and for hogs, for owls, for fish and for bonzes.

What idea does such a notion give of the Architect of so many millions of worlds, thus obliged to be continually making invisible props for perpetuating his work?

These are a very small sample of the reasons for questioning the soul's existence.

CU-SU. You reason candidly; and such a virtuous turn of mind, even if mistaken, cannot but be agreeable to the Supreme Being. You may be in error, but as you do not endeavor to deceive yourself, your error is excusable. But consider, what you have proposed to me are only doubts, and melancholy doubts. Listen to some more comforting probabilities. To be annihilated is dismal; hope then for life. A thought, you know, is not matter, nor has any affinity with it. Why, then, do you make such a difficulty of believing that God has put a divine principle in you, which, being indissoluble, cannot be subject to death? Can you say that it is impossible that you should have a soul? No, certainly. And, if it is possible that you have one, is it not also very probable? Could you reject so noble a system—so necessary to mankind? Shall a few objections withhold your assent?

KOU. I would embrace this system, but I would like it to be proved to me. It is not in my power to believe without evidence. I am always struck by this grand idea, that God has made everything, that he is everywhere, that he penetrates all things, and gives life and motion to all things. And if he is in all parts of my being, as he is in all parts of nature, I don't see that I have need of a soul. What use do I have for this little subaltern being, when I am animated by God himself? What good would this soul do for me? It is not from ourselves that we derive our ideas; we almost always formulate them despite ourselves; we have them when we are sleeping; everything takes place in us without our intervention. In vain the soul would say to the blood and animal spirits, "Be so kind as to gratify me by running this way?" They will still circulate in the manner prescribed for them by God. I prefer to be the machine of a God who is proven to me, rather than the machine of a soul, whose existence I doubt.

CU-SU. Well, if God himself animates you, never defile by any crimes this God, who is within you; and, if he has given you a soul, may this soul never offend him. In both systems you have volition, you are free; that is, you have the power to do what you will. Make use of this power to serve this God who gave it to you. If you are a philosopher, so much the better; but it is necessary for you to be just; and you will be more just, when you come to believe that you have an immortal soul.

Deign to answer me: Is it not that that God is sovereign justice?

KOU. Doubtless; and if it were possible that he should cease to be so, (which is a blasphemy) I would myself wish to act equitably.

CU-SU. Is it not true that, when you are on the throne, it will be your duty to reward virtuous actions and to punish criminal ones? Can you think of God's not doing what is incumbent on yourself to do? You know that there are, and will always be, unfortunate virtues and unpunished crimes in this life; therefore, good and evil must find their judgment in another life. It is this idea, so simple, so natural, so general, that has established among so many nations the belief in the immortality of our souls, and in divine justice that judges them when they have abandoned their mortal corpse. Is there a system more rational, more suitable to the Deity, and more beneficial to mankind?

KOU. Why, then, have several nations failed to embrace this system? You know that, in our province, we have about two hundred old Sinous families,* who formerly lived in part of Arabia Petraea; and neither they, nor their ancestors, ever believed in the immortality of the soul. They have their five books, as we have our five *Kings,* I have read a translation of them. Their laws, which necessarily resemble those of all other nations, enjoin them to respect their parents, not to steal nor lie, and to abstain from adultery and homicide; yet these same laws speak neither of rewards nor punishments in another life.

CU-SU. If this truth has not yet developed among those poor people, unquestionably their eyes will be opened some day. But what does a small obscure tribe matter to us, when the Babylonians, the Egyptians, the Indians, and all polished nations, have subscribed to this salutary doctrine? If you were sick, would you reject a remedy, approved by all the Chinese, on the pretext that a few barbarians from the mountains had refused to use it? God has endowed you with reason, and this reason tells you, that the soul must be immortal; therefore, it is God himself who tells you so.

KOU. But how can I be rewarded or punished, when I shall cease to be myself?—when I no longer have anything that constituted my person? It is only by my memory that I am always myself. I will lose my memory in my last illness; so, after my death, nothing less than a miracle can restore it to me, and thus return me to the existence I will have lost?

---

* These are the Jews from the ten tribes who during the Diaspora penetrated into China; there they are called *Sinous.*

CU-SU. That is as much as to say that if a prince had made his way to the throne by the murder of all his relatives, if had played the tyrant over his subjects, he need only say to God, "It is not I; I have lost my memory; you are mistaken, I am no longer the same person." Do you think God would be pleased with such a sophism?

KOU. Well, I acquiesce;* [16] I was in favor of doing good for my own sake, now I will do so to please the Supreme Being. I thought it was sufficient that my soul be just in this life; I will now hope that it will be happy in another. This opinion, I see, is good both for subjects and sovereigns. Still, the worship of God perplexes me.

---

* Well! Sad enemies of reason and truth, will you still say that this work teaches the mortality of the soul? This passage has been printed in all the editions. On what grounds do you thus dare to slander it? Alas, if your souls conserve their character in eternity, they will eternally be stupid and unjust souls. No, the authors of this reasonable and useful work absolutely do not tell you that the soul dies along with the body; they tell you simply that you are ignorant. Don't blush; all wise men have admitted their ignorance, none of them has been sufficiently impertinent to claim knowledge of the nature of the soul. Summarizing all that antiquity said, Gassendi tells you this: *You know that you think, but you do not know what kind of substance you are, you who think. You are like a blind man who, upon feeling the heat of the sun, thinks he has a distinct idea of that star.* Read the rest of this admirable letter to Descartes, read Locke; reread this work attentively, and you will see that it is impossible for us to have the first idea of the nature of the soul, for the good reason that it is impossible for the creature to know all of the secret mechanisms of the Creator; you will see that, without knowing the principle of our thoughts, we must strive to think with accuracy and justice, that we must be all that you are not—modest, gentle, generous, indulgent; we must resemble Cu-su and Kou, and not Thomas Aquinas or Scotus, whose souls were quite gloomy, or Calvin or Luther whose souls were hard and impetuous. Try to make your souls take a bit after ours; then you will mock yourselves prodigiously.

Fourth Dialogue

CU-SU. Why, what is there that can offend you in our Chu-king, the first canonical book, which all the Chinese emperors have so greatly respected? You plough a field with your own royal hands by way of example to the people; and the first fruits of it you offer to the Chang-ti, to the Tien, to the Supreme Being, and sacrifice to him four times every year. You are king and high-priest; you promise God to do all the good that shall be in your power. Is there anything in this that repels you?

KOU. I am very far from making any objections. I know that God has no need either of our sacrifices or prayers, but we need to offer them to him. His worship was not instituted for him, but on our account. I am delighted to give prayers, and am particularly careful that there be nothing ridiculous in them; for, were I to cry out, "That the mountain of Chang-ti is a fat mountain, and that fat mountains are not to be looked upon;" were I to put the sun to flight, and dried up the moon, will this rant be acceptable to the Supreme Being, or of any benefit to my subjects or to myself?

Especially, I cannot bear with the silliness of the sects surrounding us. On one side is Lao Tze, whom his mother conceived by the junction of heaven and earth, and was for fourscore years pregnant with him. I have no more faith in his doctrine of universal deprivation and annihilation, then in the white hairs with which he was born or the black cow on which he rode to go preach his doctrine.

The god Fo, I put on the same footing, notwithstanding he had a white elephant for his father, and promises immortal life.

One thing that particularly displeases me is that the bonzes continually preach such chimeras, thus deceiving the people, in order to govern them. They gain for themselves respect by mortifications that make nature shudder. Some deny themselves, during their whole lives, the most salutary foods, as if there were no way of pleasing God, but by a bad diet. Others carry a pillory about their necks, and sometimes they richly deserve it. They drive nails into their thighs, as if their thighs were boards; the people follow them in crowds. It the king issues an edict that does not suit their humor, they coolly declare that this edict is not to be found in the commentary of the god Fo, and that it is better to obey God then men. Now, how is such an extravagant and dangerous popular malady to be cured? Toleration, you know, is the principle of the Chinese and of all Asian governments, but isn't this quite deadly, when it exposes an empire to overthrow on account of some fanatical notions?

Cu-su. May the Chang-Ti forbid that I extinguish in you this spirit of toleration, this eminently respectable quality, which is to souls like the permission to eat is to bodies. Natural law allows everyone to believe what he will, as well as eat what he will. A doctor has no right to kill his patients for not observing the diet he has prescribed to them; neither has a sovereign the right to hang his subjects for not thinking as he thinks; but he has a right to prevent disturbances, and, if he is wise, he will very easily root out superstition. You know what happened to Daon, the sixth king of Chaldaea, about four thousand years ago?

Kou. No, I know nothing about it; I pray you oblige me with an account of it.

Cu-su. The Chaldaean priests had taken it into their heads to worship the pikes of the Euphrates, pretending that a famous fish called Oannes, had formerly taught them theology; that this fish was immortal, three feet in length, and a small crescent on its tail. In veneration of this Oannes, it was forbidden to eat pike. A violent dispute arose among the theologians, whether the fish Oannes had a soft or hard roe. The two parties excommunicated one another, and several times they came to blows. To put an end to such disturbances, king Daon made use of this expedient.

He ordered a strict fast for three days to both parties, and at the expiration of it, sent for the supporters of the hard-roed pike, who, accordingly, were present at his dinner. A pike was brought to him, three feet in length, and on the tail, a small crescent had been put. "Is this your God?" said he, to the doctors. "Yes, sire," they answered; "we know him by the crescent on the tail." The king ordered the pike to be opened. It was found to have the finest soft roe that could be. "Now," said the king, "you see that this is not your god, it being soft-roed;" and the king and his nobles ate the pike, to the great satisfaction of the hard-roed theologians, who saw that the god of their adversaries had been fried.

Immediately after, the doctors of the opposite side were sent for; they were shown a god, three feet long, with hard roe and a crescent on his tail; they assured his majesty, that this was the god Oannes, and that it had a soft roe; it was fried like the other and acknowledged as hard-roed. At this, the two parties, equally foolish, and still fasting, the good king Daon told them, that he had only pikes to give them for dinner: they greedily fell to eating, both hard- and soft-roed. The civil war ceases, all bless the good King Daon, and after that time, the citizens were allowed to eat pike as often as they pleased.

KOU. Well done, King Daon! I give my word that I will follow his example on the occasion that presents itself. As far as I can (without injuring anyone), I will prevent the worship of Fos and pikes.

I know that in the countries of Pegu and Tonquin, there are little gods and little Tapolins, who make the moon wane and clearly foretell what is to come; that is, they clearly see what is not, for the future is not. I will take care that the Tapolins not come to my kingdom to give the future for the present and make the moon wane.

It is a shame that there should be sects rambling from town to town, propagating their delusions, as quacks do their medicines. What a disgrace it is to the human mind that petty nations think that truth belongs to them alone, and that the vast empire of China is given up to error! Is then, the Eternal Being only the god of the island of Formosa or the island of Borneo? Would he abandon the rest of the universe? My dear Cu-su, he is a father to all men; he allows everyone to eat pike. The most worthy homage that can be paid to him, is being virtuous. The finest of all his temples, as the great emperor Hiao used to say, is a pure heart.

Fifth Dialogue

Cu-su. Since you love virtue; how will you practice it, when you come to be king?

Kou. In not being unjust to my neighbors, or my subjects.

Cu-su. Simply doing no harm is not enough. You will do good; you will feed the poor, by employing them in useful labor, not by rewarding sloth. You will embellish the great highways, dig canals, build public edifices, encourage all the arts, reward merit of every kind, and pardon involuntary faults.

Kou. This is what I call not being unjust: those things are so many duties.

Cu-su. Your ways of thinking become a king; but there is the king and the man, public life and private life. You will be married soon: How many wives do you think you will have?

Kou. Why, a dozen, I think will do; a greater number might prove to be a hindrance from business. I do not approve of kings, like Solomon, with three hundred wives and seven hundred concubines, and thousands of eunuchs to wait on them. This custom of having eunuchs, especially, appears to me a most execrable insult and outrage to human nature. At the very limit, I can accept that roosters are caponed; they are better to eat that way. But eunuchs haven't yet been put on the spit. What is the use of their mutilation? The Dalai Lama has fifty of them who sing in his pagoda. I would like to know whether the Chang-ti is much delighted with the clear pipes of these fifty emasculated beings.

Another most ridiculous thing is that there are bonzes who do not marry. They boast of being wiser than the other Chinese; well, then, let them produce wise children. An odd manner, indeed, of worshiping the Chang-ti, to deprive him of worshipers! A singular fashion of serving the human species by leading the way toward extinction of the human species! The good little Lama, called *Stelca Isant Erepi*,*[17] used to say that "Every priest should marry and rear as many children as possible." What this Lama taught, he practiced, and was very useful in his time. For my part, I will marry all the Lamas and Bonzes, and Lamasses and Bonzesses, who appear to have a call to the holy work. Besides making them better patriots, I shall think it no small service to my dominions.

CU-SU. What an excellent prince we shall have in you! You make me weep for joy. But you will not be satisfied with having wives and subjects, for after all, one cannot be perpetually drawing up edicts and caring for children; you will certainly have some friends.

KOU. I already have some—good ones—who alert me to my faults, and I allow myself the liberty of reproving theirs. We likewise mutually comfort and encourage one another. Friendship is the balm of life. It surpasses that of the chemist Erueil; and even the sachets of the great Hanourd are not comparable to it. I am surprised that friendship has not been made a religions precept. I have a good mind to insert it in our ritual.

CU-SU. By no means. Friendship is sufficiently sacred of itself; never make it an obligation: the heart must be free. Besides, were you to make friendship a precept, a mystery, a rite,

---

* *Stelca isant Erepi*, means in Chinese, the *abbé Castel de Saint Pierre*.

a ceremony, it would soon become ridiculous through the fantastical preaching and writing of a thousand bonzes. You mustn't expose it to such profanation.

But how will you deal with your enemies? Confucius, in no less than twenty places, directs us to love them. Doesn't this seem somewhat difficult to you?

Kou. Love one's enemies! Oh, dear doctor! Nothing is more common.

Cu-su. But what do you mean by love?

Kou. Mean by it! What it really is. I learned warfare under the prince of Decon, against the prince of Vis-Brunk;* when a wounded enemy fell into our hands, we took as much care of him as if he had been our brother. We often gave our own beds to our wounded enemies, and we lay near them on tiger's skins, spread on the bare ground. We tended and nursed them ourselves! What more could you wish? That we love them as one loves a mistress?

Cu-su. I am greatly pleased with your discourse, and wish that all nations could hear you, for I have been informed that there are some peoples, so impertinent as to assert that we know nothing of true virtue, that our good actions are only showy sins, and that we stand in need of the lessons of their Talapoins to instruct us in right principles! Poor creatures! It's only yesterday that they learned to read and write; and now, they purport to teach their masters!

SIXTH DIALOGUE

Cu-su. I shall not repeat to you the common phrases, which, for these five or six thousand years past, have been spread among us, relating to all the virtues. Some of them concern only ourselves, as

---

* It is a remarkable thing, that in reversing Decon and Vis-Brunk, which are Chinese names, we find Condé and Brunswik, reflecting how broadly great men are celebrated throughout the world.

prudence in the guidance of our souls; temperance in the government of our bodies; but these are rather dictates of policy, and care of health. The real virtues are those that promote the welfare of society, like fidelity, magnanimity, beneficence, toleration, etc. Thank Heaven, these are the first things every old woman among us teaches her grandchildren. They are the rudiments of the rising generation, both in town and country; but, I am sorry to say, there is a great virtue that is sadly on the decline among us.

KOU. Which one? Quickly name it, and I will attempt to revive it.

CU-SU. It is hospitality; for, since inns have been established among us, this social virtue—this sacred tie of mankind—becomes more and more relaxed. That pernicious institution, the hotel, came to us, it is said, from certain Western savages. These wretches apparently have no houses to welcome travelers. My heart melts with delight, when I have the happiness of entertaining, in the vast city of Lou, in Honcham, that superb square, in my delicious house Ki, some generous stranger from Samarcand, to whom, from that moment, I become sacred, and who, by all laws human and divine, is bound to entertain me on any call I may have into Tartary; and to be and remain my cordial friend.

The savages I am speaking of, do not admit strangers into their huts, filthy as they are, without their paying, and dearly too, for such sordid reception; and yet these wretches, I hear, think themselves above us; and that our morality is nothing in comparison to theirs—that their preachers preach better than Confucius. In a word, they think they can teach us what true justice is, because they sell bad wine in public places, and their women roam the streets as if mad, and dance while ours are breeding silkworms.

KOU. I much approve of hospitality, and the practice of it gives me pleasure; but I am afraid of its abuse. Near Tibet dwells a people, who, besides the poverty of their habitations, being of a roving disposition, will, for any trifle, go from one end of the world to the other; and when you go to Tibet, to profit from the right to hospitality, you will find neither a bed, nor a stew pot. This is enough to cause disgust with courtesy.

CU-SU. This disappointment may easily be remedied, by entertaining such persons only as come well recommended. Every virtue has its dangers, and it is from this danger that the practice of virtue takes much of its glory and excellence.

How wise and holy is our Confucius! There is not a virtue that he does not encourage. Every sentence is pregnant with the happiness of mankind. Here is one that comes to my memory; it's the fifty-third:

"Acknowledge kindnesses with kindness, and never avenge injuries."

What a maxim! What law could the western people propose in comparison to such a pure morality? How many times does Confucius recommend humility! If this virtue were practiced, there would be an end to all quarrels.

KOU. I have read all that Confucius, and the sages before him, wrote about humility; but none of them, I think, has ever given a sufficiently accurate definition of it. There may, perhaps, be little humility in presuming to censure them; but I at least have the humility to admit that they are beyond my comprehension. What is your idea of humility?

CU-SU. I will obey humbly. I take humility to be mental modesty; for external modesty, is nothing more than civility. Humility cannot consist in denying to oneself the superiority we may have acquired above another. A skilled doctor cannot hide from himself that he is possessed of knowledge beyond that of his delirious patient. The teacher of astronomy must admit to himself that he is more learned than his followers. He cannot prevent himself from believing it, but he must not be deceived by this. Humility is not debasement, but a corrective to self-love, just as modesty is the corrective of pride.

Kou. Well, it is in the practice of all these virtues, and the worship of one simple and universal God, that I propose to live, far from the chimeras of sophists, and the illusions of false prophets. The love of humankind will be my virtue on the throne, and the love of God my religion. As to the god Fo, and Lao Tze, and Vishnou, who has so often become incarnate among the Indians; and Sammonocodom, who came down from heaven to fly a kite among the Siamese, together with the Camis, who went from the moon to visit Japan,—I will scorn them all.

Woe to a people who are stupid and barbarous enough to think there is a God exclusively for their province! It is downright blasphemy. What! The light of the sun brightens all eyes, and the light of God would shine only for a little insignificant tribe, in a corner of this globe! What outrage and what stupidity! The Deity speaks to the heart of all men, and they should, from one end of the universe to the other, be linked together in the bonds of charity.

Cu-su. O wise Kou! You have spoken like one inspired by the great Chang-ti himself! You will make a worthy prince. I was your teacher, and you have become mine.

Catéchisme Du Curé / The Country-Priest's Catechism

Ariston. So, my dear Theotimus, you are going to be a country-priest?

Theotimus. Yes, I have had a small parish conferred upon me, and I like it better than a larger. I have only a small share of intelligence and energy. Having but one soul myself, the direction of seventy thousand souls would certainly be too much for me; and I have always admired the confidence of those who have taken on the care of those immense districts. I do not feel capable of such a charge. A large flock really frightens me, but, with a small one I may perhaps do some good. I have studied enough law to prevent, with my careful endeavors, my poor parishioners from ruining one another by litigation. I know enough medicine to prescribe to them simple remedies when they are ill. I have sufficient knowledge of agriculture so that my advice may sometimes be of service to them. The lord of the manor and his lady are good people, and not excessively devout; they will second my endeavors to do good. I flatter myself that I will live quite happily; and that those, among whom I am to live, will not be the worse for my company.

ARISTON. But aren't you upset at not having a wife? It would be a great comfort; it would be sweet after preaching, singing, confessing, communicating, baptizing, and burying, to be welcomed at your return home by an affectionate, agreeable, and virtuous wife who would take care of your linen and person, divert you when in health, tend you in sickness, and make you pretty children, whose good education would be of public advantage. I really pity you who serve humankind, being deprived of a comfort so necessary to men.

THEOTIMUS. The Greek Church makes a point of encouraging marriage in their priests. The Church of England and the Protestants act with the like wisdom; the Latin Church has a contrary wisdom, and I must submit to it. Perhaps today, when the philosophical spirit has made such great progress, a Church council would make decrees more favorable to human nature than those of the council of Trent; but until that time, I must conform to the present laws. It is a great sacrifice, I know, but so many people of greater worth than I have submitted to this law; it is not for me to murmur.

ARISTON. You have a great share of learning, and are likewise master of a wise eloquence. How do you intend to preach before a congregation of villagers?

THEOTIMUS. As I would before kings. I will insist on morality, and never meddle with controversy. God forbid that I should go about diving into concomitant grace, effectual grace, which may be resisted, sufficient grace, which does not suffice; or examining whether the angels, who ate with Abraham and Lot, had a body, or only feigned to eat. There are a thousand things my congregation would never understand, nor I, either. My endeavor will be to make them good, and to be so myself, but I will make no theologians, and I will be one as little as possible.

ARISTON. Oh, the good priest! I think I must purchase a country house in your parish. Tell me, I pray, how will you manage confession?

THEOTIMUS. Confession is an excellent thing, a strong curb to vice, invented in the very earliest times. Confession was practiced at the celebration of all the ancient mysteries; and we imitated and sanctified this wise custom. It is useful for persuading hearts filled with hatred to forgive, and for inducing petty rogues to restore what they may have stolen from their neighbors. It has some inconveniences. There are many indiscreet confessors, chiefly among the monks, who sometimes teach girls more foolishness than all the village boys could do to them. In confession there should be no particulars; it is no juridical interrogatory, but only a sinner's acknowledgment of his faults to the Supreme Being, before another sinner, who is soon to make the like acknowledgment. This salutary avowal is not made to gratify the curiosity of a man.

ARISTON. And excommunications—will you use them?

THEOTIMUS. No. There are rituals in which grasshoppers, sorcerers, and actors are excommunicated. I will never exclude grasshoppers from my church, since they never come there. I will never excommunicate sorcerers, seeing there are none; as for actors, since they are authorized by the magistrates, and pensioned by his majesty, it would ill become me to brand them with infamy. I will admit to you as a friend that I have a taste for the theater when it is kept within the limits of decency. I adore *Athaliah,* and *The Misanthrope,* and other plays that strike me as schools of virtue and polite manners.[18] The lord of my village has had some of these plays performed in his castle by talented young people. These performances lead to virtue through the attraction of pleasure; they form taste, and greatly contribute to a just elocution. Now, for my part, in all this I see nothing, but what is very innocent and even very useful; so that I intend, purely for my instruction, to be a spectator sometimes, but in a latticed box, to avoid giving offense to the weak.

ARISTON. The more you enlighten me in regard to your way of thinking, the more desirous I am to become your parishioner; but, one point remains, which I think of very great importance. How will you manage to restrain the peasants from intemperance on the holidays? That is their chief way of celebrating festivals. Some, overcome by a liquid poison, are seen with their heads drooping almost to their knees, their hands dangling, their sight and hearing lost; in a condition very much beneath beasts, led home reeling by their lamenting wives, incapable of going to work the next day, often sick, and sometimes irrevocably besotted. You see others, inflamed by wine, raise bloody quarrels, strike and be struck, sometimes putting an end to these awful scenes, which are the shame of the human race, with a murder. It must be recognized, that the state loses more subjects because of holidays than in battles. How will you reduce such an execrable abuse in your parish?

THEOTIMUS. I have decided; I will give them permission, even exhort them, to tend their fields on feast days after divine service, and that I shall take care to begin very early. It is their being unemployed on such days that sends them to public houses. On the working days, we hear of no riot or bloodshed. Moderate labor is good for both soul and body: besides, their labor is necessary to the State. Let us suppose, and the supposition is within bounds, five million men, who, on an average do ten pennies of work daily, and that these five million men are, by such a custom, rendered quite useless no less than thirty days in the year; consequently, the state is deprived of labor to the value of thirty times five million times ten pennies. Now, God certainly never instituted either this loss or this drunkenness.

ARISTON. Thus you will reconcile devotion and business, and both are of God's appointment. Thus you will serve God and do good to your neighbor. But amid our ecclesiastical feuds, with which party will you side?

THEOTIMUS. None. Virtue never occasions any disputes, because it comes from God; all these disputes are about opinions, which are the inventions of men.

ARISTON. Oh, the good priest! The good priest!

CATÉCHISME DU JAPONAIS / THE JAPANESE CATECHISM[19]

INDIAN. Is it so, that formerly, the Japanese knew nothing of cookery; that they had submitted their kingdom to the great Lama; that this great Lama arbitrarily prescribed what they should eat and drink; that he used, at times, to send to you an inferior Lama for receiving tributes, who, in return, gave you a sign of protection, which he made with his two forefingers and thumb?

JAPANESE. Alas! It is but too true; nay, all the places of the Canusi,* or chief cooks of our island, were disposed of by the Lama, and the love of God was quite out of the question. Further, every house of our seculars paid annually an ounce of silver to this head cook of Tibet. For compensation all he gave us were some small, rather wretched tasting dishes called *relics*. And on every new whim of his—as making war against the people of Tangut—we were saddled with fresh subsidies. Our

---

* The *Canusi* are the ancient priests of Japan.

nation frequently complained, but to no avail; all we got by it was to pay more for presuming to complain. At length, love, which does everything for the best, freed us from this servitude. One of our emperors quarreled with the great Lama about a woman; but it must be recognized that they who, in this affair, did us the best turn, were our Canusi, or Pauxcospies.* It is to them that, in fact, we owe our deliverance; and it happened in this manner.

The great Lama had a funny obsession; he insisted on always being in the right. Our Dairi and Canusi would have it that sometimes, at least, they might not be in the wrong. The great Lama derided this claim as an absurdity, our Canusi didn't budge, and they broke with him forever.

INDIAN. Well, ever since you have doubtless been happy and peaceful?

JAPANESE. Far from it: for nearly two hundred years, there was nothing but persecution, violence, and bloodshed among us. Though our Canusi wanted to be in the right, it is but a hundred years since they have had their proper reason. But, since that time, we may boldly esteem ourselves one of the happiest nations on earth.

INDIAN. How can that be, if as I have been told, you have no less than twelve different sects of cookery among you? You must have twelve civil wars every year.

JAPANESE. Why so? If there be twelve cooks, and each has a different recipe, is that a reason to cut each other's throats instead of dining? No, on the contrary, each one may regale himself at that cook's table whose manner of dressing victuals he likes best.

INDIAN. True; tastes are not to be disputed about. Yet people will make them a matter of contention, and quarrels heat up.

---

* *Pauxcospies,* anagram of Episcopalians [Episcopaux].

JAPANESE. After long disputing, men come to see the mischief of this wrangling, and at length agree upon a reciprocal toleration; and, certainly, they can do nothing better.

INDIAN. And pray, who are those cooks, who share your nation in the art of eating and drinking?

JAPANESE. First, there are the Breuxehs,* who never allow any pork or pudding. They hold with the old-fashioned cookery; they would as soon die, as lard a fowl; then they deal much in numbers, and if an ounce of silver is to be divided between them and the eleven other cooks, they instantly secure one-half to themselves, and the remainder goes to those who best know how to count.

INDIAN. I fancy you do not often sup with these folks.

JAPANESE. Never. Then there are the Pispates, who, on some days of the week, and even for a considerable time of the year, would much rather spend a fortune on turbot, trout, salmon, sturgeon than eat a Blanquette of veal that would cost almost nothing.

As for us Canusi, we are very fond of beef and a kind of pastry, in Japanese called pudding. Now, all the world allows our cooks to be infinitely more knowing than those of the Pispates. Nobody has gone farther than we in finding out what the garum of the Romans was. We surpass all others in our knowledge of the onions of ancient Egypt, the locust paste of the primitive Arabs, the Tartar horseflesh; and there is always something to be learned in the books of those Canusi, commonly known by the name of Pauxcospies.

I shall omit those who eat only according to Tarluh, those who observe the Vincal diet, the Bastistans, and others; but the Quekars deserve particular notice. Though I have very often been at table with them, I never saw one get drunk, or heard him swear an oath. It is a hard matter to cheat them, but then they never

---

* It is clear that the *Breuxeh* are the Hebrews [Hébreux], *et sic de caeteris.*

cheat you. The law of loving one's neighbor as one's self, seems to have been made especially for them; for, in truth, how can an honest Japanese talk of loving his neighbor as himself, when, for a small sum of money, he goes as a hireling, to blow his brains out, and to hew him with a four-inch broad saber, and all this in due form; then he, at the same time, exposes himself to the like fate, to be shot or sabred: so he may, with more truth, be said to hate his neighbor as himself. This is a frenzy the Quekars have never had. They say that poor mortals are earthen vessels, made to last but a very short time, and that they should not wantonly go and break themselves to pieces one against another. I admit, that were I not a Canusi, I wouldn't dislike being a Quekar. You must admit that this is no way of quarreling with such peaceable cooks. There is another, and a very numerous branch of cooks, called Diestes; with these, every one, without distinction, is welcome to their table, and you are at full liberty to eat as you like. You have larded or barded fowls, or neither larded nor barded, egg sauce, or oil; partridge, salmon, white or red wines; these things they hold as matters of indifference, provided you say a short prayer before or after dinner, and even simply before breakfast—and if you are good folks, they will banter with you about the great Lama, who won't be hurt by it, or about Turlah, Vincal and Memnon, &c.; these Diestes must simply acknowledge our Canusi to be very profound cooks; and, especially, let them never talk of curtailing our incomes: then we shall live very easily together.

INDIAN. But still there must be a dominant cookery, the king's cookery.

JAPANESE. There must, indeed; but when the king of Japan has regaled himself plentifully, he should be cheerful, and not hinder his good and loyal subjects from digesting.

INDIAN. But, should some hot-headed people take it upon themselves to eat sausages under the king's nose, when the king is known to have an aversion to that food; should a mob of four or five thousand of them get together, each with his gridiron, to broil their sausages, and insult those who are against eating them?

JAPANESE. In such a case, they ought to be punished as turbulent drunkards who disrupt the civil peace. But we have obviated this danger; none but those who follow the royal cookery are allowed to hold any State employment: all others may, indeed, eat as they please, but this humor excludes them from some offices. Gatherings are strictly forbidden, and instantly punished without mercy or mitigation. All quarrels at table are carefully restrained by a precept of our great Japanese cook, who has written, in the sacred language, *"Suti raho, cus flac, natis in usum lætitiae scyphis pugnare tracum est,"* that is, "the intent of feasting is a sober and decent mirth; but to throw glasses at one another is savage."

Under these maxims we live very happily. Our liberty is secured by our Taicosemas. We are every day growing more and more opulent. We have two hundred junks of the line, and are dreaded by our neighbors.

INDIAN. Why, then, has the pious rhymer, Recina, (son of the Indian poet, Recina,* so tender, precise, harmonious, and eloquent) said, in a didactic work in verse, entitled *Grace*, and not *The Graces*,

> *"Le Japon ou jadis brilla tant de lumiere,*
> *N'est plus qu'un triste amas de folles visions."*
> Japan, once famed for intellectual light,
> Lies sunk in vision, chimera, and night.[20]

---

* Racine, probably, Louis Racine, son of the admirable Racine.

JAPANESE. The poet Recina, is himself a grand visionary. Does this weak Indian not know, that it is we who taught his countrymen what light is? That it is to us India owes its knowledge of the course of the planets, and that it is we who have made known to man the primitive laws of nature and infinitesimal calculus?

To descend to things of more common use: by us his countrymen were taught to build Junks in mathematical proportion; they are beholden to us for those coverings of their legs, which they call woven stockings. Now, is it possible, that, after such admirable and useful inventions, we should be madmen? And, if he has rhymed on the follies of others, does that make him the only wise man? Let him leave us to our own cookery, and, if he must be versifying, I would advise him to choose more poetical subjects.*

INDIAN. What can be said? He is full of his country's prejudices, those of his party, and his own.

JAPANESE. A world of prejudices indeed!

CATÉCHISME DU JARDINIER / THE GARDENER'S CATECHISM

or Dialogue between Pasha Tuctan, and Karpos the Gardener.

TUCTAN. You sell your fruit, friend Karpos, very dear; however, it is pretty good. Pray, what religion do you profess now?

---

* NB. This Indian Recina, trusting to the visionaries of his country, has advanced that no good sauces can be made, unless Brahma himself, out of his gracious favor, teaches or inspires his particular favorites to make the sauce; that there is an infinite number of cooks, who, with the best intentions, and most earnest endeavors, are quite unable to serve a ragout; Brahma, from mere ill will, deprives them of the means. Such stuff will not be credited in Japan, where the following quotation is esteemed as an indisputable truth: "God never acts by partial, partial, but by general laws."

KARPOS. Why, indeed, my Lord Pasha, I cannot very well tell you. When our little island of Samos belonged to the Greeks, I remember that I was ordered to say, that *agion pneuma* (sacred spirit) proceeded only from *tou patrou* (the father). I was told to pray to God, standing upright, with my arms crossed, and was prohibited from eating milk during Lent. When the Venetians came, our new Italian curate ordered me to say, that *agion pneuma* proceeded both from *tou patrou* and from *tou you* (the son), permitted me to eat milk, and made me pray on my knees. On the return of the Greeks, and their expulsion of the Venetians, I was obliged again to renounce *tou you* and cream. You have, at length, expelled the Greeks, and I hear you cry out, as loud as you can, *"Allah ilia Allach!"* For my part, I no longer know what I am; but I love God with all my heart, and sell my fruit very reasonably.

TUCTAN. You have some fine figs there.

KARPOS. At your service, my lord.

TUCTAN. They say you have a fine daughter too.

KARPOS. Yes, my lord Pasha; but she is not at your service.

TUCTAN. Why so? Wretch!

KARPOS. Because I am an honest man. I may sell my figs, if I please; but I may not sell my daughter.

TUCTAN. And, pray, by what law are you allowed to sell one kind of fruit and not the other?

KARPOS. By the law of all honest gardeners. The honor of my daughter is not my property, but hers. It is not a marketable commodity.

TUCTAN. You are, then, disloyal to your Pasha?

KARPOS. Very faithful in every thing that is just, as long as you are my master.

TUCTAN. And so, if your Greek patriarch should form a plot against me, and should order you, in the name of *tou patrou* and the *tou you,* to enter into it, you would not have devotion enough to turn traitor?

KARPOS. Not I. I would be careful not to.

TUCTAN. And, pray, why should you refuse to obey your patriarch, on such an occasion?

KARPOS. Because I have taken an oath of allegiance to you; and I know that *tou patrou* does not command any one to engage in plots and conspiracies.

TUCTAN. I am glad of that, at least. But what, if the Greeks should retake the isle, and expel me; would you be faithful to me still?

KARPOS. And how could I be faithful to you then since you would no longer be my Pasha?

TUCTAN. What would become of your oath of allegiance then?

KARPOS. Something like my figs: it would no longer be yours to handle. Craving your honor's pardon, is it not true that if you were now dead, I should owe you no allegiance?

TUCTAN. The supposition is a little impolite; but your conclusion is true.

KARPOS. And would it not be the same, my lord, if you were expelled? For you would have a successor, to whom I must take a fresh oath of allegiance. Why should you require fidelity of me, when it would be no longer of use to you? That would be just as if you could not eat my figs yourself, and yet you would prevent my selling them to anybody else.

TUCTAN. You are a reasoner, I see. So you have principles?

KARPOS. Aye, such as they are. They are but few, but they serve me; and if I had more, they would get in my way.

TUCTAN. I should, indeed, be curious to know your principles.

KARPOS. They are, for example, to be a good husband, a good father, a good neighbor, and a good gardener. I go no further, and hope for the rest, that God will have mercy on me.

TUCTAN. And do you think he will show the same mercy to me, the governor of this island of Samos?

KARPOS. And, pray, how do you think I should know that? Is it for me to conjecture how God Almighty treats Pashas? That is an affair between you and him, with which I do not intermeddle in any shape. All that I believe of the matter is, that if you are as good a Pasha as I am a gardener, God will be very good to you.

TUCTAN. By Muhammad! I like this idolater very well! Farewell friend: *Allah* be your protection!

KARPOS. Thank you, my lord Pasha! God have mercy upon you.

CERTAIN, CERTITUDE / CERTAIN, CERTAINTY

WHAT is the age of your friend Christopher? Twenty-eight years. I have seen his marriage contract, and his baptismal register; I knew him in his infancy; he is twenty-eight—I am certain of it.

Scarcely have I heard the answer of this man, so sure of what he is saying, and of twenty others who confirm the same thing, when I learn that for secret reasons, and by a singular circumstance, Christopher's baptismal register has been antedated. Those to whom I had spoken as yet know nothing of it; they still have the same certainty of that which is not.

If you had asked the whole earth before the time of Copernicus: Has the sun risen? Has it set today? All men would have answered: We are quite certain of it. They were certain and they were in error.

Witchcraft, divinations, and possessions were for a long time the most certain things in the world in the eyes of all peoples. What an innumerable crowd of people who have seen all these fine things and who have been certain of them! At present this certainty is a little shaken.

A young man who is beginning to study geometry comes to me; he is only at the definition of triangles. Are you not certain, I said to him, that the three angles of a triangle are equal to two right angles? He answers that not only is he not certain of it, but that he has not the slightest idea of the proposition. I demonstrate it to him. He then becomes very certain of it, and will remain so all his life.

This is a certainty very different from the others; they were only probabilities and these probabilities, when examined, became errors; but mathematical certainty is immutable and eternal.

I exist, I think, I feel grief—is all that as certain as a geometrical truth? Yes. Why? It is that these truths are proved by the same principle that it is impossible for a thing to exist and not exist at the same time. I cannot at the same time exist and not exist, feel and not feel. A triangle cannot at the same time contain one hundred eighty degrees, which are the sum of two right angles, and not contain them.

The physical certainty of my existence, of my feelings, is of the same value as mathematical certainty, although it is of a different kind.

It is not the same with the certainty founded on appearances, or on the unanimous testimony of humankind.

But what, you will say to me, are you not certain that Peking exists? Do you not have merchandise from Peking? People of different countries and different opinions who have vehemently written against one another while preaching the truth in Peking; then are you not assured of the existence of this town? I answer that it is extremely probable that there may be a city of Peking but I would not wager my life that such a town exists, and I will at any time wager my life that the three angles of a triangle are equal to two right angles.

A very funny thing appears in the *Dictionnaire Encyclopédique.* It is there maintained that a man ought to be as certain that Marshal Saxe has risen from the dead, if all Paris tells him so, as he is sure that Marshal Saxe gained the battle of Fontenoy, upon the same testimony.[21] Pray observe the beauty of this reasoning: as I believe all Paris when it tells me a thing morally possible, I ought to believe all Paris when it tells me a thing morally and physically impossible.

Apparently the author of this article was seeking a good laugh, as was the other author of this article who goes into ecstasy at the end of this article and who writes against himself. (See article *Certitude*, Encyclopedia Dictionary)

Chaîne des Êtres Créés / Chain of Created Beings

THE first time I read Plato, and I saw this gradation of beings rising from the smallest atom to the Great Supreme, this ladder struck me with admiration, but I examined it more attentively this phantom disappears, as apparitions were wont to vanish at the crowing of the cock.

The imagination is pleased with the imperceptible transition from brute matter to organized matter, from plants to zoophytes, from zoophytes to animals, from animals to men, from men to genii, from these genii, clad in a light aerial body, to immaterial substances, and finally to a thousand different orders of these substances, rising from beauty to perfection, up to God Himself. This hierarchy is very pleasing to good folks who look upon it as upon the pope and cardinals, followed by the archbishops and bishops, after whom are the vicars, curates and priests, the deacons and sub-deacons, then come the monks, and the capuchins bring up the rear.

But there is, perhaps, a somewhat greater distance between God and His most perfect creatures than between the Holy Father and the dean of the sacred college. The dean may become pope, but the most perfect genii created by the Supreme Being cannot become God. Is there not infinity between them?

Nor does this chain, this pretended gradation, exist in vegetables and animals either; the proof is that some species of plants and animals have been entirely destroyed. We have no murex. The Jews were forbidden to eat griffin and ixion, these two species, whatever Bochart may say, have probably disappeared from the earth. Where, then, is the chain?

Supposing that we had not lost some species, it is evident that they can be destroyed. Lions and rhinoceroses are becoming very scarce.

It is probable that there have been races of men who are no longer to be found. But I hope they have all survived, like the whites, the blacks, the Kaffirs, to whom nature has given an apron of their own skin, hanging from the belly to the middle of the thigh; the Samoyeds, whose women have nipples of beautiful ebony, etc.

Is there not a manifest void between the ape and man? Is it not easy to imagine a two-legged animal without feathers having intelligence without our face or the use of speech—one that we could tame, that would answer our signs, and serve us? And again, between this new species and man, couldn't we imagine others?

Beyond man, divine Plato, you place in heaven a string of celestial substances, some of which we believe in because the faith so teaches us. But what reason do you have to believe in them? You did not speak with the genius Socrates, and though Heres, good man, came back to life expressly to tell you the secrets of the other world, he told you nothing of these substances.

In the sensible universe the supposed chain is no less interrupted.

What gradation, I pray you, is there among the planets? The moon is forty times smaller than our globe. Traveling from the moon through space, you find Venus, about as large as the earth. From thence you go to Mercury, which revolves in an ellipsis very different from the circular orbit of Venus; it is twenty-seven times smaller than the earth, the sun is a million times larger, and Mars is five times smaller. The latter goes his round in two years, his neighbor Jupiter in twelve, and Saturn in thirty; yet Saturn, the most distant of all, is not as large as Jupiter. Where is the pretended gradation?

And then, how, in so many empty spaces, do you extend a chain connecting the whole? If there is one, it can be none other than that which Newton discovered—that which makes all the globes of the planetary world gravitate one towards another in the immense void.

Oh, much admired Plato! I fear that you have told us nothing but fables, and a philosopher from the Cassideride Islands, where in your day men went about naked, has revealed to the world truths as grand as your imaginings are childish.[22]

CHAÎNE DES ÉVÉNEMENTS / CHAIN OF EVENTS

IT has long been imagined that all events are linked one with another by an invincible fatality. This is the fate which, in Homer, is superior to Jupiter himself. The master of gods and men expressly declares that he cannot prevent his son Sarpedon from dying at the time appointed. Sarpedon was born at the moment when it was necessary that he be born, and could not be born at any other; he could not die elsewhere than before Troy; he could not be buried elsewhere than in Lycia; his body must, in the appointed time, produce vegetables, which must change into the substance of some of the Lycians; his heirs must establish a new order of things in his states; that new order must influence neighboring kingdoms; thence must result a new arrangement in war and in peace with the neighbors of Lycia. So that, from link to link, the destiny of the whole earth hinged on the death of Sarpedon, which in turn depended on other events, which, ascending to higher events, were connected with the origin of things.

Had any one of these occurrences been ordered otherwise, the result would have been a different universe. Now, it was not possible for the actual universe not to exist; therefore it was not possible for Jupiter, even as Jupiter, to save the life of his son.

This doctrine of necessity and fatality was invented in our own times by Leibniz, as he himself claims, under the name of sufficient reason. It is, however, of great antiquity. It is no recent discovery that there is no effect without a cause and that often the smallest cause produces the greatest effects.

Lord Bolingbroke acknowledges that he was indebted to the petty quarrels between the Duchess of Marlborough and Mrs. Masham for the opportunity of concluding the private treaty between Queen Anne and Louis XIV. This treaty led to the peace of Utrecht; the peace of Utrecht secured the throne of Spain to Philip V; Philip V took Naples and Sicily from the house of Austria. Thus the Spanish prince, who is now king of Naples, evidently owes his kingdom to Mrs. Masham; he would not have had it, nor perhaps even have been born, if the Duchess of Marlborough had been more complaisant towards the queen of England; his existence at Naples depended on one folly more or less at the court of London.[23] Examine the situations of every people upon earth; they are in like manner founded on a train of occurrences seemingly without connection, but all connected. In this immense machine all is wheel, pulley, cord, or spring.

It is the same in physical order. A wind blowing from the southern seas and the remotest parts of Africa brings with it a portion of the African atmosphere, which, falling in showers in the valleys of the Alps, fertilizes our lands; on the other hand our north wind carries our vapors among the Negroes; we do good to Guinea, and Guinea to us. The chain extends from one end of the universe to the other.

But the truth of this principle seems to me to be strangely abused; for it is thence concluded that there is no atom, however small, the movement of which has not influenced the actual arrangement of the whole world; that the most trivial accident, whether among men or animals, is an essential link in the great chain of destiny.

Let us understand one another. Every effect evidently has its cause, ascending from cause to cause, into the abyss of eternity; but every cause has not its effect, going down to the end of ages. I grant that all events are produced one by another; if the past was pregnant with the present, the present is pregnant with the future; everything is begotten, but everything does not beget. It is exactly like a genealogical tree; every house, we know, ascends to Adam, but many members of the family have died without descendants.

The events of this world form a genealogical tree. It is indisputable that the inhabitants of Spain and Gaul are descended from Gomer, and the Russians from his younger brother Magog, This genealogy is found in so many great books! It cannot then be denied that we are indebted to Magog for the sixty thousand Russians who are presently under arms in Pomerania, and the sixty thousand French who are camped out around Frankfort; but whether Magog spat to the right or to the left near Mount Caucasus—made two or three circles in a well—or whether he lay on his right side or his left, I do not see that it could have much influence on the decision of the Russian Empress Elizabeth to send an army to help the Roman Empress Maria Theresa. Whether my dog dreams or not in his sleep, I do not see that this great affair has any connection to the doings of the grand Mogul.

It must be remembered that nature is not a plenum, and that motion is not communicated solely by direct collision until it has made the tour of the universe. Throw a body of a certain density into water, you can easily calculate that at the end of some time the movement of this body, and that which it has given to the water, will cease; the motion will be lost and rest will be restored. So the motion produced by Magog in spitting into a well cannot have influenced what is now passing in Russia and Prussia. Present events, then, are not the offspring of all past events, they have their direct lines, but a thousand small collateral lines have nothing to do with them. Once again: every being has a parent but every being does not have offspring. We will perhaps say more about this when we speak of destiny.

DE LA CHINE / ON CHINA

WE travel to China to obtain clay, as if we had none ourselves; fabric, as if we lacked fabric; and a small herb to be infused in water, as if we had no simples in our own countries. In return for these benefits, we strive to convert the Chinese. This is a very commendable zeal; but we must avoid contesting their antiquity, and also calling them idolaters. In truth, would we like it if a capuchin, after having been hospitably entertained at the château of the Montmorencys, endeavored to persuade them that they were new nobility, like the king's secretaries; and accused them of idolatry, because he found in their château two or three statues of constables, for whom they had the most profound respect?

The celebrated Wolf, professor of mathematics at the University of Halle, once delivered an excellent discourse in praise of Chinese philosophy. He praised that ancient species of the human race, differing from ourselves with respect to the beard, the eyes, the nose, the ears, and even the reasoning powers; he praised the Chinese, I say, for their adoration of a supreme God, and their love of virtue. He did that justice to the emperors of China, to the Kolaos, to the tribunals, and to the literati. The justice normally given to the bonzes is of a different kind.

It is necessary to observe, that this Professor Wolf attracted to Halle a thousand pupils of all nations. In the same university there was also a professor of theology, named Lange, who attracted no one. This man, maddened at the thought of freezing to death in his own deserted hall, formed the design, which undoubtedly was only right and reasonable, of destroying the mathematical professor. He did not fail, according to the practice of persons like himself, to accuse him of not believing in God.

Some European writers, who had never been in China, had pretended that the government of Peking was atheistic. Wolf had praised the philosophers of Peking; therefore Wolf was an atheist. Envy and hatred seldom construct the best syllogisms. Lange's argument, supported by a party and by a protector, was considered conclusive by the sovereign of the country, who dispatched a formal dilemma to the mathematician. This dilemma gave him the option of leaving Halle within twenty-four hours, or of being hanged; and as Wolf was a very accurate reasoner, he did not fail to leave. His departure deprived the king of two or three hundred thousand crowns a year, which were brought into the kingdom in consequence of the wealth of this philosopher's disciples.

This case should convince sovereigns that they should not always listen to calumny, and sacrifice a great man to the madness of a fool. But let us return to China.

Why should we concern ourselves—we who live at the extremity of the West—why should we dispute with abuse and fury, whether there were fourteen princes or not before Fo-hi, emperor of China, and whether the said Fo-hi lived three thousand or two thousand nine hundred years before our common era? I should like to see two Irishmen quarreling in Dublin, about who was the owner, in the twelfth century, of the estate I am now in possession of. Is it not clear, that they should refer to me, who possess the documents and titles relating to it? To my mind, the case is the same with respect to the first emperors of China; the tribunals of that country are the proper authority upon the subject.

Dispute as long as you please about the fourteen princes who reigned before Fo-hi, your very interesting dispute cannot possibly fail to prove that China was at that period populous, and that laws were in force there. I now ask you whether a people's being collected together, under laws and kings, is not proof of considerable antiquity? Reflect how long a time is required before, by a singular concurrence of circumstances, iron is discovered in mines, before it is applied to purposes of agriculture, before the invention of the shuttle, and all the other arts.

Some who produce children with a dash of the pen have produced very curious calculations. The Jesuit Petau, by a very singular computation, gives the world two hundred and twenty-five years after the deluge, one hundred times as many inhabitants as can be easily conceived to exist on it at present. The Cumberlands and Whistons have formed calculations equally ridiculous; had these worthies only consulted the registers of our colonies in America, they would have been perfectly astonished, and would have perceived not only how little humankind increases in number, but that frequently instead of increasing it actually diminishes.

Let us then, who are of recent origin, descendants of the Celts, who have only just finished clearing the forests of our savage territories, suffer the Chinese and Indians to enjoy in peace their fine climate and their antiquity. Let us, especially, cease calling the emperor of China, and the souba of the Deccan, idolaters. There is no need to be a zealot in estimating Chinese merit. The constitution of their empire is, in truth, the only one entirely established upon paternal authority (which does not prevent the mandarins from showering their children with blows); the only one in which the governor of a province is punished, if, on quitting his station, he does not receive the acclamations of the people; the only one that has instituted rewards for virtue, while, everywhere else, the sole object of the laws is the punishment of crime; the only one that has caused its laws to be adopted by its conquerors, while we are still subject to the customs of the Burgundians, the Franks, and the Goths, by whom we were conquered. Yet, we must confess, that the common people, governed by the bonzes, are equally knavish with our own; that everything is sold enormously dear to foreigners, as among ourselves; that, with respect to the sciences, the Chinese are still at the stage where we were two hundred years ago; that, like us, they labor under a thousand ridiculous prejudices; and that they believe in talismans and judicial astrology, as we long did ourselves.

We must admit also, that they were astonished at our thermometer, at our method of freezing fluids by means of saltpeter, and at all the experiments of Torricelli and Otto von Guericke; as we were also, on seeing for the first time those curious processes. Let us add, that their doctors do not cure mortal diseases any more than our own; and that minor diseases, both here and in China, are cured by nature alone. All this, however, does not interfere with the fact, that the Chinese, four thousand years ago, when we were unable even to read, knew everything essentially useful of which we boast at the present day.

I must again repeat, the religion of their learned is admirable. No superstitions, no absurd legends, no dogmas that insult both reason and nature, and to which the bonzes attribute a thousand different meanings because they really have none. The simplest worship has appeared to them the best for forty centuries. They are what we think Seth, Enoch, and Noah may have been; they are contented to adore one God in communion with the sages of the world, while Europe is divided between Thomas and Bonaventure, between Calvin and Luther, between Jansenius and Molina.

CHRISTIANISME / CHRISTIANITY

Historical Research on Christianity

SEVERAL learned men have testified their surprise at not finding in the historian, Flavius Josephus, any mention of Jesus Christ; for all men of true learning are now agreed that the short passage relative to him in that history has been interpolated.* The father of Flavius Josephus must, however, have been witness to all the miracles of Jesus. Josephus was of the sacerdotal race and related to Herod's wife, Marianne. He gives us long details of all that prince's actions, yet says not a word of the life or death of Jesus; nor does this historian, who disguises none of Herod's cruelties, say one word of the general massacre of the infants ordered by him on hearing that there was born a king of the Jews. The Greek calendar estimates the number of children murdered on this occasion at fourteen thousand.

This is, of all actions of all tyrants, the most horrible. There is no example of it in the history of the whole world.

Yet the best writer the Jews have ever had, the only one esteemed by the Greeks and Romans, makes no mention of an event so singular and so frightful. He says nothing of the appearance of a new star in the east after the birth of our Savior—a

---

* Christians, using one of those ruses qualified as "pious," falsified a passage in Joseph. They attribute to this Jew who was so attached to his religion, four ridiculously interpolated lines, and at the end of this passage they add, "He was the Christ." What! If Josephus had heard about so many events that overturn nature, would he only have devoted to them four lines in his history of his country! What! This obstinate Jew is supposed to have said, "Jesus was the Christ." Ah! If you had believed him to be Christ, you would have been Christian. What an absurdity to make Josephus speak as a Christian! How can there still be theologians stupid or insolent enough to try to justify this imposture of the first Christians, recognized as fabricators of other impostures a hundred times worse!

brilliant phenomenon, which could not escape the knowledge of a historian so enlightened as Josephus. He is also silent respecting the darkness that, on our Savior's death, covered the whole earth for three hours at midday, or the great number of graves that opened at that moment, and the multitude of the just that rose again.

The learned are constantly evincing their surprise that no Roman historian speaks of these prodigies, happening in the empire of Tiberius, under the eyes of a Roman governor and a Roman garrison, who must have sent to the emperor and the senate a detailed account of the most miraculous event of which mankind had ever heard. Rome itself must have been plunged for three hours in impenetrable darkness; such a prodigy would have had a place in the annals of Rome, and in those of every nation. But it was not God's will that these divine things should be written down by their profane hands.

The same learned persons also find some difficulties in the gospel history. They remark that, in Matthew, Jesus Christ tells the scribes and Pharisees that all the innocent blood that has been shed upon earth, from that of Abel the Just down to that of Zachary, son of Barac, whom they slew between the temple and the altar, shall be upon their heads.

There is not (they say) in the Hebrew history any Zachary slain in the temple before the coming of the Messiah, nor in His time, but in the history of the siege of Jerusalem, by Josephus, there is a Zachary, son of Barac, slain by the faction of the Zealots. This is in the nineteenth chapter of the fourth book. Hence they suspect that the gospel according to St. Matthew was written after the taking of Jerusalem by Titus. But every doubt, every objection of this kind, vanishes when it is considered how great a difference there must be between books divinely inspired and the books of men. It was God's pleasure to envelop in a cloud both opaque and respectable His birth, His life, and His death. His ways are in all things different from ours.

The learned have also been much tormented by the difference between the two genealogies of Jesus Christ. St. Matthew makes Joseph the son of Jacob, Jacob of Matthan, Matthan of Eleazar. St. Luke, on the contrary, says that Joseph was the son of Heli, Heli of Matthat, Matthat of Levi, Levi of Melchi, etc. They refuse to reconcile the fifty-six progenitors up to Abraham, given to Jesus by Luke, with the forty-two other forefathers up to the same Abraham, given him by Matthew; and they are quite staggered by Matthew's giving only forty-one generations, while he speaks of forty-two.

They start other difficulties about Jesus being the son, not of Joseph, but of Mary. They moreover raise some doubts respecting our Savior's miracles, quoting St. Augustine, St. Hilary, and others, who have given to the accounts of these miracles a mystic or allegorical sense; as, for example, to the fig tree cursed and blasted for not having borne figs when it was not the fig season; the devils sent into the bodies of swine in a country where no swine were kept; the water changed into wine at the end of a feast, when the guests were already too much heated. But all these learned critics are confounded by the faith, which is made purer by their cavils. The sole goal of this article is to follow the historical thread and give a precise idea of the facts about which there is no dispute.

First, then, Jesus was born under the Mosaic law; He was circumcised according to that law; He fulfilled all its precepts; He kept all its feasts; He preached only morality; He did not reveal the mystery of His incarnation; He never told the Jews He was born of a virgin; He received John's blessing in the waters of the Jordan, a ceremony to which several Jews submitted; but He never baptized any one; He never spoke of the seven sacraments; He instituted no ecclesiastical hierarchy during His life. He concealed from His contemporaries that He was the Son of God, begotten from all eternity, consubstantial with His Father; and that the Holy Ghost proceeded from the Father and the Son. He did not say that His person was composed of two natures and two wills. He left these mysteries to be announced to men in the course of time by those who were to be enlightened by the Holy Ghost. So long as He lived, He departed in nothing from the law of His fathers. In the eyes of men He was no more than a just man, pleasing to God, persecuted by the envious and condemned to death by prejudiced magistrates. He left His holy church, established by Him, to do all the rest.

Josephus, in chapter 12 of his History, speaks of a sect of rigorist Jews, newly established by a certain Galilean named Judas: "They despise the evils of the world; their constancy enables them to triumph over torments; in an honorable cause, they prefer death to life. They have undergone fire and sword, and submitted to having their very bones crushed, rather than utter a syllable against their legislator, or eat forbidden food."

It would seem, from the words of Josephus that the foregoing portrait applies to the Judahites, and not to the Essenes. For here are the words of Josephus: "Judas was the author of a new sect, completely different from the other three;" that is, the Sadducees, the Pharisees, and the Essenes. "They are," he goes on, "Jews by nation; they live in harmony with one another, and consider pleasure to be a vice." The natural meaning of this language would induce us to think that he is speaking of the Judahites.

However that may be, these Judahites were known before the disciples of Christ began to possess consideration and consequence in the world.

The Therapeutae were a society different from the Essenes and the Judahites. They resembled the Gymnosophists and Brahmins of India. "They possess," says Philo, "a principle of divine love that excites in them an enthusiasm like that of the Bacchantes and the Corybantes, and brings them to that state of contemplation to which they aspire. This sect originated in Alexandria, which was entirely filled with Jews, and prevailed greatly throughout Egypt."

The disciples of John the Baptist had spread themselves a little in Egypt, but principally in Syria and Arabia. There were some also in Asia Minor. It is mentioned in the Acts of the Apostles, 19 that Paul met with many of them at Ephesus. "Have you received," he asked them, "the holy spirit?" They answered him. "We have not even heard that there is a holy spirit." "What baptism, then," says he, "have you received?" They answered him, "The baptism of John."

There were in the first years following the death of Jesus, seven different societies or sects among the Jews, the Pharisees, the Sadducees, the Essenes, the Judahites, the Therapeutae, the disciples of John, and the disciples of Christ, whom God led along paths unknown to human wisdom.

He who contributed most to strengthen this rising society was Paul, who had himself persecuted it with the greatest violence. He was born at Tarsus in Cilicia, and was educated under one of the most celebrated professors among the Pharisees—Gamaliel, a disciple of Hillel. The Jews pretend that he quarreled with Gamaliel, who refused to let him have his daughter in marriage. Some traces of this anecdote are to be found in the sequel to the "Acts of St. Thekla." These acts relate that he had a large forehead, a bald head, united eyebrows, an aquiline nose, a short and clumsy figure, and crooked legs. Lucian, in his dialogue "Philopatres," seems to give a very similar portrait of him. It has been doubted whether he was a Roman citizen, for at that time the title was not given to any Jew; they had been expelled from Rome by Tiberius; and Tarsus did not become a Roman colony until nearly a hundred years later, under Caracalla, as Cellarius remarks in his *Geography* (book 3), and Grotius in his *Commentary on the Acts*.

The faithful had the name of Christians in Antioch, around year sixty of our common era; but they were known in the Roman Empire, as we shall see subsequently, by other names. In the beginning they were distinguished only by the name of brothers, or saints, or faithful. God, who came down upon earth to be an example in it of humanity and poverty, gave to his church the most feeble infancy, and conducted it in a state of humiliation similar to that in which he had himself chosen to be born. All the first believers were obscure persons. They labored with their hands. The apostle St. Paul himself acknowledges that he gained his livelihood by making tents. St. Peter raised from the dead Dorcas, a seamstress, who made clothes for the "brethren." The assembly of believers met at Joppa, at the house of a tanner called Simon, as appears from the ninth chapter of the "Acts of the Apostles."

The believers spread themselves secretly in Greece; and some of them went from Greece to Rome, among the Jews, who were permitted by the Romans to have a synagogue. They did not, at first, separate themselves from the Jews. They practiced circumcision; and, as we have elsewhere remarked, the first fifteen obscure bishops of Jerusalem were all circumcised.

When the apostle Paul took with him Timothy, who was the son of a heathen father, he circumcised him himself, in the small city of Lystra. But Titus, his other disciple, could not be induced to submit to circumcision. The brethren, or the disciples of Jesus, continued united with the Jews until the time when St. Paul experienced a persecution at Jerusalem, on account of his having introduced strangers into the temple. He was accused by the Jews of endeavoring to destroy the Law of Moses by that of Jesus Christ. It was with a view to clearing him of this accusation that the apostle St. James proposed to the apostle Paul that he should shave his head, and go and purify himself in the temple, with four Jews, who had made a vow of being shaved. "Take them with you," says James to him (Acts of the Apostles, 21), "purify yourself with them, and let the whole world know that what has been reported concerning you is false, and that you continue to obey the law of Moses." Thus, Paul, who had been at first the most summary persecutor of the

holy society established by Jesus—Paul, who afterwards endeavored to govern that rising society—Paul the Christian, practices
Judaism, "so that the world may know that he is calumniated when
it is said that he is a Christian." Paul does that which today passes
for an abominable crime, a crime punished by burning in Spain,
Portugal and Italy; and he does this on the advice of the apostle
James; and he does this after receiving the Holy Spirit, that is, after
being instructed by God himself that he must renounce all Jewish
rites previously instituted by God himself.

Paul was equally charged with impiety and heresy, and the
persecution against him lasted a long time; but it is perfectly
clear, from the nature of the charges against him, that he had
traveled to Jerusalem in order to fulfill the rites of Judaism.

He addressed to Faustus these very words: "I have never
offended against the Jewish law, nor against the temple." (Acts, 25)

The apostles announced Jesus Christ as a Jew, observing
Jewish law, sent by God to maintain its observance.

"Circumcision," says the apostle Paul (Letter to the Romans,
2), "is good, if you observe the law; but if you violate the law, your
circumcision becomes uncircumcision. If any uncircumcised
person keeps the law, he will be as if circumcised. The true Jew
is one who is Jewish inwardly."

When this apostle speaks of Jesus Christ in his epistles, he
does not reveal the ineffable mystery of his consubstantiality with
God. "We are delivered by him," says he (Letter to the Romans,
5), "from the wrath of God. The gift of God has been shed upon
us by the grace bestowed on one man, who is Jesus Christ. . . .
Death reigned through the sin of one man; the just shall reign
in life by one man, who is Jesus Christ."

And, in the eighth chapter: "We are heirs of God, and joint-
heirs of Christ;" and in the sixteenth chapter: "To God, who is
the only wise, be honor and glory through Jesus Christ. . . . You
are Jesus Christ's, and Jesus Christ is God's." (1 Cor. 3)

And (1 Cor. 15:27), "Everything is made subject to him, undoubtedly, excepting God, who made all things subject to him."

Some difficulty has been found in explaining the following part of the Epistle of the Philippians: "Do nothing through vain glory. Let each humbly think others better than himself. Be of the same mind with Jesus Christ, *who, being in the likeness of God, assumed not to equal himself to God.*" This passage appears exceedingly well investigated and elucidated in a letter, still extant, of the churches of Vienne and Lyons, written in the year 117, and which is a valuable monument of antiquity. In this letter the modesty of some believers is praised. "They did not wish," says the letter, "to assume the lofty title of martyrs (in consequence of certain tribulations), after the example of Jesus Christ, who, being in the likeness of God, did not assume the quality of being equal to God." Origen, also, in his commentary on John, says: "The greatness of Jesus shines out more splendidly in consequence of his self-humiliation than if he had assumed equality with God." In fact, the opposite interpretation would be a visible contradiction. What sense would there be in this exhortation: "Think others superior to yourselves; imitate Jesus, who did not think it an *assumption, a usurpation* to equate himself to God?" It would be an obvious contradiction; it would be offering an example of full pretension as an example of modesty; it would be an offence against commonsense.

Thus did the wisdom of the apostles establish the young church. That wisdom did not change its character as a consequence of the dispute that took place between the apostles Peter, James, and John, on one side, and Paul on the other. This contest occurred at Antioch. The apostle Peter—formerly Cephas, or Simon Barjona—ate with converted Gentiles, and among them did not observe the ceremonies of the law and the distinction of meats. He, Barnabas, and the other disciples, ate indifferently of pork, of animals that had been strangled, or that had cloven feet, or that did not chew the cud; but when many Jewish Christians arrived, St. Peter joined with them in abstinence from forbidden meats, and in the ceremonies of the Mosaic Law.

This conduct appeared very prudent; he wished to avoid giving offence to the Jewish Christians, his companions; but St. Paul attacked him on the subject with considerable severity. "I withstood him," says he, "to his face, because he was blamable." (Gal. 2)

This quarrel appears most extraordinary on the part of St. Paul. Having been at first a persecutor, he should have acted with greater moderation; especially as he had gone to Jerusalem to sacrifice in the temple, had circumcised his disciple Timothy, and strictly complied with the Jewish rites, for which very compliance he now scolded Cephas. St. Jerome imagines that this quarrel between Paul and Cephas was a fake one. He says, in his first homily (vol. iii) that they acted like two lawyers, who had worked themselves up to an appearance of great zeal and exasperation against each other, to gain credit with their respective clients. He says that Peter Cephas being appointed to preach to the Jews, and Paul to the Gentiles, they assumed the appearance of quarreling—Paul to gain the Gentiles, and Peter to gain the Jews. But St. Augustine is by no means of the same opinion. "I am upset," says he, in his epistle to Jerome, "that so great a man should be the patron of a lie (*patronum mendacii*)."

As for the rest, if Peter was sent to the Jews who were practicing Judaism, and Paul to the strangers, it appears probable that Peter never went to Rome. The Acts of the Apostles makes no mention of Peter's journey to Italy.

However that may be, it was about the sixtieth year of our era that Christians began to separate from the Jewish communion; and it was this which drew upon them so many quarrels and persecutions from the various synagogues of Rome, Greece, Egypt, and Asia. They were accused of impiety and atheism by their Jewish brethren, who excommunicated them in their synagogues three times every Sabbath day. But in the midst of their persecutions God always supported them.

By degrees many churches were formed, and the separation between Jews and Christians was complete before the close of the first century. This separation was unknown to the Roman government. Neither the senate nor the emperors of Rome entered into those quarrels of a small group that God had hitherto guided in obscurity, and that he exalted only by imperceptible gradations.

Let us consider the state of religion in the Roman Empire at that period. Mysteries and expiations were in credit throughout almost the entire earth. The emperors, the great, and the philosophers, had, it is true, no faith in these mysteries; but the people, who, in religious matters, give the law to the great, imposed on them the necessity of conforming in appearance to their worship. To succeed in chaining the multitude you must seem to wear the same fetters. Cicero himself was initiated in the Eleusinian mysteries. The knowledge of only one God was the principal tenet inculcated in these mysterious and magnificent festivals. It is undeniable that the prayers and hymns handed down to us as belonging to these mysteries are the most pious and most admirable of the relics of paganism.

The Christians, who likewise adored only one God, had thereby greater facility in converting some of the Gentiles. Some of the philosophers of Plato's sect became Christians; this is why during the three first centuries the fathers of the church were all Platonists.

The inconsiderate zeal of some of them in no way detracted from the fundamental truths. St. Justin, one of the primitive fathers, has been reproached with having said, in his commentary on Isaiah, that the saints would enjoy, during a reign of a thousand years on earth, every sensual pleasure. He has been charged with crime for having said, in his "Apology for Christianity," that God, having made the earth, left it in the care of the angels, who, having fallen in love with the women, begot children, who are the devils.

Lactantius, along with other fathers, has been condemned for having lent credence to sibylline oracles. He asserted that the sibyl Erythrea had made these four Greek lines, which rendered literally are:

> With five loaves and two fishes
> He shall feed five thousand men in the desert;
> And, gathering up the fragments that remain,
> With them he shall fill twelve baskets.

The primitive Christians have been reproached with inventing a few acrostic verses on the name Jesus Christ and attributing them to an ancient sibyl. They have also been reproached with forging letters from Jesus Christ to the king of Edessa, at a time when there was no king in Edessa; with having forged letters of Mary, letters from Seneca to Paul, letters and edicts by Pilate, false gospels, false miracles, and a thousand other impostures.

We have, moreover, the history or gospel of the nativity and marriage of the Virgin Mary, wherein we are told that she was brought to the temple at three years old and walked up the stairs by herself. It is related that a dove came down from heaven to give notice that it was Joseph who was to wed Mary. We have the proto-gospel of James, brother of Jesus by Joseph's first wife. It is there said that when Joseph complained of Mary's having become pregnant in his absence, the priests made each of them drink the water of jealousy, and both were declared innocent.

We have the gospel of the Infancy, attributed to St. Thomas. According to this gospel, Jesus, at five years of age, amused himself, like other children of the same age, with modeling clay, and making it into the form of little birds. He was scolded for this, upon which he gave life to the birds, and they flew away. Another time, a little boy having beaten him, he struck him dead on the spot. We have also another gospel of the Infancy in Arabic, which is much more serious.

We have a gospel of Nicodemus. This one seems more worthy of attention, for we find in it the names of those who accused Jesus before Pilate. They were the principal men of the synagogue—Ananias, Caiaphas, Sommas, Damat, Gamaliel, Judah, Nephthalim. In this history there are some things that are easy to reconcile with the received gospels, and others that are not elsewhere to be found. We here find that the woman cured of bleeding was called Veronica. We also see all that Jesus did in hell when He descended thither.

Then we have the two letters supposed to have been written by Pilate to Tiberius concerning the execution of Jesus; but the bad Latin in which they are written plainly shows that they are spurious.

This false zeal was carried to such a length that various letters circulated that were attributed to Jesus Christ. The letter is still preserved which he is said to have written to Abgarus, king of Edessa; but there had at that time ceased to be a king of Edessa.

Fifty gospels were fabricated and were afterwards declared apocryphal. St. Luke himself tells us that many persons had composed gospels. It has been believed that there was one called the Eternal Gospel, concerning which it is said in the Apocalypse, chapter 14, "And I saw an angel fly in the midst of the heavens, holding the Eternal Gospel.". . . . In the thirteenth century the Cordeliers, abusing these words, composed an "eternal gospel," by which the reign of the Holy Ghost was to be substituted for that of Jesus Christ. But never in the early ages of the church did any book appear with this title.

Letters of the Virgin were likewise invented, written to St. Ignatius the martyr, to the people of Messina, and others.

Abdias, who immediately succeeded the apostles, wrote their history, with which he mixed up such absurd fables that in time these histories became wholly discredited, although they initially had a great reputation. To Abdias we are indebted for the account of the contest between St. Peter and Simon the magician. There was at Rome, in reality, a very skilful mechanic named Simon, who not only made things fly across the stage, as we still see done, but who also revived the feat attributed to Dædalus. He made himself wings; he flew; and, like Icarus, he fell. So say Pliny and Suetonius.

Abdias, who was in Asia and wrote in Hebrew, tells us that Peter and Simon met at Rome during the reign of Nero. A young man, a close relative to the emperor, died, and the whole court begged Simon to resuscitate him. St. Peter presented himself to perform this operation. Simon employed all the powers of his art, and he seemed to have succeeded, for the dead man moved his head. "This is not enough," cried Peter; "the dead man must speak; let Simon leave the bedside, and we shall see whether the young man is alive." Simon moved away, the deceased no longer stirred, and Peter brought him to life with a single word.

Simon went and complained to the emperor that a miserable Galilean had taken upon himself to work greater wonders than he. Simon was confronted with Peter and they made a trial of skill. "Tell me," said Simon to Peter, "what I am thinking of?" "If," returned Peter, "the emperor will give me a barley loaf, you will see whether I know what you have in your heart." A loaf was given to him; Simon immediately causes two large dogs to appear and they want to devour it. Peter throws them the loaf, and while they are eating it, he says: "Well, did I not know your thoughts? You wanted to have your dogs devour me."

After this first sitting it was proposed that Simon and Peter should make a flying-match, to see who could raise himself highest in the air. Simon tried first; Peter made the sign of the cross and Simon broke his legs. This story was imitated from the one we find in *Sepher toldos Jeschut,* where it is said that Jesus Himself flew, and that Judas, who wanted to do the same, fell headlong.

Nero, vexed that Peter had broken the legs of his favorite, Simon, had Peter crucified with his head downwards. Hence the notion of St. Peter's visit to Rome, the manner of his execution and his sepulcher.

The same Abdias also established the belief that St. Thomas went and preached Christianity in India to King Gondafer, and that he went there as an architect.

The number of books of this sort, written in the early ages of Christianity, is prodigious. St. Jerome, and even St. Augustine, tell us that the letters of Seneca and St. Paul are quite authentic. In the first of these letters Seneca hopes his brother Paul is well: *"Bene te valere frater cupio."* Paul does not speak Latin quite so well as Seneca: "I received your letters yesterday," says he, "with joy."—*"Litteras tuas hilaris accepi."*— "And I would have answered them immediately if the young man had been here whom I would have sent to you."— *"Si præsentiam juvenis habuissem."* For the rest, these letters, that we might think should be instructive, are nothing more than compliments.

All these falsehoods, forged by ill-informed and falsely zealous Christians, were in no degree prejudicial to the truth of Christianity; they did not obstruct its progress; on the contrary, they show us that the Christian society was daily increasing and that each member wanted to hasten its growth.

The Acts of the Apostles do not tell us that the apostles agreed on a symbol. Indeed, if they had put together the symbol, the Creed as we now have it, St. Luke would not have omitted from his history this essential foundation of the Christian religion. The substance of the Creed is scattered through the gospels; but the articles were not collected until long after.

In short, our creed is, indisputably, the belief of the apostles; but it was not written by them. Rufinus, a priest of Aquileia, is the first who mentions it; and a homily attributed to St. Augustine is the first record of the supposed way in which this creed was made. Peter says, when they were assembled, "I believe in God the Father Almighty"; Andrew says, "And in Jesus Christ"; James adds, "Who was conceived by the Holy Ghost"; and so on.

This formula was called in Greek *symbolos;* and in Latin *collatio.* Only it must be observed that the Greek version has it: "I believe in God the Father, maker of heaven and earth." The Latin translates, *maker, former,* by *"creatorem."* But since the First Council of Nicea, *"factorem"* has been used.

Christianity first became established in Greece. The Christians there had to contend with a new sect of Jews, who, in consequence of intercourse with the Greeks, had become philosophers. This was the sect of *gnosis,* or Gnostics. Among them were some of the new converts to Christianity. All these sects, at that time, enjoyed complete liberty to dogmatize, discourse, and write. But, under Domitian, Christianity began to give some umbrage to the government.

The zeal of some Christians, which was not prescribed, did not prevent the Church from making the progress destined by God. The Christians, at first, celebrated their mysteries in sequestered houses and in caves, during the night. Hence, according to Minucius Felix, the title given them of *lucifugaces.* Philo calls them Gesséens. The names most frequently applied to them by the Gentiles, during the first four centuries, were "Galileans" and "Nazarenes"; but that of "Christians" has prevailed above all others.

Neither the hierarchy, nor the services of the church, was established all at once; the apostolic times were different from those which followed. St. Paul, in 1 Corinthians, teaches us that the brethren being assembled, whether circumcised or uncircumcised, when several prophets wished to speak, they allowed only two or three to speak, and if someone had a revelation during this time, the prophet who had the floor was supposed to be quiet. It is on the basis of this practice of the primitive Church that some Christian communions still operate, assembling without a hierarchy. At the time, everyone was allowed to speak in the church except the women. It is true that Paul forbids them to speak in his first letter to the Corinthians; but in the same letter, (Cor. 11:5), he also appears to authorize them to preach, to prophesy: "Every bare-headed women who prays or prophesies, sullies her head," as if she were shaven. So women believed they were permitted to speak, provided they were veiled.

The mass now celebrated at matins was the service performed in the evening; these usages changed in proportion as the church strengthened. A more numerous society required more regulations, and the prudence of the pastors accommodated itself to times and places.

St. Jerome and Eusebius relate that when the churches received a regular form, five different orders were gradually perceived to exist in them: the superintendents, *Episcopoi*, whence originate the bishops; the elders of the society, *Presbyteroi*, priests, servants or deacons; the *Pistoi*, believers, the initiated, that is, the baptized, who participated in the suppers of the agape, or love-feasts; and the *catechumens* and the *energumens*, who were awaiting baptism. In these five orders, no one had different garments from the others; no one was bound to celibacy, witness Tertullian's book, dedicated to his wife; witness also the example of the apostles. No paintings or sculptures were to be found in their assemblies during the first three centuries. The Christians carefully concealed their books from the Gentiles; they entrusted them only to the initiated. Even the catechumens were not permitted to recite the Lord's prayer.

That which most distinguished the Christians, and which has continued nearly to our own times, was the power of expelling devils with the sign of the cross. Origen, in his treaties against Celsus, declares—at No. 133—that Antinous, who was deified by the emperor Adrian, performed miracles in Egypt by the power of charms and magic; but he says that the devils come out of the bodies of the possessed on the mere utterance of the name of Jesus.

Tertullian goes farther; and from the recesses of Africa where he resided, he says, in his "Apology"—chapter 23— "If your gods do not confess themselves to be devils in the presence of a true Christian, we give you full liberty to shed that Christian's blood." Could any demonstration possibly be clearer?

In fact, Jesus Christ sent out his apostles to expel demons. The Jews in his time likewise had the power of expelling them; for, when Jesus had delivered some possessed persons and sent the devils into the bodies of a herd of two thousand swine, and had performed many other similar cures, the Pharisees said: "He expels devils through the power of Beelzebub." Jesus replied: "If I expel them by Beelzebub, by whom do your sons expel them?" It is incontestable that the Jews boasted of this power. They had exorcists and exorcisms. They invoked the name of the God of Jacob and Abraham. They put consecrated herbs into the nostrils of demoniacs. (Josephus relates a part of these ceremonies.) This power over devils, which the Jews have lost, was transferred to the Christians, who seem likewise to have lost it some time ago.

The power of expelling demons included that of destroying the operations of magic; for magic has always been prevalent in every nation. All the fathers of the Church bear testimony to magic. St. Justin, in his "Apology"—book 3—acknowledges that the souls of the dead are frequently evoked, and from this draws an argument in favor of the immortality of the soul. Lactantius, in the seventh book of his "Divine Institutions," says that "if any one ventured to deny the existence of souls after death, the magician would convince him of it by making them appear." Irenaeus, Clement of Alexandria, Tertullian, Cyprian the bishop, all affirm the same thing. It is true that, at present, all is changed and that there are now no more magicians than there are demoniacs. But others will be found whenever God so pleases.

When Christian societies became somewhat numerous, and many arrayed themselves against the worship established in the Roman Empire, the magistrates began to exercise severity against them, and the people more particularly persecuted them. The Jews, who possessed particular privileges, and who confined themselves to their synagogues, were not persecuted. They were permitted the free exercise of their religion, as is the case at Rome at the present day. All the different kinds of worship scattered over the empire were tolerated, although the senate did not adopt them.

But the Christians, by declaring themselves enemies to every other form of worship, and more especially so to that of the empire, were often exposed to these cruel trials.

One of the first and most distinguished martyrs was Ignatius, Bishop of Antioch, who was condemned by the Emperor Trajan himself, at that time in Asia, and sent to Rome by his orders, to be exposed to wild beasts, at a time when other Christians were not persecuted in Rome. It is not known precisely what charges were alleged against him before that emperor, otherwise so renowned for his clemency. St. Ignatius must have had violent enemies. Whatever the particulars of the case, the story of his martyrdom relates that the name of Jesus Christ was found engraved on his heart in letters of gold; and it was from this circumstance that Christians in some places assumed the name of Theophorus, which Ignatius had given himself.

A letter of his has been preserved for us in which he entreats the bishops and Christians to make no opposition to his martyrdom, whether at the time they might be strong enough to effect his deliverance, or whether any among them might have influence enough to obtain his pardon. Another remarkable circumstance is that when he was brought to Rome the Christians of that capital went to visit him; which would prove clearly that it was the individual who was punished and not the sect.

The persecutions were not continued. Origen, in his third book against Celsus, says: "The Christians who have suffered death on account of their religion may easily be numbered, for there were only a few of them and only at intervals."

God was so mindful of his Church that, notwithstanding its enemies, he so ordered circumstances that it held five councils in the first century, sixteen in the second, and thirty in the third, that is, tolerated assemblies. Those assemblies were sometimes forbidden, when the weak prudence of the magistrates feared that they might become tumultuous. But few genuine documents of the proceedings before the proconsuls and praetors who condemned the Christians to death have survived. Such would be the only evidence that would enable us to ascertain the charges brought against them and the punishments they suffered.

We have a fragment of Dionysius of Alexandria, in which he gives the following extract of the records of a proconsul of Egypt, under the Emperor Valerian. It follows:

"Dionysius, Faustus Maximus, Marcellus, and Chaeremon, having been admitted to the audience, the prefect Emilianus addressed them: 'You are sufficiently informed, through the conferences I have had with you and all that I have written to you, of the good will our princes have entertained towards you. I wish thus to repeat it to you once again. They make the continuance of your safety depend upon yourselves and place your destiny in your own hands. They require of you only one thing, which reason demands of every reasonable person—namely, that you adore the gods who protect their empire and abandon this other form of worship, so contrary to sense and nature.'"

Dionysius replied, "All do not have the same gods; and each adores those whom he thinks to be the true ones."

The prefect Emilianus replied: "I see clearly that you ungratefully abuse the goodness the emperors have shown you. This being the case, you shall no longer remain in this city; and I now order you to be conveyed to Cephro, in the heart of Libya. In accordance with the command I have received from your emperors, there shall be the place of your banishment. As to what remains, think not of holding your assemblies there, nor of offering up your prayers in what you call cemeteries. This is positively forbidden. I will permit it to none."

Nothing bears a stronger impress of truth than this document. We see from it that there were times when assemblies were prohibited. Thus the Calvinists among us are forbidden to assemble in Languedoc. Sometimes we have even hanged or broken on the wheel ministers or preachers who held assemblies in violation of the laws. Thus, in England and Ireland, Roman Catholics are forbidden to hold assemblies, and, on certain occasions, the delinquents have been condemned to death.

Notwithstanding these prohibitions declared by the Roman laws, God inspired several emperors with indulgence towards the Christians. Even Diocletian, whom the ignorant consider as a persecutor—Diocletian, the first year of whose reign is still regarded as marking the commencement of the era of martyrdom, was, for more than eighteen years, the declared protector of Christianity, and many Christians held offices of high consequence in his close circle. He even married a Christian; and, in Nicomedia, the place of his residence, he permitted a splendid church to be erected opposite his palace.

Caesar Galerius, having unfortunately taken up a prejudice against the Christians, against whom he thought he had reason to complain, influenced Diocletian to destroy the cathedral of Nicomedia. One of the Christians, with more zeal than prudence, tore the edict of the emperor to pieces; and hence arose that famous persecution, in the course of which more than two hundred persons were executed across the Roman Empire, without reckoning those who perished outside of all legal process, victims of the rage of the common people, always fanatical and always cruel.

The number of actual martyrs at different times has been so great that we should be careful not to undermine the true history of those genuine confessors of our holy religion with a dangerous mixture of fables and false martyr stories.

The Benedictine Prior Ruinart, for example, a man otherwise as well informed as he was respectable and devout, should have selected his genuine records, his *"Sincere Acts,"* with more discretion. It is not sufficient that a manuscript, whether taken from the abbey of St. Benoit on the Loire or from a Celestine convent in Paris, corresponds with a manuscript of the Feuillants, to show that the record is authentic. The record should possess a suitable antiquity, written by contemporaries, bearing, moreover, all the signs of truth.

He might have dispensed with relating the adventure of young Romanus, which occurred in 303. This young Romanus had obtained the pardon of Diocletian, at Antioch. However, Ruinart states that the judge Asclepiades condemned him to be burned, so that the Jews who were present at the spectacle, derided the young saint and reproached the Christians that their God, who had delivered Shadrach, Meshach, and Abednego out of the furnace, left *them* to be burned; that immediately, although the weather had been as calm as possible, a tremendous storm arose and extinguished the flames; that the judge then ordered young Romanus's tongue to be cut out; that the principal surgeon of the emperor, being present, eagerly acted the part of executioner and cut off the tongue at the root; that instantly the young man, who, before had an impediment in his speech, spoke with perfect freedom; that the emperor was astonished that any one could speak so well without a tongue; and that the surgeon, to repeat the experiment, directly cut out the tongue of some bystander who died on the spot.

Eusebius, from whom the Benedictine Ruinart drew this narrative, should have so far respected the real miracles performed in the Old and New Testament—which no one can ever doubt—as not to have associated with them stories so suspect and so calculated to give offence to weak minds.

This last persecution did not extend through the whole empire. There was at that time some Christianity in England, which was soon eclipsed and reappeared afterwards under the Saxon kings. The southern districts of Gaul and Spain abounded with Christians. The Caesar Constantius Chlorus afforded them great protection in all these provinces. He had a concubine who was a Christian and who was the mother of Constantine, known under the name of St. Helena, for no marriage was ever proved to have taken place between them; he even sent her away in the year 292, when he married the daughter of Maximilian Hercules; but she had retained great ascendancy over him and had inspired him with a great affection for our holy religion.

Thus divine Providence prepared the triumph of its Church in accordance with human ways. Constantius Chlorus died in 306, at York, in England, at a time when the children he had by the daughter of a Caesar were of tender age and incapable of making claims for the empire. Constantine boldly got himself elected at York by five or six thousand soldiers, the greater part of whom were German, Gaul, and English. There was no likelihood that this election, effected without the consent of Rome, of the senate and the armies, could stand; but God gave him the victory over Maxentius, who had been elected at Rome, and delivered him at last from all his colleagues. It is not to be dissembled that he at first rendered himself unworthy of the favors of heaven by murdering all his relations, including his own wife and son.

One may doubt what Zosimus reports on this subject. He states that Constantine, under the tortures of remorse from the perpetration of so many crimes, asked the pontiffs of the empire whether it were possible for him to obtain any expiation, and that they informed him that they knew of none. It is perfectly true that none had been found for Nero, and that he had not dared to attend the sacred mysteries in Greece. However, the Taurobolia were still in observance, and it is difficult to believe that a supremely powerful emperor could not find a priest who would willingly indulge him in expiatory sacrifices. Perhaps, indeed, it is less easy to believe that Constantine, occupied as he was with war, ambition, and projects, and surrounded by flatterers, had time for remorse at all. Zosimus adds that an Egyptian priest arrived from Spain who had access to him, promised him the expiation of all his crimes in the Christian religion. It has been suspected that this priest was Osius, Bishop of Cordova.

However this might be, Constantine took Christian communion, although he was never a catechumen, and put off his baptism until the moment of his death. This prince built the city of Constantinople, which became the center of the Empire and of the Christian religion. The Church then assumed a respectable form.

It should be noted that in the year 314, before Constantine resided in his new city, those who had persecuted the Christians were punished by them for their cruelties. The Christians threw Maxentius's wife into the Orontes; they cut the throats of all his relatives; they massacred, in Egypt and Palestine, the magistrates who had most strenuously declared their opposition to Christianity. The widow and daughter of Diocletian, having concealed themselves at Thessalonica, were recognized, and their bodies were thrown into the sea. It would certainly have been desirable that the Christians should have followed less eagerly the cry of vengeance; but it was the will of

God, who punishes according to justice, that the hands of the Christians be dyed with the blood of their persecutors, as soon as they were free to act.

Constantine assembled at Nicea, opposite Constantinople, the first ecumenical council, over which Osius presided. The great question touching the divinity of Jesus Christ, which so much agitated the church, was there decided. One party held the opinion of Origen, who says in his sixth chapter against Celsus, "We offer our prayers to God through Christ, who holds the middle place between natures created and uncreated, who leads us to the grace of His Father and presents our prayers to the great God in quality of our high priest." These disputants also cited several passages from St. Paul, some of which have been recorded. They particularly relied on these words of Jesus Christ: "My Father is greater than I;" and they regarded Jesus as the first-born of the creation, as a pure emanation of the Supreme Being, but not precisely as God.

The other side, who were orthodox, produced passages more in conformity with the eternal divinity of Jesus, like the following: "My Father, we are the same thing;" words which their opponents interpreted as signifying: "My Father and I have the same object, the same intention; I have no other will than that of My Father." Alexander, bishop of Alexandria, and after him Athanasius, were at the head of the orthodox; and Eusebius, bishop of Nicomedia, with seventeen other bishops, the priest Arius, and many more priests, were in the party opposed to them. The quarrel was at first exceedingly bitter, because St. Alexander called his opponents antichrists.

At last, after much disputation, the Holy Ghost decided in the council, by the mouths of two hundred and ninety-nine bishops, against eighteen: "Jesus is the only Son of God, begotten of the Father, that is, from the substance of the Father, God of God, light of light; true God of true God, of one substance with the Father. We believe also in the Holy Ghost," etc. Such was the decision of the council. We perceive by this example how the bishops carried it over the simple priests. Two thousand individuals of the latter class were of the opinion of Arius, according to the account of two patriarchs of Alexandria who have written the annals of Alexandria in Arabic. Arius was exiled by Constantine, as was Athanasius soon after, when Arius was recalled to Constantinople. But St. Macarius prayed so vehemently to God to terminate the life of Arius before he could enter the cathedral that God answered his prayer. Arius died on his way to church in 330. The Emperor Constantine ended his life in 337. He placed his will in the hands of an Arian priest and died in the arms of the Arian leader, Eusebius, bishop of Nicomedia, receiving baptism only on his deathbed, and leaving a triumphant but divided Church.

The partisans of Athanasius and of Eusebius carried on a cruel war; and what is called Arianism was for a long time established in all the provinces of the empire.

Julian the philosopher, surnamed the apostate, wished to stifle their divisions but could not succeed.

The second general council was held at Constantinople in 381. It was there laid down that the Council of Nicea had not decided quite correctly in regard to the Holy Ghost, and it added to the Nicean creed that "the Holy Ghost is the giver of life and proceeds from the Father, and with the Father and Son is to be worshipped and glorified."

It was not until roughly the ninth century that the Latin Church gradually decreed that the Holy Ghost proceeds from the Father and the Son.

In the year 431, the third council-general, held at Ephesus, decided Mary was truly the mother of God and that Jesus had "two natures and one person." Nestorius, bishop of Constantinople, who maintained that the Virgin Mary should be entitled Mother of Christ, was called *Judas* by the council; and the "two natures" were again confirmed by the council of Chalcedon.

I pass lightly over the following centuries, which are sufficiently known. Unhappily, all these disputes led to wars, and the Church was always obliged to combat. God, in order to test the patience of the faithful, also allowed the Greek and Latin churches to separate definitively in the ninth century. He likewise permitted twenty-nine bloody schisms in the West over the see of Rome.

Meanwhile, almost the whole of the Greek Church and the whole African Church became slaves under the Arabs, and afterwards under the Turks, who erected the Mohammedan religion on the ruins of the Christian. The Roman Church subsisted, but always reeking with blood, through more than six centuries of discord between the western empire and the priesthood. Even these quarrels rendered her very powerful. The bishops and abbots in Germany all became princes; and the popes gradually acquired absolute dominion in Rome and throughout a considerable territory. Thus has God tested his church, with humiliations, afflictions, crimes, and splendor.

This Latin Church, in the sixteenth century, lost half of Germany, Denmark, Sweden, England, Scotland, Ireland, and the greater part of Switzerland and Holland. She gained more territory in America by the conquests of the Spaniards than she lost in Europe; but, with more territory, she has considerably fewer subjects.

Divine Providence seemed to call upon Japan, Siam, India, and China to place themselves under obedience to the pope, in order to compensate him for Asia Minor, Syria, Greece, Egypt, Africa, Russia, and the other lost states we have mentioned. St. Francis Xavier, who carried the holy gospel to the East Indies and Japan when the Portuguese went there to seek merchandise, performed a great number of miracles, all attested by the reverend Jesuit fathers. Some state that he resuscitated nine dead persons. But the R. F. Ribadeneira, in his "Flower of the Saints," limits himself to asserting that he resuscitated only four. That is quite enough. Providence was desirous that, in less than a hundred years, there should be thousands of Catholics in the islands of Japan. But the devil sowed his tares among the good grain. The Christians entered into a conspiracy, followed by a civil war, in which all the Christians were exterminated in 1638. The nation then closed its ports to all foreigners except the Dutch, who were considered merchants and not Christians, and were first compelled to trample on the cross in order to gain leave to sell their wares in the prison in which they are shut up, when they land at Nagasaki.

The Catholic, Apostolic, and Roman religion was proscribed in China in recent times, but with less cruelty. The reverend Jesuits fathers had not, indeed, resuscitated the dead at the court of Peking; they were content with teaching astronomy, casting cannon, and being mandarins. Their unfortunate disputes with the Dominicans and others so scandalized the great Emperor Yonchin that this prince, who was justice and goodness personified, was blind enough to refuse permission to continue teaching our holy religion, with respect to which our missionaries were in such disagreement. He expelled them, but with a kindness truly paternal, supplying them with means of subsistence and conveyance to the confines of his empire.

All Asia, all Africa, half of Europe, all that belongs to the English and Dutch in America, all the unconquered American tribes, all the southern climes, which constitute a fifth of the globe, remain the prey of the demon, in order to fulfill these sacred words, "many are called, but few are chosen." If there are approximately sixteen hundred million men on earth, as certain learned persons pretend, the holy Roman Catholic Church possesses roughly sixty million, which accounts for about one twenty-sixth of the inhabitants of the known world.

LE CIEL DES ANCIENS / HEAVEN OF THE ANCIENTS

WERE a silkworm to designate the small quantity of downy substance surrounding its cocoon "heaven," it would reason just as well as all the ancients, when they applied that term to the atmosphere, which, as M. de Fontenelle has well observed in his "Plurality of Worlds," is the down of our cocoon.[24]

The vapors that rise from our seas and land and form the clouds, meteors, and thunder, were supposed, in the early ages of the world, to be the residence of gods. Homer always makes the gods descend in clouds of gold; and hence painters still represent them seated on a cloud. But since it is only fitting that the master of the gods be more at ease than the rest, he was given an eagle to carry him, because the eagle soars higher than the other birds.

The ancient Greeks, observing that the lords of cities resided in citadels on the tops of mountains, supposed that the gods might also have their citadel, and placed it in Thessaly, on Mount Olympus, whose summit is sometimes hidden in clouds, so that their palace was on the same level as their heaven.

Afterwards, the stars and planets, which appear fixed to the blue vault of our atmosphere, became the abodes of gods. Seven of them each had a planet, and the rest found a lodging where they could. The general council of gods was held in a spacious hall which lay beyond the Milky Way, for it was only reasonable that the gods should have a hall in the air, as men had town halls on earth.

When the Titans, a species of animal between gods and men, declared their just war against these same gods in order to recover a part of their patrimony, by the father's side, since they were the sons of heaven and earth, they contented themselves with piling two or three mountains upon one another, thinking that would be quite enough to make them masters of heaven and of the castle of Olympus.

Neve foret terris securior arduus æther,
Affectasse ferunt regnum coeleste gigantes;
Altaque congestos struxisse ad sidera montes.
—OVID, *Metamorph.*, i. 151–153.

Nor heaven itself was more secure than earth;
Against the gods the Titans levied wars,
And piled up mountains till they reached the stars.

This philosophy of children and old women was of prodigious antiquity; it is quite certain, however, that the Chaldaeans had ideas on the subject of what is called heaven that were just as accurate as ours. They placed the sun in the midst of our planetary system, nearly at the same distance from our globe as our calculation computes it; they supposed the earth and all planets to revolve round that star; this we learn from Aristarchus of Samos. It is the true system of the world since established by Copernicus; but the philosophers kept the secret to themselves, in order to obtain greater respect both from kings and the people, or rather, to avoid persecution.

The language of error is so familiar to mankind that we still apply the name of heaven to our vapors and the space between the earth and moon. We use the expression of "ascending to heaven," just as we say the sun turns, although we well know that it does not turn. We are probably the heaven of the inhabitants of the moon; and every planet places its heaven in that planet nearest to itself.

Had Homer been asked, to what heaven the soul of Sarpedon had fled, or where that of Hercules resided, Homer would have been greatly embarrassed and would have responded with some harmonious verses.

What assurance was there, that the ethereal soul of Hercules would be more at its ease on the planet Venus or Saturn, than on our own globe? Could it have gone to the sun? In that flaming and consuming furnace, it would appear difficult for it to endure its station. In short, what was it that the ancients meant by heaven? They knew nothing about it; they were always exclaiming, "Heaven and earth." It would be just as judicious to exclaim, and connect in the same manner, infinity and an atom. Properly speaking, there is no heaven. There are a prodigious number of globes revolving in the immensity of space, and our globe revolves like the rest.

The ancients thought that to go to heaven was to ascend; but there is no ascent from one globe to another. The heavenly bodies are sometimes above our horizon and sometimes below it. Thus, let us suppose that Venus, after visiting Paphos, should return to her own planet, when that planet had set; the goddess Venus would not in that case ascend, in reference to our horizon; she would descend, and the proper expression would be then, "descended to heaven." But the ancients did not discriminate with such subtlety; on every subject of natural philosophy, their notions were vague, uncertain and contradictory. Volumes have been composed in order to ascertain and point out what they thought about many questions of this kind. Six words would have been sufficient: "they did not think at all."

We must always make exception for a small number of sages; but they appeared quite late and few disclosed their thoughts; and when they did so, the charlatans in power took care to send them to heaven by the shortest route.

A writer named Pluche, if I am not mistaken, has tried to make Moses a great natural philosopher. Another had previously harmonized Moses with Descartes and published a book, which he called, *Cartesius Mosaisans*; according to him, Moses was the real inventor of "Vortices," and subtle matter. But we know full well that when God made Moses a great legislator and prophet, it was no part of His scheme to make him also a professor of physics. Moses instructed the Jews in their duty and did not teach them a single word of philosophy. Calmet, who compiled a great deal but never reasoned at all, talks of the system of the Hebrews; but that uncultured people never had any system. They had not even a school of geometry; the very name was utterly unknown to them. The whole of their science was comprised of money changing and usury.

We find in their books confused, incoherent ideas on the structure of heaven, worthy in every respect of a barbaric people. Their first heaven was the air, the second the firmament in which the stars were fixed. This firmament was solid and made of glass and supported the superior waters which issued from the vast reservoirs by floodgates, sluices, and cataracts, at the time of the deluge.

Above the firmament or these superior waters was the third heaven, or the empyrean, where St. Paul was elevated. The firmament was a sort of half-vault that embraced the earth. The sun did not revolve around a globe of which they had no idea. When it reached the west, it returned to the east by an unknown path; and if it was not visible, it was because, as the Baron de Feneste says, it was returning during the night.

And again, the Hebrews had adopted these fantasies from other peoples. Most nations, with the exception of the Chaldaean school, considered the sky a solid; the fixed and immobile earth was longer from east to west than from south to north by a generous third. This explains the expressions of "longitude" and "latitude" that we have adopted. It is clear that, according to this conception, there could be no antipodes. Accordingly, St. Augustine treats the idea of antipodes as an absurdity; and Lactantius, expressly says, "Can there possibly be anyone so simple as to believe that there are men whose heads are lower than their feet?" etc.

St. Chrysostom exclaims, in his fourteenth homily, "Where are they who pretend that the heavens are movable and that their form is circular?"

Lactantius says again, in the third book of his "Institutions," "I could prove to you by many arguments that it is impossible heaven should surround the earth."

The author of the "Spectacle of Nature" may repeat to M. le Chevalier as often as he pleases that Lactantius and St. Chrysostom were great philosophers. He will be told in reply that they were great saints and that to be a great saint it is not at all necessary to be a great astronomer. It will be believed that they are in heaven, although it will be admitted that it is impossible to say precisely which part.

CIRCONCISION / CIRCUMCISION

WHEN Herodotus narrates what he was told by the barbarians among whom he traveled, he narrates fooleries, after the manner of the greater part of travelers. Thus, he doesn't require that he be believed in his recital of the adventure of Gyges and Candaules; of Arion, carried on the back of a dolphin; of the oracle that was consulted in order to know what Croesus was doing and responded that he was then going to cook a tortoise in a covered pot; of Darius's horse, which, being the first out of a certain number to neigh, in fact proclaimed his master a king; and of a hundred other fables fit to amuse children and to be compiled by rhetoricians. But when he speaks of what he has seen, of the customs of people he has examined, of the antiquities he has consulted, he then addresses himself to men.

"It appears," he says, in his book *Euterpe*, "that the inhabitants of Colchis sprang from Egypt. I judge so from my own observations rather than from hearsay; for I found that, in Colchis, the ancient Egyptians were more frequently mentioned than the ancient customs of Colchis in Egypt.

"These inhabitants of the shores of the Euxine Sea believed themselves to be a colony founded by Sesostris. As for myself, I should think this probable, not merely because they are dark and woolly-haired, but because the inhabitants of Colchis, Egypt, and Ethiopia are the only people in the world who, from time immemorial, have practiced circumcision; for the Phoenicians and the people of Palestine confess that they adopted the practice from the Egyptians. The Syrians, who at present inhabit the banks of the Thermodon and Pathenia, and the Macrons, their neighbors, acknowledge that it is only recently that they have submitted to this Egyptian custom. It is principally from this usage that they are considered of Egyptian origin.

"With respect to Ethiopia and Egypt, as this ceremony is of great antiquity in both nations, I cannot by any means ascertain which has derived it from the other. It is, however, probable that the Ethiopians received it from the Egyptians; while, on the contrary, the Phoenicians have abolished the practice of circumcising new-born children since the expansion of their commerce with the Greeks."

From this passage of Herodotus it is evident that many people had adopted circumcision from Egypt, but no nation ever claimed to have received it from the Jews. To whom, then, can we attribute the origin of this custom- to a nation from whom five or six others acknowledge they took it, or to another nation, much less powerful, less commercial, less warlike, hid away in a corner of Arabia Petraea, and which never communicated any one of its usages to any other people?

The Jews admit that they were, long ago, received in Egypt out of charity. Is it not probable that the lesser people imitated a usage of the superior one, and that the Jews adopted some customs from their masters?

Clement of Alexandria relates that Pythagoras, when traveling among the Egyptians, was obliged to be circumcised in order to be admitted to their mysteries. It was, therefore, absolutely necessary to be circumcised to be a priest in Egypt. Those priests existed when Joseph arrived in Egypt. The government was of great antiquity, and the ancient ceremonies of the country were observed with the most scrupulous exactness.

The Jews acknowledge that they remained in Egypt two hundred and five years. They say that, during that period, they were not circumcised. It is clear, then, that during those two hundred and five years the Egyptians did not receive circumcision from the Jews. Would they have adopted it from them after the Jews had stolen the vessels which they had lent them and, according to their own account, fled with their plunder into the wilderness? Will a master adopt the principal symbol of the religion of a robbing and runaway slave? It is not in human nature.

It is stated in the Book of Joshua that the Jews were circumcised in the wilderness. "I have delivered you from what constituted your reproach among the Egyptians." But what could this reproach be, to a people living between Phoenicians, Arabs, and Egyptians, but something which rendered them contemptible to these three nations? How is that reproach removed? By removing a small portion of the prepuce? Must not this be considered the natural meaning of the passage?

The Book of Genesis relates that Abraham had been circumcised before. But Abraham traveled in Egypt, which had been long a flourishing kingdom, governed by a powerful king. There is nothing to prevent the supposition that circumcision was, in this very ancient kingdom, an established usage. Moreover, the circumcision of Abraham led to no continuation; his posterity was not circumcised until the time of Joshua.

But, before the time of Joshua, the Jews, by their own acknowledgment, adopted many of the customs of the Egyptians. They imitated them in several sacrifices, in several ceremonies; as, for example, in the fasts observed on the eves of the feasts of Isis; in ablutions; in the custom of shaving the heads of the priests; in the incense, the branched candlestick, the sacrifice of the red-haired cow, the purification with hyssop, the abstinence from swine's flesh, the dread of using the kitchen utensils of foreigners. Everything indicates that the little people of Hebrews, notwithstanding its aversion to the great Egyptian nation, had retained a vast number of the usages of its former masters. The goat Azazel, which was dispatched into the wilderness laden with the sins of the people, was a visible imitation of an Egyptian practice. Even the rabbis are agreed that the word Azazel is not Hebrew. Nothing, therefore, could exist to have prevented the Hebrews from imitating the Egyptians in circumcision, as did the Arabs their neighbors.

It is by no means extraordinary that God, who sanctified baptism, a practice so ancient in Asia, should also have sanctified circumcision, no less ancient among the Africans. We have already remarked that he has a sovereign right to attach his favors to any symbol that he chooses.

As for the rest, since the time when, under Joshua, the Jewish people became circumcised, it has retained that usage down to the present day. The Arabs, also, have faithfully adhered to it; but the Egyptians, who, in the earlier ages, circumcised both their males and females, in the course of time abandoned the practice entirely as to the latter, and at last applied it solely to priests, astrologers, and prophets. This we learn from Clement of Alexandria and Origen. In fact, it is not clear that the Ptolemys ever received circumcision.

The Latin authors who treat the Jews with such profound contempt as to apply to them in derision the expressions, "*curtus Apella*," "*credat Judaeus Apella*," "*curti Judaei*," never apply such epithets to the Egyptians. The whole population of Egypt is at present circumcised, but for a different reason; namely, because Mohammedanism adopted the ancient circumcision of Arabia.

It is this Arabian circumcision that has extended to the Ethiopians, among whom males and females are both still circumcised.

We must acknowledge that this ceremony of circumcision appears at first a very strange one; but we should remember that, from the earliest times, the oriental priests consecrated themselves to their deities by peculiar marks. An ivy leaf was inscribed with a punch on the wrist of the priests of Bacchus. Lucian tells us that those devoted to the goddess Isis impressed characters upon their wrist and neck. The priests of Cybele made themselves eunuchs.

It is highly probable that the Egyptians, who revered the instrument of human reproduction and bore its image in pomp in their processions, conceived the idea of offering to Isis and Osiris through whom everything on earth was produced, a small portion of that organ with which these deities had created for the perpetuation of the human species. Ancient oriental manners are so prodigiously different from our own that scarcely anything should appear extraordinary to a man of even a little reading. A Parisian is excessively surprised when he is told that the Hottentots deprive their male children of one testicle. The Hottentots are perhaps surprised that the Parisians preserve both.

CONCILES / COUNCILS

ALL councils are, doubtless, infallible, being composed of men.

It is not possible that passions, intrigues, the spirit of contention, hatred, jealousy, prejudice or ignorance should ever influence these assemblies.

But why, it will be said, have so many councils been opposed to one another? To exercise our faith. They were all right, each in its time.

Presently, the Roman Catholics believe only in such councils as are approved in the Vatican; the Greek Catholics believe only in those approved in Constantinople; and the Protestants make a jest of both the one and the other: so that every one ought to be content.

We shall examine here only the great councils; the lesser ones are not worth the trouble.

The first was that of Nicea. It assembled in the year 325 of the modern era, after Constantine had written and sent by way of Osius his noble letter to the rather turbulent clergy of Alexandria: "You are quarreling about a trifling matter. These subtleties are unworthy of reasonable people." It was debated whether Jesus was created or uncreated. This in no way concerned morality, which is the essential thing. Whether Jesus was in time or before time, it is not the less our duty to be honest. After much altercation, it was at last decided that the Son was as old as the Father, and *consubstantial* with the Father. This decision is not easy to comprehend, which makes it all the more sublime. Seventeen bishops protest against the decree, and an old Alexandrian chronicle, preserved at Oxford, says that two thousand priests likewise protested. But prelates don't make much account of mere priests, who are in general poor. However, there was nothing said of the Trinity in this first council. The formula runs thus: "We believe Jesus to be consubstantial with the Father, God of God, light of light, begotten, not made; we also believe in the Holy Ghost." It must be acknowledged that the Holy Ghost was treated very cavalierly.

In the supplement to the Council of Nice, it is related that the fathers, being much perplexed to find out which were the authentic and which the apocryphal books of the Old and the New Testament, laid them all upon an altar, and the books which they were to reject fell to the ground. What a pity that so fine a procedure has been lost in our times!

After the first Council of Nicea, composed of three hundred and seventeen infallible bishops, another council was held at Rimini, on which occasion the number of the infallible was four hundred, without counting a strong detachment, at Seleucia, of about two hundred. These six hundred bishops, after four months of contention, unanimously took from Jesus his *consub-stantiality*. It has since been restored to him, except by the Socinians: so nothing is amiss.

One of the great councils was that of Ephesus, in 431. Nestorius, Bishop of Constantinople, a great persecutor of heretics, was himself condemned as a heretic for having maintained that, although Jesus was really God, yet His mother was not absolutely mother of God, but mother of Jesus. It was St. Cyril who procured the condemnation of Nestorius; but the partisans of Nestorius also procured the deposition of St. Cyril in the same council, which put the Holy Ghost in considerable perplexity.

Here, gentle reader, carefully observe that the Gospel says not one syllable of the consubstantiality of the Word, nor of Mary's having had the honor of being mother of God, no more than of the other disputed points which brought together so many infallible councils.

Eutyches was a monk, who had cried out sturdily against Nestorius, whose heresy was nothing less than supposing two persons in Jesus, which is quite frightful. The monk, the better to contradict his adversary, affirmed that Jesus had but one nature. A certain Flavian, Bishop of Constantinople, maintained against him that there must absolutely be two natures in Jesus. Thereupon, a numerous council was held at Ephesus in 449, and the argument used was the cudgel, as in the lesser council of Cirta, in 355, and in a certain conference held at Carthage. Flavian's nature was well thrashed, and Jesus was reduced to a single nature. But at the Council of Chalcedon in 451, two natures were assigned to him. It is true that he still only had one person.

I pass by councils held on less weighty questions and come to the sixth general Council of Constantinople, assembled to ascertain precisely whether Jesus, with only one person, might have two wills. It is obvious how important this knowledge is to doing the will of God.

This council was convoked by Constantine the Bearded, as all the others had been by the preceding emperors. The legates from the bishop of Rome were on the left hand, and the patriarchs of Constantinople and Antioch on the right. The train-bearers at Rome may, for aught I know, assert that the left hand is the place of honor. However that may be, the result was that Jesus obtained two wills.

The Mosaic Law forbade images. Painters and sculptors had never made their fortunes among the Jews. We do not find that Jesus ever had any pictures, excepting perhaps that of Mary, painted by Luke. But Jesus Christ nowhere recommends the worship of images. Nevertheless, the primitive Christians began to worship them around the end of the fourth century, when they had become familiar with the fine arts. In the eighth century this abuse had arrived at such a pitch that Constantine Copronymus assembled in Constantinople a council of three hundred and twenty bishops who anathematized image-worship and declared it to be idolatry.

The empress Irene, the same who afterwards had her son's eyes torn out, convoked the second Council of Nicea in 787. The adoration of images was reestablished. Today, to justify this council, it is said that this adoration was the worship of *dulia* and not of *latria*.

Whether *latria* or *dulia*, in 794, Charlemagne had another council held at Frankfort, which declared the second of Nicea idolatrous. Pope Adrian I sent two legates to it, but he did not convoke it.

The first great council convoked by a pope was the first of Lateran, in 1139; there were about a thousand bishops assembled, but scarcely anything was done, except that all those were anathematized who said that the Church was too rich.

In 1179, another great council of Lateran was held by Alexander III, in which the cardinals, for the first time, took precedence over the bishops. The discussions were confined to matters of discipline.

Another great council was of Lateran in 1215. Pope Innocent III stripped the count of Toulouse of all his possessions, by virtue of his excommunication. It was the first council to mention *transubstantiation*.

In 1245, general council in Lyons, then an imperial city, in which Pope Innocent IV excommunicated the emperor Frederick II and consequently deposed him and forbade him the use of fire and water. On this occasion, a red hat was given to the cardinals, to remind them that they must imbrue their hands in the blood of the emperor's partisans. This council was the cause of the destruction of the house of Swabia and of thirty years of anarchy in Italy and Germany.

General council held at Vienne in Dauphiné in 1311, in which the Order of the Templars was abolished: its principal members having been condemned to the most horrible deaths, on charges most imperfectly established.

The great Council of Constance, in 1414, contented itself with dismissing Pope John XXIII, convicted of a thousand crimes, but had Jan Hus and Jerome of Prague burned for being obstinate, obstinacy being a much more grievous crime than murder, rape, simony, and sodomy.

In 1430, the great council of Basel, not recognized by Rome because it deposed Pope Eugenius IV, who would not be deposed.

The Romans reckon among the general councils the fifth Council of Lateran in 1512, convoked against Louis XII, king of France, by Pope Julius II; but since this warlike pope was dead, the council came to nothing.

Lastly, we have the great Council of Trent, which is not accepted in France in matters of discipline; but its doctrine is indisputable, since, as Fra Paolo Sarpi tells us, the Holy Ghost arrived in Trent from Rome every week in the courier's bag. But Fra Paolo Sarpi was a little tainted with heresy.

(by M. Abauzit the younger)

CONFESSION / CONFESSION

IT is still a problem—simply speaking from a political perspective—to determine whether confession does more good than evil. Confession was practiced in all the mysteries of Isis, Orpheus, and Ceres, in the presence of the hierophant and the initiates. Since these mysteries were expiations, it was obligatory to admit that one had crimes to expiate. The Christians adopted confession during the first centuries of the Church, just as they adopted most of the rites of antiquity, like temples, altars, incense, candles, processions, lustral water, sacerdotal clothing, and several of the formulas from the mysteries—the *sursum corda*, the *ite missa est,* and many others. The scandal occasioned by the public confession of women in Constantinople in the fourth century led to the abolishment of confession.

It is said that the practice of auricular confession did not begin in the west until about the seventh century. The abbots began to require that their monks come and acknowledge all their offences to them twice a year. It was these abbots who invented the formula: "I absolve thee to the utmost of my power and your need." It would surely have been more respectful towards the Supreme Being, as well as more just, to say: "May He forgive both your faults and mine!"

The good which confession has done is that it has sometimes procured restitution from petty thieves. The ill is that, in the internal troubles of states, it has sometimes forced the penitents to be conscientiously rebellious and blood-thirsty. The Guelph priests refused absolution to the Ghibellines, and the Ghibelline priests were careful not to absolve the Guelphs. Whether a Sforza, a Medici, a Prince of Orange, or a King of France was to be assassinated, the parricides always prepared themselves by the sacrament of confession.

Louis XI and the Marchioness de Brinvilliers always confessed as soon as they had committed any great crime; and they confessed often, as gluttons take medicines to increase their appetite.

If it were possible to be astounded by anything, it would be the bull issued by His Holiness Pope Gregory XV on August 30, 1622, in which he ordered the revelation of confessions in certain cases.

The response from the Jesuit Coton to Henry IV will outlast the Jesuit order. Would you reveal the confession of a man resolved to assassinate me? "No, but I would place myself between you and him."

CONVULSIONS / CONVULSIONS

AROUND the year 1724, there was dancing in the cemetery of St. Médard, and many miracles were performed there.[25] The following epigram by the duchess of Maine gives an account of one of them:

> *Un décrotteur à la Royale,*
> *Du talon gauche estropié,*
> *Obtint, pour grâce spéciale*
> *D'être boiteux de l'autre pied.*

> A Port-Royal shoe-black, who had *one* lame leg,
> To make both alike the Lord's favor did beg;
> Heaven listened, and straightway a miracle came,
> For quickly he rose up, with *both* his legs lame.

The miraculous convulsions continued, as is well known, until a guard was stationed at the cemetery.

> *De par le roi, défense à Dieu*
> *De plus fréquenter en ce lieu.*
> Louis to God:—To keep the peace,
> Your frequentations here must cease.

It is also well known that the Jesuits, being no longer able to perform similar miracles, since their Xavier had exhausted the Company's stock of grace by resuscitating nine dead persons at one time, had the bright idea of having an engraving printed of Jesus Christ dressed as a Jesuit, in order to counterbalance the credit of the Jansenists. A wit from the Jansenist party, as is, again, well known, wrote at the bottom of this print:

> *Admirez l'artifice extrême*
> *De ces moines ingénieux;*
> *Ils vous ont habillé comme eux,*
> *Mon Dieu, de peur qu'on ne vous aime.*

Admire the extreme artifice,
Of these ingenious monks;
They have clothed you just like themselves,
My God, for fear that you be loved.

The Jansenists, on the other hand, to better prove that Jesus Christ could not have assumed the habit of a Jesuit, filled Paris with convulsions and attracted great crowds of people to their courtyard. The counselor of parliament, Carré de Montgeron, went to present to the king a quarto collection of all these miracles, attested by a thousand witnesses. He was very properly shut away in a chateau, where attempts were made to restore his senses by regimen. But the truth always prevails over persecution, and the miracles lasted for thirty years all told, without interruption. Sister Rose, Sister Illuminated, Sister Promised and Sister Candied would show up at someone's house. They would have themselves whipped, without showing any marks the next day. They were beaten with tree limbs on their well-padded and stuffed stomachs without injury. They were placed before a large fire, their face rubbed with a certain pomade, and they were not burned. At length, just as every art advances towards perfection, swords were eventually stuck into their flesh, and they were crucified. Even a famous theologian had the benefit of being crucified. All of this was done to convince the world that a certain papal bull was ridiculous, a fact that might easily have been proved without so much trouble. However, Jesuits and Jansenists all united against the *Spirit of Laws*,[26] and against . . . and against . . . . and against . . . and . . . And after all this we dare to ridicule Laplanders, Samoyeds, and Negroes!

CORPS / BODY

JUST as we don't know what a spirit is, so also we are ignorant of what a body is; we see various properties, but what is the subject in which those properties reside? "There is nothing but body," said Democritus and Epicurus; "there is no such thing as body," said the disciples of Zeno of Elia.

Berkeley, Bishop of Cloyne, is the last who, by a hundred captious sophisms, has claimed to prove that bodies do not exist. They have, says he, neither color, nor smell, nor heat; all these modalities are in your sensations, not in the objects. He might have spared himself the trouble of proving this truth for it was already sufficiently known. But from there he went on to extent and solidity, which are essential to the body, and he thinks he has proven that there is no extent in a piece of green cloth because the cloth is not in reality green; the sensation of green being in ourselves only, therefore the sensation of extent is likewise in ourselves only. Having thus destroyed extent, he concludes that solidity, which is attached to it, falls of itself, and therefore that there is nothing in the world but our ideas. So that, according to this doctor, ten thousand men killed by ten thousand cannon shots are in reality nothing more than ten thousand apprehensions of our understanding.

Surely, the Bishop of Cloyne might have saved himself from falling into this excessive absurdity. He thinks he has shown that there is no extent because a body has appeared to him four times as large through a telescope as to his naked eye, and four times as small through another lens. Hence he concludes that, since a body cannot be at the same time four feet, sixteen feet, and but one foot in extent, there is no extent at all, therefore there is nothing. He had only to take any measure and say: Of whatever extent this body may appear to me to be, it extends to so many of these measures.

He might very easily see that extent and solidity were quite different from sound, color, taste, smell, etc. It is quite clear that these are sensations excited in us by the configuration of parts. But extent is not a sensation. When this burning wood goes out, I am no longer warm; when the air is no longer struck, I cease to hear; when this rose withers, I no longer smell it: but the wood, the air, and the rose have extent without me. Berkeley's paradox is not worth refuting.

It is worth knowing how Berkeley was drawn into this paradox. A long while ago I had some conversation with him, and he told me that his opinion originated in our being unable to conceive what the subject of this extension is. And certainly, in his book, he triumphs when he asks Hylas what this subject, this substratum, this substance is? It is the extended body, answers Hylas. Then the bishop, under the name of Philonous, laughs at him, and poor Hylas, finding that he has said that extension is the subject of extension, and has therefore talked nonsense, remains quite confused, acknowledges that he understands nothing at all; that there is no such thing as a body; that the material world does not exist, and that there is none but an intellectual world.

Hylas should only have said to Philonous: We know nothing of the subject or substance of this extension, solidity, divisibility, mobility, figure, etc.; I know no more of it than I do of the subject of thought, feeling, and will, but the subject does not the less exist, for it has essential properties of which it cannot be deprived.

We all resemble the greater part of the Parisian ladies who eat well without knowing what is put in their stews; just so do we enjoy bodies without knowing of what they are composed. Of what does a body consist? Of parts and these parts resolve themselves into other parts. What are these last parts? They, too, are bodies; you divide incessantly without making any progress.

In short, a subtle philosopher, observing that a picture is made of ingredients of which no single ingredient is a picture, and a house of materials of which no one material is a house, imagined (in a slightly different fashion) that bodies are composed of an infinity of small things that are not bodies, and these are called monads. This system is not without its merits, and, were it revealed, I should think it very possible. These little beings would be so many mathematical points, a sort of souls, waiting only for clothing to put on. There would be a continual metempsychosis. A monad would sometimes go into a whale, other times into a tree, other times into a dice player. This system is as good as another; I like it quite as well as the declination of atoms, substantial forms, versatile grace, and the vampires of Dom Calmet.

CREDO / CREED

I recite my Pater Noster and my Creed every morning. I am not like Broussin, of whom Reminiac said:

> Broussin, dès l'âge le plus tendre,
> Posséda la sauce Robert,
> Sans que son précepteur lui pût jamais apprendre
> Ni son credo, ni son pater.

> *Broussin, almost from infancy,*
> *Could distinguish a brown mustard sauce,*
> *But his tutor was never able to teach him*
> *Either his creed or his Pater Noster.*

The term *symbol* or *collation* comes from the word *symbolein,* and the Latin Church adopts this word because it has taken everything from the Greek Church. Even slightly learned theologians know that the symbol, which we call apostolic, is not that of all the apostles.

Symbol, among the Greeks, signified the words and signs by which those initiated into the mysteries of Ceres, Cybele, and Mythra, recognized one another; and Christians in time had their symbol. If it had existed in the time of the apostles, it seems that St. Luke would have spoken of it.

A history of the symbol is attributed to St. Augustine in his one hundred and fifteenth sermon. He is made to say in this sermon that Peter commenced the symbol by saying: "I believe in God, the Father Almighty." John added: "Maker of heaven and earth;" James proceeded: "I believe in Jesus Christ, His only Son, our Lord," and so on with the rest. This fable has been expunged from the last edition of Augustine. I defer to the reverend Benedictine fathers, to declare whether this curious little article ought to be left out or not.

The fact is that no person heard anything of this "creed" for more than four hundred years. People say that Paris was not built in a day, and the common people are often right in their proverbs. The apostles had our symbol in their hearts, but they put it not into writing. One was formed in the time of St. Irenaeus, which does not at all resemble the one we recite. Our symbol, such as it is at present, is of the fifth century. It is posterior to the Nicean creed. The passage which says that Jesus descended into hell and the one that speaks of the communion of saints are not found in any of the symbols that preceded ours. And, indeed, neither the gospels, nor the Acts of the Apostles, say that Jesus descended into hell. But it was an established opinion, from the third century, that Jesus descended into Hades, or Tartarus, words we translate by that of hell. Hell, in this sense, is not the Hebrew word "*sheol*," which signifies "under ground," "the pit." For this reason, St. Athanasius has since taught us how our Savior descended into hell. "His humanity," he says, "was not entirely in the tomb, nor entirely in hell. It was in the sepulcher, according to the body, and in hell, according to the soul."

St. Thomas affirms that the saints, who arose at the death of Jesus Christ, died again to rise afterwards with him, which is the most general sentiment. All these opinions are absolutely foreign to morality. We must be good men, whether the saints were raised once or twice. Our symbol has been formed recently, I confess, but virtue is from all eternity.

If it is permitted to quote moderns on so grave a matter, I will here repeat the creed of the Abbé de St. Pierre,[27] as it was written with his own hand, in his book on the purity of religion, which has not been printed, but which I have copied faithfully:

"I believe in one God alone, and I love Him. I believe that He enlightens all souls coming into the world; thus says St. John. By that, I understand all souls that seek Him in good faith.

I believe in one God alone, because there can be but one soul of the Great All, a single vivifying being, a sole Creator.

"I believe in God, the Father Almighty; because He is the common Father of nature and of all men, who are equally His children. I believe that He who has caused all to be born equally, who arranges the springs of their life in the same manner, who has given them the same moral principles, which they perceive as soon as they reflect, has made no difference between His children but that of crime and virtue.

"I believe that a just and righteous Chinese is more precious to Him than the caviling and arrogant European scholar.

"I believe that since God is our common Father, we are bound to regard all men as our brothers.

"I believe that the persecutor is abominable, and that he follows immediately after the poisoner and parricide.

"I believe that theological disputes are at once the most ridiculous farce and the most dreadful scourge of the earth, immediately after war, pestilence, famine, and the pox.

"I believe that ecclesiastics should be paid and well paid, as servants of the public, moral teachers, keepers of registers of births and deaths; but there should be given to them neither the riches of farmers-general, nor the rank of princes, because both corrupt the soul; and nothing is more revolting than to see such rich and proud men make meagerly paid clerics preach humility and the love of poverty.

"I believe that all priests who serve a parish should be married, not only to have an honest woman to take care of their household, but to be better citizens, to give good subjects to the State, and to have plenty of well raised children.

"I believe that monks must be taken away from the monastic form of life, for the sake of the country and themselves. They are men whom Circe has changed into hogs; the wise Ulysses must restore to the human form."

Paradise to the beneficent!

CRITIQUE / CRITICISM[28]

I have no intention of discussing here scholastic criticism, which so poorly reconstructs the texts of ancient authors who were previously clearly understood. I won't touch either on those true critics who have deciphered the little we can know about ancient history and philosophy. I have in sight those critics who tend towards satire.

A lover of literature was reading Tasso with me one day; he came across this passage:

> *Chiama gli habitator dell'ombre eterne,*
> *Il rauco suon della tartarea tromba,*
> *Treman le spazioze atre caverne,*
> *E l'aer ceco a quel rumor rimbomba,*
> *Ne stridendo cosi dalle superne*
> *Regioni del cielo il fulgor piomba;*
> *Ne si scossa giamai trema la terra,*
> *Quando i vapori in sen gravida serra.*[29]

He then read several other stanzas of equal force and harmony. "So!" he cried, "is this what your Boileau called flashiness? So is this how he tried to devalue a great man who had lived a century before him, in order to elevate another great man who had lived sixteen hundred years earlier and who himself would have admired Tasso?"

"Don't get worked up," I told him; "let's look at Quinault's operas." At the beginning of his works, we found something that made us angry with Boileau's criticism. Armida's admirable poem appeared before us, in which we found these words:

> *Sidonie:* *La haine est affreuse et barbare,*
> *L'amour contraint les coeurs dont*
> *il s'empare,*
> *A souffrir des maux rigoureux.*
> *Si votre sort est en votre puissance,*
> *Faites choix de l'indifférence,*
> *Elle assure un sort plus heureux.*
>
> *Armide:* *Non, non, il ne m'est pas possible*
> *De passer de mon trouble en un*
> *état paisible,*
> *Mon coeur ne se peut plus calmer;*

Renaud m'offense trop, il n'est
que trop aimable,
C'est pour moi désormais un
choix indispensable
De le haïr ou de l'aimer.[30]

We read the whole text of *Armide*, in which the genius of Tasso is endowed with new charms, thanks to Quinault. "Well," I said to my friend, "this is nevertheless the same Quinault whom Boileau always attempted to portray as the most contemptible writer. He even persuaded Louis XIV that this writer, so graceful, touching, moving and elegant, had no merit of his own and owed his success entirely to the composer Lully."

"That makes sense to me," my friend responded; "Boileau was not jealous of the musician, but he was of the poet. What faith should we put in the opinion of a man who, in order to create a rime ending in *aut*, chose to insult *Boursaut*, or *Hainaut*, or *Quinaut*, depending on whether he was on good or bad terms with these gentlemen at the time? But to cool our indignation against such injustice, let's look out this window and contemplate the handsome facade of the Louvre, which immortalizes the name of Perrault. This talented man was the brother of a learned member of the Academy who was quarreling with Boileau. That was sufficient for him to be labeled an ignorant architect."

After reflecting for a moment, my friend continued, "Human nature is made this way. In his *Memoirs*, the Duke de Sully characterizes the Cardinal d'Ossat and Secretary de Villeroi as dishonest ministers. Louvois did everything he could not to admire the great Colbert."

"They didn't publish insults about one another during their lifetime," I replied; "that is a foolishness found only in literature, legal chicanery and theology. There was a man of great merit, La Motte, who wrote beautiful stanzas:

Quelquefois au feu qui la charme
Résiste une jeune beauté,
Et, contre elle-même elle s'arme
D'une pénible fermeté.
Hélas cette contrainte extrême
La prive du vice qu'elle aime,
Pour fuir la honte qu'elle hait.
Sa sévérité n'est que faste,
Et l'honneur de passer pour chaste
La résout à l'être en effet.

En vain ce sévère stoïque
Sous mille défauts abattu
Se vante d'une âme héroïque
Tout vouée à la vertu;
Ce n'est point la vertu qu'il aime,
Mais son coeur ivre de lui-même
Voudrait usurper les autels;
Et par sa sagesse frivole
Il ne veut que parer l'idole
Qu'il offre au culte des mortels.

Les champs de Pharsale et d'Arbelle
Ont vu triompher deux vainqueurs,
L'un et l'autre digne modèle
Que se proposent les grands coeurs.
Mais le succès a fait leur gloire;
Et si le seau de la victoire
N'eût consacré ces demi-dieux,
Alexandre aux yeux du vulgaire,
N'aurait été qu'un téméraire,
Et César qu'un séditieux.[31]

"This author," he said, "was a wise man who more than once enhanced philosophy with the graces of verse. If he had always written stanzas of such quality, he would be the greatest of the lyric poets; nevertheless, at that same time as he was such beautiful pieces, one of his contemporaries was calling him,

Certain oison gibier de basse-cour:
In another passage, he says about La Motte:
De ses discours l'ennuyeuse beauté
And in another, he says:

. . . Je n'y vois qu'un défaut
C'est que l'auteur les devait faire en prose.
Ces odes-là sentent bien le Quinaut.[32]

He pursues him ceaselessly; he reproaches him particularly with dryness and a lack of harmony.

Would you like to see the odes composed several years later by this same critic who judged La Motte so imperiously and denounced him as an enemy? Read."

Cette influence souveraine
N'est pour lui qu'une illusoire chaîne
Qui l'attache au bonheur d'autrui;
Tous les brillants qui l'embellissent,
Tous les talents qui l'anoblissent
Sont en lui, mais non pas à lui.

Il n'est rien que le temps n'absorbe, ne dévore,
Et les faits qu'on ignore
Sont bien peu différents des faits non avenus.

La bonté qui brille en elle
De ses chamres les plus doux,
Est une image de celle
Qu'elle voit briller en vous.

Et par vous seule enrichie
Sa politesse affranchie
Des moindres obscurités,
Est la lueur réfléchie
De vos sublimes clartés.

Ils ont vu par ta bonne foi
De leurs peuples troublés d'effroi
La crainte heureusement déçue,
Et déracinée à jamais
La haine si souvent reçue
En survivance de la paix.

Dévoile à ma vue empressée
Ces déités d'adoption,
Synonymes de la pensée,
Symboles de l'abstraction.

N'est-ce pas une fortune,
Quand d'une charge commune
Deux moitiés portent le faix?
Que la moindre le réclame;
Et que du bonheur de l'âme,
Le corps seul fasse les frais?[33]

"No doubt," said my judicious lover of letters, "he shouldn't have offered such detestable works as models to the author he had criticized with so much bitterness. He would have done better to allow his adversary to enjoy his reputation in peace and to maintain the bit that he had himself. But what do you expect? Le *gens irritabile vatum*[34] is still inflicted with the same bile that tormented the ancient poets. Readers show indulgence for such feeble efforts because readers only want to be amused. They read in an allegory entitled *Pluto* about judges condemned to be skinned alive and to sit in hell on a throne covered with their own skin rather than royal finery. The reader cares little whether these judges deserve this punishment, or if the plaintiff who calls them to stand before Pluto is right or wrong. The reader recites these lines exclusively for his pleasure; if they amuse him, he asks for nothing more; if they displease him, he puts aside this allegory and wouldn't lift a single finger to confirm or challenge the verdict.

"Racine's inimitable tragedies were all criticized, and incompetently so, because the critiques were done by his rivals. Artists are competent judges of artistry, it is true, but these competent judges are almost always corrupt.

"An excellent critic would have to be an artist possessing great knowledge and taste, devoid of prejudice and envy. That is difficult to find."

DAVID / DAVID [35]

IF a young peasant, in searching after she-asses finds a kingdom, it is no common affair. If another peasant cures his king of insanity by playing the harp, that is still more extraordinary. But when this petty player on the harp becomes king because he has met a village priest in a corner, who pours a bottle of olive oil on his head, the affair is more marvelous still.

When and by whom were these marvels written? I know nothing of it, but I am certain that it was neither Polybius nor Tacitus. I strongly revere the worthy Jew, whoever he may be, who wrote the true history of the powerful Hebrew kingdom for instruction of the universe, guided by the God of all the worlds who inspired this good Jew. But I am upset that my friend David starts out by assembling a band of robbers numbering four hundred, and that, at the head of this troop of honest men, David reaches an understanding with the high priest Abimelech who arms with the sword of Goliath and gives him hallowed bread. (1 Kings, 21:13)

I am a bit scandalized that David, the Lord's anointed, the man according to God's heart, having revolted against Saul, another of the Lord's anointed, sets off with four hundred bandits, puts the region to contribution, robs the good man Nabal, and that immediately thereafter Nabal turns up dead and David weds his widow without delay. (1 Kings, 25:10-11)

I have some scruples about his conduct toward the great King Achish, the possessor (if I'm not mistaken) of five or six villages in the district of Gath. David, at the head of five or six hundred *banditti*, made inroads upon the allies of his benefactor Achish. He pillaged everything, killed everything, old men, women, and children at the breast. And why did he slaughter the children at the breast? "For fear," says the divine Jewish author, "that these children should carry the news to King Achish." (1 Kings, 27: 8-9-11)

These bandits become angry with him, they want to stone him. What does this Jewish mandarin do? He consults the Lord, and the Lord responds that he must attack the Amalekites and that these bandits will take good spoils there and be enriched. (1 Kings, 30)

In the meantime, the Lord's anointed, Saul, loses a battle against the Philistines and is slain. A Jew carries the news to David. David, who apparently had nothing to give as the *buona nuncia* to the messenger, has him killed for his pains. (2 Kings, 1:10)

Ishbosheth succeeds his father, Saul; David is strong enough to make war upon him. Finally Ishbosheth is assassinated.

David takes control of the whole kingdom; he surprises the little town or village of Rabbah and puts all the inhabitants to death by the most extraordinary devices—they are sawed in two, destroyed with harrows and axes of iron, and burned in brick kilns; a completely generous and noble way of waging war. (2 Kings, 12)

After these expeditions there is a famine in the country for three years. I quite readily it since, with the good David's mode of making war, the lands must necessarily have been poorly cultivated. The Lord was consulted as to the causes of the famine. The answer was easy. In a country that produces corn with difficulty, when laborers are baked in brick kilns and sawed into pieces, few people remain to cultivate the earth. The Lord, however, replies that it is because Saul had formerly slain some Gibeonites.

What is David's speedy remedy? He assembles the Gibeonites, informs them that Saul had committed a great sin in making war upon them, and that Saul not being like him, a man after God's own heart, it would be proper to punish him in his posterity. He therefore makes them a present of seven grandsons of Saul to be hanged, who were accordingly hanged because there had been a famine. (2 Kings, 21)

It is a pleasure to see how that imbecile Dom Calmet justifies and canonizes all these actions that would cause shivers of horror if they weren't incredible.

I shall not speak here of the murder of Uriah, and of the adultery with Bathsheba: these facts are sufficiently well known, and the ways of God are not the ways of men, since He permitted the descent of Jesus Christ from this very Bathsheba, everything being rendered pure by this holy mystery.

I do not now ask how the preacher Jurieu had the audacity to persecute the wise Bayle for not approving all the actions of the good King David. I only inquire why it is tolerated that a man like Jurieu molests a man like Bayle.

DÉLITS LOCAUX (DES) / LOCAL OFFENSES (ON)

IF we travel throughout the whole earth, we still find that theft, murder, adultery, and calumny are regarded as offences that society condemns and represses; but that which is approved in

England and condemned in Italy, ought it to be punished in Italy, as if it were one of the crimes against all of humanity? This is what I call a local offense. Doesn't that which is a crime only in the precincts of some mountains or between two rivers, require more indulgence from judges than those outrages that are regarded with horror in all countries? Ought not the judge say to himself, I would not dare to punish in Ragusa what I punish at Loretto? Shouldn't this reflection soften his heart and moderate the hardness that is all too easily contracted in the long exercise of his employment?

The "Kermesses" (fairs) of Flanders are well known; they were carried in the last century to a degree of indecency that might revolt the eyes of those who were not accustomed to such spectacles.

The following is the manner in which Christmas was celebrated in some towns. First, a young man appears, half-naked, with wings on his shoulders; he repeated the Ave Maria to a young girl, who replied "fiat," and the angel kissed her on the mouth; after which a child, shut up in a great pasteboard rooster, imitated the crowing of the cock: "*Puer natus est nobis.*" A great ox bellowed out "*ubi*"; a sheep baaed out "Bethlehem"; an ass brayed "*hihanus*," to signify "*eamus*"; and a long procession, preceded by four fools with bells and baubles, brought up the rear. There still remain some traces of this popular devotion, which among a civilized and educated people would be taken for profanation. A Swiss, out of patience, and possibly more intoxicated than the performers of the ox and the ass, exchanged words with them at Louvain, blows were exchanged; they wanted to hang the Swiss who barely escaped.

The same man had a violent quarrel at The Hague for aggressively taking the part of Barnevelt against a radical Gomarist. He was imprisoned at Amsterdam for saying that priests were the scourge of humanity and the source of all our misfortunes. "How!" said he, "if we maintain that good works are necessary to salvation, we are sent to a dungeon; and if we laugh at a rooster and an ass, we risk hanging!" As ridiculous as this adventure was, it is sufficient proof that one may be criminal in one or two spots in our hemisphere, and innocent in the rest of the world.

DESTIN / DESTINY

OF all the books that have come down to us, Homer is the most ancient. In his works we find the manners of profane antiquity, coarse heroes, and coarse gods, made after the image of man. But we also find the seeds of philosophy and more particularly the idea of destiny, which is the master of the gods, just as the gods are masters of the world.

In vain Jupiter wants to save Hector. He consults the destinies; he weighs in a balance the destinies of Hector and Achilles. He finds that the Trojan must inevitably be killed by the Greek; he is unable to oppose it. From that moment Apollo, the guardian genius of Hector, is compelled to abandon him. (*Iliad*, book 22) It is not to be denied that Homer often displays contradictory ideas in his poem, according to the privilege of antiquity; but yet he is the first in whom we encounter the notion of destiny. It may be concluded, then, that in his days it was a prevalent one.

The Pharisees, among the small nation of Jews, did not adopt the idea of a destiny until several centuries later. For these Pharisees themselves, who were the most learned class among the Jews, were but of very recent date. They mixed up, in Alexandria, a portion of the dogmas of the Stoics with their ancient Jewish ideas. St. Jerome goes so far as to claim that their sect is but a little anterior to our vulgar era.

Philosophers have never required the aid of Homer, or of the Pharisees, to be convinced that everything is performed according to immutable laws, that everything is ordained, that everything is a *necessary effect*.

Either the world subsists by its own nature, by its own physical laws, or a Supreme Being has formed it according to His supreme laws: in both cases these laws are immovable; in both cases everything is necessary; heavy bodies tend towards the center of the earth without having any power or tendency to rest in the air. Pear-trees cannot produce pineapples. The instinct of a spaniel cannot be the instinct of an ostrich; everything is arranged, adjusted, and fixed.

Man can have only a certain number of teeth, hairs, and ideas; and a period arrives when he necessarily loses his teeth, hair, and ideas.

It is contradictory to say that which was yesterday was not; or that today does not exist; it is just as contradictory to assert that that which must be might not have to be.

If you could derange the destiny of a single fly there would be no possible reason why you should not control the destiny of all other flies, of all other animals, of all men, of all nature. You would find, in fact, that you were more powerful than God.

Weak-minded persons say: "My physician has brought my aunt safely through a mortal disease; he has made my aunt live ten years longer than she ought." Others who claim more subtlety say: "The prudent man makes his own destiny."

> *Nullum numen abest, si sit Prudentia, sed nos*
> *Te facimus fortuna Deam coeloque locamus.*
> —JUVENAL, *Sat.* x. v. 365.

> We call on Fortune, and her aid implore,
> While Prudence is the goddess to adore.

But frequently the prudent man succumbs under his destiny instead of making it; it is destiny that makes men prudent.

Profound politicians assure us that if Cromwell, Ludlow, Ireton, and a dozen other parliamentary leaders had been assassinated eight days before Charles I had his head cut off, that king would have continued to live and would have died in his bed; they are right; and they may add that if all England had been swallowed up in the sea, that king would not have perished on a scaffold near Whitehall. But things were so arranged that Charles was to have his head cut off.

Cardinal d'Ossat was unquestionably more clever than an idiot of Bedlam; but isn't it evident that the organs of the wise d'Ossat were differently formed than those of that crazy man? Just as the organs of a fox are different from those of a crane or a lark?

Your physician saved your aunt, but in so doing he certainly did not contradict the order of nature, but followed it. It is clear that your aunt could not prevent her birth in a certain place, that she could not help being affected by a certain malady, at a certain time; that the physician could be in no other place than where he was, that your aunt could not but call him, that he could not but prescribe medicines that cured her.

A peasant thinks that it hailed upon his field by chance; but the philosopher knows that there is no chance, and that it was absolutely impossible, according to the constitution of the world, for it not to have hailed at that very time and place.

There are some who, being shocked by this truth, concede only half of it, like debtors who offer one moiety of their property to their creditors and ask remission for the other. There are, they say, some events which are necessary, and others that are not. It would be curious for one part of the world to be pre-ordered and the other not; that one part of what happens should happen inevitably, and another fortuitously. When we examine the question closely, we see that the doctrine opposed to that of destiny is absurd and contrary to the idea of eternal Providence; but many people are destined to be bad reasoners, others not to reason at all, and others to persecute those who reason.

There are some who say, "Do not believe in fatalism, for, if you do, everything appearing to you unavoidable, you will exert yourself for nothing; you will sink down in indifference; you will regard neither wealth, nor honors, nor praise; you will be careless about acquiring anything whatever; you will consider yourself worthless and powerless; no talent will be cultivated, and all will be overwhelmed in apathy."

Do not be afraid, gentlemen; we shall always have passions and prejudices, since it is our destiny to be subjected to prejudices and passions. We shall very well know that it no more depends upon us to have great merit or superior talents than to have a fine head of hair or a beautiful hand; we shall be convinced that we ought to be vain of nothing, and yet we shall always be vain.

I have necessarily the passion for writing as I now do; and, as for you, you have the passion for censuring me; we are both equally fools, both equally the sport of destiny. Your nature is to do ill, mine is to love truth and to publish it in spite of you.

The owl, while supping upon mice in his ruined tower, said to the nightingale, "Stop your singing there in your beautiful arbor, and come to my hole that I may eat you." The nightingale replied, "I am born to sing where I am and to laugh at you."

You ask me what is to become of liberty. I do not understand you; I do not know what the liberty you speak of really is. You have been so long disputing about the nature of it that you do not understand it. If you are willing, or rather, if you are able to examine with me coolly what it is, turn to the letter L.

DIEU / GOD

IN the reign of Arcadius, Logomachos, a theologue from Constantinople, went into Scythia and stopped at the foot of Mount Caucasus in the fruitful plains of Zephirim, on the borders of Colchis. The good old man Dondindac was in his great hall between his large sheepfold and his extensive barn; he was on his knees with his wife, his five sons and five daughters, his kinsmen and servants; and all were singing the praises of God, after a light repast. "What are you doing, idolater?" Logomachos said to him. "I am not an idolater," said Dondindac "You must be an idolater," said Logomachos, "for you are Scythian and not Greek. Come, tell me what you were singing in your barbarous Scythian jargon?" "All tongues are alike to the ears of God," answered the Scythian; "we were singing His praises." "Very extraordinary!" returned the theologue; "a Scythian family praying to God without having been instructed by us!" He soon entered into conversation with the Scythian Dondindac; for the theologue knew a little Scythian, and the other a little Greek. This conversation has been found in a manuscript preserved in the library of Constantinople.

LOGOMACHOS

Let us see if you know your catechism. Why do you pray to God?

DONDINDAC

Because it is just to adore the Supreme Being, from whom we have everything.

LOGOMACHOS

Not bad for a barbarian. And what do you ask of him?

DONDINDAC

I thank Him for the blessings I enjoy, and even for the trials He sends me; but I am careful to ask nothing of Him; for He knows our wants better than we do; besides, I should be afraid of asking for fair weather while my neighbor was asking for rain.

LOGOMACHOS

Ah! I thought he would say some nonsense or other. Let us begin farther back. Barbarian, who told you that there is a God?

DONDINDAC

All nature tells me.

LOGOMACHOS

That is not enough. What idea do you have of God?

DONDINDAC

The idea of my Creator, my master, who will reward me if I do good and punish me if I do evil.

LOGOMACHOS

Trifles! Trash! Let us come to some essentials. Is God infinite *secundum quid*, or according to essence?

DONDINDAC

I don't understand you.

LOGOMACHOS

Brute beast! Is God in one place, or in no place, or in every place?

DONDINDAC

I know not . . . . just as you please.

LOGOMACHOS

Ignoramus! . . . Can He cause that which has been not to have been, or that a stick shall not have two ends? Does He see the future as future or as present? How does He draw being from nothing, and how does He reduce being to nothing?

DONDINDAC

I have never examined these things.

LOGOMACHOS

What a stupid fellow! Well, I must come nearer to your level. . . . Tell me, my friend, do you think that matter can be eternal?

DONDINDAC

What matters it to me whether it exists for all eternity or not? I do not exist for all eternity. God is always my Master. He has given me the notion of justice; it is my duty to follow it: I do not seek to be a philosopher; I wish to be a man.

LOGOMACHOS

One has a great deal of trouble with these blockheads. Let us proceed step by step. What is God?

DONDINDAC

My sovereign, my judge, my father.

LOGOMACHOS

That is not what I ask. What is His nature?

DONDINDAC

To be mighty and good.

LOGOMACHOS

But is He corporeal or spiritual?

DONDINDAC

How should I know that?

LOGOMACHOS

What! do you not know what a spirit is?

DONDINDAC

Not in the least. What good would that do me? Would I be more just? Would I be a better husband, a better father, a better master, or a better citizen?

LOGOMACHOS

You must absolutely be taught what a spirit is. Listen. It is—it is—it is—I will tell you that another time.

DONDINDAC

I much fear that you will tell me rather what it is not than what it is. Permit me, in turn, to ask you one question. Some time ago, I saw one of your temples: Why do you paint God with a long beard?

LOGOMACHOS

That is a very difficult question that requires preliminary instruction.

Before I receive your instruction, I must relate to you a thing that happened to me one day. I had just built a closet at the end of my garden, when I heard a mole arguing thus with a June bug: "This is a fine construction," said the mole; "it must have been a very powerful mole that performed this work." "You jest," replied the June bug; "the architect of this edifice is a June bug of great genius." From that time I resolved never to dispute.

DIVINITÉ DE JÉSUS / DIVINITY OF JESUS

THE Socinians, who are regarded as blasphemers, do not recognize the divinity of Jesus Christ. They dare to pretend, with the philosophers of antiquity, with the Jews, the Mohammedans, and so many other nations, that the idea of a god-man is monstrous; that the distance from God to man is infinite; and that it is impossible that the infinite, immense, and eternal Being was contained in a perishable body.

They have the confidence to quote Eusebius, bishop of Cæsarea, in their favor, who, in his "Ecclesiastical History," i., 9, declares that it is absurd to imagine the uncreated and unchangeable nature of Almighty God taking the form of a man. They cite the fathers of the Church, Justin and Tertullian, who have said the same thing: Justin, in his "Dialogue with Triphonius"; and Tertullian, in his "Discourse against Praxeas."

They quote St. Paul, who never calls Jesus Christ "God," and who calls Him "man" very often. They carry their audacity so far as to affirm that the Christians passed three entire ages in forming by degrees the apotheosis of Jesus; and that they only raised this astonishing edifice by the example of the pagans, who had deified mortals. At first, according to them, Jesus was only regarded as a man inspired by God, and then as a creature more perfect than others. They gave Him some time after a place above the angels, as St. Paul tells us. Every day added to His greatness. He in time became an emanation, proceeding from God. This was not enough; He was even given a birth before time. At last He was made God consubstantial with God. Crellius, Voquelsius, Natalis Alexander, and Horneck have supported all these blasphemies by arguments which astonish the wise and mislead the weak. Above all, Faustus Socinus spread the seeds of this doctrine in Europe; and at the end of the sixteenth century a new species of Christianity was established. There were already more than three hundred.

DOGMES / DOGMAS

"ON Feb. 18, 1763, of the vulgar era, the sun entering the sign of the fishes, I was transported to heaven, as all my friends can bear witness. The mare Borac, of Mohammad, was not my steed, neither was the fiery chariot of Elijah my carriage. I was not carried on the elephant of Somonocodom, the Siamese; nor on the horse of St. George, the patron of England; nor on St. Anthony's pig. I avow with frankness that my journey was made I know not how.

"It will be easily believed that I was dazzled; but it will not so easily be credited that I witnessed the judgment of the dead. And who were the judges? They were—do not be displeased at it—all those who have done good to man. Confucius, Solon, Socrates, Titus, Antoninus, Epictetus, and all the great men who, having taught and practiced the virtues that God requires, seemed to be the only persons possessing the right of pronouncing his decrees.

"I shall not describe on what thrones they were seated, nor how many celestial beings were prostrated before the eternal architect of all worlds, nor what a crowd of the inhabitants of these innumerable worlds appeared before the judges. I shall only give an account of several little interesting peculiarities that were exceedingly striking.

"I remarked that every spirit who pleaded his cause and displayed his specious pretensions had beside him all the witnesses of his actions. For example, when the Cardinal of Lorraine boasted of having caused some of his opinions to be adopted by the Council of Trent and demanded eternal life as the price of his orthodoxy, there immediately appeared around him twenty ladies of the court, all bearing on their foreheads the number of their interviews with the cardinal. I also saw those who had established with him the foundations of the infamous League. All the accomplices of his wicked designs surrounded him.

"Over against the Cardinal of Lorraine was C....,[36] who boasted, in his gross *patois*, of having trampled upon the papal idol, after others had overthrown it. 'I have written against painting and sculpture,' said he; 'I have made it apparent that good works are of no avail, and I have proved that it is diabolical to dance a minuet. Quickly send away the Cardinal of Lorraine, and place me by the side of St. Paul.'

"As he spoke there appeared by his side a lighted pyre; a dreadful specter, wearing round his neck a half-burned Spanish frill arose from the midst of the flames, with dreadful shrieks. 'Monster,' cried he; 'execrable monster, tremble! Recognize S...., whom you caused to perish by the most cruel torments, because he had disputed with you on the manner in which three persons can form one substance.' Then all the judges commanded that the Cardinal of Lorraine should be thrown into the abyss, but that Calvin should be punished still more rigorously.

"I saw a prodigious crowd of spirits, each of which said, 'I have believed, I have believed!' but on their forehead it was written, 'I have acted,' and they were condemned.

"The Jesuit Letellier appeared boldly with the bull *Unigenitus* in his hand. But there suddenly arose at his side a heap, consisting of two thousand *lettres-de-cachet*. A Jansenist set fire to them, and Letellier was burned to a cinder; while the Jansenist, who had cabaled no less than the Jesuit, had his share of the flames.

"I saw approach, from right and left, troops of fakirs, talapoins, bonzes, and black, white, and gray monks, who all imagined that, to make their court to the Supreme Being, they must either sing, scourge themselves, or walk quite naked. I heard a terrible voice that asked them, 'What good have you done to men?' A dead silence followed this question. No one dared to answer; and they were all conducted to the madhouse of the universe, one of the largest buildings imaginable.

"One cried out that he believed in the metamorphoses of Xaca, another in those of Somonocodom. 'Bacchus stopped the sun and moon!' said this one. 'The gods resuscitated Pelops!' said the other. 'Here is the bull *in coena Domini*!' said a newcomer — and the officer of the court exclaimed, 'To Bedlam, to Bedlam!'

"When all these causes were gone through, I heard this proclamation: 'BY THE ETERNAL CREATOR, PRESERVER, REWARDER, REVENGER, FORGIVER, etc., be it known to all the inhabitants of the hundred thousand million million worlds that it hath pleased us to form, that we never judge any sinners in reference to their own shallow ideas, but only as to their actions. Such is our Justice.'

"I admit that this was the first time I ever heard such an edict; all those I had read back on the little grain of dust where I was born, ended with these words: 'Such is our *pleasure.*'"[37]

ÉGALITÉ / EQUALITY

WHAT does a dog owe to a dog, and a horse to a horse? Nothing, no animal depends on its kind. But since human beings have been endowed with that gleam of Divinity known as reason, what is the result? It means that we are the slaves of almost the entire world.

If the earth were in fact what it might be supposed it should be, that is, if men found upon it everywhere an easy and certain subsistence and a climate congenial to their nature, it would be evidently impossible for one man to subjugate another. Let the globe be covered with wholesome fruits; let the air on which we depend for life convey to us no diseases and premature death; let man require no other lodging than the deer or roebuck; in that case the Genghis Khans and Tamerlanes will have no other attendants than their own children, who will be sufficiently worthy persons to assist them in their old age.

In that state of nature enjoyed by all quadrupeds, birds and reptiles, man would be just as happy as they are. Domination would be a mere chimera, an absurdity no one would think of, for why should servants be sought for when no service is required?

If it should enter the mind of any individual of a tyrannical disposition and nervous arm to subjugate his less powerful neighbor, the thing would be impossible; the oppressed would be a hundred leagues away before the oppressor had completed his preparations.

All men, then, would necessarily be equal if they were without needs. It is the misery attached to our species which places one man in subjection to another; inequality is not the real grievance, but dependence. It is of little consequence for one man to be called his highness and another his holiness, but it is hard to serve either one.

A numerous family has cultivated a good soil; two small neighboring families live on lands unproductive and barren. It will therefore be necessary for the two poor families to serve the rich one or to destroy it. This is easily accomplished. One of the two indigent families goes and offers its services to the rich one in exchange for bread; the other makes an attack upon it and is conquered. The serving family is the origin of domestics and laborers; the one conquered is the origin of slaves.

It is impossible in our melancholy world to prevent men living in society from being divided into two classes, one of the rich who command, the other of the poor who serve, and these two are subdivided into a thousand others, which have also their respective shades of difference.

Every man is born with an eager inclination for power, wealth, and pleasure, and also with a great taste for indolence. Every man, consequently, would wish to possess the fortunes and the wives or daughters of others, to be their master, to retain them in subjection to his caprices, and to do nothing, or at least nothing but what is perfectly agreeable. You clearly perceive that with such amiable dispositions, it is as impossible for men to be equal as for two preachers or divinity professors not to be jealous of each other.

The human race, constituted as it is, cannot exist unless there be an infinite number of useful individuals possessed of no property at all, for most certainly a man in easy circumstances will not leave his own land to come and cultivate yours; and if you want a pair of shoes you will not get a lawyer to make them for you. Equality, then, is both the most natural and the most chimerical thing possible.

As men carry everything to excess if they have it in their power to do so, this inequality has been pushed too far; it has been maintained in many countries that no citizen has a right to quit that in which he was born. The meaning of such a law must evidently be: "This country is so wretched and ill-governed we prohibit every individual from leaving it, under an apprehension that otherwise everyone would leave it." Do better; make all your subjects desire to stay and foreigners a desire to come.

Every man has a right to entertain a private opinion of his own equality to other men, but it follows not that a cardinal's cook should take it upon him to order his master to prepare his dinner. The cook, however, may say: "I am a man like my master; I was born like him in tears and he will die like me in anguish, attended by the same common ceremonies. We both perform the same animal functions. If the Turks get possession of Rome, and I then become a cardinal and my master a cook, I will take him into my service." This language is perfectly reasonable and just, but, while waiting for the Grand Turk to get possession of Rome, the cook is bound to do his duty, or all human society is subverted.

With respect to a man who is neither a cardinal's cook nor invested with any office whatever in the state, with respect to an individual who has no connections, and is disgusted at being everywhere received with an air of protection or contempt, who sees quite clearly that many men of quality and title have no more knowledge, wit, or virtue than himself, and who is wearied by being occasionally in their antechambers—what ought such a man to do? He ought to go away.

ENFER / HELL

WHEN men came to live in society, they must have perceived that a great number of criminals eluded the severity of the laws; the laws punished public crimes; it was necessary to establish a check upon secret crimes; this check was to be found only in religion. The Persians, Chaldaeans, Egyptians, and Greeks, entertained the idea of punishments after the present life, and of all the nations of antiquity that we are acquainted with, the Jews were the only ones who admitted solely temporal punishments. It is ridiculous to believe, or pretend to believe, from some excessively obscure passages, that hell was recognized by the ancient laws of the Jews, by their Leviticus, or by their Decalogue, when the author of those laws says not a single word that can bear the slightest relation to the chastisements of a future life. We might have some right to address the compiler of the Pentateuch in such language as the following: "You are a man of no consistency, as destitute of probity as understanding, and totally unworthy of the name you arrogate to yourself of legislator. What! You are familiar with that doctrine as repressive, as necessary to the common people as the doctrine of hell, and yet you do not explicitly announce it? And, while it is accepted by all the nations that surround you, you are content to leave it for some commentators who will come four thousand years after you, to suspect that this doctrine might possibly have been entertained by you, and to twist and torture your expressions, in order to find that in them that which you never said? Either you are an ignoramus who does not know that this belief was universal in Egypt, Chaldaea, and Persia; or you have committed a great error in judgment, in not having made it the foundation-stone of your religion."

The authors of the Jewish laws could at most only answer: "We confess that we are excessively ignorant; that we did not learn the art of writing until a late period; that our people were a wild and barbarous horde, that wandered, as our own records admit, for nearly half a century in impracticable deserts, and at length obtained possession of a petty territory by the most odious rapine and detestable cruelty ever mentioned in the records of history. We had no commerce with civilized nations, and how could you suppose that we (the most earthly of men) could invent an entirely spiritual?"

We employed the word which most nearly corresponds with soul, merely to signify life; we knew our God and His ministers, His angels, only as corporeal beings; the distinction of soul and body, the idea of a life beyond death, can only be the fruit of long meditation and refined philosophy. Ask the Hottentots and Negroes, who inhabit a country a hundred times larger than ours, whether they know anything of a life to come? We thought we had done enough in persuading the people under our influence that God punished offenders to the fourth generation, either by leprosy, by sudden death, or by the loss of the little property one might possess.

To this apology it might be replied: "You have invented a system, the ridicule and absurdity of which are immediately apparent; for the offender who enjoyed good health, and whose family were in prosperous circumstances, must absolutely have mocked you."

The apologist for the Jewish law would here rejoin: "You are much mistaken; since for one criminal who reasoned correctly, there were a hundred who never reasoned at all. The man who, after he had committed a crime, found no punishment of it attached to himself or his son, would yet tremble for his grandson. Besides, if after the time of committing his offence he was not speedily seized with some festering sore, such as our nation was extremely subject to, he would experience it in the course of years. Calamities are always occurring in a family, and we easily instilled the belief that these calamities were inflicted by a divine hand taking vengeance for secret offences."

It would be easy to reply to this answer by saying: "Your apology is worth nothing; for it happens every day that very worthy and excellent persons lose their health and their property; and, if there were no family that did not experience calamity, and that calamity at the same time was a chastisement from God, all the families of your community must have been made up of scoundrels."

The Jewish priest might again answer and say that there are some calamities inseparable from human nature, and others expressly sent by God. But, in return, we should point out to such a reasoner that it is ridiculous to think that fever and hail-stones are in some cases a divine punishment and in others a natural effect.

In short, the Pharisees and the Essenes among the Jews did admit, in their own way, the belief in hell. This dogma had already passed from the Greeks to the Romans and was adopted by the Christians.

Several fathers of the church rejected the doctrine of eternal punishments. It appeared to them absurd to burn to all eternity an unfortunate man for stealing a goat. Virgil may have said in the sixth book of the *Aeneid*:

> . . . *Sedit eternumque sedebit*
> *Infelix Theseus.*
> Unhappy Theseus, doomed forever there,
> Is fixed by fate on his eternal chair.

—DRYDEN

But it is vain that he claims that Theseus is forever fixed to his chair and that this position constitutes his punishment. Others have imagined Theseus to be a hero who is not seated in hell, and who is to be found in the Elysian Fields.

Not long ago, a good Huguenot minister preached and wrote that the damned would at some future period be pardoned, that there must be some proportion between the sin and the penalty, and that a momentary trespass can in no way merit an infinite punishment. The rest of the ministers of his association expelled this indulgent judge. One of them said to him: "My good friend, I no more believe in the eternity of hell than you; but it is no bad thing for your servant, your tailor, and your lawyer to believe in it."

ENTHOUSIASME / ENTHUSIASM

THIS Greek word signifies "emotion of the bowels, internal agitation." Was the word invented by the Greeks to express the vibrations experienced by the nerves, the dilation and shrinking of the intestines, the violent contractions of the heart, the precipitous course of those fiery spirits which mount from the viscera to the brain whenever we are strongly and vividly affected?

Or was the term "enthusiasm," of a painful affection of the bowels, first applied to the contortions of the Pythia who, on the Delphian tripod, received the inspiration of Apollo in a place apparently intended to receive only bodies?

What do we understand by enthusiasm? How many shades are there in our affections! Approbation, sensibility, emotion, distress, impulse, passion, transport, insanity, rage, fury. Such are the stages through which the miserable human soul is liable to pass.

A geometrician attends the performance of a touching tragedy. He remarks only that it is well written. A young man who sits next to him is so moved by the performance that he makes no remark at all; a lady sheds tears over it; another young man is so transported that to his great misfortune he goes home determined to compose a tragedy himself. He has caught the disease of enthusiasm.

The centurion or military tribune who considered war simply as a profession by which he might make a small fortune, went to battle coolly, like a shingler ascending the roof of a house. Caesar wept at seeing the statue of Alexander.

Ovid spoke of love only with his mind. Sappho expressed the genuine enthusiasm of the passion, and if it be true that she sacrificed her life to it, her enthusiasm must have advanced to madness. Party politics tend to excite enthusiasm astonishingly; there is no faction that has not its devoted and possessed partisans.

Enthusiasm is connected particularly closely with ill-conceived religious devotion. The young fakir who fixes his eye on the tip of his nose when saying his prayers, gradually kindles in devotional ardor until he at length believes that if he burdens himself with chains of fifty pounds weight the Supreme Being will be obliged and grateful to him. He goes to sleep with an imagination totally absorbed by Brahma, and is sure to have a sight of him in a dream. Occasionally even in the intermediate state between sleeping and waking, sparks radiate from his eyes; he beholds Brahma resplendent with light; he falls into ecstasies, and the disease frequently becomes incurable.

What is most rarely to be met with is the combination of reason with enthusiasm. Reason consists in constantly perceiving things as they really are. He, who, under the influence of intoxication, sees objects double, is at the time deprived of reason. Enthusiasm is precisely like wine, it has the power to excite such ferment in the blood vessels, and such strong vibrations in the nerves, that reason is completely destroyed by it. But it may also occasion only slight agitations so as not to convulse the brain, but merely to render it more active, as is the case in grand bursts of eloquence and more especially in sublime poetry. Reasonable enthusiasm is the patrimony of great poets. This reasonable enthusiasm is the perfection of their art. It is this which formerly occasioned the belief that poets were inspired by the gods, a notion which was never applied to other artists. How is reasoning to control enthusiasm? A poet should initially make a sketch of his design. Reason then holds the pencil. But when he wants to animate his characters and give them passions? Then his imagination kindles, enthusiasm is in full operation and urges him on like a fiery courser in his career. But his course has been previously traced with coolness and judgment.

ESPRIT FAUX / FALSE UNDERSTANDING

WE have blind, one-eyed, cross-eyed, and squinting people, and visions long, short, clear, confused, weak, or indefatigable. All this is a faithful image of our understanding; but we know scarcely any *false* vision. There are not many men who always mistake a rooster for a horse, or a chamber pot for a house. How is it that we often meet with minds, otherwise judicious, that are absolutely wrong in some things of importance? How is it that the same Siamese man who can never be fooled when he is supposed to receive three rupees, firmly believes in the metamorphoses of Sammonocodom? By what strange whim do men of sense resemble Don Quixote, who beheld giants where other men saw nothing but windmills? Yet was Don Quixote more excusable than the Siamese, who believes that Sammonocodom came several times upon earth or the Turk, who is persuaded that Mohammad put half of the moon into his sleeve? Don Quixote, impressed with the idea that he is to fight with a giant, may imagine that a giant must have a body as big as a mill and arms as long as the sails; but from what supposition can a man of sense set out to arrive at a conclusion that half the moon went into a sleeve, and that a Sammonocodom came down from heaven to fly kites in Siam, to cut down a forest, and to exhibit sleight-of-hand?

The greatest geniuses may have their minds warped with regard to a principle they have received without examination. Newton was very wrong-headed when he was writing his commentary on the Apocalypse.

All that certain tyrants of souls desire, is that the men whom they teach may have their intellects distorted. A fakir brings up a child of great promise; he employs five or six years in driving it into his head, that the god Fo appeared to men in the form of a white elephant; and he persuades the child, that if he does not believe in these metamorphoses, he will be flogged after death for five hundred thousand years. He adds, that at the end of the world, the enemy of the god Fo will come and fight against that divinity.

The child studies, and becomes a prodigy; he develops arguments based on his master's lessons; he finds that Fo could not change himself into anything but a white elephant, because that is the most beautiful of animals. The kings of Siam and Pegu, he says, went to war with one another for a white elephant: certainly, had not Fo been concealed in that elephant, these two kings would not have been so mad as to fight for the possession of a mere animal.

Fo's enemy will come and challenge him at the end of the world: this enemy will certainly be a rhinoceros; for the rhinoceros fights the elephant. Thus does the fakir's learned pupil reason in mature age, and he becomes one of the lights of the Indies: the more subtle his intellect, the more crooked it is; and he, in his turn, forms other intellects as distorted as his own.

If these besotted beings are shown a little geometry, they learn it easily enough; but, strange to say, this does not set them right. They perceive the truths of geometry; but it does not teach them to weigh probabilities: they have taken their bent; they will reason falsely all their lives; and I am sorry for them.

ÉTATS, GOUVERNEMENTS / STATES, GOVERNMENTS

Which is the best?

I have not hitherto known any person who has not governed some state. I speak not of messieurs the ministers, who really govern; some two or three years, others six months, and others six weeks; I speak of all other men, who, at supper or in their closet, unfold their systems of government, and reform armies, the Church, the magistracy, and finances.

The Abbé de Bourzeis began to govern France towards the year 1645, under the name of the Cardinal de Richelieu, and made the "Political Testament," in which he would enlist the nobility into the cavalry for three years, make chambers of accounts and parliaments pay the poll tax, and deprive the king of the produce of the excise tax.[38] He asserts, above all, that to start a military campaign with fifty thousand men, it is essential to economize that a hundred thousand should be raised. He affirms that "Provence alone has more fine seaports than Spain and Italy together."

The Abbé de Bourzeis had not traveled. As to the rest, his work abounds with anachronisms and errors; and as he makes the Cardinal de Richelieu sign in a manner in which he never signed, so he makes him speak as he had never spoken. Moreover, he fills a whole chapter with saying that reason should guide a state, and in endeavoring to prove this discovery. This work of obscurities, this bastard of the Abbé de Bourzeis, has long passed for the legitimate offspring of the Cardinal de Richelieu; and all academicians, in their reception speeches, never failed to praise extravagantly this political masterpiece.

The Sieur Gatien de Courtilz, seeing the success of Richelieu's *Testament Politique*, published at The Hague the *Testament de Colbert*, with a fine letter from M. Colbert to the king. It is clear that if this minister made such a testament, it would have been necessary to suppress it; yet this book has been quoted by several authors. Another ignoramus, whose name is unknown, did not fail to produce the *Testament de Louvois*, still worse, if possible, than that of Colbert. An abbé of Chevremont also made Charles, duke of Lorraine, form a testament. We have had the political testaments of Cardinal Alberoni, Marshal Belle-Isle, and finally that of Mandrin.

M. de Boisguillebert, author of the *Détail de la France*, published in 1695, produced the impracticable project of the royal tithe, under the name of the marshal de Vauban.

A madman, named La Jonchere, wanting bread, wrote, in 1720, a finance plan in four volumes; and some fools have quoted this production as a work of La Jonchere, the treasurer-general, imagining that a treasurer could not write a bad book on finance.

But it must be confessed that some very wise men, perhaps very worthy to govern, have written on the administration of states in France, Spain, and England. Their books have done much good; not that they have corrected ministers who were in place when these books appeared, because a minister does not and cannot correct himself. He has attained his full growth; no more instruction, no more counsel, he hasn't the time to listen to them; the current of affairs carries him away. But these good books shape the young people destined for office; they shape princes, and the second generation is instructed.

The strength and weakness of all governments has been narrowly examined in recent times. Tell me, then, you who have traveled, who have read and have seen, in what state, under what sort of government, would you like to have been born? I conceive that a great landed lord in France would have no objection to being born in Germany: he would be a sovereign instead of a subject. A peer of France would be very glad to have the privileges of the English peerage: he would be a legislator.

The magistrate and the financier would find themselves better off in France than elsewhere.

But what country would a wise, free man choose—a man of small fortune, without prejudices?

A rather learned member of the council of Pondicherry was returning to Europe by land with a Brahmin, more learned most. "How do you find the government of the Great Mogul?" said the counselor. "Abominable," answered the Brahmin; "how can you expect a state to be happily governed by Tartars? Our rajahs, our omras, and our nabobs are very contented, but the citizens are by no means so; and millions of citizens are something."

The counselor and the Brahmin traversed all Upper Asia, reasoning on their way. "I reflect," said the Brahmin, "that there is not a single republic in all this vast part of the world." "There was formerly that of Tyre," said the counselor, "but it didn't last long; there was another near Arabia Petraea, in a little nook called Palestine—if we can honor with the name of republic a horde of thieves and usurers, sometimes governed by judges, sometimes by a sort of kings, sometimes by high priests, who became slaves seven or eight times and were finally driven from the country they had usurped."

"I fancy," said the Brahmin, "that we should find very few republics on earth. Men are seldom worthy to govern themselves. This happiness should only belong to small countries, secluded on islands or between mountains, like rabbits that steal away from carnivorous animals but at length are discovered and devoured."

When the travelers arrived in Asia Minor, the counselor said to the Brahmin, "Would you believe that there was a republic formed in a corner of Italy that lasted more than five hundred years and possessed Asia Minor, Asia, Africa, Greece, the Gauls, Spain, and the whole of Italy?" "It must soon have turned into a monarchy?" said the Brahmin. "You have guessed it," said the other; "but this monarchy fell, and every day we make fine dissertations to explain the causes of its decay and fall."[39] "Your efforts are useless," said the Indian: "this empire fell because it existed. All must fall. I hope that the same will happen to the empire of the Great Mogul."

"Apropos," said the European, "do you believe that more honor is required in a despotic state and more virtue in a republic?" The term "honor" being first explained to the Indian, he replied that honor was more necessary in a republic and that there is more need of virtue in a monarchical state. "For," said he, "a man who aspires to be elected by the people, will not be so, if he is dishonored; while at court he can easily obtain a place, according to the maxim of a great prince, that to succeed, a courtier should have neither honor nor temper. With respect to virtue, it is prodigiously required in a court, in order to dare to tell the truth. The virtuous man is much more at his ease in a republic, having nobody to flatter."

"Do you believe," said the European, "that laws and religions can be formed for climates, the same as furs are required at Moscow and gauze fabric at Delhi?" "Yes, doubtless," said the Brahmin; "all laws dealing with physics are calculated for the meridian we inhabit; a German requires only one wife, and a Persian must have three or four.

"Religious rites are of the same nature. If I were a Christian, how would you have me say mass in my province where there is neither bread nor wine? With regard to dogmas, that it is another matter; climate has nothing to do with them. Didn't your religion start in Asia where it has been eliminated? Doesn't it exist around the Baltic Sea where it was previously unknown?"

"In what state, under what dominion, would you like to live?" said the counselor. "Anywhere but in my country," said his companion, "and I have found many Siamese, Tonquinese, Persians, and Turks who said the same." "But still," said the European, "what state would you choose?" The Brahmin answered, "The one where the laws alone are obeyed." "That is an old answer," said the counselor. "It is none the worse for that," said the Brahmin. "Where is this country?" said the counselor. The Brahmin: "We must seek it." (See article "Geneva.")[40]

ÉVANGILE / GOSPEL

IT is a matter of high importance to ascertain which are the first gospels. It is a solid truth, whatever Abbadie may assert to the contrary, that none of the first fathers of the Church, down to Irenaeus, quotes any passage from the four gospels with which we are acquainted. On the contrary, the Alogi, the Theodosians, constantly rejected the gospel of St. John, and always spoke of it with contempt; as we are informed by St. Epiphanius in his thirty-fourth homily. Our enemies further observe that the most ancient fathers do not merely fail to quote anything from our gospels, but relate many passages or events which are to be found only in the apocryphal gospels rejected from the canon.

St. Clement, for example, relates that our Lord, having been questioned concerning the time when His kingdom would come, answered, "That will be two are but one, when what is without shall resemble that within, and when there shall be neither male nor female." But we must admit that this passage does not occur in any of our gospels. There are a hundred examples that prove this truth; they may be consulted in the "Critical Examination" of M. Fréret, perpetual secretary of the Academy of Belles Lettres at Paris.

The learned Fabricius took the pains to collect the ancient gospels which time has spared; that of James appears to be the first; and it is certain that it still possesses considerable authority with some of the Oriental churches. It is called "the first gospel." There remain the passion and the resurrection, supposedly written by Nicodemus. This gospel of Nicodemus is quoted by St. Justin and Tertullian. It is there we find the names of our Lord's accusers—Annas, Caiaphas, Soumas, Dathan, Gamaliel, Judas, Levi, and Napthali; the attention and particularity with which these names are given confer upon the work an appearance of truth and sincerity. Our adversaries have inferred that since so many false gospels were forged, which at first were recognized as true, those that today constitute the foundation of our faith may have been forged also. They emphatically insist on the faith of the first heretics who died for these apocryphal gospels. There were evidently, they say, forgers, seducers, and misguided individuals who died in defense of that error; it is, therefore, no proof of the truth of our religion that martyrs who have died for it.

They add further that the martyrs were never asked, "Do you believe the gospel of John or the gospel of James" The Pagans could not base interrogations on books with which they were not at all acquainted; the magistrates punished some Christians as disturbers of the public peace, but they never put particular questions to them in relation to our four gospels. These books only began to be known to the Romans during the reign of Trajan, and they came into the hands of the public only at the close of Diocletian's reign. The rigid Socinians do not consider our four gospels in any other light than as clandestine works, fabricated about a century after the time of Jesus Christ, and carefully concealed from the Gentiles for another century beyond that; works, they say, of a coarse and vulgar character, written by coarse and vulgar men who for a long time addressed only the populace. We will not here repeat their other blasphemies. This sect, although considerably diffused and numerous, is at present as much concealed as were the first gospels. The difficulty of converting them is so much the greater, since they listen only to reason. The other Christians contend against them only with the weapons of the Holy Scripture: it is thus impossible that, being always in conflict, they should ever unite in their conclusions.

(by the Abbé de Tilladet)

D'ÉZÉCHIEL / ON EZEKIEL

On some curious passages from this prophet,
and several ancient customs.

IT is well known that we ought not to judge ancient usages by modern ones; he who would reform the court of Alcinous in the "Odyssey" on the model of the Grand Turk or Louis XIV would not meet with a very gentle reception from the learned; he who is disposed to reprehend Virgil for having described King Evander covered with a bear's skin and accompanied by two dogs at the introduction of ambassadors would be a poor critic.

The manners of the ancient Egyptians and Jews are still more different from ours than those of King Alcinous, his daughter Nausicáa, and the worthy Evander. Ezekiel, when in slavery among the Chaldaeans, had a vision near the small river Chobar, which falls into the Euphrates.

We ought not to be in the least astonished at his having seen animals with four faces, four wings, and with calves' feet; or wheels revolving without aid and possessing the "spirit of life"; these images are pleasing to the imagination; but many critics have been shocked at the order given him by the Lord to eat, for a period of three hundred and ninety days, bread made of barley, wheat, or millet, covered with human excrement.

The prophet exclaimed, "Ah! Ah! My soul has not hitherto been polluted"; and the Lord replied, "Well, I will allow you instead of human excrement to use that of the cow, and with the latter you shall knead your bread."

As it is now unusual to eat such jam on one's bread, most men find these orders unworthy of the Divine Majesty. Yet it must be admitted that cow dung and all the diamonds of the great Mogul are perfectly equal, not only in the eyes of a Divine Being, but in those of a true philosopher; and, with regard to the reasons God might have for ordering such a lunch for the prophet, we have no right to inquire into them.

It is enough for us to show that commands that appear to us very strange did not appear so to the Jews. It must be admitted that the synagogue, in the time of St. Jerome, did not permit Ezekiel to be read before the age of thirty; but this was because, in the eighteenth chapter, he says that the son shall not bear the iniquity of his father, and it shall not be any longer said the fathers have eaten sour grapes, and the children's teeth are set on edge.

On these points, he was in direct contradiction with Moses who, in the twenty-eighth chapter of Numbers, declares that the children bear the iniquity of the fathers, even to the third and fourth generation.

Ezekiel, again, in the twentieth chapter, makes the Lord say that He has given to the Jews precepts that are not good. Such are the reasons for which the synagogue forbade young people to read an author likely to raise doubts on the irrefragability of the laws of Moses.

The censorious critics of the present day are still more astonished with the sixteenth chapter of Ezekiel. In that chapter he thus takes it upon him to expose the crimes of the city of

Jerusalem. He introduces the Lord speaking to a young woman; and the Lord said to her, "When you were born, your navel string was not cut, you were not salted, you were quite naked, I had pity on you; you did increase in stature, your breasts were fashioned, your hair sprouted, I passed by, I saw you, I knew that the time of lovers was come, I covered your shame, I spread my cloak over you; you became mine; I washed and perfumed you, and dressed and shod you well; I gave you a scarf of linen, and bracelets, and a chain for you neck; I placed a jewel in you nose, pendants in you ears, and a crown upon you head."

"Then, confiding in you beauty, you played the harlot with every passer-by. . . . And you built a high place of profanation . . . and you prostituted yourself in public places, and opened your legs to everyone who passed . . . and you committed fornication with the Egyptians . . . and finally you paid lovers and made them presents, that they might lie with you . . . and by hiring them, instead of being hired, you have done differently from other harlots. . . . The proverb is, as is the mother, so is the daughter, and that proverb is used of you," etc.

They protest even more against the twenty-third chapter. A mother had two daughters, who lost their virginity early. The elder was called Ohola, and the younger Oholibah . . . . "*Oholah was crazy for the young lords, magistrates, and captains, and lay with the Egyptians from her early youth . . . . Oholibah, her sister, committed still greater fornication with officers, magistrates, and well-made cavaliers; she discovered her shame, she multiplied her fornications, she sought eagerly for the embraces of those whose member was like that of an ass, and who spread their seed like horses.*"

These descriptions, which so madden weak minds, signify, in fact, no more than the iniquities of Jerusalem and Samaria; these expressions, which appear to us licentious, were not so then. The same naïveté is displayed in many other parts of Scripture without the slightest apprehension. It is often spoken of opening the vulva. The terms used to express the coupling of Boaz with Ruth, and of Judah with his daughter-in-law, are not indelicate in the Hebrew language, but would be so in our own.

People who are not ashamed of nakedness, never cover it with a veil. In the days, how could anyone blush at the mention of the testicles, since they were actually touched by the person who bound himself by any promise to another; it was a mark of respect, a symbol of fidelity, as formerly among ourselves, feudal lords put their hands between those of their sovereign.

We have translated the term adverted to by the word "thigh." Eliezer puts his hand under Abraham's thigh. Joseph puts his hand under the thigh of Jacob. This custom was very ancient in Egypt. The Egyptians were so far from attaching any disgrace to the thing we don't dare to uncover or mention that they bore in procession a large image of the male member, called Phallus, in order to thank the gods for making this member serve in the perpetuation of the human species.

All this affords sufficient proof that our sense of decorum and propriety is different from that of other nations. At what point in their history did Romans appear to have been more polished than in the time of Augustus? Yet Horace doesn't hesitate to say, in one of his moral pieces: "*Nec metuo, ne dum futuo vir rure recurrat.*" (satire 2, book 1, v. 127)

Augustus uses the same expression in an epigram on Fulvia.

The man who pronounced among us the word in our language that corresponds to futuo, would be regarded as a drunken porter; that word, as well as various others used by Horace and other authors, appears to us even more indecent than the expressions of Ezekiel. Let us then do away with our prejudices when we read ancient authors or travel among distant nations. Nature is the same everywhere, and usages are everywhere different.

I once met at Amsterdam a rabbi quite brimful of this chapter. "Ah! my friend," says he, "how very much we are obliged to you. You have displayed all the sublimity of the Mosaic Law, Ezekiel's breakfast; his delightful left-sided attitudes; Oholah and Oholibah are admirable things; they are types, my brother—types that show that one day the Jewish people will be masters of the whole world; but why did you admit so many others of nearly equal strength? Why did you not represent the Lord saying to the sage Hosea, in the second verse of the first chapter, 'Hosea, take a harlot, and make to her the children of a harlot?' Such are the very words. Hosea took the young woman and had a son by her, and afterwards a daughter, and then again a son; and it was a type, and that type lasted three years. That is not all; the Lord says in the third chapter, 'Go and take a woman who is not merely a harlot, but an adulteress.' Hosea obeyed, but it cost him fifteen crowns and eighteen bushels of barley; for, you know, there was very little wheat in the promised land. But do you know the meaning of all this?" "No," said I to him. "Nor do I," said the rabbi.

A grave scholar then advanced towards us and said they were ingenious fictions and abounding in exquisite beauty. "Ah, sir," remarked a young man of great learning, "if you are inclined for fictions, believe me, give preference to those of Homer, Virgil, and Ovid. He who prefers the prophecies of Ezekiel deserves to dine with him."

FABLES / FABLES

AREN'T the most ancient fables the most visibly allegorical ones? The earliest one we know of, in accordance with our way of reckoning time, isn't it the one recorded in the ninth chapter of the book of Judges? It was necessary to choose a king among the trees. The olive tree did not want to abandon the care of its oil, nor the fig tree the care of its figs, nor the vine the care of its grapes, nor the other trees the care of their fruit. The bramble who was good for nothing became king because it had thorns and could cause harm.

Isn't the ancient fable of Venus, as related by Hesiod, an allegory of all of nature? Reproductive parts fell from the skies by the seashore; Venus is born from this precious foam; her first name is the lover of reproduction; could there be a more telling image? This Venus is the goddess of beauty. Beauty ceases to be lovely if unaccompanied by the graces. Beauty produces love. Love has features that pierce all hearts; he wears a headband that conceals the faults of those beloved.

Wisdom is conceived in the brain of the chief of the gods, under the name of Minerva. The soul of man is a divine fire that Minerva shows to Prometheus, who uses this divine fire to animate mankind.

It is impossible, in these fables, not to recognize a lively picture of pure nature. Most other fables are either corruptions of ancient histories or caprices of the imagination. It is with ancient fables as with our modern tales; some convey charming morals, and others are very insipid.

The fables of the ingenious peoples of antiquity have been grossly imitated by unenlightened peoples—witness the tales of Bacchus, Hercules, Prometheus, Pandora, and many others, which were the amusement of the ancient world. The barbarians, who confusedly heard them spoken of, adopted them into their own savage mythology, and afterwards they dared to claim that they invented them. Alas! poor unknown and unknowing peoples, who knew no art either useful or agreeable and to whom even the name of geometry was foreign, can you say that you have invented anything? You have not known either how to discover truth or to lie adroitly.

Fanatisme / Fanaticism

FANATICISM is, in reference to superstition, what delirium is to fever, or rage to anger. He who is involved in ecstasies and visions, who takes dreams for realities, and his own imaginations for prophecies, is an enthusiast; he who backs up his folly with murder is a fanatic. Living off in Nuremberg, John Bartholomew Diaz, who was completely convinced that the pope was the Antichrist of the Apocalypse bearing the sign of the beast, was simply an enthusiast. His brother, Alfonso Diaz, who left Rome to commit the holy assassination of his brother and who, in fact, killed him for the love of God, was one of the most abominable fanatics that superstition has ever succeeded in creating.

Polyeuctes, who went to the temple on a day of solemn festival, to throw down and destroy the statues and ornaments, was a fanatic less horrible than Diaz, but not less foolish. The assassins of Francis, Duke of Guise, of William, Prince of Orange, of King Henry III, of King Henry IV, and various others, were equally possessed, equally laboring under morbid fury, with Diaz.

The most striking example of fanaticism is that exhibited on the night of St. Bartholomew, when the people of Paris rushed from house to house to stab, slaughter, throw out of the window, and tear into pieces their fellow citizens who did not attend mass.[41]

There are some cold-blooded fanatics; such as those judges who sentence men to death for no other crime than that of thinking differently from themselves, and these judges are all the more guilty and deserving of the execration of humankind, since, not laboring under madness like the Clements, Châtels, Ravaillacs, and Damiens, they might be deemed capable of listening to reason.

When once fanaticism has gangrened the brain of any man, the disease may be regarded as nearly incurable. I have seen Convulsionaries who, while speaking of the miracles of St. Paris, gradually worked themselves up to higher and more vehement degrees of agitation till their eyes became inflamed, their whole frames shook, their countenances became distorted by rage, and had any man contradicted them he would inevitably have been murdered. There is no other remedy for this epidemical malady than that spirit of philosophy, which, extending itself from individual to individual, at length civilizes and softens the manners of men and prevents the access of the disease. For when the disorder has made any progress, we should flee and wait till the air has become purified from contagion. Law and religion are not completely efficient against the spiritual pestilence. Religion, indeed, so far from affording proper nutriment to the minds of patients laboring under this infection, is converted into poison. These wretches have incessantly before their eyes the example of Ehud, who assassinated the king of Eglon; of Judith, who cut off the head of Holofernes while in bed with him; of Samuel, hewing into pieces King Agag. They do not perceive that these instances, which are respectable in antiquity, are in the present day abominable. They derive their fury from the religion that condemns it.

Laws are yet more powerless against these paroxysms of rage; it's like reading a decree of council to a man in a frenzy. Such people are fully convinced that the Holy Spirit which animates and fills them is above all laws; that their own enthusiasm is the only law they are bound to obey.

What can be said in answer to a man who says he prefers to obey God than men, and who consequently feels certain of meriting heaven by cutting your throat?

Fanatics are nearly always under the direction of knaves, who place the dagger in their hands. These knaves resemble the "Old Man of the Mountain," who, it is said, made weak persons imagine that they really had experienced the joys of paradise, and promised them a whole eternity of such delights as they had sampled, if they would go and assassinate all those he should point out to them. There has been only one religion in the world that has not been polluted by fanaticism and that is the religion of the learned in China. The different sects of ancient philosophers were not merely exempt from this pest of human society, but they were antidotes to it. For the effect of philosophy is to render the soul tranquil, and fanaticism and tranquility are totally incompatible. That our own holy religion has been so frequently polluted by this infernal fury must be imputed to the folly and madness of humankind. Thus Icarus abused the wings that he received for his benefit. They were given to him for his salvation and they insured his destruction:

> *Ainsi du plumage qu'il eut*
> *Icare pervertit l'usage;*
> *Il le reçut pour son salut,*
> *Il s'en servit pour son dommage.*
> —Bertaut, Bishop of Séez

FAUSSETÉ DES VERTUS HUMAINES / FALSENESS OF HUMAN VIRTUES

WHEN the Duke de la Rochefoucauld wrote his "Thoughts on Self-Love," and uncovered this motor of human action, one M. Esprit of the Oratory, wrote a captious book entitled *Of the Falseness of Human Virtues*.[42] This author says that there is no virtue; but by grace, he terminates each chapter by referring to Christian charity. So, according to M. Esprit, neither Cato, Aristides, Marcus Aurelius, nor Epictetus was a good man; such can be found only among the Christians. Among the Christians, again, there is no virtue except among the Catholics; among the Catholics, the Jesuits must be excepted as the enemies of the Oratory; ergo, virtue is scarcely to be found anywhere except among the enemies of the Jesuits.

This M. Esprit commences by asserting that prudence is not a virtue; and his reason is that it is often deceived. It is as if he had said that Caesar was not a great captain because he was conquered at Dyrrachium.

If M. Esprit had been a philosopher, he would not have examined prudence as a virtue, but as a talent, as a useful and fortunate quality; for a great rascal may be very prudent, and I have known many such. Oh, what an outrage to claim that *"Nul n'aura de vertu que nous et nos amis!"*—None are virtuous but ourselves and our friends!

What is virtue, my friend? It is to do good; let us then do it, and that will suffice. But we give you credit for the motive. What, then! According to you, there is no difference between the President de Thou and Ravaillac? Between Cicero and Popilius, whose life he saved and who afterwards cut off his head for money? And you will pronounce Epictetus and Porphyrius rogues because they did not follow our dogmas? Such insolence is disgusting; but I will say no more, for I am getting angry.

Fin, Causes Finales / End, Final Causes

It would appear that a man must be supposed to have lost his senses before he can deny that stomachs are made for digestion, eyes to see, and ears to hear.

On the other hand, a man must have a singular partiality for final causes, to assert that stone was made for building houses, and that silkworms are produced in China so that we may have satin in Europe.

But, it is urged, if God has evidently done one thing by design, he has then done all things by design. It is ridiculous to admit Providence in the one case and to deny it in the others. Everything that is done was foreseen, was arranged. There is no arrangement without an object, no effect without a cause; all, therefore, is equally the result, the product of a final cause; it is, therefore, as correct to say that noses were made to bear spectacles, and fingers to be adorned with rings, as to say that the ears were formed to hear sounds, the eyes to receive light.

I believe this difficult can be illuminated without difficulty. When the effects are invariably the same in all times and places, and when these uniform effects are independent of the beings to which they belong, then there is visibly a final cause.

All animals have eyes and see; all have ears and hear; all have mouths with which they eat; stomachs, or something similar, by which they digest their food; all have suitable means for expelling the feces; all have a reproductive organ; and these naturally function in them without any application or intermixture of art. Here are final causes clearly established; and to deny a truth so universal would be a perversion of the faculty of reason.

But stones, in all times and places, do not constitute the materials of buildings. All noses do not bear spectacles; all fingers do not carry a ring; all legs are not covered with silk stockings.[43] A silkworm, therefore, is not made to cover my legs, exactly as your mouth is made for eating and your bottom for going to the toilet. There are, therefore, immediate effects produced from final causes, and numerous effects that cannot be labeled in this way.

But both are equally part of the design of general Providence: doubtless, nothing is done despite or even without Providence. Everything belonging to nature is uniform, immutable, and the immediate work of its author. It is he who has established the laws by which the moon contributes three-fourths to the cause of the flux and reflux of the ocean, and the sun the remaining fourth. It is he who has given a rotational motion to the sun, in consequence of which that orb communicates its rays of light in the space of five and a half minutes to the eyes of men, crocodiles, and cats.

But if, after a course of ages, we took a mind to invent shears and spits, to clip the wool of sheep with the one, and with the other to roast them in order to eat them, what else can be inferred from such circumstances, but that God formed us in such a manner that, at some time or other, we could not avoid becoming ingenious and carnivorous?

Sheep, undoubtedly, were not made expressly to be roasted and eaten, since many nations abstain from this horror. Humankind is not created essentially to massacre one another, since the Brahmins and the Quakers kill no one. But the clay from which we are kneaded frequently produces massacres, just as it produces calumnies, vanities, persecutions, and impertinences. It is not that the form of man is the final cause of our madness and folly, for a final cause is universal, and invariable in every age and place; but the horrors and absurdities of the human race are none the less included in the eternal order of things. When we thresh our grain, the flail is the final cause of the separation of the grain. But if that flail, while threshing my grain, crushes to death a thousand insects, this does not occur by an express and determinate act of my will, nor, on the other hand, is it by mere chance; the insects were, on this occasion, actually under my flail and could not but be there.

It is a consequence of the nature of things that a man should be ambitious; that he should enlist other men; that he should be a conqueror, or that he should be defeated; but it can never be said, "Man was created by God to be killed in war."

The organs with which nature has supplied us cannot always be final causes in action that have an inevitable effect. The eyes which are bestowed for seeing are not constantly open. Every sense has its rest periods. There are even some senses that are not used. For example, an imbecile and wretched female, shut up in a cloister at the age of fourteen years, closes forever the door by which a new generation was supposed to exit; but the final cause, nevertheless, continues to exist and will operate whenever it is free to.

Foi / Faith

PRINCE Pico della Mirandola once met Pope Alexander VI at the house of the courtesan Emilia, while Lucretia, the holy father's daughter, was confined in childbirth, and the people of Rome were discussing whether the child belonged to the pope, to his son the Duke de Valentinois, or to Lucretia's husband, Alphonso of Aragon, who was considered by many as impotent. The conversation immediately became quite animated. Cardinal Bembo relates a portion of it. "My little Pico," says the pope, "whom do you think the father of my grandson?" "I think your son-in-law," replied Pico. "What! How can you possibly believe such nonsense?" "I believe it by faith." "But surely you know that an impotent man cannot be a father." "Faith," replied Pico, "consists in believing things because they are impossible; and, besides, the honor of your house demands that Lucretia's son should not be reputed the offspring of incest. You require me to believe more incomprehensible mysteries. Am I not bound to believe that a serpent spoke; that from that time all men were damned; that the ass of Balaam also spoke with great eloquence; and that the walls of Jericho fell down at the sound of trumpets?" Pico thus proceeded with a long train of all the admirable things in which he believed. Alexander fell back upon his sofa with laughing. "I believe all that as well as you," says he, "for I well know that I can be saved only by faith, as I can certainly never be so by works." "Ah, Holy Father!" says Pico, "you need neither works nor faith; they are well enough for such poor, profane creatures as we are; but you, who are absolutely a vice-god—you may believe and do just whatever you please. You have the keys of heaven; and St. Peter will certainly never shut the door in your face. But with respect to myself, who am nothing but a poor prince, I freely confess that I should have found some very powerful protection necessary, if I had lain with my own daughter, or had employed the stiletto and poison as often as Your Holiness." Alexander VI understood the teasing. "Let us speak seriously," says he to the prince. "Tell me what merit there can be in a man's saying to God that he is persuaded of things of which, in fact, he cannot be persuaded? What pleasure can this afford to God? Between ourselves, a man who says that he believes what is impossible to be believed is a liar."

Pico della Mirandola at this crossed himself in great agitation. "My God!" says he, "I beg Your Holiness' pardon; but you are not a Christian." "No," says the pope, "upon my faith." "I suspected so," said Pico della Mirandola.

(by a descendant of Rabelais)[44]

II

What is faith? Is it to believe that which is evident? No. It is perfectly evident to my mind that there exists a necessary, eternal, supreme, and intelligent Being. This is no matter of faith, but of reason. I have no merit in thinking that this eternal and infinite Being, who is the essence of virtue and goodness, is desirous that I should be good and virtuous. Faith consists in believing not what seems true, but what seems false to our understanding. The Asiatics can only by faith believe the journey of Mohammad to the seven planets, and the incarnations of the god Fo, of Vishnu, Xaca, Brahma, and Sommonocodom. They submit their understanding; they tremble to examine; they wish to avoid being either impaled or burned, they say: "I believe."

There is a faith for astonishing things, and a faith for contradictory and impossible things.

Vishnu became incarnate five hundred times; this is extremely astonishing, but it is not, however, physically impossible; for if Vishnu possessed a soul, he may have transferred that soul into five hundred different bodies, for his own enjoyment. The Indian, indeed, does not have a very lively faith; he is not intimately and decidedly persuaded of these metamorphoses; but he will nevertheless say to his bonze, "I have faith; it is your will and pleasure that Vishnu has undergone five hundred incarnations, which is worth to you an income of five hundred rupees: very well; you will inveigh against me, and denounce me, and ruin my trade if I have no faith; very well, I have faith, and here are ten rupees that I give you." The Indian may swear to the bonze that he believes without taking a false oath, for, after all, there is no demonstration that Vishnu has not actually made five hundred visits to India.

But if the bonze requires him to believe what is contradictory or impossible, as that two and two make five, or that the same body may be in a thousand different places, or that to be and not to be are precisely one and the same thing; in that case, if the Indian says he has faith he lies, and if he swears that he believes, he commits perjury. He says, therefore, to the bonze: "My reverend father, I cannot declare to you that I believe in these absurdities, even though they should be worth to you an income of ten thousand rupees instead of five hundred."

"My son," the bonze answers, "give me twenty rupees and God will give you grace to believe all that you now do not believe."

"But how can you expect or desire," rejoins the Indian, "that God should do to me that which He cannot do even to Himself? It is impossible that God should either perform or believe contradictions; otherwise he would no longer be God. I am very willing to say, in order to give you satisfaction that I believe obscure things, but I cannot say that I believe that which is impossible. It is the will of God that we should be virtuous, and not that we should be absurd. I have already given you ten rupees; here are twenty more; believe in thirty rupees; be an honest man, if you can, and do not trouble me any more."

FOLIE / MADNESS

THERE is no question of replicating the book by Erasmus, which would today be a rather insipid commonplace.[45]

We call madness the disease of the brain that necessarily hinders a man from thinking and acting like other men. Not being able to manage his property, the madman is withheld from it; incapable of ideas suitable to society, he is shut out from it; if he be dangerous, he is confined altogether; and if he be furious, he is bound.

It is important to observe, however, that this man is not deprived of ideas; waking, he possesses them like other men, and often when he sleeps. We might inquire how his spiritual and immortal soul, lodged in his brain, receiving all its ideas correctly and distinctly from the senses, is nevertheless powerless to formulate a sane judgment. It perceives objects, as the souls of Aristotle, of Plato, of Locke, and of Newton, perceived them. It hears the same sounds and possesses the same sense of feeling; how, therefore, receiving impressions like the wisest, does the soul of the madman connect them extravagantly, without being able to dispense with them?

If this simple and eternal substance enjoys the same properties as the souls that are lodged in the sagest brains, it ought to reason like them. What can prevent it from doing so? If my madman sees a thing red, while the wise men see it blue; if when my sages hear music, my madman hears the braying of an ass; if when they attend a sermon, he imagines himself to be listening to a comedy; if when they understand yes, he understands no; then I conceive clearly that his soul ought to think contrary to theirs. But my madman has the same perceptions they have; there is no apparent reason why his soul, having received all the necessary materials, cannot make a proper use of them. It is pure, they say, and subject to no infirmity; it is provided with all the necessary assistance; whatever may happen in the body that contains it, nothing can change its essence; yet, wrapped in its sheath, it is conveyed to Bedlam.

This reflection may lead us to suspect that the faculty of thought, bestowed by God upon man, is subject to derangement like the other senses. A madman is an invalid whose brain is diseased, just as the gouty man is one who suffers in his feet and hands. People think by means of the brain, and walk on their feet, without knowing anything of the source of either this incomprehensible ability to walk or the equally incomprehensible ability to think; gout may be in the head, instead of the feet. In short, after a thousand arguments, faith alone can convince us of the possibility of a simple and immaterial substance liable to disease.

The learned may say to the madman: "My friend, although you are deprived of common sense, your soul is as pure, as spiritual, and as immortal, as our own; but our souls are happily lodged, yours poorly. The windows of its dwelling are closed; it lacks air and is stifled." The madman, in a lucid interval, would reply to them: "My friends, you beg the question, as usual. My windows are as wide open as your own, since I can perceive the same objects and hear the same words. It necessarily follows that my soul makes a bad use of my senses; or that my soul is a vitiated sense, a depraved faculty. In a word, either my soul is itself diseased, or I have no soul."

One of the doctors may reply: "My brother, God has possibly created foolish souls, just as he created wise ones." The madman will answer: "If I believed what you say, I should be a still greater madman than I am. Have the kindness, you who know so much, to tell me why I am mad?"

If the doctors retain a little sense, they will say: "We know nothing about the matter." They do not understand why one brain has incoherent ideas. Neither are they better able to comprehend why another brain has regular, coherent ideas. They call themselves sages, and are as mad as their patient.

FRAUDE / FRAUD

Whether pious frauds should be practiced upon the people.[46]
ONE day the fakir Bambabef met one of the disciples of Confutzee (whom we call Confucius), and this disciple was named Whang. Bambabef maintained that the common people need to be deceived, and Whang asserted that we should never deceive any one. Here is a sketch of their dispute:

BAMBABEF. We must imitate the Supreme Being, who does not show us things as they are. He makes us see the sun with a diameter of two or three feet, although it is a million times larger than the earth. He makes us see the moon and the stars affixed to the same blue surface, while they are at different elevations; he chooses that a square tower should appear round to us at a distance; he chooses that fire should appear to us to be hot, although it is neither hot nor cold; in short, he surrounds us with errors suitable to our nature.

WHANG. What you call error is not. The sun, such as it is, placed at millions of millions of lis* from our globe, is not that which we see. Actually, we perceive, and we can only perceive the sun that is painted on our retina at a determinate angle. Our eyes were not given us to know sizes and distances: to know these, other aids and other operations are necessary.

Bambabef seemed much astonished at this position. Whang, being very patient, explained to him the theory of optics; and Bambabef, having some conception, was convinced by the demonstrations of the disciple of Confucius. He then resumed in these terms:

BAMBABEF. If God does not, as I thought, deceive us by the ministry of our senses, you will at least acknowledge that our physicians are constantly deceiving children for their good. They tell them that they are giving them sugar, when in reality they are giving them rhubarb. I, a fakir, may then deceive the people, who are as ignorant as children.

WHANG. I have two sons; I have never deceived them. When they have been sick, I have said to them: "Here is a nauseous medicine; you must have the courage to take it; if it were pleasant,

---

* One li equals 124 steps.

it would injure you." I have never allowed their nurses and tutors to make them afraid of ghosts, goblins, and witches. I have thereby made them wise and courageous citizens.

BAMBABEF. The common people are not born so happily as your family.

WHANG. Men all nearly resemble one another; they are born with the same dispositions. Fakirs are the ones who corrupt human nature.

BAMBABEF. We teach them errors, I admit; but it is for their good. We make them believe that if they do not buy our blessed nails, if they do not expiate their sins by giving us money, they will, in another life, become post-horses, dogs, or lizards. This intimidates them, and they become good people.

WHANG. Do you not see that you are perverting these poor folks? There are many more among them than you think who reason, who mock your miracles and your superstitions; who see very clearly that they will not be turned into lizards, nor into posthorses. What is the consequence? They have enough good sense to perceive that you are preaching an impertinent religion; but they have not enough to elevate themselves to a religion pure and untrammeled by superstition, like ours. Their passions make them think there is no religion, because the only one that is taught to them is ridiculous: thus you become guilty of all the vices into which they plunge.

BAMBABEF. Not at all, for we teach them none but good morals.

WHANG. The people would stone you if you taught impure morals. Men are so constituted that they willingly do evil, but they will not have it preached to them. But a wise morality should not be mixed up with absurd fables: for by these impostures, which you might do without, you weaken the morality that you are forced to teach.

BAMBABEF. What! do you think that truth can be taught to the people without the aid of fables?

WHANG. I firmly believe it. Our literati are made of the same stuff as our tailors, our weavers, and our laborers. They worship a creating, rewarding, and avenging God. They do not sully their worship by absurd systems, nor by extravagant ceremonies, and there are many fewer crimes among the lettered than among the people; why should we not condescend to instruct our working classes as we do our literati?

BAMBABEF. That would be a great folly; you might as well wish them to have the same politeness, or to be all jurisconsults. It is neither possible nor desirable. There must be white bread for the masters and brown for the servants.

WHANG. I admit that men should not all have the same learning; but there are some things necessary to all. It is necessary that everyone be just; and the surest way of inspiring justice in all men is to inspire in them religion without superstition.

BAMBABEF. That is a fine project, but it is impracticable. Do you think it is sufficient for men to believe in a being that rewards and punishes? You have told me that the more acute among the people often revolt against my fables. They will, in like manner, revolt against your truth. They will say: Who shall assure me that God rewards and punishes? Where is the proof? What mission have you? What miracle have you worked that I should believe in you? They will laugh at you much more than at me.

WHANG. That is your error. Do you imagine that men will shake off the yoke of an idea that is honest, likely, and useful to everyone; an idea that accords with human reason, because they reject things that are dishonest, absurd, useless, dangerous, and shocking to good sense?

The people are much disposed to believe their magistrates; and when their magistrates propose to them only a rational belief, they embrace it willingly. There is no need of prodigies to believe in a just God, who reads the heart of man: this idea is too natural to be combated. It is not necessary to know precisely how

God rewards and punishes: to believe in His justice is enough. I assure you that I have seen whole towns with scarcely any other tenets; and it is in those towns that I have seen the most virtue.

BAMBABEF. Take heed what you say. You will find philosophers in these towns who will deny both pains and rewards.

WHANG. But you will acknowledge that these philosophers will much more strongly deny your inventions; so you will gain nothing by that. Supposing that there were philosophers who didn't agree with my principles, they would all the same be honest men; they would cultivate virtue no less, which should be embraced through love and not through fear. Moreover, I maintain that no philosopher could ever be assured that Providence does not reserve pains for the wicked and rewards for the good. For, if they ask me who has told me that God punishes, I will ask them who has told them that God does not punish. In short, I maintain that the philosophers, far from contradicting me, will aid me. Will you be a philosopher?

BAMBABEF. With all my heart. But don't tell the fakirs.

GENÈSE / GENESIS

I will not anticipate what we say about Moses in his article; we will follow several major characteristics of Genesis, one after the next.

In the beginning God created the heaven and the earth.

Thus has the passage been translated, but the translation is not correct. There is no one, however slightly informed upon the subject, who is not aware that the text reads, "In the beginning the gods made (*plural* or *singular*) the heaven and the earth." This reading, moreover, perfectly corresponds with the ancient idea of the Phoenicians, who imagined that, in reducing the chaos (*Chaut Ereb*) into order, God employed the agency of inferior deities.

The Phoenicians had been long a powerful people, having a theogony of their own, before the Hebrews became possessed of a few cantons of land near their territory. It is quite natural to suppose that when the Hebrews had at length formed a small establishment near Phoenicia, they began to acquire its language, particularly when they were slaves there. At that time those who made it their business to write copied parts of the ancient theology of their masters. Such is the regular march of the human mind.

At the time in which Moses is supposed to have lived, the Phoenician philosophers were probably sufficiently enlightened to regard the earth as a mere point in the compass with the infinite orbs placed by God in the immensity of space, commonly called heaven. But the idea so very ancient, and at the same time so utterly false, that heaven was made for the earth, has almost always prevailed in the minds of the great mass of the ignorant people. It would certainly be just as correct and judicious for any person to suppose, if told that God created all the mountains and a single grain of sand, that the mountains were created for that grain of sand. It is scarcely possible that the Phoenicians, who were such excellent navigators, did not have some good astronomers; but the old prejudices generally prevailed, and those old prejudices constituted the only knowledge of the Jews.

The earth was without form (tohu bohu) and void; darkness rested upon the face of the deep, and the spirit of God moved upon the surface of the waters.

Tohu bohu means precisely chaos, disorder. It is one of those imitative words which are to be found in all languages; as, for example, in the French we have *sens dessus dessous, tintamarre, trictrac*. The earth was not as yet formed in its present state; matter existed, but the divine power had not yet arranged it. The spirit of God means literally the breath, the wind that agitated the waters. The same idea occurs in the "Fragments" of the Phoenician author

Sanchoniathon. The Phoenicians, like every other people, believed matter to be eternal. There is not a single author of antiquity who ever represented something to have been produced from nothing. Even throughout the whole Bible, no passage is to be found in which matter is said to have been created out of nothing. On the question of the eternity of the world, mankind has always been divided, but never on that of the eternity of matter. From nothing, nothing can proceed, nor into nothing can aught existent return.

De nihilo nihilum, et in nihilum nil posse gigni reverti. (Persius, Sat. iii)

Such was the opinion of all antiquity.

God said let there be light, and there was light; and he saw that the light was good, and he divided the light from the darkness; and he called the light day, and the darkness night; and the evening and the morning were the first day. And God said also, let there be a firmament in the midst of the waters, and let it divide the waters from the waters. And God made the firmament, and divided the waters which were under the firmament from the waters which were above the firmament. And God called the firmament heaven. And the evening and the morning were the second day, and he saw that it was good.

We begin with examining whether Huet, Bishop of Avranches, and Leclerc are not in the right in opposing the idea of those who consider this passage as exhibiting the most sublime eloquence.

Eloquence is not aimed at in any history written by the Jews. The style of the passage in question, like that of all the rest of the work, possesses the most perfect simplicity. If an orator, intending to give some idea of the power of God, employed for that purpose this expression, "He said, let there be light, and there was light," it would then be sublime. Exactly similar is the passage in one of the Psalms, "*Dixit, et facta sunt*"—"He spoke, and they were made." It is a trait which, being unique in this place, and introduced purposely in order to create a majestic image, elevates and transports the mind. But, in the instance under examination, the narrative is of the most simple character. The Jewish writer speaks of the light in a way no different from the other objects of creation; he expresses in the same way in each article, "and God saw that it was good." Everything is sublime in the course of creation, unquestionably, but the creation of light is no more so than that of the herbs of the field; the sublime is something that soars far above the rest, whereas all is equal throughout this chapter.

But further, it was another very ancient opinion that light did not proceed from the sun. It was seen diffused throughout the atmosphere, before the rising and after the setting of that star; the sun was supposed merely to give it greater strength; accordingly the author of Genesis accommodates himself to this popular error, and, in a singular reversal in the order of things, even states the creation of the sun and moon not to have taken place until four days after the existence of light. It was impossible to understand how there could be a morning and evening before the existence of a sun. Therein lies a confusion that is impossible to unravel. The inspired writer deigned, in this instance, to condescend to the gross and wild ideas of the nation. God did not claim to teach the Jews philosophy. He might have raised their minds to the truth, but he preferred descending to their level.

The separation of the light from the darkness also defies physics. It would seem that night and day were mixed up together, as seeds of different species that are separated from each other. It is sufficiently known that darkness is nothing but the absence of light and that there is in fact no light when our eyes receive no sensation of it; but at that period these truths were far from being known.

The idea of a firmament, again, is of the very highest antiquity. The heavens were imagined to be a solid mass, because they always exhibited the same phenomena. They rolled over our heads; they were therefore constituted of the most solid materials.

How could the amount of water that the exhalations from the land and sea supply to the clouds be computed? There was no Halley to make this calculation. The heavens therefore were conceived to contain reservoirs. These reservoirs could be supported only by a strong vault, and as this vault of heaven was actually transparent, it must necessarily have been made of crystal. In order that the waters above might descend from it upon the earth, sluices, cataracts, and floodgates were necessary, which might be opened and shut as circumstances required. Such was Jewish astronomy; and, since the author was writing for Jews, it was incumbent upon him to adopt their ideas.

God also made two great lights, one to rule the day, the other the night; He also made the stars.

Always the same ignorance of nature. The Jews did not know that the moon shines only with a reflected light. The author here speaks of stars as of mere luminous points, although they are in fact so many suns, having each of them worlds revolving round it. The Holy Spirit, then, accommodated Himself to the spirit of the times.

God said, also, let us make man in our own image, and let him have dominion over the fishes, etc.

What meaning did the Jews attach to the expression, "let us make man in our own image?"—the same as all antiquity attached to it:

Finxit in effigiem moderantum cuncta deorum. (Ovid, Metam. i. 82)

Images are made only of bodies. No nation ever imagined a God without body, and it is impossible to represent Him otherwise. We may indeed say that God is nothing that we are acquainted with, but we can have no idea of what He is. The Jews invariably conceived God to be corporeal, as well as every other people. All the first fathers of the Church, also, believe God to be corporeal until they had embraced the ideas of Plato.

He created them male and female.

If God, or the secondary or inferior gods, created mankind, male and female, after their own likeness, it would seem in that case, as if the Jews believed that God and the gods were male and female. It has been a subject of discussion, whether the author means to say that man had originally two sexes, or merely that God made Adam and Eve on the same day. But this interpretation involves an absolute contradiction to the statement of the woman's being made out of the rib of man after the seven days were concluded.

And he rested on the seventh day.

The Phoenicians, Chaldaeans, and Indians represented God as having made the world in six periods, which the ancient Zoroaster calls the six "Gahanbars," so celebrated among the Persians.

It is beyond all question that these nations possessed a theology before the Jews inhabited the deserts of Horeb and Sinai, and before they could possibly have had any writers. It is thus of the greatest probability that the allegory of six days was imitated from that of the six periods.

From this pleasant place a river went out that watered the garden, and thence it was divided into four rivers. One was called Pison, which compassed the whole land of Havilah, whence cometh gold . . . the second was called Gihon and surrounds Ethiopia . . . the third is the Tigris, and the fourth the Euphrates.

According to this version, the earthly paradise would have contained nearly a third part of Asia and of Africa. The sources of the Euphrates and the Tigris are sixty leagues distant from each other, in frightful mountains, bearing no possible resemblance to a garden. The river which borders Ethiopia and which can be no other than the Nile, commences its course at the distance of more than seven hundred leagues from the sources of the Tigris and Euphrates; and, if the Pison means the Phasis, it is not a little surprising that the source of a Scythian river and that of an African one should be situated on the same spot.

For the rest, the Garden of Eden is visibly related to the gardens of Eden at Saana in Arabia Felix, celebrated throughout all antiquity. The Hebrews, a very recent people, were an Arabian horde. They claimed for themselves the honor of the most beautiful spot in the finest district of Arabia. They have always converted to their own purposes the ancient traditions of the vast and powerful nations in the midst of whom they were ensconced.

The Lord then took the man and put him into the Garden of Eden that he might cultivate it.

It is very respectable for a man to "cultivate his garden," but it must have been difficult for Adam to cultivate a garden between seven and eight hundred leagues in length; apparently he had been supplied with assistants.

Eat not of the fruit of the tree of knowledge of good and evil.

It is not easy to conceive that there ever existed a tree that could teach good and evil, as there are trees that bear pears and apricots. And besides, why is God unwilling that man should know good and evil? Would not his free access to this knowledge, on the contrary, appear worthy of God and far more necessary to man? To our weak reason it would seem that God ought to have commanded him to eat copiously of this fruit; but we must bring our reason into submission.

If you shall eat thereof, you shall die.

Nevertheless, Adam ate of it and did not die. Many of the fathers considered the whole matter as an allegory. In fact, it might be said that all other animals have no knowledge that they shall die, but that man, by means of his reason, has such knowledge. This reason is the tree of knowledge that enables him to foresee his end. This, perhaps, is the most rational interpretation that can be given.

The Lord said, also, it is not good for man to be alone; let us make him a helpmeet for him.

We naturally expect that the Lord is about to bestow on him a wife; not at all; the Lord first brings before him all the animals.

And the name Adam gave to every animal is its true name.

That which we might naturally understand by the true name of an animal, would be a name describing all, or at least the principal properties of its species. But this is not the case in any language. In each there are some imitative words, as "*coq*" in Celtic, which bears some slight similarity to the cry of the rooster; *lupus*, in Latin, etc. But these imitative words are exceedingly few. Moreover, if Adam had thus thoroughly known the properties of various animals, he must either have previously eaten of the fruit of the tree of knowledge, or it would apparently have answered no end for God to have interdicted him from it.

It may be remarked that this is the first time the name of Adam occurs in the Book of Genesis. The first man, according to the ancient Brahmins, who were prodigiously anterior to the Jews, was called Adimo, the son of the earth, and his wife, Procris, life. This is recorded in the Vedas, which is perhaps the most ancient book in the world. Adam and Eve signified the same things in the Phoenician language.

When Adam was asleep God took one of his ribs and put flesh instead thereof; and of the rib which he had taken from Adam he formed a woman, and he brought the woman to Adam.

In the previous chapter the Lord had already created the male and the female; why, therefore, remove a rib from the man to form out of it a woman who already existed? It is answered that the author barely announces in the one case what he explains in another.

But the serpent was more subtle than all animals on the earth; he said to the woman, etc.

Throughout the whole of this article there is no mention made of the devil. Everything in it is physical. The serpent was considered by all oriental nations, not only as the most cunning of all animals, but likewise as immortal. The Chaldaeans had a fable concerning a quarrel between God and the serpent, and this fable had been preserved by Pherecydes. Origen cites it in his sixth book against Celsus. A serpent was carried in procession at the feasts of Bacchus. The Egyptians, according to the statement of Eusebius in the first book of the tenth chapter of his "Evangelical Preparation," attached a sort of divinity to the serpent. In Arabia, India, and even China, the serpent was regarded as a symbol of life; and hence it was that the emperors of China, long before the time of Moses, always bore upon their breast the image of a serpent.

Eve expresses no astonishment at the serpent's speaking to her. In all ancient histories, animals spoke; this is why no one was surprised when Pilpay and Lokman made animals talk.

The whole of this affair is so physical and so unconnected with anything allegorical, that the narrative assigns a reason why the serpent, from that time, has moved creeping on its belly, why we always are eager to crush it under our feet, and why it always attempts to bite us. Precisely as, with respect to presumed changes affecting certain animals recorded in ancient fable, reasons were stated why the crow which originally had been white is at the present day black; why the owl leaves his hole only by night; why the wolf likes carnage, etc.

I will multiply your sorrow and your conception; in sorrow shall you bring forth children. You shall be under the power of the man, and he shall rule over you.

Why, it is asked, should the multiplication of pregnancies be a punishment? It was, on the contrary, a great blessing, particularly among the Jews. The pains of childbirth are inconsiderable, except in delicate women. Those accustomed to labor are delivered with great ease, particularly in warm climates. There are some animals that experience great suffering from this process of nature: some even die under it. And with respect to the superiority or dominion of the man over the woman, it is an entirely natural thing; it is the consequence of strength of body, and even of strength of mind. Men, generally speaking, possess organs more capable of sustained attention than women, and are better suited for labors both of the head and arm. But when a woman possesses both a hand and a mind more powerful than her husband's, she everywhere possesses the dominion over him; it is then the husband who is subjected to the wife.

The Lord made for them coats of skins.

This passage decidedly proves that the Jews believed God to be corporeal, since they make him exercise the trade of tailor. A rabbi, of the name of Eliezer, wrote that God clothed Adam and Eve with the skin of the very serpent who had tempted them; and Origen maintains that this coat of skins was a new flesh, a new body, that God conferred on man.

And the Lord said; Lo! Adam is become like one of us.

Common sense must be sacrificed in order to reject the idea that the Jews originally admired several gods. It is somewhat more difficult to determine what they meant by the word "God," *Elohïm.* Some commentators have contended that the expression "one of us" signifies the Trinity. But certainly there is nothing relating to the Trinity throughout the Bible. The Trinity is not a compound of many or several Gods: it is one and the same god threefold; and the Jews never heard the slightest mention of one god in three persons. By the words "like us," or "as one of us," it is probable that the Jews understood the angels, Elohïm and that this book was not written until that people had adopted the belief in those inferior gods.

The Lord sent him forth from the Garden of Eden to cultivate the ground.

But the Lord had placed him in the Garden of Eden to *culti-vate* that garden. If Adam, instead of being a gardener, merely becomes a laborer, his situation is not made very much worse by the change. A good laborer is well worth a good gardener.

The whole of this history, generally speaking, proceeds from the idea which has prevailed in every past age, and still exists, that the first times were better and happier than those which followed. Men have always complained of the present and extolled the past. Pressed down by the labors of life, they have imagined happiness to consist in inactivity, not considering that the most unhappy of all states is that of a man who has nothing to do. They frequently saw themselves miserable and framed in their imaginations an ideal period in which all the world had been happy; it is about the same as if we said there was a time in which no tree decayed and perished, in which no beast was weak, diseased, or devoured by another. Hence the idea of the golden age; of the egg pierced by Arimanes; of the serpent who stole from the ass the recipe for obtaining a happy and immortal life, which the man had placed upon his pack-saddle; of the conflict between Typhon and Osiris, and between Opheneus and the gods; of the famous box of Pandora; and of all those ancient tales, of which some are amusing, but none instructive. "And He placed before the garden of Eden a cherub with a flaming sword, which turned all round to guard the way to the tree of life."

The word *kerub* signifies *ox*. An ox armed with a flaming sword is rather a singular exhibition, before a portal. But the Jews later represented angels in the form of oxen and hawks although they were forbidden to make any images. They evidently derived these emblems of oxen and hawks from the Egyptians, whom they imitated in so many other things. The Egyptians first venerated the ox as the emblem of agriculture, and the hawk as that of the winds; but they never converted the ox into a sentinel.

The gods Elohïm, seeing that the daughters of men were fair, took for wives those whom they chose.

This imagination, again, may be traced in the history of every people. No nation has ever existed, unless perhaps we may except China, in which some god is not described as having had offspring from women. These corporeal gods frequently descended to visit their dominions upon earth; they saw the daughters of our race, and attached themselves to those who were most beautiful: the issue of this connection between gods and mortals must of course have been superior to other men; accordingly, Genesis informs us these gods who lay with our women produced giants.

I will bring a deluge of waters upon the earth.

(See article "*Inondation* / Flood") I will merely observe here that St. Augustine, in his City of God, No. 8, says, "*Maximum illud diluvium Graeca nec Latina novit historia*"—neither Greek nor Latin history knows anything about the great deluge. In fact, none had ever been known in Greece but those of Deucalion and Ogyges. They are regarded as universal in the fables collected by Ovid, but are wholly unknown in eastern Asia.

God said to Noah, I will make a covenant with you and with your seed after you, and with all living creatures.

God make a covenant with beasts! What sort of a covenant? But if He makes a covenant with man, why not with the beast? It has feeling, and there is something as divine in feeling as in the most metaphysical meditation. Besides, beasts feel more correctly than the greater part of men think. It is clearly by virtue of this treaty that Francis of Assisi, the founder of the Seraphic order, said to the grasshoppers and the hares, "Pray sing, my dear sister grasshopper; pray browse, my dear brother hare." But what were the conditions of the treaty? That all animals should devour one another; that they should feed upon our flesh, and we upon theirs; that, after having eaten them, we should exterminate our own race with wrath—nothing being then wanting to crown the horrid series of butchery and cruelty, but devouring our fellow men, slain by our hands. Had there been actually such a treaty as this it could have been entered into only with the devil. Probably the meaning of the whole passage is neither more nor less than that God is equally the absolute master of everything that breathes.

And I will put my bow in the clouds, and it shall be a sign of my covenant.

Observe that the author does not say, I have put my bow in the clouds; he says, I *will* put: this clearly implies it to have been the prevailing opinion that there had not always been a rainbow. This phenomenon is necessarily produced by rain; yet in this place it is represented as something supernatural, exhibited in order to announce that the earth should no more be inundated. It is singular to choose the sign of rain, in order to assure men against their being drowned. But it may also be replied that in any danger of inundation, we have the cheering security of the rainbow.

And two angels arrived at Sodom in the evening, etc.

The whole history of these two angels, whom the inhabitants of Sodom wished to rape, is perhaps the most extraordinary in the records of all antiquity. But it must be considered that almost all Asia believed in the existence of the demoniacal incubus and succubus; and moreover, that these two angels were creatures more perfect than mankind, and must have possessed more beauty and stimulated more desires in a corrupt people than ordinary men.

As for Lot, who proposes his two daughters to the people of Sodom in the stead of the angels; and his wife, who was changed into a statue of salt, and all the rest of that history, what shall we venture to say? The old Arabian tale of Kinyras and Myrrha has some resemblance to the incest of Lot with his daughters; and the adventure of Philemon and Baucis is somewhat similar to the case of the two angels who appeared to Lot and his wife. With respect to the statue of salt, we know not where to find any resemblance; perhaps in the history of Orpheus and Eurydice?

Some critics have contended that all these incredible passages, which scandalize the weak, ought to be removed from the canonical books; but it has been said that those critics were corrupted hearts and ought to be burned at the stake; and that it is impossible to be a good man if one does not believe that the people of Sodom wanted to rape two angels. Such is the reasoning of a species of monsters who wish to dominate our spirits.

A few eminent fathers of the Church have had the prudence to turn all these stories into allegories, after the example of the Jews, and particularly of Philo. Some popes, still more prudent, have endeavored to prevent the translation of these books into the vulgar tongue, lest some men should be enabled to judge that which they are supposed to adore.

We are certainly justified in concluding that those who thoroughly understand this book should tolerate those who do not understand it; for if the latter understand nothing of it, it is not their own fault; on the other hand, those who comprehend nothing that it contains should tolerate those who comprehend everything in it.

GLOIRE / GLORY

THAT worthy chief of the dervishes, Ben-al-betif, said to his brethren one day: "My brethren, it is good that you should frequently use that sacred formula of our Koran, 'In the name of the most merciful God'; because God uses mercy, and you learn to do so too, by oft repeating the words that recommend virtue, without which there would be few men left upon the earth. But, my brethren, beware of imitating those rash ones who boast, on every occasion, of laboring for the glory of God. If a young simpleton defends a thesis on the categories, defense at which an ignoramus in furs presides, he is sure to write in large characters, at the head of his thesis, *'Ek alha abron doxa.'*—*'Ad majorem Dei gloriam.'*—To the greater glory of God.[47] If a good Mussulman has had his house whitewashed, he engraves this foolish inscription on the door. A saka carries water for the greater glory of God. It is an impious usage, piously used. What would you say of a little chiaoux, who, while emptying our sultan's close-stool, should exclaim: "To the greater glory of our invincible monarch?" There is certainly a greater distance between God and the sultan than between the sultan and the little chiaoux.

"You miserable earth-worms, called men, what do you have in common with the glory of the Supreme Being? Can He love glory? Can He receive it from you? Can He enjoy it? How long, you two-legged animals without feathers, will you make God after your own image? What! because you are vain, because you love glory, you would have God love it also? If there were several gods, perhaps each one would seek to gain the good opinion of his fellows. That might be the glory of a God. Such a God, if infinite greatness may be compared with extreme lowliness, would be like King Alexander or Iscander, who would enter the lists with none but kings. But you, poor creatures! What glory can you give to God? Cease to profane the sacred name. An emperor, named Octavius Augustus, forbade his being praised in the schools of Rome, lest his name should be brought into contempt. You can neither vilify nor honor the Supreme Being. Humble yourselves; adore, and be silent."

Thus spoke Ben-al-betif; and the dervishes cried out: "Glory to God! Ben-al-betif has spoken well."

GRÂCE / GRACE [48]

HOLY advisers of modern Rome, illustrious and infallible theologians, no one has more respect for your divine decisions than I; but if Paulus Æmilius, Scipio, Cato, Cicero, Cæsar, Titus, Trajan, or Marcus Aurelius revisited that Rome to which they formerly did such credit, you must confess that they would be a little astonished at your decisions on grace. What would they say if they heard you speak of healthful grace according to St. Thomas, and medicinal grace according to Cajetan; of exterior and interior grace, of free, sanctifying, cooperating, actual, habitual, and efficacious grace, which is sometimes inefficacious; of sufficient grace, which sometimes does not suffice, of the versatile and congruous—would they really comprehend it more than you and I?

What need would these poor people have of your instructions? I fancy I hear them say:

"Reverend fathers, you are terrible genii; we foolishly thought that the Eternal Being never conducted Himself by particular laws like vile human beings, but by general laws, eternal like Himself. No one among us ever imagined that God was like a senseless master, who gives an estate to one slave and refuses food to another; who orders one with a broken arm to knead a loaf, and a cripple to be his courier.

All is grace on the part of God; He showed grace to the globe we inhabit forming it; to the trees the grace of making them grow; to animals that of feeding them; but will you say, because one wolf finds in his road a lamb for his supper, while another is dying with hunger, that God has given the first wolf a particular grace? Is it a preventive grace to cause one oak to grow in preference to another in which sap is wanting? If throughout nature all being is submitted to general laws, how can a single species of animals avoid conforming to them?

Why should the absolute master of all be more occupied in directing the interior of a single man than in conducting the remainder of entire nature? By what caprice would He change something in the heart of a Courlander or a Biscayan, while He changes nothing in the general laws which He has imposed upon all the stars.

What a pity to suppose that He is continually making, unmaking, and renewing sentiments in us! And what audacity to believe that we are distinguished from all beings! And further, is it only for those who practice confession that these changes are imagined.

A Savoyard, a Bergamask, on Monday, will have the grace to have a mass said for twelve pennies; on Tuesday he will go to the tavern and have no grace; on Wednesday he will have a cooperating grace that will conduct him to confession, but he will not have the efficacious grace of perfect contrition; on Thursday there will be a sufficient grace that will not suffice, as has been already said. God will labor continuously in the head of this Bergamask—sometimes strongly, sometimes weakly— while the rest of the earth will no way concern Him! He will not deign to meddle with the interior of the Indians and Chinese! If you possess a grain of reason, reverend fathers, do you not find this system prodigiously ridiculous?

Poor, miserable man! Behold this oak that rears its head to the clouds, and this reed which bends at its feet; you do not say that efficacious grace has been given to the oak and withheld from the reed. Raise your eyes to heaven; see the eternal Demiourgos creating millions of worlds, which gravitate towards one another by general and eternal laws. See the same light reflected from the sun to Saturn, and from Saturn to us; and in this harmony of so many stars, urged onward in their rapid course, in this general obedience of all nature, dare to believe, if you can, that God is occupied in giving a versatile grace to Sister Theresa and a concomitant grace to Sister Agnes.

Atom, to whom another foolish atom has said that the Eternal has particular laws for a few atoms of your neighborhood, that He gives His grace to that one and refuses it to this; that he who did not have grace yesterday shall have it tomorrow; do repeat not this folly. God made the universe, and does not create new winds to displace pieces of straw in a corner of this universe. Theologians are like the combatants in Homer, who believed that the gods were sometimes armed for and sometimes against them. Had Homer not been admired as a poet, he would be as a blasphemer.

It is Marcus Aurelius who speaks, and not I; for God, who inspires you, has given me grace to believe all that you say, all that you have said, and all that you will say.

GUERRE / WARFARE

FAMINE, pestilence and war are the three most infamous ingredients of this lowly world. Included under the category of famine all the bad foods to which shortages force us to resort, thus shortening life in the hope of prolonging it.

Pestilence includes all contagious diseases, which number two or three thousand. These two gifts come to us from Providence; but war, which unites all these gifts, is brought to us by the imagination of three or four hundred individuals who are scattered over the surface of the globe and bear the title of prince or minister. It is perhaps for this reason that in several dedications, they are referred to as the living image of the Divinity.

The most determined of flatterers will easily agree that war always brings pestilence and famine in its train, from the little that he may have seen in the hospitals of the armies of Germany, or the few villages he may have passed through in which some great exploit of war has been performed.

It is doubtless a very fine art that desolates the countryside, destroys habitations, and in a common year causes the death of from forty thousand men out of one hundred thousand. This invention was first cultivated by nations assembled for their common good; for instance, the diet of the Greeks declared to the diet of Phrygia and neighboring nations, that they intended to depart on a thousand fishers' barks, to exterminate them if they could.

The assembled Roman people judged that it was to their interest to go and fight, before harvest, against the people of Veii or the Volscians. And some years after, all the

Romans, being exasperated against all the Carthaginians, fought them a long time on sea and land. It is not exactly the same at present.

A genealogist proves to a prince that he descends in a direct line from a count, whose parents made a family compact, three or four hundred years ago, with a house the recollection of which does not even exist. This house had distant pretensions to a province, whose last possessor died of apoplexy. The prince and his council see his right at once. This province, which is some hundred leagues distant from him, in vain protests that it knows him not; that it has no desire to be governed by him; that to give laws to its people, he must at least have their consent; these discourses do even reach the ears of the prince, whose right is incontestable. He immediately finds a great number of men who have nothing to lose, dresses them in coarse blue cloth, trims their hats with broad white ribbon, makes them turn to the right and left, and marches to glory.

Other princes who hear of this escapade, take part in it, each according to his power, and cover a small extent of country with more mercenary murderers than Genghis Khan, Tamerlane, and Bajazet employed in their train.

Distant people hear that they are going to fight, and that they may earn five or six pennies a day, if they wish to be of the party; they divide themselves into two bands, like reapers, and sell their services to whoever will employ them.

These multitudes fall upon one another, not only without having any interest in the affair, but without knowing the reason for it.

There are five or six belligerent powers at a time, sometimes three against three, sometimes two against four, and sometimes one against five; all equally detesting one another, uniting with and attacking each other by turns; all agree on a single point, that of doing all the harm possible.

The most marvelous part of this infernal enterprise is that each chief of murderers has his flags blessed and solemnly invokes God before he goes to exterminate his neighbors. If a chief only has the fortune to kill two or three thousand men, he does not thank God for it; but when he has exterminated about ten thousand by fire and sword, and, as a crowning grace, some town has been leveled with the ground, they then sing a long song in four parts, composed in a language unknown to all who have fought, and moreover replete with barbarisms.[49] The same song serves for marriages and births, as well as for murders; which is unpardonable, particularly in the nation the most renowned for new songs.

Natural religion has a thousand times prevented citizens from committing crimes. A well born soul has no inclination for it; a tender one is alarmed at it, representing to itself a just and avenging God; but artificial religion encourages all the cruelties that are carried out in groups—conspiracies, seditions, pillages, ambushes, surprises of towns, robberies, and murder. Each marches gaily to crime, under the banner of his saint.

A certain number of orators are everywhere paid to celebrate these murderous days; some are dressed in a long black close-fitting coat, with a short cloak; others have a shirt above a gown; some wear two streamers of variegated cloth over their shirts. All of them speak for a long time; they cite the example of things done of old in Palestine, as applicable to a combat in Veteravia.

The rest of the year these people preach against vices. They prove, in three points and by antitheses, that ladies who spread a little carmine on their cheeks will be the eternal objects of the eternal vengeances of the Eternal; that *Polyeuctus* and *Athalia* are works of the demon;[50] that a man who, for two hundred crowns a day, has his table furnished with fresh sea-fish during Lent, infallibly works his salvation; and that a poor man who eats two sous and a half worth of mutton will go forever to all the devils.

Of five or six thousand predications of this kind, there are three or four at most, composed by a Gaul named Massillon, that an honest man may read without disgust; but in all these discourses, you will scarcely find two in which the orator dares to say a word against the scourge and crime of war, which contains all other scourges and crimes.[51] The unfortunate orators speak incessantly against love, which is the only consolation of mankind, and the only way of replenishing it; they say nothing of the abominable efforts we make to destroy it.

You have made a very bad sermon on impurity—oh, You have made a very bad sermon on impurity—oh, Bourdaloue!—but none on these murders, varied in so many ways; on these rapines and robberies; on this universal rage that devours the world. All the united vices of all ages and places will never equal the evils produced by a single campaign.

Miserable physicians of souls! you exclaim, for five quarters of an hour about some pricks of a pin and say nothing of the malady that tears us into a thousand pieces! Moral philosophers! Burn all your books. As long as the caprice of a few men causes thousands of our brothers to be slaughtered, that part of mankind dedicated to heroism will be the most frightful thing in all of nature. Humanity, beneficence, modesty, temperance, mildness, wisdom, and piety: what do they become and what do they matter to me, while half a pound of lead, shot from the distance of six hundred steps, shatters my body, and I die at twenty years of age, in inexpressible torments, in the midst of five or six thousand dying men, while my eyes, which open for the last time, see the town in which I was born destroyed by fire and sword, and the last sounds that reach my ears are the cries of women and children expiring under the ruins, all for the pretended interests of a man whom we know not?

What is worse, war is an inevitable scourge. If we take notice, all men have worshipped Mars. Sabaoth, among the Jews, signifies the god of arms; but Minerva, in Homer, calls Mars a furious, mad, and infernal god.

HISTOIRE DES ROIS JUIFS ET PARALIPOMÈNES / KINGS AND CHRONICLES

EVERY nation, as soon as it was able to write, has written its own history, and the Jews have accordingly written theirs. Before they had kings, they lived under a theocracy; they were supposedly governed by God himself.

When the Jews were desirous of having a king, like the adjoining nations, the prophet Samuel, who was exceedingly interested in preventing it, declared to them, on behalf of God, that they were rejecting God himself. Thus the Jewish theocracy ceased when the monarchy commenced.

We may therefore remark, without the imputation of blasphemy, that the history of the Jewish kings was written like that of other nations, and that God did not take the pains Himself to dictate the history of a people whom He no longer governed.

We advance this opinion with the greatest diffidence. What may perhaps be considered as confirming it, is, that the Chronicles very frequently contradict the Book of Kings, both with respect to chronology and facts, just as our profane historians sometimes contradict one another. Moreover, if God has always written the history of the Jews, it seems only consistent and natural to think that He writes it still; for the Jews are still His cherished people. They are on some future day to be converted, and it seems that whenever that event happens, they will have as complete a right to consider the history of their dispersion as sacred, as they have now to say that God wrote the history of their kings.

We may be allowed here to make one reflection; which is, that as God was for a very long period their king, and afterwards became their historian, we are bound to entertain for all Jews the most profound respect. There is not a single Jew old-clothes seller who is not infinitely superior to Caesar and Alexander. How can we avoid bending in prostration before an old-clothes seller, who proves to us that his history has been written by God Himself, while the histories of Greece and Rome have been transmitted to us only by the profane hand of man?

If the style of the history of the Kings and of the Chronicles is divine, it may nevertheless be true that the actions recorded in these histories are not divine. David murders Uriah; Ishbosheth and Mephibosheth are murdered; Absalom murders Ammon; Joab murders Absalom; Solomon murders his brother Adonijah; Baasha murders Nadab; Zimri murders Ela; Omri murders Zimri; Ahab murders Naboth; Jehu murders Ahab and Joram; the inhabitants of Jerusalem murder Amaziah, son of Joash; Shallum, son of Jabesh, murders Zachariah, son of Jeroboam; Menahhem murders Shallum, son of Jabesh; Pekah, son of Remaliah, murders Pekahiah, son of Manehem; and Hoshea, son of Elah, murders Pekah, son of Remaliah. We pass over, in silence, many other minor murders. It must be acknowledged, that, if the Holy Spirit did write this history, He did not choose a subject particularly edifying.

Idée / Idea

WHAT is an idea?

It is an image painted upon my brain.

Are all your thoughts, then, images?

Certainly; for the most abstract thoughts are only the consequences of all the objects that I have perceived. I utter the word "being" in general, only because I have known particular beings; I utter the word "infinity," only because I have seen certain limits, and because I push back those limits in my mind to a greater and still greater distance, as far as I am able. I have ideas in my head only because I have images.

And who is the painter of this picture?

It is not myself; I cannot draw with sufficient skill; the being that made me, makes my ideas.

You must, then, I imagine, be of Malebranche's opinion, that we see all in God?

I am at least certain of this, that if we do not see things in the Great Being, we see them in consequence of His powerful and immediate action.

And what was the nature or process of this action?

I have already told you repeatedly, in the course of our conversations, that I do not know a single syllable about the subject, and that God has not communicated His secret to any one. I am completely ignorant of that which makes my heart beat, and my blood flow through my veins; I am ignorant of the principle of all my movements, and yet you seem to expect how I should explain how I feel and how I think. Such an expectation is unreasonable.

But you at least know whether your faculty of having ideas is joined to extension?

Not in the least. It is true that Tatian, in his discourse to the Greeks, says the soul is evidently composed of a body. Irenaeus, in the sixty-second chapter of his second book, says, "The Lord has taught that our souls preserve the figure of our body in order to retain the memory of it." Tertullian asserts, in his second book on the soul, that it is a body. Arnobius, Lactantius, Hilary, Gregory of Nyssa, and Ambrose, are precisely of the same opinion. It is claimed that other fathers of the Church assert that the soul is without extension, and that in this respect they adopt the opinion of Plato; this, however, may well be doubted. With respect to myself, I dare not venture to form an opinion; I see nothing but obscurity and incomprehensibility in either system; and, after a whole life's meditation on the subject, I am not advanced a single step beyond where I was on the first day.

The subject, then, was not worth thinking about?

That is true; the man who enjoys knows more of it, or at least knows it better, than he who reflects; he is happier. But what do you want? It depended not, I repeat, upon myself whether I should admit or reject all those ideas that have crowded into my brain in conflict with each other, and actually converted my medullar magazine into their field of battle.

After a hard-fought contest between them, I have obtained nothing but uncertainty from the spoils.

It is a melancholy thing to possess so many ideas, and yet to have no precise knowledge of the nature of ideas.

It is, I admit; but it is much more melancholy, and inexpressibly more foolish, for a man to believe he knows what in fact he does not.

IDOLE, IDOLÂTRE, IDOLÂTRIE /
IDOL, IDOLATER, IDOLATRY

IDOL is derived from the Greek word *eidos*, figure; *eidolos*, the representation of a figure, and *latreuein* to serve, revere, or adore. This word *adore* is Latin, and has many different meanings. It signifies *to bring the hand to the mouth in speaking respectfully, to bend over, to kneel, to greet,* and commonly, finally, *to render highest worship.*

It is useful to note here that the Trevoux Dictionary begins this article by saying that all pagans were idolaters and that the Indians are still idolatrous peoples.[52] First, no one was called pagan prior to Theodosus the younger; this name was then given to the inhabitants of the Italian villages, *pagorum incolae pagani,* who retained their former religion. Secondly, Hindustan is Mohammedan, and Mohammedans are implacable enemies of images and idolatry. Third, it is wrong to label as idolatrous many peoples in India who follow the ancient religion of the Parsis and those in certain castes that have no idols.

EXAMINATION,

Whether there has ever been an idolatrous government?

It does not appear that there were ever any people on earth who took the name of idolaters. This word is an offence, an insulting term, like that of "*gavache*," which the Spaniards formerly gave to the French; and that of "*maranes*," which the French gave to the Spaniards in return. If we had asked the senate of the Areopagus of Athens, or at the court of the kings of Persia: "Are you idolaters?" they would scarcely have understood the question. None would have answered: "We adore images and idols." This word, idolater, idolatry, is found neither in Homer, Hesiod, Herodotus, nor any other author of the religion of the Gentiles. There has never been any edict, any law, which commanded that idols should be adored; that they should be treated as gods and regarded as gods.

When the Roman and Carthaginian captains made a treaty, they called all their gods to witness. "It is in their presence," said they, "that we swear peace." Yet the statues of these gods, whose number was very great, were not in the tents of the generals. They regarded the gods as present at the actions of men as witnesses and judges. And assuredly it was not the image which constituted the divinity.

In what view, therefore, did they see the statues of their false gods in the temples? With the same view, if we may so express ourselves, that we see images of the object of our veneration. The error was not in adoring a piece of wood or marble, but in adoring a false divinity, represented by this wood and marble. The difference between them and us is not that they had images, and we had none; the difference is, that their images represented the fantastic beings of a false religion, and that our images represent real beings in a true religion. The Greeks had the statue of Hercules, and we have that of St. Christopher; they had Æsculapius and his goat, we have St. Roch and his dog; they had Jupiter armed with thunder, and we have St. Anthony of Padua and St. James of Compostella.

When the consul Pliny addresses prayers to the immortal gods in the exordium of the panegyric of Trajan, it is not to images that he addresses them. These images were not immortal.

Neither the latest nor the most remote times of paganism offer a single fact which can lead to the conclusion that they adored idols. Homer speaks only of the gods who inhabited the high Olympus. The palladium, although fallen from heaven, was only a sacred token of the protection of Pallas; it was herself that was venerated in the palladium.

But the Romans and Greeks knelt before their statues, gave them crowns, incense, and flowers, and carried them in triumph in the public places. We have sanctified these customs, and we are not idolaters.

The women in times of drought carried the statues of the Gods after having fasted. They walked barefooted with disheveled hair, and it quickly rained bucketfuls, says Petronius: "*Et statim urceatim pluebat.*" Has not this custom been consecrated; illegitimate indeed among the Gentiles, but legitimate among us? In how many towns are not corpses carried barefoot to obtain the blessings of heaven through their intercession? If a Turk, or a learned Chinese, were a witness of these ceremonies, he would, through ignorance, accuse us of putting our trust in the figures that we thus promenade in possession; but one word would suffice to correct their error.

We are surprised at the prodigious number of declamations uttered in all times against the idolatry of the Romans and Greeks; and we are afterwards still more surprised when we see that they were not idolaters.

Some temples are more privileged than others. The great Diana of Ephesus had more reputation than a village Diana. There were more miracles performed in the temple of Æsculapius at Epidaurus, than in any other of his temples. The statue of the Olympian Jupiter attracted more offerings than that of the Paphlagonian Jupiter. But since here we must always oppose the customs of a true religion to those of a false one, have we not for several ages had more devotion to certain altars than to others? Has not Our Lady of Loretto been preferred to Our Lady of the Snows? It is for us to see whether this pretext should be used to accuse us of idolatry.

There was only a single Diana, a single Apollo, a single Æsculapius and not as many Apollos, Dianas and Æsculapiuses as they had temples and statues. It is therefore proved, as much as history can prove anything, that the ancients did not believe the statue to be a divinity; that worship was not paid to this statue or image, and consequently that they were not idolaters.

A gross, superstitious and unreasoning populace, who knew neither how to doubt, deny, or believe; who visited the temples out of idleness, and because the lowly are there equal to the great; who made their contributions because it was the custom; who spoke continually of miracles without examining any of them; and who were in terms of intellect little above the brutes whom they sacrificed—such a people, I repeat, in the sight of the great Diana, or of Jupiter the Thunderer, may well have been seized with a religious horror, and adored, without consciousness, the statue itself. This is what happens now and then, in our own churches, to our ignorant peasantry, who, however, are informed that it is the blessed mortals received into heaven whose intercession they solicit, and not that of images of wood and stone; and that they should adore God alone.

The Greeks and Romans augment the number of their gods by their apotheoses. The Greeks deified conquerors like Bacchus, Hercules, and Perseus. Rome devoted altars to her emperors. Our apotheoses are of a different kind; we have saints instead of their half-gods and secondary gods, but we pay respect neither to rank nor to conquest. We have consecrated temples to the simply virtuous men, who would have been unknown on earth if they had not been placed in heaven. The apotheoses of the ancients were the effect of flattery; ours are produced by a respect for virtue. But these ancient apotheoses are one more proof that the Greeks and Romans were not idolatrous. It is clear that they no more believed in the divine virtue of statues of Augustus and Claudius than of their medals.

Cicero, in his philosophical works, allows not even a suspicion that the statues of the gods could be misunderstood and confounded them with the gods themselves. His interlocutors attack the established religion, but none of them thinks of accusing the Romans of taking marble and brass for divinities. Lucretius accuses no person of this stupidity, although he reproaches the superstitious of every class. This opinion, therefore, has never existed; there never have been idolaters.

Horace causes an image of Priapus to speak, and makes him say: "I was once the trunk of a fig tree, and a carpenter being doubtful whether he should make of me a god or a bench, at length determined to make me a divinity." What are we to gather from this pleasantry? Priapus was one of the subaltern divinities, and a subject of raillery for the wits, and this pleasantry is the strongest proof that a figure placed in the garden to frighten away the birds could not be very profoundly worshipped.

Dacier, giving way to the spirit of a commentator, observes that Baruch predicted this adventure, saying, "They became what the workmen chose to make them:" but might not this be observed of all statues?

A block of marble may as well be hewn into a cistern, as into a figure of Alexander, Jupiter, or any being still more respectable. The matter which composed the cherubim of the Holy of Holies might have been equally appropriated to the vilest functions. Is a throne or altar the less revered because it might have been formed into a kitchen table?

Dacier, instead of concluding that the Romans adored the statue of Priapus, and that Baruch predicted it, should have perceived that the Romans laughed at it. Consult all the authors who speak of the statues of the gods, you will not find one of them allude to idolatry; their testimony amounts to the express contrary. "It is not the workman," says Martial, "who makes the gods, but he who prays to them."

> *Qui finxit sacros auro vel marmore vultus*
> *Non facit ille deos, qui rogat ille facit.*

"It is Jove whom we adore in the image of Jove," writes Ovid: *Colitur pro Jove, forma Jovis.*"

"The gods inhabit our minds and bosoms," observes Statius, "and not images in the form of them:"

> *Nulla autem effigies, nulli commissa metallo.*
> *Forma Dei, mentes habitare et pectora gaudet.*

Lucan, too, calls the universe the abode and empire of God: "*Estne Dei, sedes, nisi terra, et pontus, et aer?*"

A volume might be filled with passages asserting idols to be images alone.

There remains only the case in which statues became oracles; a notion that might have led to an opinion that there was something divine about them. The predominant sentiment, however, was that the gods had chosen to visit certain altars and images, in order to give audience to mortals, and to reply to them. We read in Homer and in the chorus of the Greek tragedies, of prayers to Apollo, who delivered his responses on the mountains in such a temple, or such a town. There is not, in all antiquity, the least trace of a prayer addressed to a statue.

Those who professed magic, and who either believe, or affected to believe it a science, claimed to possess the secret of making the gods descend into their statues, not indeed, the superior gods, but the secondary gods or genii. This is what Hermes Trismegistus calls "making" gods—a doctrine which is refuted by St. Augustine in his *City of God*. But even this clearly shows that the images were not thought to possess anything divine, since it required a magician to animate them, and it seems to me that it happened very rarely that a magician was skillful enough to give a soul to a statue so that it would speak.

In a word, the images of the gods were not gods. Jupiter, and not his statue, launched his thunderbolts; it was not the statue of Neptune that stirred up tempests, nor that of Apollo that bestowed light. The Greeks and the Romans were Gentiles and Polytheists, but not idolaters.

Whether the Persians, Sabæans, Egyptians, Tartars, or Turks, have been idolaters; and the extent of the antiquity of the images called idols.

History of their worship.

It is a great error to denominate those idolaters who worship the sun and the stars. These nations for a long time had neither images nor temples. If they were wrong, it was in rendering to the stars that which belonged only to the creator of the stars. Moreover, the dogma of Zoroaster, or Zerdusht, included in the Sadder, teaches a Supreme Being, an avenger and rewarder, which opinion is very distant from idolatry. The government of China possesses no idol, but has always preserved the simple worship of the master of heaven, Kien-tien. Genghis Khan, among the Tartars, was not an idolater, and used no images. The Mohammedans, who inhabit Greece, Asia Minor, Syria, Persia, India, and Africa, call the Christians idolaters and giaours, because they imagine that Christians worship images. They break the statues which they find in Sancta Sophia, the church of the Holy Apostles; and others they convert into mosques. Appearances have deceived them, as they are eternally deceiving man, and have led them to believe that temples dedicated to saints who were formerly men, images of saints worshipped kneeling, and miracles worked in these churches, are invincible proofs of absolute idolatry. But this is not at all the case. Christians, in fact, adore one God only, and even in the blessed, only revere the virtues of God manifested in them. The iconoclasts and the Protestants have reproached the Catholic Church in the same way, and they have been given the same answer.

As men have rarely had precise ideas, and still less expressed them with precision and without ambiguity, we called the Gentiles, and still more the Polytheists, idolaters. An immense number of volumes have been written and various opinions uttered on the origins of the worship rendered to God or to several gods in the form of material figures. This multitude of books and opinions proves nothing, except ignorance.

It is not known who invented coats, shoes, and stockings, and yet we would know who invented idols. What is the importance of a passage of Sanchoniathon, who lived before the battle of Troy? What does he teach us when he says that *Chaos*—the spirit, that is to say, the breath—in love with his principles, drew slime from them, rendered the air luminous; that the wind *Colp*, and his wife *Bau*, engendered *Eon;* that *Eon* engendered *Genos*, that *Chronos*, their descendant, had two eyes behind as well as before; that he became a god, and that he gave Egypt to his son *Thaut?* Such is one of the most respectable monuments of antiquity.

Orpheus, prior to Sanchoniathon, will teach us no more in his "Theogony," which Damasius has preserved for us. He represents the principles of the world under the figure of a dragon with two heads, the one of a bull, the other of a lion; a face in the middle, which he calls the face of God, and golden wings on his shoulders.

But, from these fantastic ideas may be drawn two great truths—the one that sensible images and hieroglyphics are of the remotest antiquity; the other that all the ancient philosophers have recognized a First Principle.

As to polytheism, good sense will tell you that as long as men have existed—that is to say, weak animals capable of reason and folly, subject to all accidents, sickness and death—these men have felt their weakness and dependence. They have easily acknowledged that there is something more powerful than themselves; They have felt a force in the earth that furnishes their food; one in the air that often destroys them; one in fire that consumes; and in water that drowns them. What is more natural than for ignorant men to imagine beings which preside over these elements? What is more natural than to revere the invisible power which makes the sun and stars shine to our eyes? And, when they wished to form an idea of these powers superior to man, what more natural than to figure them in a manner accessible to the senses? Could they think otherwise? The Jewish religion, which preceded ours, and which was given by God himself, was filled with these images, under which God is represented. He deigns to speak the human language in a bush; He appears once on a mountain; the celestial spirits, which he sends, all come with a human form: finally, the sanctuary is covered with cherubs, which are the bodies of men with the wings and heads of animals. It is this which has given rise to the error of Plutarch, Tacitus, Appian, and so many others, of reproaching the Jews with adoring an ass's head. God, in spite of his prohibition to paint or form likenesses, has, therefore, deigned to adapt himself to human weakness, which required that the senses be addressed by images.

Isaiah, in chapter 6, sees the Lord seated on a throne, and the lower portion of his gown filled the temple. The Lord extends His hand, and touches the mouth of Jeremiah, in chapter 1 of that prophet. Ezekiel, in chapter 3, sees a throne of sapphire, and God appears to him like a man seated on this throne. These images do not alter the purity of the Jewish religion, which never employed pictures, statues, or idols, to represent God to the eyes of the people.

The learned Chinese, the Parsees, and the ancient Egyptians, had no idols; but Isis and Osiris were soon represented. Bel, at Babylon, was a great colossus. Brahma was a fantastic monster in the peninsula of India. Above all, the Greeks multiplied the names of the gods, statues, and temples, but always attributed the supreme power to their *Zeus*, called Jupiter by the Latins, the sovereign of gods and men. The Romans imitated the Greeks. These people always placed all the gods in heaven, without knowing what they understood by heaven and by their Olympus. It was unlikely that there superior beings lived inhabited the clouds, which are nothing but water. Seven were initially placed in the seven planets, among which the sun was included. But later, the expanse of the heavens was the abode of all the gods.

The Romans had their twelve great gods, six male and six female, whom they called "*Dii majorum gentium*"; Jupiter, Neptune, Apollo, Vulcan, Mars, Mercury, Juno, Vesta, Minerva, Ceres, Venus, and Diana; Pluto was therefore forgotten: Vesta took his place.

Afterwards, came the gods "*minorum gentium*," the gods of mortal origin; the heroes, as Bacchus, Hercules, and Æsculapius: the infernal gods, Pluto and Proserpine: those of the sea, as Tethys, Amphitrite, the Nereids, and Glaucus. The Dryads, Naiads, gods of gardens; those of shepherds, etc. They had them, indeed, for every profession, for every action of life, for children, marriageable girls, married, and lying-in women: they had even the god Peditum; and finally, they idolized their emperors. Neither these emperors nor the god Peditum, the goddess Pertunda, nor Priapus, nor Rumilia, the goddess of nipples; nor Stercutius, the god of the privy, were, in truth, regarded as the masters of heaven and earth. The emperors sometimes had temples, the petty gods—the penates—had none; but all had their representations, their idols.

There were little images with which they ornamented their closets, the amusements of old women and children, which were not authorized by any public worship. The superstition of every individual was left to act according to his own taste. These small idols are still found in the ruins of ancient towns.

If no person knows when men began to make these images, they must know that they are of the greatest antiquity, Terah, the father of Abraham, made them at Ur in Chaldaea. Rachel stole and carried off the images of Laban, her father. We cannot go back further.

But what precise notion had the ancient nations of all these representations? What virtue, what power, was attributed to them? Did they believe that the gods descended from heaven to conceal themselves in these statues; or that they communicated to them a part of the divine spirit; or that they communicated to them nothing at all? Again, there has been much useless writing on this subject; it is clear that every man judged according to the degree of his reason, credulity, or fanaticism. It is evident that the priests attached as much divinity to their statues as they possibly could, to attract more offerings. We know that the philosophers reproved these superstitions, that warriors laughed at them, that the magistrates tolerated them, and that the people, always absurd, knew not what they did. In a word, this is the history of all nations to which God has not made himself known.

The same idea may be formed of the worship which all Egypt rendered to the cow, and that several towns paid to a dog, an ape, a cat, and to onions. It appears that these were first emblems. Afterwards, a certain ox Apis, and a certain dog Anubis, were adored; they always ate beef and onions; but it is difficult to know what the old women of Egypt thought of the holy cows and onions.

Idols also often spoke. On the day of the feast of Cybele at Rome, those fine words were commemorated which the statue pronounced when it was translated from the palace of King Attilus: "I wished to depart; take me away quickly; Rome is the worthy residence of every god."

> *Ipsa peti volui; ne sit mora, mitte volentum;*
> *Dignus Roma locus quo Deus omnis eat.*
> —OVIDS, *Fasti,* iv, 269–270

The statue of Fortune spoke; the Scipios, the Ciceros, and the Cæsars, indeed, believed nothing of it; but the old woman, to whom Encolpus gave a crown to buy geese and gods, might credit it.

Idols also gave oracles, and priests hidden in the hollow of the statues spoke in the name of the divinity.

How can it be, in the midst of so many gods and different theogonies and particular forms of worship, that there were never any religious wars among the people called idolaters? This peace was a good produced from an evil, even from error; for each nation, acknowledging several inferior gods, found it good that its neighbors should also have theirs. If you except Cambyses, who is reproached with having killed the ox Apis, you will not see any conqueror in profane history who ill-treated the gods of a vanquished people. The Gentiles had no exclusive religion, and the priests thought only of multiplying the offerings and sacrifices.

The first offerings were fruits. Soon after, animals were required for the table of the priests; they killed them themselves, and became cruel butchers; finally, they introduced the horrible custom of sacrificing human victims, and above all, children and young girls. The Chinese, Parsees, and Indians, were never guilty of these abominations; but at Hieropolis, in Egypt, according to Porphyrius, men were immolated.

Strangers were sacrificed at Taurida: happily, the priests of Taurida never had much of a following. The first Greeks, the Cypriots, Phoenicians, Tyrians, and Carthaginians, possessed this abominable superstition. The Romans themselves fell into this religious crime; and Plutarch relates, that they immolated two Greeks and two Gauls to expiate the gallantries of three vestals. Procopius, contemporary with the king of the Franks, Theodobert, says that the Franks sacrificed men when they entered Italy with that prince. The Gauls and Germans commonly made these frightful sacrifices. We can scarcely read history without conceiving horror at mankind.

It is true that among the Jews, Jephthah sacrificed his daughter, and Saul was ready to immolate his son; it is also true that those who were devoted to the Lord by anathema could not be redeemed, as other beasts were, but were doomed to perish. The Jewish priest Samuel hacked to bits with a holy chopping knife the king Agag, a prisoner of war whom Saul had pardoned, and Saul was blamed for having respected human rights with this king. But God, the master of men, can claim their lives when he wishes, as he wishes, using whomever he wishes; and it is not for men to put themselves in the place of the master of life and death, or to usurp the rights of the Supreme Being.

To console mankind for this horrible picture, for these pious sacrifices, it is important to know, that amongst almost all nations called idolatrous, there have been holy theologies and popular error, secret worship and public ceremonies; the religion of sages, and that of the vulgar. To know that one God alone was taught to those initiated into the mysteries, it is only necessary to look at the hymn attributed to the ancient Orpheus, which was sung in the mysteries of the Eleusinian Ceres, so celebrated in Europe and Asia: "Contemplate divine nature; illuminate thy mind; govern thy heart; walk in the path of justice, that the God of heaven and earth may be always present to your eyes: He is unique, he alone exists by himself, all beings derive their existence from Him; He sustains them all; He has never been seen by mortals, and He sees all things."

We may also read the passage of the philosopher Maximus of Madaura, in his letter to Augustine: "What man is so gross and stupid as to doubt that there is a supreme, eternal, and infinite God, who has engendered nothing like Himself, and who is the common father of all things?"

There are a thousand proofs that the ancient sages not only abhorred idolatry, but polytheism.

Epictetus, that model of resignation and patience, that man so great in a humble condition, never speaks of but one God. Here is one of his maxims: "God has created me; God is within me; I carry Him everywhere. Can I defile Him by obscene thoughts, unjust actions, or loathsome desires? My duty is to thank God for all, to praise Him for all; and only to cease blessing Him in ceasing to live." All the ideas of Epictetus turn on this principle.

Marcus Aurelius, perhaps as great on the throne of the Roman Empire as Epictetus was in slavery, often speaks, indeed, of the gods, either to conform himself to the received language, or to express intermediate beings between the Supreme Being and men; but in how many places does he show that he recognizes one eternal, infinite God alone? "Our soul," says he, "is an emanation from the divinity. My children, my body, my mind, are derived from God."

The Stoics and Platonics admitted a divine and universal nature; the Epicureans denied it. The pontiffs spoke only of a single God in their mysteries. Where then were the idolaters?

As to the rest, it is one of the greatest errors of the *Dictionary* of Moreri to say, that in the time of Theodosius the younger, there remained no idolaters except in the distant countries of Asia and Africa. Even in the seventh century there were still many heathen people in Italy. The north of Germany, from the Weser, was not Christian in the time of Charlemagne. After his death, Poland and all the north long remained in what was called idolatry. Half of Africa, all the kingdoms beyond the Ganges, Japan, the populace of China, and a hundred hordes of Tartars, have preserved their ancient religion. In Europe there are only a few Laplanders, Samoyeds, and Tartars, who have persevered in the religion of their ancestors.

Let us conclude with the remark, that in the time which we call the middle ages, we called the country of the Mohammedans *the Pagan lands*. We treated as idolaters and adorers of images, a people who hold all images in abhorrence. Let us once more avow that the Turks are more excusable in believing us idolaters, when they see our altars loaded with images and statues.

INONDATION / FLOOD

WAS there ever a time when the globe was entirely inundated? It is physically impossible. It is possible that the sea may successively have covered every land, one part after another; and even this can only have happened by very slow gradation, and in a prodigious number of centuries. In the course of five hundred years the sea has withdrawn from Aigues-Mortes, Fréjus, and Ravenna, which were considerable ports, and left about two leagues of land dry. According to the ratio of such progression, it is clear that it would require two million and two hundred and fifty thousand years to produce the same effect through the whole circuit of the globe. It is very remarkable that this period of time nearly falls in with that which the axis of the earth would require to be raised, so as to coincide with the equator; a very likely movement, which we only began to suspect about fifty years ago, and which could only be completed in the space of two million three hundred thousand years.

The beds or strata of shells, which have been discovered at the distance of some leagues from the sea, are an incontestable evidence that it has gradually deposited these marine productions on tracts which were formerly shores of the ocean; but that the water should have ever covered the whole globe at once is an absurd chimera in physics, demonstrated to be impossible by the laws of gravitation, by the laws of fluids, and by the insufficient quantity of water for the purpose. We do not, by these observations, at all mean to impeach the truth of the universal deluge, reported in the Pentateuch; on the contrary, that is a miracle, so it must be believed; it is a miracle, and therefore could not have been accomplished by physical laws.

All is miracle in the story of the deluge—a miracle that forty days of rain should have inundated the four quarters of the world and raised the water to the height of fifteen cubits above the tops of the loftiest mountains; a miracle that there should have been cataracts, floodgates, and openings in the heavens; a miracle that all sorts of animals should have been collected in the ark from all parts of the world; a miracle that Noah found the means of feeding them for a period of ten months; a miracle that all the animals with all their provisions could have been accommodated in the ark; a miracle, that the greater part of them did not die; a miracle, that after quitting the ark, they found food enough to survive; and a further miracle, but of a different kind, that a person, by the name of Pelletier, thought himself capable of explaining how all the animals could be contained and fed in Noah's ark naturally.

But the history of the deluge being the most miraculous event of which the world has ever heard, it must be the height of folly and madness to attempt an explanation of it: it is one of the mysteries that are believed by faith; and faith consists in believing that which reason does not believe—which is again another miracle.

The history of the universal deluge, therefore, is like that of the tower of Babel, of Balaam's ass, of the falling of the walls of Jericho at the sound of trumpets, of waters turned into blood, of the passage of the Red Sea, and of the whole of the prodigies which God condescended to perform in favor of his chosen people. These are depths the human understanding cannot fathom.

INQUISITION / INQUISITION

THE Inquisition is well known to be an admirable and truly Christian invention for increasing the power of the pope and monks, and for making hypocrites of whole kingdoms.

St. Dominic is usually considered the person to whom the world is indebted for originating this institution. In fact, we still have a patent granted by that great saint, conceived in the following words: "I, brother Dominic, reconcile to the Church Roger, the bearer of these orders, on condition of his being scourged by a priest on three successive Sundays from the entrance of the city to the church doors; of his abstaining from meat all his life; of his fasting for the space of three Lents in a year; of his never drinking wine; of his carrying about him the 'san benito' with crosses; of his reciting the breviary every day, and ten paternosters in the course of the day, and twenty at midnight; of his preserving perfect chastity, and of his presenting himself every month before the parish priest, etc.; the whole under pain of being treated as heretical, perjured, and impenitent."

Although Dominic was the real founder of the Inquisition, Louis de Paramo, one of the most respectable writers and most brilliant luminaries of the Holy Office, relates, in the second chapter of his second book, that God was the first institutor of the Holy Office, and that he exercised the power of the preaching brethren against Adam. In the first place Adam is cited before the tribunal: *"Adam ubi es?"*—Adam, where art thou? And in fact, adds Paramo, the want of this citation would have rendered the whole procedure of God null.

The clothing formed of skins, which God made for Adam and Eve, were the model of the *"san benito,"* which the Holy Office requires to be worn by heretics. It is true that, according to this argument, God was the first tailor; but it is no less evident that he was the first inquisitor.

Adam was deprived of the immovable property he possessed in the terrestrial paradise, and hence the Holy Office confiscates the property of all whom it condemns.

Louis de Paramo remarks, that the inhabitants of Sodom were burned as heretics because sodomy is a formal heresy. He thence passes to the history of the Jews: and in every part of it discovers the Holy Office.

Jesus Christ is the first inquisitor of the new law; the popes were inquisitors by divine right; and at last they communicated their power to St. Dominic.

He afterwards estimates the number of all those whom the Inquisition has put to death; he states it to be considerably above a hundred thousand.

His book was printed in 1589, at Madrid, with the approbation of doctors, praise from the bishop, and the privilege of the king. We can today scarcely form any idea of horrors so extravagant and abominable; but at that time nothing seemed more natural and edifying. All men resemble Louis de Paramo when they are fanatics.

Paramo was a plain, direct man, very exact in dates, omitting no interesting fact, and calculating with precision the number of human victims immolated by the Holy Office throughout the world.

He relates, with great naïveté, the establishment of the Inquisition in Portugal, and is in perfect accordance with four other historians who have all spoken like he. They are unanimous in this account.

Pope Boniface had long before, at the beginning of the fifteenth century, delegated some Dominican friars to go to Portugal, from one city to another, to burn heretics, Mussalmans, and Jews; but these were itinerant; and even the kings sometimes complained of their vexations caused. Pope Clement VII wanted to give them a fixed residence in Portugal, as they had in Aragon and Castile. Difficulties arose between the court of Rome and that of Lisbon; tempers became irritated, the Inquisition suffered by it, and was far from being perfectly established.

In 1539, there appeared at Lisbon a legate of the pope, who came, he said, to establish the holy Inquisition on unshakeable foundations. He delivered letters to King John III from Pope Paul III. He had other letters from Rome for the chief officers of the court; his patents as legate were duly sealed and signed; and he exhibited the most ample powers for creating a grand inquisitor and all the judges of the Holy Office. He was an impostor of the name of Saavedra, who had the talent of counterfeiting handwriting, seals, and coats-of-arms. He had acquired the art at Rome, and had perfected it in Seville, from whence he came in company with two other knaves. His train was magnificent, consisting of more than a hundred and twenty domestics. To defray this enormous expense, he and his two associates borrowed in Seville large sums in the name of the apostolic chamber of Rome; everything was coordinated with the most dazzling art.

The king of Portugal was at first astonished that the pope had sent to him a legate *a latere* without any previous announcement. The legate haughtily replied that in a concern as urgent as that of establishing the Inquisition on a firm foundation, his holiness could admit of no delays, and that the king might consider himself honored by the Holy Father's having appointed a legate to be the first person to announce his intention. The king did not venture to reply. The legate on the same day constituted a grand inquisitor, and sent about collectors to receive the tenths; and before the court could obtain answers from Rome, the legate had brought two hundred victims to the stake, and collected more than two hundred thousand crowns.

However, the Marquis of Villanova, a Spanish nobleman, from whom the legate had borrowed at Seville a very considerable sum upon forged bills, determined, if possible, to repay himself the money with his own hands, instead of going to Lisbon and exposing himself to the intrigues and influence of the swindler there. The legate was at this time making his circuit along the borders of Spain. The marquis advanced upon him with fifty men well armed, carried him off prisoner, and conducted him to Madrid.

The whole imposture was speedily discovered at Lisbon; the Council of Madrid condemned the legate Saavedra to be flogged and sent to the galleys for ten years; but the most admirable circumstance was, that Pope Paul IV confirmed subsequently all that the impostor had established; out of the plenitude of his divine power he rectified all the little irregularities of the various procedures, and rendered sacred that which before had been merely human.

> *"Qu'importe de quel bras Dieu daigne se servir?"*
>
> (Zaïre, II,i)
>
> What does it matter which arm God deigns to employ?

Such was the manner in which the Inquisition became established at Lisbon; and the whole kingdom wondered at the workings of Providence.

For the rest, the methods adopted by this tribunal are generally known; it is well known how strongly they are opposed to the false equity and blind reason of all other tribunals in the world. Men are imprisoned on the mere accusation of the most disreputable persons; a son may denounce his father and the wife her husband; the accused is never confronted with the accusers; property is confiscated for the benefit of the judges: such at least were the ways of the Inquisition until our own times. Surely in this there is something divine; for it is incomprehensible that men should have patiently submitted to this yoke.

Finally Count Aranda has obtained the blessings of all Europe by paring the nails and filing the teeth of the monster; but it still breathes.

JEPHTÉ / JEPHTHAH

OR ON SACRIFICES OF HUMAN BLOOD

IT is evident from the text of the Book of Judges that Jephthah promised to sacrifice the first person that should come out of his house to congratulate him on his victory over the Ammonites. His only daughter came before him; he tore his garments and immolated her, after allowing her to go mourn in the mountains the misfortune of dying a virgin. The daughters of Israel long continued to celebrate this adventure, devoting four days in the year to lamentation for the daughter of Jephthah. (See Judges, 12)

In whatever period this history was written, whether it was imitated from the Greek story of Agamemnon and Idomeneus, or was the model from which that story was taken; whether it might be anterior or posterior to similar Assyrian narratives, is not the point I am now examining. I keep strictly to the text. Jephthah vowed to make his daughter a burnt offering, and fulfilled his vow.

It was expressly commanded by the Jewish law to sacrifice men devoted to the Lord: "Every man that shall be devoted shall not be redeemed, but shall be put to death without remission." The Vulgate translates, *non redimetur, sed morte morietur.* (Lev.27:29)

It was in virtue of this law that Samuel hewed in pieces King Agag, whom, as we have already seen, Saul had pardoned. In fact, it was for sparing Agag that Saul was rebuked by the Lord and lost his kingdom.

Thus, sacrifices of human blood were clearly established; there is no point of history more incontestable: we can only judge of a nation by its own archives, and by what it relates concerning itself.

JOB / JOB

GOOD day, my friend Job![53] You are one of the most ancient originals of which books make mention; you were not a Jew; we know that the book that bears your name is more ancient than the Pentateuch. If the Hebrews, who translated it from the Arabic, made use of the word "Jehovah" to signify God, they borrowed it from the Phoenicians and Egyptians, as men of learning know well. The word "Satan" was not Hebrew; it was Chaldaean, as is well known.

You dwelt near the border of Chaldaea. Commentators worthy of their profession claim that you believed in the resurrection, because, lying on your dunghill, you said, in your nineteenth chapter, *that you would rise up from it* one day. A patient who is hoping for his cure does not, for that reason, also wish for resurrection; but I would speak to you of other things.

Confess that you were a great babbler; but your friends even more so. It is said that you possessed seven thousand sheep, three thousand camels, one thousand cows, and five hundred she-asses. I will reckon up their value:

	LIVRES.
Seven thousand sheep, at three pounds ten pennies apiece..	22,500
I estimate the three thousand camels at fifty crowns apiece	450,000
A thousand cows, one with the other, cannot be valued at less than	80,000
And five hundred she-asses, at twenty francs an ass.	10,000
The whole amounts to	562,500

without reckoning thy furniture, rings and jewels.

I have been much richer than you; and though I have lost a great part of my property and am ill, like you I have not murmured against God, as your friends seem to reproach you with doing sometimes.

I am not at all pleased with Satan, who, to induce you to sin, and to make you forget God, asks permission to take away all your property and to give you the itch. It is in this state that men always have recourse to the Divinity. It is prosperous people who forget God. Satan was not familiar enough with the world; he has improved himself since; and when he would be sure of someone, he makes him a farmer-general, or something better if possible, as our friend Pope has clearly shown in his story of the knight Sir Balaam.

Your wife was an impertinent, but your supposed friends Eliphaz the Temanite, Bildad the Shuite, and Zophar, the Naamathite, were much more intolerable than she. They exhorted you to patience in a manner that would have roused the mildest of men; they made long sermons for you more tiresome than those preached by the knave V————e at Amsterdam, and by so many other people.

It is true that you did not know what you were saying, when you exclaimed—"My God, am I a sea or a whale, to be shut up by You as in a prison?" But your friends knew no better when they answered you, "that the bulrush cannot bud without humidity, and that the grass of the field cannot grow without water." Nothing is less consolatory than this axiom.

Zophar of Naamath reproached you with being a prater; but none of these good friends lent you a crown. I would not have treated you thus. Nothing is more common than people who advise; nothing more rare than those who assist. Friends are not worth much, from whom we cannot procure a drop of broth if we are in misery. I imagine that when God restored your riches and health, these eloquent personages dared not present themselves before you; hence *the comforters of Job* have become a proverb.

God was displeased with them, and told them sharply, in chapter 42, that they were tiresome and imprudent, and he condemned them to a fine of seven bullocks and seven rams, for having talked nonsense. I would have condemned them for not having assisted their friend.

I pray you, tell me if it is true, that you lived a hundred and forty years after this adventure. I like to learn that honest people live long; but men of the present day must be great rogues, since their lives are comparatively so short.

As to the rest, the book of Job is one of the most precious of all antiquity. It is evident that this book is the work of an Arab who lived before the time in which we place Moses. It is said that Eliphaz, one of the interlocutors, is of Teman, which was an ancient city of Arabia. Bildad was of Shua, another town of Arabia. Zophar was of Naamath, a still more eastern country of Arabia.

But what is more remarkable, and which shows that this fable cannot be that of a Jew, is, that three constellations are spoken of, which we now call the Bear, Orion, and the Hyades. The Hebrews never had the least knowledge of astronomy; they did not even have a word to express this science; all that regards the mental sciences was unknown to them, including even the term geometry.

The Arabs, on the contrary, living in tents, and being continually led to observe the stars, were perhaps the first who regulated their years by the inspection of the heavens.

The more important observation is that one God alone is spoken of in this book. It is an absurd error to imagine that the Jews were the only people who recognized a sole God; it was the doctrine of almost all the East, and the Jews were only plagiarists in that as in everything else.

In chapter 37 God Himself speaks to Job from the midst of a whirlwind, which has been since imitated in Genesis. We cannot too often repeat that the Jewish books are very modern. Ignorance and fanaticism exclaim that the Pentateuch is the most ancient book in the world. It is evident that those of Sanchoniathon, and those of Thaut, eight hundred years anterior to those of Sanchoniathon; those of the first Zerdusht, the "Shasta," the "Vedas" of the Indians, which we still possess; the "Five Kings of China"; and finally the Book of Job, are of a much remoter antiquity than any Jewish book. It is demonstrated that this little people could only have had annals when they had a stable government; that they only had this government under their kings; that its jargon was only formed in the course of time from a mixture of Phoenician and Arabic. These are incontestable proofs that the Phoenicians cultivated letters a long time before them. Their profession was pillage and brokerage; they were writers only by chance. We have lost the books of the Egyptians and Phoenicians, the Chinese, Brahmins, and Guebres; the Jews have preserved theirs. All these monuments are curious, but they are monuments of human imagination alone, in which not a single truth, either physical or historical, is to be learned. There is not at present a single little physical treatise that would not be more useful than all the books of antiquity.

The good Calmet, or Dom Calmet (for the Benedictines like us to give them their Dom), that naïve compiler of so many reveries and imbecilities; that man whom simplicity has rendered so useful to whoever would laugh at ancient nonsense, faithfully relates the opinion of those who would discover the malady with which Job was attacked, as if Job was a real personage. He does not hesitate in saying that Job had smallpox, and he heaps passage upon passage, as usual, to prove that which is not. He had not read the history of smallpox by Astruc; for Astruc, being neither a father of the Church nor a doctor of Salamanca, but a very learned physician, the good man, Calmet did not know that he existed. Monkish compilers are poor creatures!

(by an invalid at the waters of Aix-la-Chapelle)

Joseph / Joseph

THE story of Joseph, considering it merely as an object of curiosity and literature, is one of the most precious monuments of antiquity to have reached us. It appears to be the model of all Oriental writers; it is more touching than Homer's "Odyssey"; for a hero who pardons is more touching than one who avenges.

We regard the Arabs as the first authors of these ingenious fictions, which have passed into all languages; but I see among them no adventures comparable to those of Joseph. Almost everything in it is wonderful, and the conclusion makes tears of tenderness flow. He is a young man of sixteen years of age, whose brothers are jealous; he is sold by them to a caravan of Ishmaelite merchants, conducted into Egypt, and bought by a eunuch of the king. This eunuch had a wife, which is not at all extraordinary; the Kislar-aga, a perfect eunuch, who has had everything cut off, today has a seraglio in Constantinople; he still has his eyes and his hands, and nature has not altogether lost its power over his heart. Other eunuchs, who have only had removed the two companions of the reproductive organ, still use this organ often; and Potiphar, to whom Joseph was sold, could very well be counted among the number of these eunuchs.

The wife of Potiphar falls in love with the young Joseph, who, faithful to his master and benefactor, rejects the advances of this woman. She is irritated at it, and accuses Joseph of attempting to seduce her. Such is the history of Hippolytus and Phædra, of Bellerophon and Zenobia, of Hebrus and Damasippa, of Tennes and Periboea, of Myrtilus and Hippodamia, of Peleus and Demenette.

It is difficult to know which is the original of all these stories; but among the ancient Arabian authors there is a tale relating to the adventure of Joseph and Potiphar's wife, which is very ingenious. The author supposes that Potiphar, uncertain between the assertions of his wife and Joseph, did not look at Joseph's tunic, which his wife had torn as a proof of the young man's outrage. There was a child in a cradle in his wife's chamber; and Joseph said that she had seized and torn his tunic in the presence of this infant. Potiphar consulted the child, whose mind was very advanced for its age. The child said to Potiphar: "See if the tunic is torn in back or in front; if in front, it is a proof that Joseph tried to embrace your wife by force, and that she defended herself; if in back, it is a proof that your wife tried to detain Joseph." Potiphar, thanks to the genius of the child, recognized the innocence of his slave. It is thus that this adventure is related in the Koran, after the Arabian author. It informs us not to whom the infant belonged, who judged with so much wit. If it was not a son of Potiphar, Joseph was not the first whom this woman had seduced.

However that may be, according to Genesis, Joseph is put in prison, where he finds himself in company with the butler and baker of the king of Egypt. These two prisoners of state both dream during the night. Joseph explains their dreams; he predicts that in three days the butler will be restored to favor, and that the baker will be hanged; which did not fail to happen.

Two years afterwards the king of Egypt also dreams, and his butler tells him that there is a young Jew in prison who is the first man in the world for the interpretation of dreams. The king has the young man brought to him, who foretells seven years of abundance and seven of sterility.

Let us interrupt here the thread of the story to consider the prodigious antiquity of the interpretation of dreams. Jacob saw in a dream the mysterious ladder at the top of which was God Himself. In a dream he learned a method of multiplying his flocks, a method which never succeeded with any but himself. Joseph himself had learned by a dream that he should one day govern his brothers. Abimelech, a long time before, had been warned in a dream that Sarah was the wife of Abraham. (See article *Songes* / Dreams)

To return to Joseph: after explaining the dream of Pharaoh, he was made first minister on the spot. We doubt if at present a king could be found, even in Asia, who would bestow such an office in return for an interpreted dream. Pharaoh gave to Joseph in marriage a daughter of Potiphar. It is said that this Potiphar was high-priest of Heliopolis; he was not therefore the eunuch, his first master; or if it was the latter, he had another title besides that of high-priest; and his wife had been a mother more than once.

In the meantime, the famine happened, as Joseph had foretold; and Joseph, to merit the good graces of his king, forced all the people to sell their land to Pharaoh, and all the nation became slaves to procure wheat. This is apparently the origin of despotic power. It must be confessed, that never had a king made a better bargain; but also the people must hardly have blessed the prime minister.

Finally, the father and brothers of Joseph also needed wheat, for "the famine was sore in all lands." It is scarcely necessary to relate here how Joseph received his brothers; how he pardoned and enriched them. In this story is found all that constitutes an interesting epic poem—exposition, crisis, recognition, adventures, and the marvelous; nothing is more strongly marked with the stamp of Oriental genius.

What the good man Jacob, the father of Joseph, replied to Pharaoh, ought to strike all those who know how to read. "How old are you?" the king said to him. "I am one hundred thirty," said the old man, "and I have not yet had one happy day in this short pilgrimage."

JUDÉE / Judaea

I have never been in Judea, thank God! And I never will go there. I have met with men of all nations who have returned from it, and they have all told me that the situation of Jerusalem is horrible; that all the land round it is stony; that the mountains are bare; that the famous river Jordan is not more than forty feet wide; that the only good spot in the country is Jericho; in short, they all speak of it as St. Jerome did, who long resided in Bethlehem, and who describes the country as the refuse of nature. He says that in summer there isn't even water to drink. This country, however, must have appeared to the Jews a delightful place, in comparison with the deserts in which they originated. If the wretched inhabitants of the Landes left their home for some of the mountains of Lampourdan, they would boast in the change; and if they hoped eventually to penetrate into the fine and fruitful districts of Languedoc, that would be for them the land of promise!

Such is precisely the story of the Jews. Jericho and Jerusalem are Toulouse and Montpellier, and the desert of Sinai is the country between Bordeaux and Bayonne.

But if the God who guided the Israelites wished to bestow upon them a pleasant and fruitful land; if these wretches had in fact dwelt in Egypt, why didn't he leave them in Egypt? To this the only reply is theological mumblings.

Judea, it is said, was the Promised Land. God said to Abraham: "I will give thee all the country between the river of Egypt and the Euphrates." (Genesis, 15)

Alas! my friends, you never have had possession of those fertile banks of the Euphrates and the Nile. You have been made fools of. The masters of the Nile and the Euphrates have in turn been your masters. You have almost always been slaves. To promise and to perform, my poor Jews, are different things. There was an old rabbi once among you, who, when reading your sagacious prophecies that announce for you a land of milk and honey, remarked that you had been promised more butter than bread. Be assured that were the great Turk this very day to offer me the lordship (*seigneurie*) of Jerusalem, I would positively decline it.

Frederick II, when he saw this detestable country, said, loudly enough to be distinctly heard, that Moses must have been very ill advised to conduct his tribe of lepers to such a place as that. "Why," says Frederick, "did he not go to Naples?" Adieu, my dear Jews; I am extremely sorry that Promised Land is lost land.

(by the baron de Broukana)

JULIEN LE PHILOSOPHE / JULIAN THE PHILOSOPHER

ROMAN EMPEROR[54]

JUSTICE often comes very late. Two or three authors, either venal or fanatical, eulogize the cruel and effeminate Constantine as if he had been a god, and treat as an absolute miscreant the just, the wise, and the great Julian. All the authors copying from these repeat both the flattery and the calumny, and so they become almost an article of faith. At length the age of healthy criticism arrives; and at the end of fourteen hundred years, enlightened men revise the cause which had been decided by ignorance. In Constantine we see a man of successful ambition, who scoffed at things divine as well as human. He has the insolence to pretend that God sent him a sign in the air to assure him of victory. He bathes himself in the blood of all his relatives, and is lulled to sleep in all the effeminacy of luxury; but he was a Christian, and so he was canonized.

Julian is sober, chaste, disinterested, brave, and clement; but he was not a Christian—he has long been considered a monster.

At the present day—after having compared facts, memorials and records, the writings of Julian and those of his enemies—we are compelled to acknowledge that, if he was not partial to Christianity, he was somewhat excusable in hating a sect stained with the blood of all his family; and that although he had been persecuted, imprisoned, exiled, and threatened with death by the Galileans under the reign of the cruel and sanguinary Constantius, he never persecuted them, but on the contrary even pardoned ten Christian soldiers who had conspired against his life. His letters are read and admired: "The Galileans," says he, "under my predecessor, suffered exile and imprisonment; and those who, according to the change of circumstances, were called heretics, were reciprocally massacred in their turn. I have called home their exiles, I have liberated their prisoners, I have restored their property to those who were proscribed, and have compelled them to live in peace; but such is the restless rage of these Galileans that they now deplore their inability to devour one another." What a letter! What a judgment, dictated by philosophy, against persecuting fanaticism!

In short, on investigating facts with impartiality, we are obliged to admit that Julian possessed all the qualities of Trajan, with the exception of that depraved taste so long pardoned of the Greeks and Romans; all the virtues of Cato, without either his obstinacy or ill-humor; everything admirable in Julius Caesar but with none of his vices. He possessed the continence of Scipio. Finally, he was in all respects equal to Marcus Aurelius, who was reputed the first of men.

There are none who will now venture to repeat, after that slanderer Theodoret, that he sacrificed a woman in the temple of Carres in order to propitiate the gods. It is no longer said that when he was dying he tossed several drops of his blood towards the heavens, calling out to Jesus Christ: "You have won, Galilean;" as if he had fought against Jesus in making war upon the Persians; as if this philosopher, who died with such perfect resignation, had with alarm and despair recognized Jesus; as if he had believed that Jesus was in the air, and that the air was heaven! These ridiculous absurdities of those so-called fathers of the Church are happily no longer repeated nowadays.

They were finally reduced to using ridicule against him, as did the frivolous citizens of Antioch. He is reproached for his ill-combed beard and the manner of his walk. But you, M. Abbé de la Bletterie, never saw him walk; you have, however, read his letters and his laws, the monuments of his virtues. Of what consequence was it, comparatively, that he had a slovenly beard and an abrupt, headlong walk, as long as his heart was full of magnanimity and all his steps tended to virtue!

One important fact remains to be examined at the present day. Julian is reproached with attempting to invalidate the prophecy of Jesus Christ by rebuilding the temple of Jerusalem. Fires, it is asserted, came out of the earth and prevented the continuance of the work. It is said that this was a miracle, and that this miracle did not convert Julian, nor Alypius, the superintendent of the enterprise, nor any individual of the imperial court. The Abbé de la Bletterie expresses himself thusly: "The emperor and the philosophers of his court undoubtedly employed all their knowledge of natural philosophy to deprive the Deity of the honor of so striking and impressive a prodigy. Nature was always the favorite resource of unbelievers; but she serves the cause of religion so very seasonably that they might surely suspect some collusion between them."

1. It is not true that it is said in the Gospel that the Jewish temple should never be rebuilt. It is true that the gospel of Matthew, which was evidently written after the destruction of Jerusalem by Titus, prophesies that not one stone should remain upon another of the temple of the Idumæan Herod; but no evangelist says that it shall never be rebuilt.

2. Of what consequence could it be to the Supreme Being whether there was a Jewish temple, a magazine, or a mosque, on the spot where the Jews were in the habit of slaughtering bullocks and cows?

3. It is not ascertained whether these so-called fires that burned the workmen started within the circuit of the walls of the city, or within the temple. But it is not very obvious why Jesus would burn the workmen of the emperor Julian and not those of the caliph Omar, who long afterwards built a mosque upon the ruins of the temple; or those of the great Saladin who rebuilt the same mosque. Had Jesus such a particular predilection for the mosques of the Muslims?

4. Jesus, notwithstanding his having predicted that there would not remain one stone upon another in Jerusalem, did not prevent the rebuilding of that city.

5. Jesus predicted many things which God has not permitted to come to pass. He predicted the end of the world, and his coming in the clouds with great power and majesty, before or about the end of the then existing generation. The world, however, has lasted to the present moment, and in all probability will last much longer.

6. If Julian had written an account of this miracle, I should say that he had been deceived by a false and ridiculous report; I should think that the Christians, his enemies, employed

every artifice to oppose his enterprise, that they themselves killed the workmen, and excited and promoted the belief of their being destroyed by a miracle; but Julian does not say a single word on the subject. The war against the Persians at that time fully occupied his attention; he put off the rebuilding of the temple to some other time, and he died before he was able to commence the building.

7. This prodigy is related by Ammianus Marcellinus, who was a Pagan. It is very possible that it may have been an interpolation of the Christians. They have been charged with committing numberless others which have been clearly proved.

But it is not even less probable that at a time when nothing was spoken of but prodigies and stories of witchcraft, Ammianus Marcellinus would have reported this fable on the faith of some credulous narrator. From Titus Livius to de Thou, inclusively, all histories have been infected with prodigies.

8. If Jesus performed miracles, would it be in order to prevent the rebuilding of a temple in which he had himself sacrificed, and in which he was circumcised? Or would he not rather perform miracles to convert to Christianity the various nations who at present ridicule it? Or rather still, to render more humane, more kind, Christians themselves, who, from Arius and Athanasius down to Roland and the Paladins of the Cévennes, have shed torrents of human blood, and conducted themselves nearly as might be expected from cannibals?

Hence I conclude that nature is not in "collusion," as La Bletterie expresses it, with Christianity, but that La Bletterie is in collusion with some old women's stories, one of those persons, as Julian phrases it, "*quibus cum stolidis aniculis negotium erat.*"

La Bletterie, after having done justice to some of Julian's virtues, yet concludes the history of that great man by observing that his death was the effect of "divine vengeance." If that be the case, all the heroes who have died young, from Alexander to

Gustavus Adolphus, have, we must infer, been punished by God. Julian died the noblest of deaths, in the pursuit of his enemies, after many victories. Jovian, who succeeded him, reigned a much shorter time than he did, and reigned in disgrace. I see no divine vengeance in the matter; and I see in La Bletterie himself nothing more than a disingenuous, dishonest declaimer. But where are the men to be found who dare to speak the truth?

Libanius the Stoic was one of these extraordinary men. He celebrated the brave and clement Julian in the presence of Theodosius, the wholesale murderer of the Thessalonians; but Le Beau and La Bletterie fear to praise him in the hearing of their own puny parish officers.

(taken from M. Boulanger)

DU JUSTE ET DE L'INJUSTE / ON THE JUST AND THE UNJUST

WHO has given us the perception of just and unjust? God, who gave us a brain and a heart. But when does your reason tell you that there are such things as vice and virtue? Just at the same time it teaches us that two and two make four. There is no innate knowledge, for the same reason that there is no tree that bears leaves and fruit when it first sprouts above the earth. There is nothing innate, that is to say, fully developed; but—we repeat here what we have often said—God causes us to be born with organs, which, as they mature, make us feel all that is necessary for our species to feel for the conservation of that species.

How is this continual mystery performed? Tell me, you yellow inhabitants of the Isles of Sunda, you black Africans, you beardless Canadians; and you—Plato, Cicero, and Epictetus. You all equally feel that it is better to give the superfluity of your bread, your rice, or your manioc to the poor man who meekly requests it than to kill him or put out his eyes. It is evident to the whole world that a good action is more honorable than an outrage, that gentleness is preferable to fury.

The only thing required, then, is to exercise our reason in discriminating the various shades of what is right and wrong. Good and evil are often neighbors; our passions confound them; who shall enlighten and direct us? Ourselves, when we are calm and undisturbed. Whoever has written on the subject of human duties, in all countries throughout the world, has written well, because he wrote only with reason. All have said the same thing; Socrates and Epictetus, Confucius and Cicero, Marcus Antoninus and Amurath II had the same morality.

Let us repeat every day to the whole of the human race: Morality is uniform and invariable; it comes from God: dogmas are different; they come from ourselves.

Jesus never taught any metaphysical dogmas; He wrote no theological courses; He never said: I am consubstantial; I have two wills and two natures with only one person. He left for the Cordeliers and the Jacobins, who would come along twelve hundred years after Him the delicate and difficult topic of argument of whether His mother was conceived in original sin. He never pronounced marriage to be the visible sign of a thing invisible; He never said a word about concomitant grace; He instituted neither monks nor inquisitors; He appointed nothing of what we see at the present day.

God had given the knowledge of just and unjust, right and wrong, throughout all the ages which preceded Christianity. God never changed nor can change; the constitution of our souls, our principles of reason and morality, will ever be the same. How is virtue promoted by theological distinctions, by dogmas founded on those distinctions, by persecutions founded on those dogmas? Nature, terrified and horror-struck at all these barbarous inventions, calls aloud to all men: Be just, and not persecuting sophists.

You read this admirable maxim in the "*Zend-Avesta*," which is the summary of the laws of Zoroaster: "When it is doubtful whether the action you are about to perform is just or unjust, abstain from doing it." What legislator ever spoke better? This is no the system of "probable opinions," invented by people who call themselves "the Society of Jesus."

LETTRES, GENS DE LETTRES, OU LETTRÉS / LETTERS, MEN OF LETTERS

IN our barbarous past when the Franks, Germans, Bretons, Lombards, and Spanish Mozarabians did not know how to read or write, schools and universities composed almost entirely of ecclesiastics were instituted. These ecclesiastics, knowing only their own jargon, taught this jargon to those who would learn it. Academies were not founded until long after, and though they despised the follies of the schools, they have not always dared to oppose them, because there are follies which we respect when they are attached to respectable things.

Men of letters who have rendered the most service to the small number of thinking beings scattered over the earth are isolated scholars, true sages shut up in their studies, who have neither publicly disputed in the universities, nor said things by halves in the academies; such men have almost all been persecuted. Our miserable race is so created that those who walk in the beaten path always throw stones at those who would show them a new path.

Montesquieu says that the Scythians put out the eyes of their slaves that they might be more attentive to the making of their butter. It is thus that the Inquisition acts and almost every one is blinded in the countries in which this monster reigns. In England people have had two eyes for more than a hundred years. The French are beginning to open one eye—but sometimes the men in power don't even want to allow us to be one-eyed.

These miserable statesmen are like Doctor Balouard of the Italian comedy, who will only be served by the fool Harlequin, and who fears to have too penetrating a servant.

Compose odes in praise of Lord Superbus Fadus, madrigals for his mistress; dedicate a book of geography to his porter, and you will be well received. Enlighten men, and you will be crushed.

Descartes is obliged to quit his country; Gassendi is calumniated; Arnaud passes his days in exile; all philosophers are treated as the prophets were among the Jews.

Who would believe that in the eighteenth century, a philosopher has been dragged before the secular tribunals and treated as impious by reasoning theologians for having said that men could not practice the arts if they had no hands? I expect that they will soon condemn to the galleys the first who shall have the insolence to say that a man could not think if he had no head; for a learned student will say to him that the soul is a pure spirit, the head is only matter; God can place the soul in the heel as well as in the brain; therefore I denounce you as a blasphemer.

The greatest misfortune a man of letters can experience is perhaps not to be the object of the jealousy of his brothers, the victim of cabals, and denigrated by the powerful of the world—it is to be judged by fools. Fools sometimes go very far, particularly when fanaticism is joined to folly, and folly to the spirit of vengeance. Further, the great misfortune of a man of letters is generally to be attached to nothing. A bourgeois citizen buys some small position, and is maintained by his fellow citizens. If any injustice is done to him, he soon finds defenders. The literary man is without aid; he resembles the flying fish; if he rises a little, the birds devour him; if he dives, the fishes eat him up.

Every public man pays tribute to malignity; but he is repaid in money and honors. The man of letters pays the same tribute without receiving anything in return. He enters the arena for his own pleasure; he condemns his own self to the lions.

De la Liberté / On Liberty

A. A battery of cannon is discharged at our ears; have you the liberty to hear it or not hear it, as you please?

B. Undoubtedly I cannot hinder myself from hearing it.

A. Do you wish that these cannon might take off your head, and those of your wife and daughter who walk with you?

B. What a question! I cannot, at least while I am in my right senses, wish such a thing; it is impossible.

A. Good; you necessarily hear these cannon, and you do not necessarily wish for you and your family to die from a canon shot while out walking. You have neither the power to not hear it, nor the power to wish to remain here.

B.* That is clear.[55]

A. I perceive that you have as a result advanced thirty paces in order to be out of the reach of the cannon; you have had the power of walking these few steps with me.

B. That is also very clear.

A. And if you had been paralyzed, you could not have avoided being exposed to this battery; you would not have had the power to be where you are, you necessarily would have heard and received a cannon shot; and you would have as necessarily died.

B. Nothing is more true.

---

* A poor idiot objects in a small, honest, polite, and particularly logical work, that if the prince orders B. to remain exposed to the cannons, he will remain there. Yes, no doubt, if he has more courage, or rather more fear of shame, than love of life, as is often the case. First, the matter at hand here is an entirely different case. Secondly, when the instinct for the fear of shame overrules the instinct for self-preservation, the man is required to remain exposed to the cannon, just as much as he is required to flee when it is not shameful to flee. The poor idiot was required to make ridiculous objections and insults; and *philosophers* feel that they are required to mock him a bit and to forgive him.

A. In what then consists your liberty, if not in the power that your body has acquired of performing that which from absolute necessity your will requires?

B. You embarrass me. Liberty then is nothing more than the power of doing what I wish?

A. Reflect; and see whether liberty can be understood otherwise.

B. In this case, my hunting dog is as free as myself; he has necessarily the desire to run when he sees a hare; and the power of running, if there is nothing the matter with his legs. I have therefore nothing above my dog; do you mean to reduce me to the state of the beasts?

A. These are poor sophisms, and they are poor sophists who have instructed you. You are miserable to find yourself to be free like your dog. Do you not eat, sleep, and propagate like him, and nearly in the same attitudes? Would you smell otherwise than by your nose? Why would you possess liberty differently from your dog?

B. But I have a soul that reasons all the time, and my dog scarcely reasons at all. He has nothing beyond simple ideas, while I have a thousand metaphysical ideas.

A. Well, you are a thousand times more free than he is; you have a thousand times greater power of thought than he has; but still you are not free in any other manner than your dog is free.

B. What! Am I not free to will what I like?

A. What do you understand by that?

B. I understand what all the world understands. Is it not every day said that the will is free?

A. An adage is not a reason; explain yourself better.

B. I understand that I am free to will as I please.

A. With your permission, that makes no sense; see you not that it is ridiculous to say—I want to will? Consequently, you necessarily will only those ideas which are presented to you. Do you wish to marry, yes or no?

B. Suppose I answer that I want neither the one nor the other.

A. In that case you would answer like he who said: Some believe Cardinal Mazarin dead, others believe him living; I believe neither the one nor the other.

B. Well, I want to marry!

A. Aye, that is an answer. Why do you wish to marry?

B. Because I am in love with a young, beautiful, sweet, well-educated, rich girl, who sings very well, whose parents are very honest people, and I flatter myself that I am beloved by her and welcomed by her family.

A. There is a reason. You see that you cannot will without a reason. I declare to you that you are free to marry, that is to say, that you have the power of signing the contract.

B. What! I cannot will without a motive? Then what will become of the other proverb—"*Sit pro ratione voluntas*"—my will is my reason—I will because I will?

A. It is an absurd one, my dear friend; you would then have an effect without a cause.

B. What! When I play at odd or even, have I a reason for choosing even rather than odd?

A. Undoubtedly.

B. And what is the reason, if you please?

A. It is, that the idea of even is presented to your mind rather than the opposite idea. It would be extraordinary if there were cases in which we will because there is a motive, and others in which we will without one. When you would marry, you evidently perceive the predominant reason for it; you perceive it not when you play at odd or even, and yet there must be one.

B. Therefore, once more, I am not free.

A. Your will is not free, but your actions are. You are free to act when you have the power of acting.

B. But all the books that I have read on the liberty of indifference—

A. — are junk; there is no such thing as the liberty of indifference, it is a word devoid of sense, invented by people with almost no sense of their own.

LIBERTÉ DE PENSER / LIBERTY OF THOUGHT

TOWARDS the year 1707, the time at which the English won the battle of Saragossa, protected Portugal, and for some time gave a king to Spain, Lord Boldmind, a general officer who had been wounded, was at the waters of Baréges. He there met with Count Medroso, who, having fallen from his horse behind the baggage train, a league and a half from the field of battle, also came to take the waters. He was a familiar of the Inquisition, while Lord Boldmind was only familiar in conversation.[56] One day after their wine, he held this dialogue with Medroso:

BOLDMIND. You are then a sergeant of the Dominicans? You exercise a villainous trade.

MEDROSO. It is true; but I found I preferred to be their servant than their victim, and I have preferred the unhappiness of burning my neighbor to that of being roasted myself.

BOLDMIND. What a horrible alternative! You were a hundred times happier under the yoke of the Moors, who freely suffered you to abide in all your superstitions, and conquerors as they were, arrogated not to themselves the strange right of keeping souls in chains.

MEDROSO. What would you have? It is not permitted us either to write, speak, or even to think. If we speak, it is easy to misinterpret our words, and still more our writings; and as we cannot be condemned in an *auto-da-fé* for our secret thoughts, we are menaced with being burned eternally by the order of God himself if we do not think like the Jacobins. They have persuaded the government that if we had common sense the entire state would be in flames, and the nation would become the most miserable upon earth.

BOLDMIND. Do you believe that we English, who cover the seas with vessels and win battles for you in the south of Europe, can be so unhappy? Do you see that the Dutch, who have taken from you almost all your discoveries in India and who at present are ranked as your protectors, are cursed by God for having given full liberty to the press, and for making a business out of the thoughts of men? Has the Roman Empire been less powerful because Tullius Cicero wrote freely?

MEDROSO. Who is this Tullius Cicero? I have never heard of him, and this is not about Cicero, it is about our holy father the pope, and Saint Anthony of Padua, and I have always heard it said that the Roman religion is lost if men begin to think for themselves.

BOLDMIND. It is not for you to believe it; for you are sure that your religion is divine, and that the gates of hell cannot prevail against it. If that is the case, nothing will ever destroy it.

MEDROSO. No; but it may be reduced to very little; and it is for having thought that Sweden, Denmark, your entire island, and the half of Germany groan under the frightful misfortune of not being subjects of the pope. It is even said that if men continue to follow their false lights, they will soon limit themselves merely to the simple adoration of God and of virtue. If the gates of hell ever prevail so far, what will become of the holy office?

BOLDMIND. If the first Christians had not the liberty of thought, does it not follow that there would have been no Christianity?

MEDROSO. What do you mean? I do not understand you at all.

BOLDMIND. I'm sure of it, I mean that if Tiberius and the first emperors had fostered Jacobins, who would have prevented the first Christians from having pens and ink; and had it not been a long time permitted in the Roman Empire to "think freely, it would have been impossible for the Christians to establish their dogmas. If, therefore, Christianity was only formed by liberty of opinion, by what contradiction, by what injustice, would you now destroy the liberty on which alone it is founded?

When some affair of interest is proposed to you, do you not examine it for a long time before drawing any conclusions? What greater interest could there be in the world than our eternal happiness or misery? There are a hundred religions on earth which all condemn us if we believe your dogmas, which *they* call impious and absurd; why, therefore, not examine these dogmas?

MEDROSO. How can I examine them? I am not a Jacobin.

BOLDMIND. You are a man, and that is sufficient.

MEDROSO. Alas! You are more of a man than I am.

BOLDMIND. You have only to teach yourself to think; you are born with a mind, you are a bird in the cage of the Inquisition, the holy office has clipped your wings, but they will grow again. He who knows not geometry can learn it: all men can instruct themselves. Is it not shameful to put your soul into the hands of those to whom you would not entrust your money? Dare to think for yourself.

MEDROSO. It is said that if the world thought for itself, it would produce strange confusion.

BOLDMIND. Quite the contrary. When we go to a show, every one freely tells his opinion of it, and the public peace is not thereby disturbed; but if some insolent patron of a poet would force all people of taste to proclaim that to be good which appears to them bad, blows would follow, and the two parties would throw apples of discord at one another's heads, as once happened at London. Tyrants over mind have caused a part of the misfortunes of the world. We have only been happy in England for as long as every one has freely enjoyed the right to speak his mind.

MEDROSO. We are all very tranquil at Lisbon, where no person dares speak his.

BOLDMIND. You are tranquil, but you are not happy: it is the tranquility of galley-slaves, who row in cadence and in silence.

MEDROSO. You believe, then, that my soul is at the galleys?

BOLDMIND. Yes, and I would deliver it.

MEDROSO. But if I am happy at the galleys?

BOLDMIND. Why, then, you deserve to be there.

DES LOIS / ON LAWS

FIRST SECTION

SHEEP live in society very mildly and agreeably; their character passes for being a very gentle one, because we do not see the prodigious quantity of animals devoured by them. We may, however, conceive that they eat them very innocently and without knowing it, just as we do when we eat Sassenage cheese. The republic of sheep is a faithful image of the age of gold.

A hen-roost exhibits the most perfect representation of monarchy. There is no king comparable to a rooster. If he marches haughtily and fiercely in the midst of his people, it is not out of vanity. If the enemy is advancing, he does not content himself with issuing an order to his subjects to go and be killed for him, in virtue of his unfailing knowledge and resistless power; he goes himself, ranges his hens behind him and fights to the last gasp. If he conquers, it is he who sings the "*Te Deum.*" In his civil or domestic life, there is nothing so gallant, so respectable, and so disinterested. He possesses all of the virtues. Whether he has in his royal beak a grain of corn or a grub-worm, he bestows it on the first of his female subjects that comes within his presence. In short, Solomon in his harem was not to be compared to a rooster in a farmyard.

If it be true that bees are governed by a queen to whom all her subjects make love, that is a more perfect government still.

Ants are considered as constituting an excellent democracy. This is superior to every other state, as all are equal and every individual works for the happiness of all.

The republic of beavers is superior even to that of ants; at least, if we may judge by their performances in masonry.

Monkeys are more like a group of acrobats than a regularly governed people; they do not appear associated under fixed and fundamental laws, like the species previously mentioned.

We resemble monkeys more than any other animals in our gift for imitation, in the levity of our ideas, and in that inconstancy which has always prevented our having uniform and durable laws.

When nature formed our species, and imparted to us a certain portion of instinct, self-love for our own preservation, benevolence for the safety and preservation of others, love which is common to all species, and the inexplicable gift of combining more ideas than all the inferior animals together—after bestowing on us our lot she said to us: "Go, and do the best you can."

There is not a good code of laws in any single country. The reason is obvious: laws have been made for particular purposes, according to time, place, exigencies, etc.

When the exigencies upon which laws were founded are changed or removed, the laws themselves become ridiculous. Thus the law which forbade eating pork and drinking wine was perfectly reasonable in Arabia, where pork and wine are injurious; but in Constantinople it is absurd.

The law that confers the whole fief or landed property on the eldest son is a very good one in a time of general anarchy and pillage. The eldest is then the commander of the castle, which sooner or later will be attacked by brigands; the younger brothers will be his chief officers, and the laborers his soldiers. All that is to be feared is that the younger brother may assassinate or poison the elder, his liege lord, in order to become himself the master of the premises; but such instances are uncommon, because nature has so combined our instincts and passions that our horror at the thought of assassinating our elder brother is greater than our desire to succeed to his authority and estate.

But this law, suitable enough to the owners of little castles in the days of Chilperic, is detestable when it is a question of the division of family property in a city.

To the disgrace of mankind, the laws of play or gaming are, it is well known, the only ones that are throughout just, clear, inviolable, and carried into impartial and perfect execution. Why is the Indian who laid down the laws of a game of chess willingly and promptly obeyed all over the world, while the decrees of the popes, for example, are at present an object of horror and contempt? The reason is, that the inventor of chess combined everything with caution and exactness for the satisfaction of the players, and that the popes in their decrees looked solely to their own advantage. The Indian sought to at the same time exercise the minds of men and furnish them with amusement; the popes wanted to stupefy them. Accordingly, the game of chess has remained substantially the same for upwards of five thousand years, and is common to all the inhabitants of the earth; while the decrees are known only at Spoleto, Orvieto, and Loretto, and even there are secretly despised and scorned by the most shallow and contemptible of the practitioners.

Second Section

During the reigns of Vespasian and Titus, when the Romans were disemboweling the Jews, a rich Israelite with no desire whatsoever to be disemboweled fled with all the gold he had accumulated as a usurer, taking his entire family to Ezion-Geber. This family consisted of his elderly wife, a son and a daughter as well as two eunuchs, one of whom acted as a cook and the other as a laborer and wine-grower. A pious Essene, who knew the Pentateuch by heart, acted as his chaplain. All these embarked at the port of Ezion-Geber, traversed the sea commonly called Red, although it is far from being so, and entered the Persian Gulf to go in search of the land of Ophir, without knowing where it was. As you may well imagine, a dreadful tempest soon came on, which drove the Hebrew family towards the coast of India; and the vessel was wrecked on one of the Maldive islands now called Padrabranca, but which was at that time uninhabited.

The old usurer and his wife were drowned; the son and daughter, the two eunuchs, and the almoner were saved. They took as many provisions from the wreck as they were able; erected little cabins for themselves on the island, and lived there comfortably enough. You are aware that the island of Padrabranca is within five degrees of the line, and that it furnishes the largest coconuts and the best pineapples in the world; it was pleasant to have such a lovely asylum at a time when the favorite people of God were elsewhere being slaughtered; but the Essene wept at the thought that perhaps those on that happy island were the only Jews remaining on the earth, and that the seed of Abraham was to be annihilated.

"It is up to you to revive it," said the young Jew; "marry my sister." "I would willingly," said the almoner, "but it is against the law. I am an Essene; I have made a vow never to marry; the law enjoins the strictest observance of a vow; the Jewish race may come to an end, if it must be so; but I will certainly not marry your sister in order to prevent it, however beautiful she may be."

"My two eunuchs," resumed the Jew, "can be of no service in this affair; if you have no objection I will therefore get her with child myself, and you shall bestow the usual marriage benediction."

"I had a hundred times rather be disemboweled by the Roman soldiers," said the chaplain, "than to be instrumental to your committing incest; were she your sister on your father's side only, the law would allow your marriage; but as she is your sister by the same mother, such a marriage would be abominable."

"I can readily admit," returned the young man, "that it would be a crime at Jerusalem, where I might find other young women, but in the isle of Padrabranca, where I see nothing but coconuts,

pineapples, and oysters, I consider the case to be very allowable."
The Jew accordingly married his sister, and had a daughter by her,
notwithstanding all the protestations of the Essene; and this was
the only offspring of a marriage which one of them thought very
legitimate, and the other absolutely abominable.

After fourteen years, the mother died; and the father said to
the chaplain, "Have you at length got rid of your old prejudices?
Will you marry my daughter?" "God preserve me from it," said
the Essene. "Then," said the father, "I will marry her myself,
come what will of it; for I cannot bear that the seed of Abraham
should be totally annihilated." The Essene, struck with inexpressible horror, would dwell no longer with a man who thus
violated and defiled the law, and fled. The new-married man
loudly called after him, saying, "Stay here, my friend. I am
observing the law of nature, and doing good to my country; do
not abandon your friends." The other suffered him to call and
call, in vain; his head was full of the law; and he did not stop until
he had swum to another island.

This was the large island of Attola, well-populated and
civilized; and as soon as he landed he was made a slave. He complained bitterly of the inhospitable manner in which he had
been received; he was told that such was the law, and that, ever
since the island had been very nearly surprised and taken by the
inhabitants of the island of Ada, it had been wisely enacted that
all strangers landing at Attola should be made slaves. "This cannot be a law," said the Essene, "for it is not in the Pentateuch."
He was told in reply that it was to be found in the digest of the
country, and he remained a slave: fortunately he had a kind and
wealthy master, who treated him very well, and to whom he
became strongly attached.

Some murderers once came to the house to kill his master and
carry off his treasure. They inquired of the slaves if he was at
home, and if he had much money? "We assure you, on our oaths,"

said the slaves, "that he has no money and that he is not at home."
But the Essene said: "The law does not allow lying; I swear to you
that he is at home, and that he has a great deal of money." The
master was, in consequence, robbed and murdered; the slaves
accused the Essene, before the judges, of having betrayed his master. The Essene said that he would not lie, and that nothing in the
world should induce him to lie; and he was hanged.

This story was told to me, along with many similar ones, on
the last voyage I made from India to France. When I had
arrived, I went to Versailles on business and saw a beautiful
woman in the street, followed by several other beautiful women.
"Who is that beautiful woman?" I asked the barrister who had
accompanied me; for I had a case then pending before the
Parliament of Paris about some clothes that I had had made in
India, and I wanted to have my counsel with me as much as possible. "She is the daughter of the king," said he, "she is amiable
and benevolent; it is a great pity that under no circumstances
whatever can such a woman as that become queen of France."
"What!" I replied, "if we had the misfortune, God forbid, to lose
all her relations and the princes of the blood, would not she, in
that case, succeed to the throne of her father?" "No," said the
counselor; "the Salic law expressly forbids it." "And who made
this Salic law?" said I to the counselor. "I do not at all know," said
he; "but they say that among an ancient people called the Salii,
who were unable either to read or write, there existed a written
law according to which in Salic territory a daughter should not
inherit, and this law was then adopted in non-Salic lands." "And
I," said I to him, "I break that law; you assure me that this
princess is amiable and benevolent; she would, therefore have
an incontestable right to the crown, should the calamity occur
of her being the last existing person of royal blood: my mother
inherited from her father; and I am resolved that this princess
shall inherit from hers."

On the ensuing day, my suit was decided in one of the chambers of parliament, and I lost everything by a single vote; my counselor told me, that in another chamber I should have gained everything by a single vote. "That is a very curious circumstance," said I: "at that rate each chamber follows its own law." "That is just the case," said he: "there are twenty-five commentaries on the common law of Paris: that is to say, it is proved five and twenty times over that the common law of Paris is equivocal; and if there had been five and twenty chambers of judges, there would be just as many different systems of jurisprudence. We have a province called Normandy," continued he, "fifteen leagues distant from Paris, where the judgment in your cause would have been very different from what it was here." This statement gave me a strong desire to see Normandy; and I accordingly went there with one of my brothers. At the first inn, we met with a young man in a state of despair. I inquired of him what his misfortune was; he told me it was having an elder brother. "Where," said I, "can be the great calamity of having a brother? The brother I have is my elder, and yet we live very happily together." "Alas! sir," said he to me, "the law of this place gives everything to the elder brother, and of course leaves nothing for the younger ones." "You are right to be angry," I said; "among us everything is divided equally; and still sometimes brothers love each other no more for it."

These little adventures caused me to make some observations, which of course were very ingenious and profound, upon the subject of laws; and I saw that it is with them as it is with our garments: I must wear a doliman at Constantinople, and a coat at Paris.

"If all human laws," said I, "are matters of convention, but the only thing to do is to make a good bargain." The citizens of Delhi and Agra say that they have made a very bad one with Tamerlane: those of London congratulate themselves on having made a very good one with King William of Orange. A citizen of London once said to me: "Laws are made by necessity, and observed through force." I asked him if force did not also occasionally make laws, and if William, the bastard and conqueror, had not chosen simply to issue his orders without condescending to make any convention or bargain with the English at all. "True," said he, "it was so: we were oxen at that time; William brought us under the yoke, and drove us with a goad; since that period we have been metamorphosed into men; the horns, however, remain with us still, and we use them as weapons against every man who attempts making us work for him and not for ourselves."

With my mind full of all these reflections, I could not help feeling a sensible gratification in thinking that there exists a natural law entirely independent of all human conventions: The fruit of my labor ought to be my own: I am bound to honor my father and mother: I have no right over the life of my neighbor, nor has my neighbor over mine, etc. But when I considered, that from Chedorlaomer to Mentzel, colonel of hussars, every one kills and plunders his neighbor according to law, and with a license in his pocket, I was greatly distressed.

I was told that laws existed even among robbers, and that there were laws also in war. I asked what the laws of war were. "They are," said some one, "to hang a brave officer for maintaining a weak post without cannon; to hang a prisoner, if the enemy has hanged any of yours; to ravage with fire and sword those villages which shall not have delivered up their means of subsistence by an appointed day, agreeably to the commands of the gracious sovereign of the region." "Well," said I, "that is the true spirit of laws."[57]

After acquiring a good deal of information, I found that there existed some wise laws, by which a shepherd is condemned to nine years' imprisonment and labor in the galleys for having given his sheep a little foreign salt. My neighbor was ruined by a suit on account of two oaks belonging to him, which he had cut down in his wood, because he had omitted a technicality which he couldn't have known about; as a result, his wife died in misery and his son leads a miserable life. I admit that these laws are just, although their execution is a little severe; but I am no fan of laws that authorize a hundred thousand men to loyally set about cutting the throats of a hundred thousand neighbors. It appears to me that the greater part of mankind have received from nature enough common sense to make laws, but that not everyone has enough justice to make good laws.

Gather together simple, peaceful farmers from every part of the world and they will easily agree that everyone should be free to sell his excess corn to his neighbor, and that every law contrary to it is both inhuman and absurd; that the value of money, being the representative of commodities, ought no more to be tampered with than the produce of the earth; that the father of a family should be master in his own house; that religion should collect men together to unite them and not to make them fanatics and persecutors; and that those who labor ought not to deprive themselves of the fruits of their labor in order to endow superstition and idleness. They could make thirty laws of this sort in the course of an hour, all beneficial to mankind.

But let Tamerlane arrive and subjugate India, and you will then see nothing but arbitrary laws. One will oppress and grind down a whole province, merely to enrich one of Tamerlane's collectors of revenue; another will make it a crime of high treason to speak contemptuously of the mistress of a rajah's chief valet; a third will extort half of his harvest from the farmer, and dispute with him the right to the remainder; in short, there will be laws by which a Tartar sergeant will be authorized to seize your children in the cradle and make the sturdy one a soldier and the weak one a eunuch—and thus to leave the father and mother without assistance and without consolation.

But which would be preferable, being Tamerlane's dog or his subject? It is evident that the condition of his dog would be by far superior.

LOIS CIVILES ET ECCLÉSIASTIQUES / CIVIL AND ECCLESIASTICAL LAWS

THE following notes were found among the papers of a lawyer, and are perhaps deserving some consideration:

That no ecclesiastical law should be of any force without the express sanction of government. It was in this way that Athens and Rome were never involved in religious quarrels. These quarrels fall to the lot of those nations not yet civilized, or again reduced to barbarism.

That the magistrate alone should have authority to permit or prohibit work on festival days, because it is not the role of priests to forbid men to cultivate their fields.

That everything relating to marriages depends solely upon the magistrate, and that the priests should be confined to the august function of blessing them.

That lending money at interest is purely an object of civil law, as it alone presides over commerce.

That all ecclesiastical persons should be in all cases under the control of the government because they are subjects of the state.

That men should never be so disgracefully ridiculous as to pay to a foreign priest the first year's revenue of an estate conferred by citizens upon a priest who is their fellow citizen.

That no priest should have the authority to deprive a citizen of even the smallest of his rights, under the pretext that the citizen is a sinner; because the priest, himself a sinner, ought to pray for sinners and not to judge them.

That magistrates, laborers, and priests should contribute equally to the expenses of the state, because all belong equally to the state.

That there should be only one system of weights and measures, and usages.

That the punishment of criminals should be rendered useful. A hanged man is no longer useful; but a man condemned to the public works is still useful to his country, and serves as a living lesson.

That every law should be clear, uniform, and precise. Interpretation leads almost inevitably to corruption. That nothing should be held infamous but vice.

That taxes should be imposed always in just proportion.

That law should never be in contradiction to custom; for, if the custom is good, the law is worth nothing. (See "Poem on Natural Law")[58]

Luxe / Luxury

Luxury has been denounced for two thousand years, both in verse and prose; and yet it has been always liked.

What has not been said of the Romans? When these bandits ravaged and carried off their neighbor's harvests; when, in order to augment their own wretched village, they destroyed the poor villages of the Volsci and Samnites, they were men disinterested and virtuous. They could not as yet carry away gold, silver, or jewels because the towns which they sacked and plundered had none; nor did their woods and swamps produce partridges or pheasants; yet people extol their temperance.

When, from one to the next, they had pillaged and robbed every country from the recesses of the Adriatic to the Euphrates, and had sense enough to enjoy the spoils for seven or eight years; when they cultivated all the arts and tasted all the pleasures of life, and then even communicated them to the conquered nations; then, we are told, they ceased to be wise and good.

All such declamations tend just to prove this—that a robber ought not to eat the dinner he has taken, nor wear the habit he has stolen, nor wear the ring he has plundered from another. They say that in order to live like good people all this should be thrown into the river; say rather one should not steal in the first place. Condemn the brigands when they plunder; but do not treat them as fools or madmen for enjoying their plunder.* [59] In good faith, when a number of English sailors have obtained their prize money for the capture of Pondicherry, or Havana, can they be blamed for purchasing a little pleasure in London, in return for the labor and pain they have suffered in the uncongenial climes of Asia or America?

Do these critics really think men should bury the riches that might be accumulated by the fortune of war, or by agriculture, commerce, and industry in general? They cite Lacedæmon; why do they not also cite the republic of San Marino? What benefit did Sparta do to Greece? Had she ever a Demosthenes, a Sophocles, an Apelles, or a Phidias? The luxury of Athens formed great men of every description. Sparta had certainly some great captains, and even those in smaller number than other cities. But allowing that a small republic like Lacedæmon may maintain its poverty, men uniformly die, whether they are in want of everything or enjoying the various means of rendering life agreeable. The savage of Canada subsists and attains old age as well as the English citizen who has fifty thousand guineas a year. But who will ever compare the country of the Iroquois to England?

---

* The poor idiot whom we have previously quoted, having read this passage in a bad edition where there was a period after the words "*good faith,*" believed that the author meant to say that thieves enjoyed their plunder in good faith. We are quite aware that this poor idiot is mean, but, in good faith, he is incapable of being dangerous.

Let the republic of Ragusa and the canton of Zug enact sumptuary laws; they are right to do so, for the poor must not spend beyond their means; but I read somewhere, "Know above all that luxury makes the large state rich, even as it bankrupts a small one:"

> *Sachez surtout que le luxe enrichit*
> *Un grand Etat, s'il en perd un petit.*[60]

If by luxury you mean excess, we know that excess is universally pernicious in abstinence as well as gluttony, in parsimony or generosity. I do not know how it happened, that in those of my own villages where the soil is poor and meager, the taxes heavy, and the prohibition against a man's exporting the corn he himself has sown and reaped intolerable, there is hardly a single colonist who is not well clothed, well shod and well fed.[61] Should this colonist go to plow in his best clothes and with his hair dressed and powdered, there would in that case exist the greatest and most absurd luxury; but were a wealthy citizen of Paris or London to appear at the play in the dress of this peasant, he would exhibit the grossest and most ridiculous parsimony.

> *Est modus in rebus, sunt certi denique fines,*
> *Quos ultra citraque nequit consistere rectum.*
> —HORACE, I Sat. i. v. 106
> *Some certain mean in all things may be found,*
> *To mark our virtues, and our vices, bound.*
> —FRANCIS

When scissors were invented, which are certainly not so far off in antiquity, what criticism was not made of those who pared their nails and cut off some of the hair that hung down over their noses? They were undoubtedly considered prodigals and dandies, who bought at an extravagant price a vain instrument just to spoil the work of the Creator. What an enormous sin to pare the horn which God Himself made to grow at our fingers' ends! It was absolutely an insult to the Divine Being Himself. When shirts and socks were invented, it was even worse. It is well known with what wrath and indignation the old counselors, who had never worn socks, exclaimed against the young magistrates who encouraged so dreadful and fatal a luxury.

MAÎTRE / MASTER

How can one man become the master of another? And by what kind of incomprehensible magic has he been able to become the master of several other men? A great number of good volumes have been written on this subject, but I give the preference to an Indian fable, because it is short, and fables explain everything.

Adimo, the father of all the Indians, had two sons and two daughters with his wife Pocriti. The eldest was a vigorous giant, the youngest was a little hunchback, and the two girls were pretty. As soon as the giant was of an age, he lay with his two sisters, and caused the little hunchback to serve him. Of his two sisters, the one was his cook, the other his gardener. When the giant wanted to sleep, he began by chaining his little brother to a tree; and when the latter fled from him, he caught him in four strides, and gave him twenty lashes with a bullwhip.

The dwarf became submissive and the best subject in the world. The giant, satisfied with seeing him fulfill his duties as a subject, permitted him to sleep with one of his sisters that he was tired of. The children who sprang from this marriage were not quite hunchbacks, but they were still somewhat deformed. They were brought up in the fear of God and of the giant. They received an excellent education; they were taught that their uncle was a giant by divine right—that he could do what he pleased with his entire family; that if he had some pretty niece or grand-niece, he should have her without difficulty, and no one else could sleep with her until he no longer wished to himself.

The giant dying, his son, who was neither as strong or as large, believed himself to be like his father, a giant by divine right. He purported to make all the men work for him, and all the girls sleep with him. The family leagued against him: he was killed, and they became a republic.

The Siamese pretend, that on the contrary the family started out by being republican; and that the giant only came along after a great many years and dissensions: but all the authors of Benares and Siam agree that men lived an infinity of ages before they had the wit to make laws, and they prove it by an unanswerable argument, which is that even at present, when all the world prides itself on its wit, we have not yet found the means of making a score of passably good laws.

It is still, for example, an insoluble question in India, whether republics were established before or after monarchies; if confusion appeared more horrible to men than despotism. I do not know what happened in the order of time, but in that of nature we must agree that men are all born equal: violence and ability made the first masters; laws have made the most recent.

MARTYRE / MARTYRDOM

WE are fooled with martyrs who make us break out into laughter. The Tituses, the Trajans, the Marcus Aureliuses, all models of virtue, are painted as monsters of cruelty. Fleury, Abbé of Loc Dieu, has disgraced his ecclesiastical history by tales which a sensible old woman would not tell to little children.

Can it be seriously repeated that the Romans condemned seven virgins, each seventy years old, to pass through the hands of all the young men of the city of Ancyra—those Romans who punished the Vestals with death for the least gallantry?

For the entertainment of innkeepers, someone invented the story of a Christian innkeeper named Theodotus asked God to kill these seven virgins rather than put them at risk of losing their antique virginities. God answered the prayers of the bashful innkeeper and the proconsul had the seven maids drowned in a lake. As soon as they were drowned, they came back to Theodotus to complain about the bad turn he had done them, and begged him on the spot to at least prevent them from being eaten by the fishes. Theodotus took three drunks from his tavern with him to the lake, preceded by a celestial flame and a celestial knight, fished out the seven old women, buried them and was eventually hanged.

Diocletian meets a little boy named St Romain, who stuttered; he wants to have him burned because he is a Christian; three Jews who happened to be passing by began to laugh at the idea that Jesus Christ would let a little boy belonging to him be burned. They cried out that their religion was obviously better than the Christian religion, since God delivered Sidrac, Mizac and Abdenago from the fiery inferno. No sooner had they said it than the flames that surrounded the young Roman without hurting him parted to burn the three Jews.

Quite surprised, the emperor declared that he didn't want to argue with God, but an unscrupulous village judge condemned the little stutterer to have his tongue cut out. The emperor's chief doctor was honest enough to perform the operation himself; once he had cut the little Roman boy's tongue out, the child began suddenly to chatter with a volubility that delighted the entire assembly.

A hundred tales of this sort are found in the martyrologies. We meant to render the ancient Romans odious, and instead we have rendered ourselves ridiculous. Do you want some good, well-authenticated barbarities—a good, well-documented massacre, rivers of blood which have actually flowed—fathers, mothers, husbands, wives, infants at the breast, who have in fact had their throats cut and been heaped on one another? Persecuting monsters! Seek these truths in your own annals: you will find them in the crusades against the Albigenses, in the massacres of Merindol and Cabrière, in the horrific day of St. Bartholomew, in the massacres of Ireland, in the valleys of the Pays de Vaud. It becomes you well, barbarians as you are, to impute extravagant cruelties to the best of emperors; you who have deluged Europe with blood and covered it with dying corpses in order to prove that the same body can be in a thousand places at once, and that the pope can sell indulgences! Cease to calumniate the Romans, your law-givers, and ask pardon of God for the abominations of your forefathers.

It is not the torture, you say, which makes a martyr; it is the cause. Well! I agree with you that your victims ought not to be designated by the name of martyr, which signifies witness; but what name shall we give to your executioners? The Phalaris and the Busiris were the gentlest of men in comparison with you. Does not your Inquisition, which still persists, make reason, nature, and religion shudder? Great God! If mankind should reduce that infernal tribunal to ashes, would they be unacceptable in your avenging eyes?

MATIÈRE / MATTER

WHEN wise men are asked what the soul is, they answer that they know not. If they are asked what matter is, they make the same reply. It is true that there are professors, and particularly scholars, who know all this perfectly; and when they have repeated that matter has extent and divisibility, they think they have said it all; being pressed, however, to say what this thing is that is extended, they find themselves somewhat embarrassed. It is composed of parts, they say. And what are these parts composed of? Are the elements of the parts divisible? Then they are mute, or they talk a great deal; which are equally suspicious. Is this almost unknown being called matter eternal? Such was the belief of all antiquity. Has it of itself force? Many philosophers have thought so. Have those who deny it a right to deny it? You do not conceive that matter can have anything in itself; but how can you be assured that it has not of itself the properties necessary to it? You are ignorant of its nature, and you refuse it the modes which nevertheless are in its nature: for it can no sooner have been, than it has been in a certain fashion—it has had shape, and having necessarily shape, is it impossible that it should not have had other modes attached to its configuration? Matter exists, but you know it only by your sensations. Alas! To what avail have all the subtleties of the mind been since man first reasoned? Geometry has taught us many truths, metaphysics very few. We weigh matter, we measure it, we decompose it; and if we seek to advance one step beyond these crude operations, we turn inward to find ourselves powerless, and outward to see before us an immeasurable abyss.

Pray forgive all mankind who were deceived in thinking that matter existed by itself. Could they do otherwise? How are we to imagine that what is without succession has not always been? If it were not necessary for matter to exist, why should it exist? And if it were necessary that it should be, why should it not have been forever? No axiom has ever been more universally received than this: "Nothing comes from nothing." Indeed the contrary is incomprehensible. With every nation, chaos preceded the arrangement which a divine hand made of the whole world. The eternity of matter has with no people been injurious to the worship of the Divinity. Religion was never startled at the recognition of an eternal God as the master of an eternal matter. We of the present day are so fortunate as to know by faith that God brought matter out of nothing; but no nation has ever been instructed in this dogma;

even the Jews were ignorant of it. The first verse of Genesis says, that the gods—*Eloïm*, not *Eloi*—made heaven and earth. It does not say that heaven and earth were created out of nothing.

Philo, who lived at the only time when the Jews had any erudition, says, in his chapter on the creation, "God, being good by nature, bore no envy against substance, matter; which of itself had nothing good, having by nature only inertness, confusion, and disorder. It was bad, and He deigned to make it good."

The idea of chaos put into order by a God is to be found in all ancient theogonies. Hesiod repeated the opinion of the Orientals, when he said in his *Theogony*, "Chaos was that which first existed." The whole Roman Empire spoke in these words of Ovid: "*Sic ubi dispositam quisquis fuit ille Deorum Congeriem secuit.*"

Matter then, in the hands of God, was considered like clay under the potter's wheel, if these feeble images may be used to express His divine power.

Matter, being eternal, must have had eternal properties, such as configuration, the force of inertia, motion, and divisibility. But this divisibility is only a consequence of motion; for without motion nothing is divided, nor separated, nor arranged. Motion therefore was regarded as essential to matter. Chaos had been a confused motion, and the arrangement of the universe a regular motion, communicated to all bodies by the Master of the world. But how can matter have motion by itself, as it has, according to all the ancients, extent and divisibility?

But it cannot be conceived to be without extent, and it may be conceived to be without motion? To this it was answered: It is impossible that matter should not be permeable; and being permeable, something must be continually passing through its pores. Why should there be passages, if nothing passes?

Reply and rejoinder might thus be continued forever. Like all other systems, the system of the eternity of matter has very great difficulties. That of the formation of matter out of nothing is no

less incomprehensible. We must admit it, and not flatter ourselves
with accounting for it; philosophy does not account for everything. How many incomprehensible things are we not obliged to
admit, even in geometry! Can any one conceive two lines constantly approaching each other, yet never meeting?

Geometricians indeed will tell you, the properties of asymp-
totes are demonstrated; you cannot help admitting them—but
creation is not; why then admit it? Why is it hard for you to believe,
like all the ancients, in the eternity of matter? The theologian will
press you on the other side, and say: "If you believe in the eternity
of matter then you acknowledge two principles—God and
matter—you fall into the error of Zoroaster and of Manes."

No answer can be given to the geometricians, for those folks
know of nothing but their lines, their superficies, and their
solids; but you may say to the theologians: "In what way am I a
Manichaean? Here are stones, which an architect has not made,
but of which he has erected an immense building. I do not admit
two architects; the rough stones have obeyed power and genius."

Happily, whatever system a man embraces, it is in no way hurt-
ful to morality; for what imports it whether matter is made or
arranged? God is still our absolute master. Whether chaos was created out of nothing, or only reduced to order, it is still our duty to
be virtuous; scarcely any of these metaphysical questions affect the
conduct of life. It is with such disputes as with table talk; each one
forgets after dinner what he has said, and goes wherever his interest or inclination calls him.

MÉCHANT / WICKED

WE are told that human nature is essentially perverse; that man
is born a child of the devil, and wicked. Nothing can be more
injudicious; for you, my friend, who preach to me that all the
world is born perverse, warn me that you are also born such, and

that I must mistrust you as I would a fox or a crocodile. Oh, no! you say; I am regenerated; I am neither a heretic nor an infidel; you may trust me. But the rest of mankind, which are either heretic, or what you call infidel, will be an assemblage of monsters, and every time that you speak to a Lutheran or a Turk, you may be sure that they will rob and murder you, for they are children of the devil, they are born wicked; the one is not regenerated, the other is degenerated. It would be much more reasonable, much nobler, to say to men: "You are all born good; see how dreadful it would be to corrupt the purity of your being." All mankind should be dealt with as are all men individually. If a canon leads a scandalous life, we say to him: "Is it possible that you would dishonor the dignity of canon?" We remind a lawyer that he has the honor of being a counselor to the king, and that he should set an example. We say to a soldier to encourage him: "Remember that you are of the regiment of Champagne." We should say to every individual: "Remember your dignity as a man."

And indeed, notwithstanding the contrary theory, we always return to that; for what else signifies the expression, so frequently used in all nations: "Be yourself again?" If we are born of the devil, if our origin was criminal, if our blood was formed of infernal liquor, this expression: "Be yourself again," would signify: "Consult, follow your diabolical nature; be an impostor, thief, and assassin; it is the law of your nature."

Man is not born wicked; he becomes so, as he becomes sick. Physicians present themselves and say to him: "You are born sick." It is very certain these doctors, whatever they may say or do, will not cure him, if the malady is inherent in his nature; besides, these reasoners are often very ill in their own right.

Assemble all the children of the universe; you will see in them only innocence, mildness, and fear; if they were born wicked, mischievous, and cruel, they would show some signs of it, as little serpents try to bite, and little tigers to tear. But nature not having given to men more offensive arms than to pigeons and rabbits, she cannot have given them an instinct that leads them to destroy. Man, therefore, is not born bad; why, therefore, are several infected with the plague of wickedness? It is because those who lead them, being taken with the malady, they communicate it to the rest of men: just as a woman who has been attacked with the disease Christopher Columbus brought from America spreads the poison from one end of Europe to the other. The first ambitious man corrupted the earth.

You will tell me that this first monster has sowed the seeds of pride, plunder, fraud, and cruelty, which are in all men. I confess that in general most of our brethren can acquire these qualities; but does everyone have putrid fever or kidney stones though everyone is exposed to it?

There are whole nations which are not wicked: the Philadelphians, the Banians, have never killed any one. The Chinese, the people of Tonquin, Lao, Siam, and even Japan, have not known war for more than a hundred years. In ten years we scarcely see one of those great crimes which astonish human nature in the cities of Rome, Venice, Paris, London, and Amsterdam; towns in which cupidity, the mother of all crimes, is nonetheless extreme.

If men were essentially wicked—if they were all born submissive to a being as mischievous as unfortunate, who, to revenge himself for his suffering, inspired them with all his mad rages— we should every morning see husbands assassinated by their wives, and fathers by their children; as at break of day we see fowls strangled by a weasel who comes to suck their blood.

If there be a thousand million men on the earth, that is a great many; that makes about five hundred million of women, who sew, spin, nourish their little ones, keep their houses or cabins in order, and slander their neighbors a little. I see not what great harm these poor innocents do on earth. Of this number of inhabitants of the globe, there are at least two hundred million children, who certainly neither kill nor steal, and about as many old people and invalids, who have not the power of doing so. That leaves at most a hundred million robust young people capable of crime. Of this hundred million, there are ninety continually occupied in forcing the earth, by prodigious labor, to furnish them with food and clothing; these hardly have time to do ill.

The ten million remaining will include idle people and good company, who would enjoy themselves at their ease; men of talent occupied in their professions; magistrates, priests, visibly interested in leading a pure life, at least in appearance. Therefore, of truly wicked people, there will only remain a few politicians, either secular or regular, who are always looking to disrupt the world, and some thousand vagabonds who hire their services to these politicians. Now, there are never a million of these ferocious beasts at work at the same time, and in this number I reckon highwaymen. You have therefore on the earth, in the most stormy times, only one man in a thousand whom we can call wicked, and even he is not always so.

There is, therefore, infinitely less wickedness on the earth than we are told and believe there is. There is still too much, no doubt; we see misfortunes and horrible crimes; but the pleasure of complaining of and exaggerating them is so great that at the least scratch we say that the earth flows with blood. Have you been deceived?—all men are perjurers. A melancholy mind, which has suffered injustice, sees the earth covered with the damned, just as a young rake, dining with his lady after the opera, imagines that there are no unfortunates.

MESSIE / MESSIAH

MESSIAH or *Messias* in Hebrew; *Christus* or *Eleimmenos* in Greek; or in Latin *Unctus* or *Oint.*

In the Old Testament we see that the word "Messiah" was often given to idolatrous kings and princes. It is said (II Kgs 8:12–14) that God sent a prophet to anoint Jehu, king of Israel, and announced sacred unction to Hazael, king of Damascus and Syria; those two princes being the Messiahs of the Most High, to revenge the crimes and abominations of the house of Ahab.

But in Isaiah, 45:1, the name of Messiah is expressly given to Cyrus: "Thus saith the Lord to Cyrus, His anointed, His Messiah, whose right hand I have taken that I might subdue nations before him." etc.

Ezekiel, in the twenty-eighth chapter of his revelations, gives the name of Messiah to the king of Tyre, whom he also calls Cherubim. "Son of man," says the Eternal to the prophet, "take up a lamentation upon the king of Tyre, and say unto him, Thus said the Lord God; You were the seal of God's likeness, full of wisdom, and perfect in beauty. You have been the Lord's Garden of Eden" (or, according to other versions, "You were all the Lord's delight.") "Your clothes were made of sardius, topaz, and diamond; beryl, onyx, and jasper; sapphire, emerald, carbuncle, and gold: the workmanship of your drums and pipes was already prepared in you the day you were created. You were Cherubim, a Messiah.

This name of *Messiah, Christ,* was given to the kings, prophets, and high priests of the Hebrews. We read, in I Kings, 12:5: "The Lord and his Messiah are witness"; that is, the Lord and the king whom he has set up. And elsewhere: "Touch not my Anointed; do not hurt my prophets. . . . ." David, animated by the Spirit of God, repeatedly gives his father-in-law Saul, whom he had no cause to love—the name and title of Anointed, or Messiah of the Lord. "God preserve me," he says frequently, "from laying my hand upon the Lord's Anointed, upon God's Messiah."

Herod, being anointed, was called *Messiah* by his followers, who for a while formed a small sect of their own.

If the fine title of Messiah, or Anointed of the Eternal, was given to idolatrous kings, to cruel and tyrannical princes, it has very often been used in our ancient oracles to designate the real Anointed of the Lord, the quintessential Messiah, Christ, son of God, in fact God Himself.

If we compare all these different oracles ordinarily applied to the Messiah, a few obvious and almost irreconcilable contradictions result, which the Jews have prevailed upon in order to justify, if this is possible, their obstinacy. A number of great theologians acknowledge that in the state of oppression under which the Jewish people were groaning, and after all the glorious promises which the Eternal had so often made them, they must have longed for the coming of a victorious Messiah who would liberate them, and that they are therefore to an extent excusable for not having recognized this liberator in the person of the Lord Jesus, even more so given that there is not a single passage in the Old Testament that says "Believe in the Messiah."

It was written in the divine plan that the spiritual ideas of the true Messiah be unknown to the blind multitude; indeed, they were unknown to such a degree that the Jewish scholars decided to deny that the passages which we claim must be understood as concerning the Messiah. Some of them maintain that their oracles have been misunderstood; that it is in vain to long for the coming of a Messiah, since He has already come in the person of Ezechias. Such was the opinion of the famous Hillel. A great many others assert that the belief in the coming of a Messiah is not a fundamental article of faith, and that as this dogma is not found either in the commandments or in Leviticus it is nothing more than a consolatory hope.

Some rabbis will tell you that they do not doubt that the Messiah came at the time indicated, as it is written in the ancient oracles, but that he did not age and remains hidden here on earth, waiting to come forth until such a time as Israel will properly honor the Sabbath.

The celebrated rabbi, Solomon Jarchi or Raschi who lived at the beginning of the twelfth century, says, in his *Talmudes* that the ancient Hebrews believed the Messiah to have been born on the day of the last destruction of Jerusalem by the Roman armies. This is indeed calling in the physician when the man is dead.

The rabbi Kimchi, who also lived in the twelfth century, announced that the Messiah, whose coming he believed to be very near, would drive the Christians out of Judea, which was then in their possession; and it is true that the Christians lost the Holy Land; but it was Saladin who vanquished them. Had that conqueror but protected the Jews, and declared for them, it is not unlikely that in their enthusiasm they would have made him their Messiah.

Sacred writers, and our Lord Jesus Himself, often compare the reign of the Messiah and eternal beatitude to a nuptial festival or a banquet; but the Talmudists have strangely abused these parables; according to them, the Messiah will give to his people, assembled in the land of Canaan, a repast in which the wine will be that which was made by Adam himself in the terrestrial paradise, and which is kept dry, in vast cellars, by the angels at the center of the earth.

At the first course will be served up the famous fish called the great Leviathan, which swallows up at once a smaller fish, which smaller fish is nevertheless three hundred leagues long; the whole mass of the waters is carried upon Leviathan. In the beginning God created a male and a female of this fish; but lest they should overturn the land, and fill the universe with their kind, God killed the female and salted her for the Messiah's feast.

The rabbis add that the bull Behemoth, who is so large that he eats the hay from a thousand mountains every day, will also be killed for this repast. The female of this bull was killed in the beginning of the world, to prevent so prodigious a species from multiplying, since this could only have injured the other creatures; but they assure us that the Eternal did not salt her, because dried cow is not as good as she-Leviathan. The Jews still put such faith in these rabbinical reveries that they often swear by their share of the bull Behemoth, as some impious Christians swear by their portion of the bull Behemoth.

After such gross ideas of the coming of the Messiah, and of His reign, is it astonishing that the Jews, ancient as well as modern, and also some of the primitive Christians unhappily tinctured with all these reveries, could not elevate themselves to the idea of the divine nature of the Lord's Anointed, and did not consider the Messiah as God? Observe how the Jews express themselves on this point in the work entitled *Judæi Lusitani Quæstiones ad Christianos* (Quaest. 1, 2, 4, 23, etc.). "To acknowledge a God-man," say they, "is to abuse your own reason, to make to yourself a monster—a centaur—the strange compound of two natures which cannot coalesce." They add that the prophets do not teach that the Messiah is God-man; that they expressly distinguish between God and David, declaring the former to be Master and the latter servant.

It is well enough known that the Jews, slaves to the literal sense of text as they are, have never been able to penetrate the true meaning of scripture the way we have.

When the Savior appeared, Jewish prejudice rose up against him. Jesus Christ Himself, in order to not rouse their blind thinking, seems to have been very reserved concerning His divinity. "He wished," says St. Chrysostom, "insensibly to accustom His auditors to the belief of a mystery so far above their reason." If He takes upon Him the authority of a God, by pardoning sin, this action raises up against Him all who are witnesses of it. His most evident miracles cannot even convince of His divinity even those in whose favor they are worked. When, before the tribunal of the Sovereign Sacrificer, He acknowledges, by a modest intimation, that He is the Son of God, the high priest tears his robe and cries,

'Blasphemy!' Before the sending of the Holy Ghost, even the apostles did not suspect the divinity of their dear Master. He asks them what the people think of Him; and they answer, that some take Him for Elias, other for Jeremiah, or some other prophet. St Peter needed an individual revelation in order to recognize that Jesus is the Christ, the Son of the living God."

The Jews, revolting against the divinity of Christ, have resorted to all sorts of expedients to destroy this great mystery; they distort the meaning of their own oracles, or do not apply them to the Messiah; they assert that the name of God, "*Eloi*," is not peculiar to the Divinity, but is given, even by sacred writers, to judges, to magistrates, and in general to such as are high in authority; in fact they cite a great many passages of the Holy Scriptures that justify this observation, but which do not in the least affect the express terms of the ancient oracles concerning the Messiah.

Lastly, they assert that if the Savior, and after Him the evangelists, the apostles, and the first Christians, call Jesus the Son of God, this august term did not in evangelical times signify anything but the opposite of son of Belial—that is, a good man, a servant of God, in opposition to a wicked man, one without the fear of God.

If the Jews have disputed with Jesus Christ His quality of Messiah and His divinity, they have missed no opportunity to make him contemptible, to cast all the ridicule and opprobrium that their criminal malevolence could imagine on His birth, His life, and His death.

Of all the works which the blindness of the Jews has produced, there is none more odious and more extravagant than the ancient book entitled *Sepher Toldos Jeschu*, brought to light by Wagenseil, in the second volume of his work entitled *Tela Ignea*, etc.

In this *Sepher Toldos Jeschu*, we find a monstrous history of the life of our Savior, forged with the utmost passion and disingenuousness. For instance, they have dared to write that one Panther, or Pandera, an inhabitant of Bethlehem, fell in love with a young woman married to Jokanam. By this impure commerce he had a son called Jesua or Jesu. The father of this child was obliged to fly, and retired to Babylon. As for young Jesu, he was sent to the schools; but—adds our author—he had the insolence to raise his head and uncover himself before the sacrificers, instead of appearing before them with his head bent down and his face covered, as was the custom—a piece of effrontery which was warmly rebuked; this caused his birth to be inquired into, which was found to be impure, and soon exposed him to ignominy.

This detestable book, *Sepher Toldos Jeschu*, was known in the second century: Celsus confidently cites it and Origen refutes it in his ninth chapter.

There is another book also entitled *Toledos Jeschu*, published by Huldric in 1705, which more closely follows the "Gospel of the Infancy," but which is full of the grossest anachronisms. It places both the birth and death of Jesus Christ in the reign of Herod the Great, stating that complaints were made of the adultery of Panther and Mary, the mother of Jesus, to that prince.

The author, who takes the name of Jonathan, and calls himself a contemporary of Jesus Christ, living at Jerusalem, pretends that Herod consulted, in the affair of Jesus Christ, the senators of a city in the land of Cæsarea. We will not follow so absurd an author through all his contradictions.

Yet it is under cover of all these calumnies that the Jews keep up their implacable hatred against the Christians and the gospel. They have done their utmost to alter the chronology of the Old Testament, and to raise doubts and difficulties respecting the time of our Savior's coming.

Ahmed-ben-Cassum-la-Andacousy, a Moor of Granada, who lived about the close of the sixteenth century, cites an ancient Arabian manuscript, which was found, together with sixteen plates of lead engraved with Arabian characters, in a grotto near Granada. Don Pedro y Quinones, archbishop of Granada, has himself borne testimony to this fact. These leaden plates, called the plates of Granada, were afterwards carried to Rome, where, after several years' investigation, they were at last condemned as apocryphal, during the pontificate of Alexander VII; they contain only fabulous stories relating to the lives of Mary and her Son.

The name of Messiah, coupled with the epithet "false," is still given to those impostors who, at various times, have sought to abuse the credulity of the Jewish nation. There were some of these false Messiahs even before the coming of the true Anointed of God. The wise Gamaliel mentions (Acts 5:34–36) one Theodas, whose history we read in Josephus' *Jewish Antiquities*, book 20, chapter 2. He boasted of crossing the Jordan without wetting his feet; he drew many people after him; but the Romans, having fallen upon his little troop, dispersed them, cut off the head of their unfortunate chief, and exposed it in Jerusalem.

Gamaliel also speaks of Judas the Galilean, who is doubtless the same of whom Josephus makes mention in the second chapter of the second book of the "Jewish War." He says that this false prophet had gathered together nearly thirty thousand men; but hyperbole is characteristic of the Jewish historian.

In the apostolic times, there was Simon, surnamed the Magician (Acts 8-9), who contrived to bewitch the people of Samaria, so that they considered him as "the great power of God."

In the following century, in the years 178 and 179 of the Christian era, in the reign of Adrian, the false Messiah Barcochebas appeared at the head of an army. The emperor sent Julius Severus against them, who, after several encounters, enclosed them in the town of Bither; after an obstinate defense it was carried, and Barcochebas taken and put to death. Adrian thought he could not better prevent the continual revolt of the

Jews than by issuing an edict, forbidding them to go to Jerusalem; he also had guards stationed at the gates of the city, to prevent the rest of the people of Israel from entering it.

We read in Socrates, an ecclesiastical historian, (Hist. eccl. 2.38) that in the year 434, there appeared in the island of Candia a false Messiah calling himself Moses. He claimed he was the ancient deliverer of the Hebrews, raised from the dead to deliver them again.

A century afterwards, in 530, there was in Palestine a false Messiah named Julian; he announced himself as a great conqueror, who, at the head of his nation, would destroy by arms the whole Christian people. Seduced by his promises, the armed Jews butchered a number of Christians. The emperor Justinian sent troops against him; battle was given to the false Christ; he was taken, and condemned to be tortured to death.

At the beginning of the eighth century, Serenus, a Spanish Jew, gave himself out as a Messiah, preached, had some disciples, and, like them, died in misery.

Several false Messiahs arose in the twelfth century. One appeared in France in the reign of Louis the Young; he and all his adherents were hanged without the name of the master or of the disciples ever being known.

The thirteenth century was fruitful in false Messiahs; there appeared seven or eight in Arabia, Persia, Spain, and Moravia; one of them, calling himself David el Roy, passed for a very great magician; he seduced the Jews, and found himself at the head of a considerable party; but this Messiah was assassinated.

James Zeigler, of Moravia, who lived in the middle of the sixteenth century, announced the approaching manifestation of the Messiah, born, as he declared, fourteen years before; he had seen him, he said, at Strasburg, and he kept for him with great care a sword and a scepter, to place them in his hands as soon as he should be old enough to teach.

In the year 1624, another Zeigler confirmed the prediction of the former.

In the year 1666, Sabatei Sevi, born at Aleppo, called himself the Messiah foretold by the Zeiglers. He began with preaching on the highways and in the fields, the Turks laughed at him while his disciples admired him. It appears that he did not at first gain over the mass of the Jewish nation; for the heads of the synagogue at Smyrna passed sentence of death against him; but he escaped with the fear only, and with banishment.

He contracted three marriages, of which it is asserted he did not consummate a one, saying that it was beneath him so to do. He took into partnership one Nathan Levi; the latter played the role of the prophet Elias, who was to precede the Messiah. They repaired to Jerusalem, and Nathan there announced Sabatei Sevi as the deliverer of nations. The Jewish populace declared for them, but those who had anything to lose anathematized them.

To avoid the storm, Sevi fled to Constantinople, and thence to Smyrna, where Nathan Levi sent four ambassadors to him, who acknowledged and publicly saluted him as the Messiah. This embassy imposed on the people, and also on some of the doctors, who declared Sabatei Sevi to be the Messiah, and king of the Hebrews. But the synagogue of Smyrna condemned its king to be impaled.

Sabatei put himself under the protection of the cadi of Smyrna, and soon had the whole Jewish people on his side; he had two thrones prepared, one for himself, the other for his favorite wife; he took the title King of Kings and gave his brother, Joseph Sevi, that of King of Judah. He promised the Jews the certain conquest of the Ottoman Empire; and even carried his insolence so far as to have the emperor's name struck out of the Jewish liturgy, and his own substituted.

He was thrown into prison at the Dardanelles; and the Jews gave out that his life was spared only because the Turks well knew he was immortal. The governor of the Dardanelles grew rich by the presents which the Jews lavished on him in order to visit their king, their imprisoned Messiah, who, though in irons, retained all his dignity, and made them kiss his feet.

Meanwhile the sultan, who was holding his court at Adrianople, resolved to put an end to this farce: he sent for Sevi, and told him that if he was the Messiah he must be invulnerable; to which Sevi assented. The grand signor then had him placed as a mark for the arrows of his *icoglans*. The Messiah confessed that he was not invulnerable, and protested that God sent him only to bear testimony to the holy Mussulman religion. Being beaten by the ministers of the law, he turned Mohammedan; he lived and died equally despised by the Jews and Muslims; which cast such discredit on the profession of false Messiah that Sevi was the last that appeared.

MÉTAMORPHOSE, MÉTEMPYSCOSE / METAMORPHOSIS, METEMPSYCOSIS

IT may very naturally be supposed that the metamorphoses with which our earth abounds suggested the imagination to the Orientals—who have imagined everything—that the souls of men passed from one body to another. An almost imperceptible point becomes a grub, and that grub becomes a butterfly; an acorn is transformed into an oak; an egg into a bird; water becomes cloud and thunder; wood is changed into fire and ashes; everything, in short, in nature, appears to be metamorphosed. What was thus obviously and distinctly perceptible in grosser bodies was soon conceived to take place with respect to souls, which were considered slight, shadowy, and scarcely material figures. The idea of metempsychosis is perhaps the most ancient dogma of the known world, and prevails still in a great part of India and of China.

It is highly probable, again, that the various metamorphoses which we witness in nature produced those ancient fables which Ovid has collected in his admirable work. Even the Jews had their metamorphoses. If Niobe was changed into a stone, Edith, the wife of Lot, was changed into a statue of salt. If Eurydice remained in hell for having looked behind her, it was for precisely the same indiscretion that Lot's wife was deprived of her human nature. The village in which Baucis and Philemon resided in Phrygia is changed into a lake; the same thing happens to Sodom. The daughters of Anius converted water into oil; we have in Scripture a metamorphosis very similar, but more true and more sacred. Cadmus was changed into a serpent; the rod of Aaron becomes a serpent also.

The gods frequently change themselves into men; the Jews never saw angels but in the form of men; angels ate with Abraham. Paul, in his Second Epistle to the Corinthians, says that an angel of Satan has slapped him: "*Angelus Satanæ me colaphizet.*"

MIRACLES / MIRACLES

A miracle, according to the true meaning of the word, is something admirable; in which case, all is miracle. The stupendous order of nature, the revolution of a hundred millions of worlds around a million of suns, the activity of light, the life of animals, all are grand and perpetual miracles.

According to common acceptation, we call a miracle the violation of these divine and eternal laws. A solar eclipse at the time of the full moon, or a dead man walking two leagues and carrying his head in his arms, we call that a miracle.

Many natural philosophers maintain, that in this sense there are no miracles; and advance the following arguments:

A miracle is the violation of mathematical, divine, immutable, eternal laws. By the very exposition itself, a miracle is a contradiction in terms: a law cannot at the same time be immutable and violated. But they are asked, cannot a law, established by God Himself, be suspended by its author? They have the hardihood to reply that it cannot; and that it is impossible a being infinitely wise can have made laws only to then violate them. He could not, they say, alter the machine but with a view of making it work better; but it is evident that being God, all wise and omnipotent, he originally made this immense machine, the universe, as good and perfect as He was able. If He saw that some imperfections would arise from the nature of matter, He provided for that in the beginning; and, accordingly, He will never change anything in it.

Moreover, God can do nothing without reason; but what reason could induce him to disfigure for a time His own work?

It is done, they are told, in favor of mankind. They reply: We must presume, then, that it is in favor of all mankind; for it is impossible to conceive that the divine nature should concern itself with only a few men in particular, and not with the whole human race; and even the whole human race itself is a very small concern; it is less than a small anthill in comparison with all the beings inhabiting the immensity. But is it not the most absurd of all extravagances to imagine that the Infinite Supreme should, in favor of three or four hundred ants on this little heap of earth, derange the operation of the vast machinery that moves the universe?

But, admitting that God chose to distinguish a small number of men by particular favors, is there any necessity that, in order to accomplish this object, He should change what He established for all periods and for all places? He certainly can have no need of this inconstancy in order to bestow favors on any of His creatures: His favors consist in His laws themselves: he has foreseen all and arranged all, with a view to them. All invariably obey the force which He has impressed forever on nature.

For what purpose would God perform a miracle? To accomplish some particular design upon a few living beings? He would then, in reality, be supposed to say: "I have not been able to fulfill a particular plan by my construction of the universe, by my divine decrees, by my eternal laws, a particular object; I am now going to change my eternal ideas and immutable laws on order to accomplish what I have not been able to do by means of them." This would be an avowal of His weakness, not of His power; it would appear in such a being the most inconceivable contradiction. Accordingly, therefore, to dare to ascribe miracles to God is actually to insult him (if man can in reality insult God.) It is saying to Him: "You are a weak and inconsistent Being." It is therefore absurd to believe in miracles; it is, in a way, dishonoring the divinity.

These philosophers are challenged, they are told "You can exalt as much as you please the immutability of the Supreme Being, the eternity of His laws, and the regularity of His infinitude of worlds; but our little heap of dirt has been completely covered over with miracles. History relates as many prodigies as natural events. The daughters of the high priest Anius changed whatever they pleased to corn, wine, and oil; Athalide, the daughter of Mercury, came back to life again several times; Æsculapius resuscitated Hippolytus; Hercules rescued Alcestes from the hand of death; and Heres returned to the world after having passed fifteen days in hell. Romulus and Remus were the offspring of a god and a vestal. The Palladium descended from heaven on the city of Troy; the hair of Berenice was changed into a constellation; the cot of Baucis and Philemon was converted into a superb temple; the head of Orpheus delivered oracles after his death; the walls of Thebes spontaneously constructed themselves to the sound of a flute, in the presence of the Greeks; the cures effected in the temple of Æsculapius were absolutely innumerable, and we still have monuments containing the very names of persons who were eyewitnesses of his miracles."

Mention to me a single nation in which the most incredible prodigies have not been performed, especially in those periods in which the people scarcely knew how to read or write.

The philosophers respond to these objections by slightly raising their shoulders and by a smile; but the Christian philosophers say: "We are believers in the miracles of our holy religion; we believe them by faith and not by our reason, which we are very cautious about listening to; for when faith speaks, it is well known that reason ought to be silent. We have a firm and entire faith in the miracles of Jesus Christ and the apostles, but permit us to entertain some doubt about many others: permit us, for example, to suspend our judgment on what is related by a very simple man, although he has obtained the title of great. He assures us, that a certain monk was so much in the habit of performing miracles, that the prior at length forbade him to exercise his talent in that line. The monk obeyed; but seeing a poor tiler fall from the top of a house, he hesitated for a moment between the desire to save the unfortunate man's life, and the sacred duty of obedience to his superior. He merely ordered the tiler to stay in the air till he should receive further instructions, and ran as fast as his legs would carry him to communicate the urgency of the circumstances to the prior. The prior absolved him from the sin he had committed in beginning the miracle without permission, and gave him leave to finish it, provided he stopped there and never again repeated his fault." The philosophers may certainly be excused for entertaining a little doubt of this legend.

But how can you deny, they are asked, that St. Gervais and St. Protais appeared in a dream to St. Ambrose, and informed him of the spot in which were deposited their relics? That St. Ambrose had them disinterred? And that they restored sight to a man that was blind? St. Augustine was at Milan at the very time, and it is he who relates the miracle, using the expression, in the twenty-second book of his work called the *City of God,* "*immenso populo teste*"—in the presence of an immense number of people. Here is one of the very best attested and established miracles. The philosophers, however, say that they do not believe one word about Gervais and Protais appearing to any person whatever; that it is a matter of very little consequence to mankind where the remains of their carcasses lie; that they have no more faith in this blind man than in Vespasian's; that it is a useless miracle, and that God does nothing that is useless; and they adhere to the principles they began with. My respect for St. Gervais and St. Protais prevents me from being of the same opinion as these philosophers: I merely state their incredulity. They lay great stress on the well-known passage of Lucian, to be found in the death of Peregrinus: "When an expert juggler turns Christian, he is sure to make his fortune." But as Lucian is a profane author, we ought surely to set him aside as of no authority.

These philosophers cannot even make up their minds to believe the miracles performed in the second century. Never mind that eyewitnesses write that after the bishop of Smyrna, St. Polycarp, was condemned to be burned and thrown into the midst of the flames they heard a voice from heaven exclaiming: "Courage, Polycarp! Be strong, and show yourself a man"; that the flames then drew back from his body and formed a pavilion of fire above his head, and from the midst of the pile there flew out a dove. In the end, Polycarp's enemies had to cut off his head. For what good, say these incredulous men, for what good was this miracle? Why did the flames lose their nature, and the axe of the executioner retain all its power of destruction? Whence comes it that so many martyrs escaped unhurt out of boiling oil, but were unable to resist the edge of the sword? It is answered, such was the will of God. But the philosophers would wish to see and hear all this themselves, before they believe it.

Those who strengthen their reasonings by learning will tell you that the fathers of the Church have frequently declared that miracles were no longer performed in their days. St. Chrysostom says expressly: "The extraordinary gifts of the spirit were bestowed even on the unworthy, because the Church at that time had need of miracles; but now, they are not bestowed even on the worthy, because the Church has need of them no longer." He afterwards declares, that there is no one now who raises the dead, or even who heals the sick.

St. Augustine himself, notwithstanding the miracles of Gervais and Protais, says, in his City of God: "Why are not such miracles as were wrought formerly wrought now?" and he assigns the same reason as St. Chrysostom for it. *Cur inquiunt, nunc illa miracula quæ prædicatis facta esse non fiunt? Possem quidem dicere necessaria prius fuisse, quam crederet mundus, ad hoc ut crederet mundus.*

It is objected to the philosophers that St. Augustine, notwithstanding this avowal, mentions nevertheless an old cobbler of Hippo, who, having lost his garment, went to pray in the chapel of the twenty martyrs and on his return found a fish, in the body of which was a gold ring; and that the cook who dressed the fish said to the cobbler: "See what a present the twenty martyrs have made you!"

To this the philosophers reply, that there is nothing in this story that goes against the laws of nature; that natural philosophy is not contradicted or shocked by a fish's swallowing a gold ring, or a cook's delivering such ring to a cobbler; that, in short, there is no miracle at all in the case.

If these philosophers are reminded that, according to St. Jerome, in his "Life of Paul the Hermit," that hermit had many conversations with satyrs and fauns; that a raven carried half of a loaf for his dinner to him every day for thirty years, and a whole one on the day that St. Anthony went to visit him, they might reply again, that all this is not absolutely inconsistent with natural philosophy; that satyrs and fauns may have existed; and that, at all events, whether the narrative be a recital of facts, or only a story fit for children, it has nothing at all to do with the miracles

of our Lord and His apostles. Many good Christians have con-
tested the "History of St. Simeon Stylites," written by Theodoret;
many miracles considered authentic by the Greek Church have
been called in question by many Latins, just as the Latin miracles
have been suspected by the Greek Church. Afterwards, the
Protestants appeared on the stage, and treated the miracles of
both churches certainly with very little respect or ceremony.

A learned Jesuit (*Ospinian.* p. 230), who was long a preacher
in the Indies, deplores that neither his colleagues nor himself
had ever been able to perform a miracle. Xavier laments in many
of his letters that he has not the gift of languages. He says that
among the Japanese he is merely like a dumb statue: yet the
Jesuits have written that he resuscitated nine people from
the dead, which is quite a lot, but it must be recollected that he
resuscitated them six thousand leagues from here. Since that
time there are people who have claimed that the abolition of the
Jesuits in France is a much greater miracle than any performed
by Xavier and Ignatius.

However that may be, all Christians agree that the miracles
of Jesus Christ and the apostles are incontestably true; but that
we may certainly be permitted to doubt some stated to have
been performed in our own times, and which have not been
completely authenticated.

It would certainly be very desirable, for example, if any miracles to be authenticated be performed in the presence of the
Academy of Sciences of Paris, or the Royal Society of London, and
the Faculty of Medicine, assisted by a detachment of guards to
keep in due order and distance the populace, who might by their
rudeness or indiscretion prevent the operation of the miracle.

A philosopher was once asked what he should say if he saw
the sun stand still, that is to say, if the motion of the earth around
that star were to cease; if all the dead were to rise again; and if
the mountains were to go and throw themselves together into

the sea, all in order to prove some important truth, like for instance, that of versatile grace. "What should I say?" answered the philosopher; "I should become a Manichaean; I should say that one principle counteracted the performance of another."

MOÏSE / MOSES

IN vain several scholars* have maintained that the Pentateuch could not have been written by Moses. They say that even Scripture itself affirms that the first known copy was found in the time of King Josiah, and that this single copy was brought to

---

* Is it true that there was a Moses? If a man who controlled all of nature had existed among the Egyptians, wouldn't such remarkable events have been included in the main part of the history of Egypt? Wouldn't Sanchoniathon, Manetho, Megasthenes, and Herodotus have spoken of him? The historian Josephus collected all possible testimony in favor of the Jews. He does not dare to maintain that any of authors he cites said a single word about the miracles of Moses. What! The Nile was turned to blood, an angel slaughtered all the first born in Egypt, the sea parted, its waters suspended to the left and right, and no author spoke of it! The great nations forgot these marvels, and a small people of barbarous slaves are the only ones to tell us this story thousands of years after the fact?

Who then is this Moses, unknown to the whole earth, until the time when Ptolemy, it is said, was curious enough to have the writings of the Jews translated into Greek. For many centuries, Eastern fables attributed to Bacchus all that the Jews have said about Moses. Bacchus had crossed the Red Sea with dry feet; Bacchus had changed water into blood; Bacchus had operated daily miracles with his staff. All these things were sung in the Bacchic orgies before there was the least contact with the Jews, even before this pitiful people had books. Isn't it of the greatest likelihood that, along with the Phoenician language, this people — of such recent origin, having wandered for so long, so lately established in Palestine — also adopted Phoenician fables, upon which it is still elaborating, just like all vulgar imitators? So poor, so ignorant and so foreign to the arts, could this people have done otherwise than to copy its neighbors? Aren't we are aware that even the names Adonai, Idaho, Elohim and Eloah, which mean God among the Jewish nation, were all Phoenician?

the king by the secretary Shaphan. Now, between the time of
Moses and this adventure of the secretary Shaphan, there were
one thousand one hundred and sixty-seven years, by the Hebrew
computation. For God appeared to Moses in the burning bush
in the year of the world 2213, and the secretary Shaphan published the book of the law in the year of the world 3380. This
book found under Josiah, was unknown until the return from
the Babylonian captivity; and it is said that it was Esdras, inspired
by God, who brought the Holy Scriptures to light.

But whether it was Esdras or another who wrote down this
book is absolutely indifferent once it is inspired. It is not said in
the Pentateuch, that Moses was the author; we might, therefore,
be permitted to attribute it to another man, to whom the divine
spirit would have dictated it, if the Church had not decided that
the book is by Moses.

Some opponents add that no prophet has quoted the
books of the Pentateuch, that there is no mention of it either
in the Psalms or in the books attributed to Solomon, in
Jeremiah or Isaiah, or, in short, in any canonical book of the
Jews. Words answering to those of Genesis, Exodus, Numbers,
Leviticus, Deuteronomy, are not found in any other text recognized by them as authentic.

Others, still bolder, have put the following questions:

1. In what language could Moses have written in a savage
desert? It could only have been in Egyptian; for by this same
book we are told that Moses and all his people were born in
Egypt. It is therefore probable that they spoke no other language. The Egyptians had yet made no use of papyrus; they
engraved hieroglyphics on tables of wood or marble. It is
even said, that the tables of the commandments were
engraved on polished stones, which required prodigious
time and labor.

2. Is it likely, that in a desert where the Jewish people had neither shoemaker nor tailor—in which the God of the universe was obliged to work a continual miracle to preserve the old clothes and shoes of the Jews—men could be found clever enough to engrave the five books of the Pentateuch on marble or wood? You will say that they obviously found laborers who made a golden calf in one night, and who afterwards reduced the gold into powder—an operation impracticable to common chemistry (which was not yet discovered), who then constructed the tabernacle, who ornamented thirty columns of brass with capitals of silver, who wove and embroidered veils of linen with hyacinth, purple, and scarlet, but all that only supports the opinion of the contradictors. They answer, that it was not possible for them to perform works so intricate in a desert, where they were in want of everything; that they must have begun by making shoes and tunics; that those who want for the necessary do not dabble in luxuries; and that it is an evident contradiction to say that they had founders, engravers, and embroiderers when they had neither clothes nor bread.

3. If Moses had written the first chapter of Genesis, would all young people have been forbidden to read the first chapter? Would so little respect have been paid to the legislator? If it was Moses who said that God punished the iniquity of the fathers to the fourth generation, would Ezekiel have dared to say the contrary?

4. If Moses wrote Leviticus, could he have contradicted it in Deuteronomy? Leviticus forbids a woman to marry her brother, Deuteronomy commands it.

5. Could Moses have spoken of towns which existed not in his time? Would he have said that towns which, in regard to him, were on the east of the Jordan, were on the west?

6. Would he have assigned forty-eight cities to the Levites, in a country in which there were never ten, and in a desert in which he had always wandered without habitation?

7. Would he have prescribed rules for the Jewish kings, when not only there were no kings among this people, but they were held in horror, and it was not likely they had ever had any? What! Would Moses have given precepts for the conduct of kings who did not come along until five hundred years after him, and have said nothing in relation to the judges and priests who succeeded him? Does not this reflection lead us to believe that the Pentateuch was composed in the time of kings, and that the ceremonies instituted by Moses had been no more than a tradition?

8. Is it even possible that he might have said to the Jews: I have made you depart to the number of six hundred thousand combatants from the land of Egypt under the protection of your God? Would not the Jews have answered him: You must have been very timid not to lead us against Pharaoh of Egypt; he could not have opposed to us an army of two hundred thousand men. There never was such an army on foot in Egypt; we should have conquered them easily; we should have been the masters of their country. What! has the God who talks to you slain all the first-born of Egypt to please us, which, if there were in this country three hundred thousand families, makes three hundred thousand men destroyed in one night, simply to avenge us, and yet you have not seconded your God and given us that fertile country which nothing could withhold from us? On the contrary, you have made us depart from Egypt as thieves and cowards, to perish in the desert between mountains and precipices. You might, at least, have conducted us by the direct road to this land of Canaan, to which we have no right, but which you have promised us, and which we have not yet been able to enter.

It was natural that, from the land of Goshen, we should march towards Tyre and Sidon, along the Mediterranean; but you made us entirely pass the Isthmus of Suez, and re-enter Egypt go back up as far as Memphis, we find ourselves at Beel-Sephor on the borders of the Red Sea, turning our backs on the land of Canaan, having journeyed eighty leagues in this Egypt which we wished to avoid, at last to nearly perish between the sea and the army of Pharaoh!

If you had wished to deliver us to our enemies, you could not have taken a different route and other measures. God has saved us by a miracle, you say; the sea opened to let us pass; but after such a favor, should He let us die of hunger and fatigue in the horrible deserts of Kadesh-barnea, Mara, Elim, Horeb, and Sinai? All our fathers perished in these frightful solitudes; and you come tell us after forty years that God took particular care of them!

This is what these murmuring Jews, these unjust children of the Jewish vagabonds who died in the desert, might have said to Moses, if he had read Exodus and Genesis to them. And what might they not have said and done on the article of the golden calf? What! You dare to tell us that your brother made a calf for our fathers, when you were with God on the mountain? You, who sometimes tell us that you have spoken to God face to face, and sometimes that you could only see His back! But no matter, you were with this God, and your brother cast a golden calf in one day, and gave it to us to adore it; and instead of punishing your unworthy brother, you make him our chief priest, and order your Levites to slay twenty-three thousand men of your people. Would our fathers have suffered this? Would they have allowed themselves to be sacrificed like so many victims by sanguinary priests? You tell us that, not content with this incredible butchery, you have further massacred twenty-four thousand of our poor followers because one of them slept with a Midianitish woman,

while you yourself espoused a Midianite; and yet you add, that
you are the mildest of men! A few more instances of such mildness and not a soul would have remained.

No; if you have been capable of all this cruelty, if you could
have exercised it, you would be the most barbarous of men, and
no punishment would suffice to expiate so great a crime.

These are nearly the objections which all scholars make to
those who think that Moses is the author of the Pentateuch.
But we answer them that the ways of God are not those of men;
that God has proved, conducted, and abandoned His people by
a wisdom which is unknown to us; that the Jews themselves, for
more than two thousand years, have believed that Moses is the
author of these books; that the Church, which has succeeded
the synagogue, and which is equally infallible, has decided this
point of controversy; and that scholars should remain silent
when the Church pronounces.

MORALE / MORALITY

I have just read these words in a piece of declamation in fourteen volumes, entitled, *The History of the Lower Empire:*

"The Christians had a morality, but the Pagans had none."

Oh, M. Le Beau! Author of these fourteen volumes, where
did you pick up this absurdity? What becomes of the morality of
Socrates, of Zaleucus, of Charondas, of Cicero, of Epictetus, and
of Marcus Aurelius?

There is but one morality, M. Le Beau, as there is but one
geometry. But you will tell me that the greater part of mankind
is ignorant of geometry. True; but if they apply themselves a little to the study of it, all men draw the same conclusions.
Agriculturists, manufacturers, artisans, do not go through a regular course of morality; they read neither the *De Finibus* of
Cicero, nor the *Ethics* of Aristotle; but as soon as they reflect, they

are, without knowing it, disciples of Cicero. The Indian dyer, the Tartarian shepherd, and the English seaman are acquainted with justice and injustice. Confucius did not invent a system of morals, as men construct system in the physical sciences. He found his in the hearts of all mankind.

This morality existed in the heart of the praetor Festus when the Jews pressed him to put Paul to death for having taken strangers into their temple. "Learn," said he, "that the Romans never condemn any one unheard."

If the Jews were deficient in a moral sense the Romans were not, and paid it homage.

There is no morality in superstition; it exists not in ceremonies, and has nothing to do with dogmas. We cannot repeat too frequently that dogmas differ, but that morality is the same among all men who make use of their reason. Morality thus proceeds from God, like light; our superstitions are only darkness. Reflect, reader; pursue the truth, and draw the consequences.

NÉCESSAIRE / NECESSARY

OSMIN

Do you not assert that everything is necessary?

SELIM

If all be not necessary, it would follow that God would have done unnecessary things.

OSMIN

So, it was necessary for the Divine Nature to do all that it has done?

SELIM

I believe, or at least I suspect so. There are men who think differently. I do not understand them; but possibly they are right. I fear to dispute on this subject.

OSMIN

I wish to speak to you about another necessary thing, however.

SELIM

What then? Would you speak of what is necessary to an honest man to live, or the evil to which people are reduced who lack the bare essentials of life?

OSMIN

No; for that which is necessary to one is not always necessary to another. It is necessary for an Indian to possess rice, for an Englishman to eat meat, as Russians must wear furs, and Africans gauze. One man believes that he has need of a dozen coach-horses, another limits himself to a pair of shoes, and a third walks gaily on his bare feet. I wish to speak to you of that which is necessary to all men.

SELIM

It appears to me that God has given this species all that is necessary in this sense: eyes to see, feet to walk, a mouth to eat, a gullet to swallow, a stomach to digest, a brain to reason, and organs to produce their kind.

OSMIN

How happens it then that men are sometimes born who are deprived of a part of these necessary faculties?

SELIM

Because the general laws of nature are liable to accidents which produce monsters; but in general man is provided with all things necessary to his existence in society.

OSMIN

Are there not notions common to all men necessary to this purpose?

SELIM

Yes; I have traveled with Paul Lucas,[62] and wherever I went I saw that man respected his father and mother; that he thought himself bound to keep his promise; that he pitied oppressed innocence; that he detested persecution; that he regarded freedom of thinking as a right of nature, and the enemies of that freedom as the enemies of the human race. They who think differently appear to me to be badly organized, and monsters, like those who are born without eyes or hands.

OSMIN

These necessary things—are they necessary in all times, and in all places?

SELIM

Yes: otherwise they would not be necessary to human kind.

OSMIN

Therefore, a new creed is not necessary to mankind. Men were perfectly capable of living in society, and performing all their duties towards God, even before they believed that Mohammed had frequent conversations with the angel Gabriel.

SELIM

Nothing is more evident; it would be ridiculous to think that man could not perform his duties before Mohammed came into the world. It was no way necessary for men to believe the Koran. The world went on before the appearance of Mohammed precisely as it goes on today. If Mohammedanism was necessary to the world, it would have existed from the beginning, in all places. God, who has given each of us two eyes to see his sun, would have bestowed upon each of us some means of seeing the truths of the Mohammedan religion. That sect is therefore no more than the arbitrary laws which change according to times and places, like fashions or like the opinions of physicians which succeed one another.

The Mohammedan religion cannot therefore be essentially necessary to man

OSMIN

But since it exists, God has permitted it.

SELIM

Yes, just as He permits all the world to abound in absurdities, errors, and calamities. This is not saying that men were all absolutely created in order to be foolish and unhappy. God permits some men to be eaten by serpents, but we ought not to say that God made man to be eaten by serpents.

OSMIN

What do you mean by saying that God permits? Can anything happen but by His orders? To permit, to will, and to do—are they not for Him the same thing?

SELIM

He permits crime, but does not commit it.

OSMIN

To commit a crime is to act against Divine justice—to disobey God. Therefore, as God cannot disobey Himself, He cannot commit crime; but He has so made man that man commits it frequently. How does that arise?

SELIM

Somemen can tell, but I am not one of them. All that I know is that the Koran is ridiculous, though here and there one may find some fairly good things. The Koran, however, is certainly not necessary to man—that I maintain. I perceive clearly that which is false, but know very little of that which is true.

OSMIN

I thought that you would instruct me, but you teach me nothing.

SELIM

Is it not a great deal to know the men who deceive you, and the gross and dangerous errors they spout to you?

OSMIN

I should have cause to complain of a physician who gave me a lesson on poisonous plants, without showing me any of those which are salutary.

SELIM

I am no physician, nor are you a sick man; but it appears to me that I would be giving you a very useful prescription if I said to you: Distrust the inventions of charlatans; worship God; be an honest man; and believe that two and two make four.

ORGUEIL / PRIDE

CICERO, in one of his letters, says familiarly to his friend: "Send to me the persons to whom you wish me to give the Gauls." In another, he complains of being tired of the letters from I know not what princes, who thank him for causing their provinces to be erected into kingdoms; and he adds that he does not even know where these kingdoms are situated.

It is even possible that Cicero, who had often seen the Roman people, the sovereign people, applaud and obey him and who was thanked by kings whom he knew not, had experienced some twinges of pride and vanity.

Though the sentiment is not at all consistent in so pitiful an animal as man, yet we can pardon it in a Cicero, a Caesar, or a Scipio; but when in the extremity of one of our half barbarous provinces, a man who may have bought an insignificant office, and printed poor verses, takes it into his head to be proud, it is very laughable.[63]

PAPISME (SUR LE) / POPERY (ON)

PAPIST. His highness has within his principality Lutherans, Calvinists, Quakers, Anabaptists, and even Jews; and you wish that he would admit Unitarians?

TREASURER. If these Unitarians bring with them wealth and industry, what harm will they do us. You will only be the better paid for your wages.

PAPIST. I must confess that a diminution of my income would be more disagreeable to me than the admission of these persons; but they do not believe that Jesus Christ is the Son of God.

TREASURER. What does it matter to you, provided that you are permitted to believe it, and are well lodged, well clothed, and well fed? The Jews are far from believing that He is the Son of God, and yet you are quite pleased to find Jews here, with whom you deposit your money at six percent. St. Paul himself never spoke of the divinity of Jesus Christ. He frankly calls him a man. "Death," says he, "entered into the world by the sin of one man . . . the just will reign by one sole man who is Jesus . . . you belong to Jesus and Jesus belongs to God." (Romans) All the early fathers of your Church thought like Paul. It is evident that, for three hundred years, Jesus was content with His humanity; imagine yourself a Christian of one of the first three centuries.

PAPIST. Yes, sir; but neither do they believe in eternal punishments.

TREASURER. Nor I either; be eternally damned if you please; for my own part, I have no such plans.

PAPIST. Ah, sir! it is very hard not to be able to damn at will all the heretics in the world; but the rage which the Unitarian displays for rendering everybody happy in the end is not my only complaint. You know that these monsters no more believe in the resurrection of the body than the Sadducees. They say that we are all anthropophagi, and that the particles which compose our grandfathers and great-grandfathers, having been necessarily dispersed in the atmosphere, have become carrots and asparagus, and that it is impossible that you not have devoured a few small bits of your ancestors.

TREASURER. Be it so; my children will do as much by me; it is but repayment, and the same goes for Papists. This is no reason for driving you from the estates of his highness; and nor is it a reason for him to evict the Unitarians. Rise again, if you are able; it matters little to me whether or not the Unitarians rise again, provided they are useful during their lives.

PAPIST. And what, sir, do you say to original sin, which they so boldly deny? Are you not scandalized by their assertion, that the Pentateuch says not a word about it, that the bishop of Hippo, St. Augustine, is the first who decidedly taught this dogma, although it is evidently indicated by St. Paul?

TREASURER. Truly, if the Pentateuch does not mention it, that is not my fault. Why not add a text or two about original sin to the Old Testament, as it is said you have added so many other things? I know nothing of these subtleties; my job is to pay you your stipend, when I have the money to do so.

PATRIE / FATHERLAND

A country is a composition of many families; and as a family is commonly supported on the principle of self-love, in the absence of an opposing interest the same self-love extends to one's city, or one's town, which one calls one's country.

The larger this country becomes, the less we love it; for love is weakened by diffusion. It is impossible to dearly love a family so numerous that all the members can scarcely be known.

He who is burning with ambition to be aedile, tribune, praetor, consul, or dictator, exclaims that he loves his country, while he loves only himself. Every man wishes to possess the power of sleeping quietly at home, without any other man appropriating the power of sending him to sleep elsewhere. Everyone would be certain of his property and his life. Thus, all forming the same wishes, it comes about that the particular interest becomes the general. The welfare of the republic is spoken of, while all that is signified is love of self.

It is impossible that a state was ever formed on earth, which was not governed in the first instance as a republic: it is the natural march of human nature. A few families come together against the bears and the wolves; he who has grain provides it in exchange to the man who has only wood.

When we discovered America, we found all of the peoples divided into republics; there were but two kingdoms in all that part of the world. Of a thousand nations, but two were found to be subjugated.

It was the same in the ancient world; all was republican in Europe before the little kinglings of Etruria and of Rome. There are yet republics in Africa. Tripoli, Tunis, and Algeria, in the north, are republics of bandits. The Hottentots, towards the south, still live as people are said to have lived in the first ages of the world—free, equal, without masters, without subjects, without money, and almost without wants. The flesh of their sheep feeds them; they are clothed with their skins; huts of wood and clay form their habitations. They are the smelliest of all men, but they feel it not, but live and die more gently than we do.

There remain eight republics in Europe without monarchs—Venice, Holland, Switzerland, Genoa, Lucca, Ragusa, Geneva, and San Marino. Poland, Sweden, and England may be regarded as republics under a king, but Poland is the only one of them which takes the name.

But which of the two is to be preferred—that your country be a monarchy or a republic? The question has been agitated for four thousand years. Ask the rich, and they will tell you an aristocracy; ask the people, and they will reply a democracy; kings alone prefer royalty.

Why, then, is almost all the earth governed by monarchs? Put that question to the rats who proposed to hang a bell around the cat's neck. In truth, the genuine reason is, as it has been said, because men are very rarely worthy of governing themselves.

It is lamentable, that to be a good patriot we must become the enemy of the rest of mankind. That good citizen, the ancient Cato, always proclaim his opinion in the Senate, "Carthage must be destroyed." To be a good patriot is to wish that one's own country be enriched by commerce and powerful by arms. It is clear that one country cannot win without another losing, and that it cannot triumph without causing misery to its neighbors.

Such is the condition of mankind, that to wish the greatness of one's own country is often to wish evil to one's neighbors. He who could bring himself to wish that his country never be greater or smaller, richer or poorer, but should always remain as it is would be a citizen of the universe.

PAUL / PAUL

QUESTIONS ON PAUL

WAS Paul a Roman citizen, as he boasted? If he was a native of Tarsus in Cilicia, all antiquarians agree that Tarsus was not a Roman colony until a hundred years after his death. If he belonged to the little town or village of Gescala, as St. Jerome believed, this town was in Galilee, and certainly the Galileans were not Roman citizens.

Is it true that St. Paul entered into the rising society of Christians, who at that time were still half Jewish, only because Gamaliel, whose disciple he was, refused him his daughter in marriage? It seems to me that this accusation is to be found exclusively in the Acts of the Apostles as received by the Ebionites, acts reported and refuted by the Bishop Epiphanius in his thirtieth chapter.

Is it true, that St. Thecla sought out St. Paul disguised as a man, and were the acts of St. Thecla admissible? Tertullian, in the thirteenth chapter of his book *Baptism*, maintains that this history was composed by a priest attached to Paul. Jerome and Cyprian, in refuting the story of the lion baptized by St. Thecla, affirm the truth of these acts, in which we find that singular portrait of St. Paul, which we have already recorded. "He was fat, short, and broad shouldered; his dark eyebrows united across his aquiline nose; his legs were crooked, his head bald, and he was full of the grace of the Lord."

This is pretty nearly his portrait in the "Philopatris" of Lucian, with the exception of "the grace of God," with which Lucian unfortunately had no acquaintance.

Is Paul to be excused for his reproof of the practice of Judaism by St. Peter, when he himself practiced Judaism for eight days in the temple of Jerusalem?

When the Jews took Paul before the governor of Judea for having introduced strangers into the temple, was it proper for him to say to the governor that he was prosecuted because of his teaching the resurrection of the dead, when there was never any question of the resurrection of the dead at all. (Acts, 24)

Did Paul do right in circumcising his disciple Timothy, after having written to the Galatians, "If you have yourself circumcised Jesus will not do you any good"?

Did he do right to write to the Corinthians (chapter 9): "Have we not the right to eat and drink at your expense and to bring to along a woman?" etc. Was it proper to write in his Second Epistle to the Corinthians, that he will pardon none of them, neither those who have sinned nor others? What should we think at present of a man who would claim the right to live at our expense, him and his wife; and to judge and punish us, confounding the innocent with the guilty?

What are we to understand by the ascension of Paul into the third heaven?—what is the third heaven?

Which is the most probable—humanly speaking—that St. Paul become a Christian as a result of being thrown from a horse by the appearance of a great light at noon day, and that a celestial voice cried out to him: "Saul, Saul, why do you persecute Me?" or that Paul was irritated against the Pharisees, either by the refusal of Gamaliel to give him his daughter or by some other cause?

In all other history, would not the refusal of Gamaliel appear more probable than the celestial voice; especially if we were not obliged to believe in this miracle?

I only ask these questions in order to be instructed; and I request all those who are willing to instruct me to speak reasonably.

PÉCHÉ ORIGINEL / ORIGINAL SIN

THIS is a subject on which the Socinians or Unitarians supposedly triumph. They call this foundation of Christianity the "original sin." It is an insult to God, they say; it is accusing Him of the most absurd barbarity to dare to assert that He formed all the successive generations of mankind in order to torment them with eternal tortures under the pretext that their original ancestor ate a fruit in a garden. This sacrilegious imputation is so much the more inexcusable among Christians insofar as there is not a single word referring to this same invention of original sin in the Pentateuch, the prophets, or the gospels, whether apocryphal or canonical, or in any of the writers who are called the "first fathers of the Church."

It is not even related in the Book of Genesis that God condemned Adam to death for eating an apple. God says to him, indeed, "in the day that you eat thereof you shall surely die." But the very same Book of Genesis makes Adam live nine hundred and thirty years after indulging in this criminal repast. The animals, the plants, which had not partaken of this fruit, died at the respective periods prescribed for them by nature. Man is evidently born to die, like all the rest.

Moreover, the punishment of Adam was never present in any way in the Jewish law. Adam was no more a Jew than he was a Persian or Chaldaean. The first chapters of Genesis—at whatever period they were composed—were regarded by all the learned Jews as an allegory, and even as a dangerous fable, since it was forbidden to read that book before the age of twenty-one.

In a word, the Jews knew no more about original sin than they did about Chinese ceremonies; and, although divines generally discover in the Scripture everything they wish to find there, either "*totidem verbis*," or "*totidem literis*," we may safely assert that no reasonable divine will ever discover in it this surprising mystery.

Let us admit that St. Augustine was the first to lend credit to this strange notion; a notion worthy of the warm and romantic brain of an African debauchee and penitent, Manichaean and Christian, tolerant and persecuting, who passed his life in perpetual self-contradiction.

What an abomination, exclaim the strict Unitarians, to so atrociously calumniate the Author of Nature as to even impute to Him perpetual miracles, in order that He may damn mankind to all eternity, whom he makes to be born for so short a time! Either He created souls from all eternity, in which case, being necessarily, infinitely more ancient than the sin of Adam they can have no possible connection with it; or these souls are formed whenever man and woman sexually associate; in which case the Supreme Being must be supposed continually watching for all the rendezvous in the universe so that he may create spirits that He will render eternally miserable; or, finally, God is Himself the soul of all mankind, and so damns Himself. Which of these three suppositions is the most absurd and abominable? There is no fourth, for the opinion that God waits six weeks before He creates a damned soul in a fetus is, in fact, no other than that which creates it at the moment of sexual connection: the difference of six weeks cannot be of the slightest consequence in the argument.

I have merely related the opinion of the Unitarians; but men have now attained such a degree of superstition that I can scarcely relate it without trembling.

(article by the late M. Boulanger)[64]

PERSÉCUTION / PERSECUTION

I will not call Diocletian a persecutor, for he protected the Christians for eighteen years; and if, during his latter days, he did not save them from the resentment of Galerius, he was no more than a prince seduced, like many others, by intrigue and cabal, into a conduct unworthy of his character.

I will still less give the name of persecutor to the Trajans or the Antonini. I should regard myself as uttering blasphemy.

What is a persecutor? He whose wounded pride and mad fanaticism incite princes and magistrates against innocent men, whose only crime is that of being of a different opinion. "Impudent man! you worship God; you preach and practice virtue; you have served and assisted man; you have protected the orphan, have succored the poor; you have changed deserts, in which slaves dragged on a miserable existence, into fertile countryside peopled with happy families; but I have discovered that you despise me, and have never read my controversial work: you know that I am a rogue, that I counterfeited the handwriting of G——, that I stole some ____; you might very well say so, so I must warn you, I will seek the confessor of the prime minister, or the magistrate. I will show them again, with outstretched neck and twisted mouth, that you hold an erroneous opinion in relation to the cells in which the Septuagint were kept; that already ten years ago you spoke disrespectfully of Tobit's dog, which you assert to have been a spaniel, when I proved that it was a greyhound. I will denounce you as the enemy of God and man!" Such is the language of the persecutor; and if these words do not precisely issue from his lips, they are engraved on his heart with the graver of fanaticism steeped in the gall of envy.

It was thus that the Jesuit Letellier dared to persecute the Cardinal de Noailles, and that Jurieu persecuted Bayle.

When the persecution of the Protestants commenced in France, it was not Francis I, nor Henry II, nor Francis II, who sought out these unfortunate people, who hardened themselves against them with reflective bitterness, and who delivered them to the flames in the spirit of vengeance. Francis I was too busy with the Duchess d'Étampes; Henry II with his ancient Diana, and Francis II was but a child. Who, then, initiated these persecutions? Jealous priests, who enlisted in their service the prejudices of magistrates and the policy of ministers.

If these monarchs had not been deceived, if they had foreseen that these persecutions would produce half a century of civil war, and that half of the nation would be mutually exterminated, they would have extinguished with their tears the first pyres which they allowed to be lighted.

Oh, God of mercy! if any man can resemble that malignant being who is described as actually employed in the destruction of Your works, is it not the persecutor?

PHILOSOPHE / PHILOSOPHER

PHILOSOPHER, "lover of wisdom, that is to say, of truth." All philosophers have possessed this twofold character; there is not a one among those of antiquity who did not give examples of virtue to mankind, and lessons of moral truth. They might all have been mistaken on subjects of natural science; but that is of so little importance to the conduct of life that philosophers had no need of it. Ages were required to discover only part of the laws of nature. A single day is sufficient for a wise man to know the duties of man.

The philosopher is no enthusiast; he does not set himself up as a prophet; he does not claim to be inspired by the gods. I shall not therefore place in the rank of philosophers the ancient Zoroaster, or Hermes, or Orpheus, or any of those legislators boasted about by the countries of Chaldaea, Persia, Syria, Egypt, and Greece. Those who called themselves the sons of gods were the fathers of imposture; and if they employed falsehood to inculcate truths, they were unworthy of inculcating them; they were not philosophers; they were at best only very careful liars.

By what destiny, disgraceful perhaps to the nations of the West, has it come about that we are obliged to travel to the extremity of the East in order to find a sage of simple manners and character, without arrogance and without imposture, who taught men how to live happily six hundred years before our era, at a period when the whole of the North was ignorant of the use of letters and the Greeks had scarcely begun to distinguish themselves by their wisdom? That sage is Confucius, who as a legislator never sought to deceive mankind. What finer example or rule of conduct has ever been given since his time, in the whole world? "Rule a state as you rule a family; a man cannot govern his family well without giving a good example.

"Virtue should be common to the laborer and the monarch.

"Be active in preventing crimes, that you may lessen the trouble of punishing them.

"Under the good kings Yao and Xu, the Chinese were good; under the bad kings Kie and Chu, they were wicked.

"Do to another as to thyself.

"Love mankind in general, but cherish those who are good; forget insults but never forget kindnesses.

"I have seen men incapable of the sciences, but never any incapable of virtue."

Let us acknowledge that no legislator ever announced truths more useful to the human condition.

A multitude of Greek philosophers taught afterwards a morality equally pure. Had they distinguished themselves only by their vain systems of natural philosophy, their names would now be mentioned only in derision. If they are still respected, it is because they were just, and because they taught mankind to be so.

It is impossible to read certain passages of Plato, and particularly the admirable exordium of the laws of Zaleucus, without experiencing an ardent love of honorable and generous actions. The Romans have their Cicero who alone is perhaps more valuable than all the philosophers of Greece. After him come men more respectable still, but whom we may almost despair of imitating; these are Epictetus in slavery, and the Antonines and Julians upon a throne.

Who among us would deprive himself, like Julian, Antoninus, and Marcus Aurelius, of all the refined accommodations of our soft and effeminate lives? Who would, like them, sleep on the bare ground? Who would restrict himself to their frugal habits? Who would, like them, march bareheaded and barefoot at the head of the armies, exposed sometimes to the burning sun, other times to the freezing blast? Who would, like them, keep perfect mastery of all his passions? We have among us devout people, but where are the wise men? Where are the just and tolerant souls, serene and undaunted?

There have been some closet philosophers in France; and all of them, with the exception of Montaigne, have been persecuted. It seems to me the ultimate manifestation of the malignity of our nature, to wish to oppress those who seek to correct and improve it.

I can easily conceive of the fanatics of one sect slaughtering those of another sect; that the Franciscans should hate the Dominicans, and that a bad artist should cabal and intrigue for the destruction of an artist more gifted than he; but that the sage Charron should have been threatened with death; that the learned and noble-minded Ramus should have been assassinated; that Descartes should have been obliged to withdraw to Holland in order to escape the rage of ignorant people; that Gassendi should have been compelled more than once to withdraw to Digne, away from the calumnies of Paris—these events are the eternal shame of a nation.

One of the most persecuted philosophers was the immortal Bayle, the honor of human nature. I shall be told that the name of Jurieu, his slanderer and persecutor, has become execrable and I acknowledge that it is so; that of the Jesuit Letellier has likewise become so; but is it the less true that the great men whom he oppressed ended their days in exile and penury?[65]

One of the pretexts used to attack Bayle and reduce him to poverty was his article on David in his valuable dictionary. He was reproached with not praising actions which were in themselves unjust, sanguinary, atrocious, contrary to good faith, or grossly offensive to decency.

It is true that Bayle did not praise David for having, according to the Hebrew historian, gathered together six hundred vagabonds overwhelmed with debts and crimes; for having pillaged his countrymen at the head of these bandits; for having resolved to destroy Nabal and his whole family, because he refused paying contributions to him; for having hired out his services to King Achish, the enemy of his country; for having afterwards betrayed Achish, notwithstanding his kindness to him; for having sacked the villages in alliance with that king; for having massacred in these villages every human being, including even infants at the breast, out of fear that one day one would bear witness to his depredations, as if an infant could have possibly disclosed his villainy; for having destroyed all the inhabitants of some other villages under saws, and harrows, and axes, and in brick-kilns; for having wrested the throne from Ishbosheth, the son of Saul, by an act of perfidy; for having despoiled of his property and afterwards put to death Mephibosheth, the grandson of Saul, and son of his own peculiar friend and generous protector, Jonathan; or for having delivered up to the Gibeonites two other sons of Saul, and five of his grandsons who perished by the gallows.

All this without mentioning the extreme incontinence of David, his numerous concubines, his adultery with Bathsheba, or his murder of Uriah.

What then! Is it possible that the enemies of Bayle should have expected him to eulogize all these cruelties and crimes? Ought he to have said: Go, ye princes of the earth, and imitate the man after God's own heart; massacre without pity the allies of your benefactor; destroy or deliver over to destruction the whole family of your king; lie with all the women, while you are pouring out the blood of the men and you will be a model of virtue, especially if, in addition to all the rest, you do but compose a book of psalms?

Was not Bayle perfectly correct in his observation, that if David was the man after God's own heart, it must have been by his penitence, and not by his crimes? Did not Bayle perform a service to the human race when he said that God, who undoubtedly dictated all of Jewish history, has not consecrated all the crimes recorded in that history?

However, Bayle was persecuted, and by whom? By the very men who had been elsewhere persecuted themselves; by refugees who in their own country would have been burned; and these refugees were opposed by other refugees called Jansenists, who had been driven from their own country by the Jesuits; who have in turn been themselves driven out in the end.

Thus all the persecutors declare against each other mortal war while the philosopher, oppressed by them all, contents himself with pitying them.

It is not generally known, that Fontenelle, in 1713, was on the point of losing his pension, position, and freedom, for having published twenty years earlier in France, the learned Van Dale's "Treatise on Oracles," from which he had carefully removed everything which might cause alarm among fanatics.[66] A Jesuit had written against Fontenelle and he had not deigned to reply; which was enough to make the Jesuit Letellier, confessor to Louis XIV, accuse Fontenelle of atheism before the king.

But for the fortunate mediation of M. d'Argenson, the son of a forger, solicitor of Vire and known forger in his own right, would have proscribed Corneille's nephew in his old age.

It is so easy for a confessor to seduce his penitent, that we ought to bless God that Letellier did no more harm than is justly imputed to him. There are two situations in the world in which seduction and calumny cannot easily be resisted—the bed and the confessional.

We have always seen philosophers persecuted by fanatics. But can it be really possible, that men of letters engage in this business as well, sharpening the same weapons for use against their brethren by which they are themselves almost all destroyed or wounded in their turn?

Unhappy men of letters, does it become you to turn informers? Did the Romans ever find a Garasse, a Chaumieux, or a Hayet, to accuse a Lucretius, a Posidonius, a Varro, or a Pliny?

How low it is to be a hypocrite! But how much more horrible it is to be a mischievous and malignant hypocrite! There were no hypocrites in ancient Rome, which reckoned us but a small portion of its subjects. There were impostors, I admit, but not religious hypocrites, which are the most profligate and cruel kind of all. Why is it that we see none such in England, and whence does it arise that there are still such in France? Philosophers, you will solve this problem with ease.

PIERRE / PETER

IN Italian *Piero*, or *Pietro*; in Spanish *Pedro*; in Latin *Petrus*; in Greek *Petros*; in Hebrew *Cepha*.

Why have the successors of St. Peter possessed so much power in the West and none in the East? This is just the same as to ask why the bishops of Würzburg and Salzburg appropriated regal prerogatives in a period of anarchy, while the Greek bishops always remained subjects. Time, opportunity, the ambition of some, and the weakness of others, have done and will do everything in the world.

Opinion has joined itself to this anarchy, and opinion is the queen of mankind. Not that, in fact, they have any very clear and definite opinion of their own, but words serve in its place.

It is told in the Gospel that Jesus said to Peter; "I will give to you the keys of the kingdom of heaven." The zealous partisans of the bishop of Rome contended, about the eleventh century, that whoever gives the greater gives the less; that heaven surrounded the earth; and that, as Peter had the keys of the container, he had also the keys of what was contained. If by heaven we understand all the stars and planets, it is evident, according to Tomasius, that the keys given to Simon Barjonas, surnamed Peter, were a universal passport. If we understand by heaven the clouds, the atmosphere, the ether, and the space in which the planets revolve, no locksmith in the world, as Meursius observes, could ever make a key for such gates as these. Keys in Palestine were wooden latches with strings to them. Jesus says to Barjonas, "Whatsoever you shall bind on earth shall be bound in heaven." The pope's clergy concluded from these words that the popes had received the authority to bind and unbind the people's oath of fidelity to their kings, and to dispose of kingdoms as they pleased. This certainly was concluding magnificently. The Commons in the states-general of France, in 1302, say, in their request to the king, that "Boniface VIII was a b— who believed that God bound and imprisoned in heaven what Boniface bound on earth." A famous German Lutheran—the great Melancthon—could not endure the idea of Jesus having said to Simon Barjonas, Cepha or Cephas, "You are Peter (*Pierre*), and upon this rock (*pierre*) will I build my assembly, my church." He could not conceive that God would use such a play of words, and that the power of the pope could have been established on a pun.

Peter has been considered as having been bishop of Rome; but it is well known that in the apostolic age and long after, there was no one particular bishopric. The society of Christians did not assume a regular form until about the middle of the second century.

It may be true that Peter went to Rome, and even that he was crucified with his head downwards, although that was not the usual mode of crucifixion; but we have no proof whatever of all this. We have a letter under his name, in which he says that he is at Babylon: acute and shrewd canonists have contended that by Babylon we ought to understand Rome. On the same principle, if he had dated the letter from Rome, we might have concluded that it had been written at Babylon. Men have long been in the habit of drawing such conclusions as these; and it is in this manner that the world has been governed.

There was once a clergyman who had been made to pay extortionately for a benefice at Rome—an offense known by the name of simony. He was asked some time afterwards whether he thought Simon Peter had ever been in that city, to which he replied, "I do not think that Peter was ever there, but I am sure Simon was."

With respect to the personal character and behavior of Peter, it must be acknowledged that Paul is not the only one who was scandalized at his conduct. There were those who stood up to his face, to him, and to his successors. St. Paul vehemently reproached him with eating forbidden meats: that is, pork, blood-pudding, hare, eels, the ixion, and the griffin; Peter vindicated himself by saying that he had seen heaven opened about the sixth hour, and as it were a great sheet descending from the four corners of it, which was filled with creeping things, quadrupeds, and birds, while the voice of an angel called out to him, saying, "Kill and eat." This, says Woolston, seems to have been the same voice that has called out to so many pontiffs since, "Kill everything; eat up the substance of the people."

Casaubon could not bring himself to approve the manner in which Peter treated Ananias and Sapphira, his wife. "By what right," says Casaubon, "did a Jewish slave of the Romans order or permit that all those who believed in Jesus should sell their inheritance, and lay down the proceeds at his feet?" If an Anabaptist in London were to order all the money belonging to his brethren to be brought and laid at his feet, would he not be apprehended as a seditious seducer, as a thief who would certainly be hanged at Tyburn? Was it not abominable to kill Ananias, because, after having sold his property and delivered over the bulk of the produce to Peter, he had secretly retained for himself and his wife a few crowns out of necessity? Ananias was scarcely dead before his wife comes before Peter. Peter, instead of charitably warning her that he had just destroyed her husband by apoplexy for having kept back a few oboli, and cautioning her therefore to look well to herself, leads her intentionally into the trap. He asks her if her husband has given all his money to the saints; the poor woman answers yes, and dies instantly. This is severe.

Corringius asks, why Peter, who thus killed those who had given him alms and showed him kindness, did not rather go and destroy all the learned doctors who had brought Jesus Christ to the cross, and who more than once had he himself whipped. "Oh, Peter!" says Corringius, "you put to death two Christians who bestowed alms on you, and at the same time suffer to live those who crucified your God!"

It is pretty evident that Corringius was not in the country of the Inquisition when he published his bold remarks. Erasmus, in relation to St. Peter, remarked an extremely curious thing, which is that the chief of the Christian religion began his apostleship with denying Jesus Christ, and that the first pontiff of the Jews had commenced his ministry by making a golden calf and worshipping it.

However that may be, Peter is portrayed to us as a poor man instructing the poor. He resembles those founders of orders who lived in indigence, and whose successors have become great lords and even princes.

The pope, the successor of Peter, has sometimes gained and sometimes lost; but there are still about fifty millions persons in the world submitting in many points to his laws, besides his own immediate subjects.

To give oneself a master three or four hundred leagues from home; to wait to think until this man seems to have thought; to not dare to pronounce a final decision on a cause relating to certain of one's fellow citizens but through commissioners appointed by this stranger; to not dare to take possession of certain fields and vineyards granted by one's own sovereign without paying a considerable sum to this foreign master; to violate the laws of our country, which prohibit a man's marriage with his niece, and marry her legitimately by giving this foreign master an even more considerable sum; to not dare to cultivate one's field on the day this stranger wishes one to celebrate the memory of some unknown person whom he has chosen to introduce into heaven by his own sole authority; such are only a part of what it is to admit the jurisdiction of a pope; such are the liberties of the Gallican Church.

There are some other nations that carry their submission further. We have, in our own time, actually seen a sovereign request permission of the pope to try in his own courts certain monks accused of parricide, able neither to obtain this permission nor to venture on such trial without it!

It is well known that, formerly, the power of the popes extended further. They were far above the gods of antiquity; for the latter only seemed to control empires, whereas the popes disposed of them in fact.

Sturbinus says that we may pardon those who entertain doubts of the divinity and infallibility of the pope, when we reflect.

That forty schisms have profaned the chair of St. Peter, twenty-seven of which have been marked by blood;

That Stephen VII, the son of a priest, disinterred the corpse of Formosus, his predecessor, and had the head of it cut off;

That Sergius III, convicted of assassinations, had a son by Marozia, who inherited the popedom;

That John X, the paramour of Theodora, was strangled her in her bed;

That John XI, son of Sergius III., was known only by his gross intemperance;

That John XII was assassinated in the apartments of his mistress;

That Benedict IX both bought and sold the pontificate;

That Gregory VII was the author of five hundred years of civil war, carried on by his successors;

That, finally, among so many ambitious, sanguinary, and debauched popes, there was an Alexander VI, whose name is pronounced with the same horror as those of Nero and Caligula.

It is, we are told, a proof of the divinity of their character, that it has subsisted in connection with so many crimes; but according to this if the caliphs had displayed still more atrocious and abominable conduct, they would have been still more divine. Dermius reasoned in this fashion, but the Jesuits refuted him.

PRÉJUGÉS / PREJUDICES

PREJUDICE is an opinion without judgment. Thus, throughout the world, children are inspired with opinions before they can judge. There are universal and necessary prejudices, and these even constitute virtue. In all countries, children are taught to acknowledge a rewarding and punishing God; to respect and love their fathers and mothers; to regard theft as a crime, and self-interested lying as a vice, before they can tell what is a virtue or a vice. There are therefore good prejudices, which is to say those verified by judgment through the process of reason.

Sentiment is not simply prejudice, it is something much stronger. A mother loves not her son because she is told that she must love him; she fortunately cherishes him in spite of herself. It is not through prejudice that you run to the aid of an unknown child about to fall down a precipice, or be devoured by a beast.

But it is through prejudice that you will respect a man dressed in certain clothes, one who walks and talks in a grave manner. Your parents have told you that you must bend to this man; you respect him before you know whether he merits your respect; you grow in age and knowledge; you come to realize that this man is a quack, filled with pride, interest, and artifice; you despise that which you revered, and so prejudice yields to judgment. Through prejudice, you have believed the fables with which your infancy was lulled: you were told that the Titans made war against the gods, that Venus was amorous of Adonis; at twelve years of age you take these fables for truth; at twenty, you regard them as ingenious allegories.

Let us briefly examine the different kinds of prejudices, in order to organize our ideas. We shall perhaps be like those who, in the time of the John Law's System, perceived that they had calculated upon imaginary riches.

Prejudices of the Senses

Is it not an amusing thing that our eyes always deceive us, even when we see very well, and that on the contrary our ears do not? When your properly-formed ear hears: "You are beautiful; I love you," it is very certain that the words are not: "I hate you; you are ugly;" but you see a smooth mirror—it is proven that you are deceived; it is a very rough surface. You see the sun about two feet in diameter; it is proven that it is a million times larger than the earth.

It seems that God has put truth into your ears, and error into your eyes; but study optics, and you will see that God has not deceived you, and that in the present state of things it is impossible for objects to appear to you otherwise than you see them.

PHYSICAL PREJUDICES

The sun rises, the moon also, the earth is immovable; these are natural physical prejudices. But that crabs are good for the blood, because when boiled they are of the same color; that eels cure paralysis, because they frisk about; that the moon influences our diseases, because an invalid was one day observed to have an increase of fever during the wane of the moon: these ideas and a thousand others were the errors of ancient charlatans, who judged without reason, and who, being themselves deceived, deceived others.

HISTORICAL PREJUDICES

The greater part of history has been believed without question, and this confidence is a prejudice. Fabius Pictor relates, that, several ages before him, a vestal of the town of Alba was raped while going to draw water in her pitcher; that she then gave birth to Romulus and Remus, and that they were nourished by a she-wolf. The Roman people believed this fable; they did not question whether at that time there were vestals in Latium; whether it was likely that the daughter of a king should go out of her convent with a pitcher, or whether it was probable that a she-wolf should suckle two children, instead of eating them. The prejudice was thus established.

A monk writes that Clovis, being in great danger at the battle of Tolbiac, made a vow to become a Christian if he escaped; but is it natural that he should address a strange god on such an occasion?[67] Would not the religion in which he was born have acted the most powerfully? Where is the Christian who, in a battle against the Turks, would not rather address himself to the holy Virgin Mary, than to Mohammed? He adds, that a pigeon brought the holy vial in his beak to anoint Clovis, and that an angel brought the oriflamme to guide him: the prejudiced believe all the little stories of this kind. Those who are acquainted with human nature well know, that the usurper Clovis, and the usurper Rollo, or Rol, became Christians in order to govern the Christians more securely; as the Turkish usurpers became Muslims to govern the Muslims more securely.

Religious Prejudices

If your nurse has told you, that Ceres presides over corn, or that Vishnu and Xaca transformed themselves into men several times, or that Sammonocodom cut down a forest, or that Odin expects you in his hall near Jutland, or that Mohammed, or some other, made a journey to heaven; finally, if your preceptor afterwards stuffs into your brain what your nurse has engraved upon it, you will possess it for life. If your judgment would rise above these prejudices, your neighbors, and the women in particular, will exclaim "impiety!" and frighten you; your dervish, fearing to see his revenue diminished, accuses you before the cadi; and this cadi, if he can, causes you to be impaled, because he would command fools, and he believes that fools obey better than others; which state of things will last until your neighbors and the dervish and cadi begin to comprehend that folly is good for nothing, and that persecution is abominable.

PRÊTRE / **PRIEST**

PRIESTS are to the State what preceptors are in private families: it is their province to teach, pray, and provide a model. They can have no authority over the masters of the house; at least until it can be proved that he who gives the wages ought to obey him who receives them. Of all religions the one that most positively excludes the priesthood from civil authority is without question that of Jesus. "Give unto Caesar the things which are Caesar's."—"Among you there is neither first nor last."—"My kingdom is not of this world."

The quarrels between the empires and the priesthood, which have bloodied Europe for more than six centuries, have therefore been, on the part of the priests, nothing but rebellion against both God and man, and a continual sin against the Holy Ghost.

From the time of Calchas, who assassinated the daughter of Agamemnon, until Gregory XII, and Sixtus V, two bishops who wanted to deprive Henry IV of the kingdom of France, sacerdotal power has been injurious to the world.

Prayer is not dominion, nor exhortation despotism. A good priest ought to be a physician to the soul. If Hippocrates had ordered his patients to take hellebore under pain of being hanged, he would have been more insane and barbarous than Phalaris, and would have had few followers. When a priest says: Worship God; be just, indulgent, and compassionate; he is then a good physician; when he says: Believe me, or you shall be burned; he is an assassin.

The magistrate ought to support and restrain the priest in the same manner as the father of a family insures respect for the preceptor, and prevents him from abusing it. *The agreement of Church and State* is of all systems the most monstrous, for as soon as we seek this partnership we necessarily presume division; rather, we ought to say *the protection given by the State to the priesthood or church.*

But what is to be said and done in respect to countries in which the priesthood has obtained dominion, as in Salem, where Melchisedek was priest and king; in Japan, where the dairo has been for a long time emperor? I answer, that the successors of Melchisedek and the dairos have been dispossessed.

The Turks are wise in this; they religiously make a pilgrimage to Mecca; but they will not permit the sherif of Mecca to excommunicate the sultan. Neither will they purchase from Mecca permission to not observe the Ramadan, or to marry their cousins or their nieces. They are not judged by imans, whom the sherif delegates; nor do they pay the first year's revenue to the sherif. What is to be said of all that? Reader, it is up to you to speak for yourself.

PROPHÈTES / PROPHETS

THE prophet Jurieu was hissed; the prophets of the Cévennes were hanged or racked; the prophets who went from Languedoc and Dauphine to London were put in the pillory; the Anabaptist prophets were condemned to various modes and degrees of torture; and the prophet Savonarola was cooked at Florence. St. John the Baptist was beheaded.

Zachariah is claimed to have been assassinated; but, happily, this is not absolutely proved. The prophet Jeddo, or Addo, who was sent to Bethel on the condition that he neither to eat nor drink, having unfortunately tasted a morsel of bread, was devoured in his turn by a lion; and his bones were found on the highway between the lion and his ass. Jonah was swallowed by a fish, and while it is true that he did not remain in the fish's stomach more than three days and three nights it still means he spent seventy-two extremely uncomfortable hours.

Habakkuk was transported through the air to Babylon, suspended by the hair of his head; while in truth this was not a fatal or permanent calamity, it must still have been an exceedingly uncomfortable means of transport. A man could not help but suffer a great deal, suspended by his hair for a journey of three hundred miles. I certainly should have preferred a pair of wings, or the mare Borak, or the Hippogriffe.

Micaiah, the son of Imla, having seen the Lord seated on His throne, surrounded by His army of celestial spirits; and the Lord having inquired who could be found to go and deceive King Ahab, the devil having volunteered himself for that purpose, and being accordingly charged with the commission; Micaiah, on the part of the Lord, gave King Ahab an account of this celestial adventure. It is true that his only reward was a tremendous slap from the hand of the prophet Zedekiah, it is also true that he was only shut up for a few days in a dungeon, but still, it is unpleasant and painful enough for a man divinely inspired to be slapped about and stuffed in a damp and dirty hole of a prison.

It is believed that King Amaziah had the teeth of the prophet Amos pulled out to prevent him from speaking; not that a person without teeth is absolutely incapable of speaking, as we see many chatty but toothless old ladies; but a prophecy must be uttered with great distinctness; and a toothless prophet is never listened to with the respect that is his due.

Baruch experienced various persecutions. Ezekiel was stoned by his fellow slaves. We do not know whether Jeremiah was stoned or sawed in two.

Isaiah is commonly considered to have been sawed to death by order of Manasseh, mini-king of Judah.

It cannot be denied that the occupation of a prophet is exceedingly irksome and dangerous. For every one who, like Elijah, sets off on his tour among the planets in a fine chariot of light, drawn by four white horses, there are a hundred who travel on foot, and are obliged to beg their dinner from door to door. They may be compared to Homer, who, we are told, was reduced to begging in the same seven cities who since sharply dispute with each other the honor of being his birth-place. His commentators have attributed to him an infinity of allegories which he never even thought of; and prophets have frequently had similar honor conferred upon them. I by no means deny that they may have been very knowledgeable about the future. The only thing left to do is for a man to work up his soul to a high state of exaltation, as in the case of one of our fine philosophers or madmen, who wished to dig a hole through to the Antipodes, and cure the sick by covering them all over with pitch-plaster. The Jews possessed this faculty of exalting and exciting the soul to such a degree that they saw every future event as clearly as possible; only unfortunately, it is difficult to decide whether by Jerusalem the prophets always meant eternal life; whether Babylon means London or Paris; whether, when they speak of a grand dinner, they really mean a fast, and whether red wine means blood, and a red mantle faith, and a white mantle charity. Indeed, the correct and com-plete understanding of the prophets is the most arduous attainment of the human mind, which is why I will say no more on the subject.

RELIGION / **RELIGION**

FIRST QUESTION

WARBURTON, Bishop of Gloucester, author of one of the most learned works ever written, thus expresses himself ("Divine Legation of Moses," i, 8): "A religion, a society, which is not founded on the belief of another life, must be supported by an extraordinary Providence. Judaism is not founded on the belief of another life; therefore, Judaism was supported by an extraordinary Providence."

Many theologians rose up against him; and, as all arguments are retorted, so was his retorted upon himself; he was told:

"Every religion which is not founded on the dogma of the immortality of the soul, and on everlasting rewards and punishments, is necessarily false. Now these dogmas were unknown to the Jews; therefore Judaism, far from being supported by Providence, was, according to your own principles, a false and barbarous religion by which Providence was attacked."

This bishop had some other adversaries, who maintained against him that the immortality of the soul was known to the Jews even in the time of Moses; but he proved to them very clearly that neither the Decalogue, nor Leviticus, nor Deuteronomy had said one word of such a belief; and that it is ridiculous to strive to distort and corrupt some passages of other books, in order to draw from them a truth which is not announced in the book of the law.

The bishop, having written four volumes to demonstrate that the Jewish law proposed neither pains nor rewards after death, has never been able to answer his adversaries in a very satisfactory manner. They said to him: "Either Moses knew this dogma, and so deceived the Jews by not communicating it, or he did not know it, in which case he did not know enough to found a good religion. Indeed, if the religion had been good why should it have been abolished? A true religion must be for all times and all places; it must be as the light of the sun, enlightening all nations and generations."

This prelate, enlightened as he is, has found it no easy task to extricate himself from so many difficulties. But what system is free from them?

SECOND QUESTION

Another man of learning, and a much greater philosopher, who is one of the most profound metaphysicians of our time, advances very strong arguments to prove that polytheism was the primitive religion of mankind, and that men began with believing in several gods before their reason was sufficiently enlightened to acknowledge only one Supreme Being.

On the contrary, I venture to believe that in the beginning they acknowledged only one God, and that afterwards human weakness adopted several. My conception of the matter is this:

It is indubitable that there were villages before large towns were built, and that all men have been divided into petty commonwealths before they were united in great empires. It is very natural that the people of a village, being terrified by thunder, afflicted at the loss of its harvests, ill-used by the inhabitants of a neighboring village, feeling every day its own weakness, feeling everywhere an invisible power, might soon have said: There is some Being above us who does us good and harm.

It seems to me to be impossible that they might have said: There are two powers; for why more than one? In all things we begin with the simple; then comes the compound; and after, by superior understanding, we go back to the simple again. Such is the march of the human mind!

But what is this being who would first have been invoked? Is it the sun? Is it the moon? I do not think so. Let us examine what passes in the minds of children; they are nearly like those of uninformed men. They are struck, neither by the beauty nor by the utility of the star which animates nature, nor by the assistance lent us by the moon, nor by the regular variations of her course; they think not of these things; they are too much accustomed to them. We adore, we invoke, we seek to appease, only that which we fear. All children look upon the sky with indifference; but when the thunder growls they tremble and run to hide themselves. The first men undoubtedly did likewise. It could only be a sect of philosophers who first observed the courses of the planets, made them admired, and caused them to be adored; mere tillers of the ground, without any information, did not know enough of them to embrace so noble an error.

A village then would confine itself to saying: There is a power which thunders and hails upon us, which makes our children die; let us appease it. But how shall we appease it? We see that by small presents we have calmed the anger of irritated men; let us then make small presents to this power. It must also receive a name. The first that presents itself is that of "chief," "master," "lord." This power then is styled "My Lord." For this reason perhaps it was that the first Egyptians called their god "knef"; the Syrians, "Adonai"; the neighboring nations, "Baal," or "Bel," or "Melch," or "Moloch"; the Scythians, "Papæus"; all these names signifying "lord," "master."

Thus was nearly all America found to be divided into a multitude of petty tribes, each having its protecting god. The Mexicans, too, and the Peruvians, forming great nations, had only one god—the one adoring Manco Capak, the other the god of war. The Mexicans called their warlike divinity "*Huitzilipochtli*," as the Hebrews had called their Lord "*Sabaoth*."

It was not from a superior and cultivated reason that every people thus began to acknowledge only one Divinity; had they been philosophers, they would have adored the God of all nature, and not the god of a village; they would have examined those infinite relations among all things which prove a Being creating and preserving; but they examined nothing—they felt. Such is the progress of our feeble understanding. Each village would feel its weakness and its need of a protector; it would imagine that tutelary and terrible being residing in the neighboring forest, or on a mountain, or in a cloud. It would imagine only one, because the clan had but one chief in war; it would imagine that one corporeal, because it was impossible to represent it otherwise. It could not believe that the neighboring tribe had not also its god. Therefore it was that Jephthah said to the inhabitants of Moab: "You possess lawfully what your god Chemoth has made you conquer; you should, then, let us enjoy what our god has given us by his victories."

This language, used by one foreigner to other foreigners, is very remarkable. The Jews and the Moabites had dispossessed the natives of the country; neither had any right but that of force; and the one says to the other: "Your god has protected you in your usurpation; suffer our god to protect us in ours."

Jeremiah and Amos both ask what right the god Melchem had to seize the country of Gad. From these passages it is evident that the ancients attributed to each country a protecting god. We still find traces of this theology in Homer.

It is very natural that, men's imaginations being heated, and their minds having acquired some confused knowledge, they should soon have multiplied their gods, and assigned protectors to the elements, the seas, the forests, the fountains, and the fields. The more they would have observed the stars, the more they would have been struck with admiration. How, indeed, could they have not adored the sun, adoring as they did the divinity of a brook? The first step being taken, the earth would soon be covered with gods; and from the stars eventually all the way down to cats and onions.

Reason, however, must necessarily work towards perfection; time at length found philosophers who saw that neither onions, nor cats, nor even the stars, had arranged the order of nature. All those philosophers—Babylonians, Persians, Egyptians, Scythians, Greeks, and Romans—admitted a supreme, rewarding, and avenging God.

They did not at first tell it to the people; for whosoever should have spoken ill of onions and cats before priests and old women would have been stoned; whosoever should have reproached certain of the Egyptians for eating their gods would himself have been eaten—as Juvenal relates that an Egyptian was in reality killed and eaten quite raw in a controversial dispute.

What did they do? Orpheus and others established mysteries, which the initiated swore by horrible oaths not to reveal—the principal mystery of which was the adoration of a supreme God. This great truth made its way through half the world, and the number of the initiated became immense. It is true that the ancient religion still existed; but as it was not contrary to the dogma of the unity of God, it was allowed to exist. And why should it have been abolished? The Romans acknowledged the "*Deus optimus maximus*," and the Greeks had their Zeus—their supreme god. All the other divinities were only intermediate beings; heroes and emperors were ranked with the gods, i. e., with the blessed; though clearly Claudius, Octavius, Tiberius, and Caligula were not regarded as the creators of heaven and earth.

In short, it seems proved that, in the time of Augustus, all who had a religion acknowledged a superior, eternal God, with several orders of secondary gods, whose worship was called idolatry.

The laws of the Jews had never favored idolatry; for, although they admitted the Malachim, angels and celestial beings of an inferior order, their law did not ordain that they should worship these secondary divinities. They adored the angels, it is true; that is, they prostrated themselves when they saw them; but as this did not often happen, there was no ceremonial or legal worship established for them. The cherubim of the ark received no homage. It is beyond a doubt that the Jews, from at least Alexander's time onwards, openly adored only one God, as the innumerable multitude of the initiated secretly adored Him in their mysteries.

THIRD QUESTION

It was at the time when the worship of a Supreme God was universally established among all the wise in Asia, in Europe, and in Africa that the Christian religion took its birth.

Platonism assisted materially the understanding of its dogmas. The "*Logos*" which with Plato meant the "wisdom," the reason of the Supreme Being, became with us the "word," and a second person of God. Profound metaphysics, above human intelligence, were an inaccessible sanctuary in which religion was enveloped.

It is not necessary here to repeat how Mary was afterwards declared to be the mother of God; how the consubstantiality of the Father and the "word" was established; as also the proceeding of the "*pneuma*," the divine organ of the divine *Logos*; as also the two natures and two wills resulting from the hypostasis; and lastly, the superior manducation—the soul nourished as well as the body, with the flesh and blood of the God-man, adored and eaten in the form of bread, present to the eyes, sensible to the taste, and yet annihilated. All mysteries have been sublime.

In the second century devils began to be cast out in the name of Jesus; before they were cast out in the name of Jehovah or Ihaho; for St. Matthew relates that the enemies of Jesus having said that He cast out devils in the name of the prince of devils, He answered, "If I cast out devils by Beelzebub, by whom do your sons cast them out?"

It is not known at what time the Jews recognized Beelzebub, who was a strange god, as the prince of devils; but it is known, for Josephus tells us, that there were at Jerusalem exorcists appointed to cast out devils from the bodies of the possessed; that is, of such as were attacked by singular maladies, which were then in a great part of the world attributed to the malefic genii.

These demons were then cast out by the true pronunciation of Jehovah, which is now lost, and by other ceremonies now forgotten.

This exorcism by Jehovah or by the other names of God, was still in use in the first ages of the church. Origen, disputing against Celsus, says to him: "If, when invoking God, or swearing by Him, you call Him 'the God of Abraham, Isaac, and Jacob,' you will by those words do things, the nature and force of which are such that the evil spirits submit to those who pronounce them; but if you call him by another name, as 'God of the roaring sea,' etc., no effect will be produced. The name of 'Israel,' rendered in Greek, will work nothing; but pronounce it in Hebrew with the other words required, and you will effect the conjuration."

The same Origen has these remarkable words: "There are names which are powerful from their own nature, such as those used by the sages of Egypt, the Magi of Persia, and the Brahmins of India. What is called 'magic,' is not a vain and chimerical art, as the Stoics and Epicureans pretend. The names '*Sabaoth*' and '*Adonai*' were not made for created beings, but belong to a mysterious theology which has reference to the Creator; hence the virtue of these names when they are arranged and pronounced according to rule."

Origen, when speaking thus, is not giving his private opinion; he is but repeating the universal opinion. All the religions then known admitted a sort of magic, which was divided into celestial magic, and infernal magic, necromancy and theurgy—all was prodigy, divination, and oracle. The Persians did not deny the miracles of the Egyptians, nor the Egyptians those of the Persians. God permitted the primitive Christians to be persuaded of the truth of the oracles attributed to the Sibyls, and left them a few other unimportant errors, which were in no way detrimental to the core of their religion.

Another thing, still quite remarkable, is that the Christians of the primitive ages held temples, altars, and images in abhorrence. Origen acknowledges this (No. 347). Everything was afterwards changed, with the discipline, when the Church assumed a permanent form.

FOURTH QUESTION

WHEN once a religion is established in a state, the tribunals are all employed in preventing the continuance of most of the things that were done in that religion before it was publicly received.

The founders used to assemble in private, in spite of magistrates; but now no assemblies are permitted but public ones under the eyes of the law, and all concealed associations are forbidden. The maxim formerly was, that "it is better to obey God than man"; the opposite maxim is now adopted, that "to follow the laws of the state is to obey God." All anyone heard talk of was obsessions and possessions; the devil was then let loose upon the world, but now the devil stays at home. Prodigies and predictions were necessary then but now are no longer admitted: a man who predicted calamities in the town square would now be sent to a madhouse. The founders secretly received the money of the faithful; but now, a man who gathered money for his own disposal without being so authorized by the law, would be brought before a court of justice. Thus we no longer use a single one of the scaffoldings that served to build the edifice.

FIFTH QUESTION

After our own holy religion, which indubitably is the only good one, what religion would be the least objectionable?

Would it not be the simplest? Would it not be a religion that would teach much morality and very little dogma; that would tend to make men just, without making them absurd; that would not ordain the belief of things impossible, contradictory, injurious to the Divinity, and pernicious to mankind; nor dare to threaten with eternal pains whosoever should possess common sense? Would it not be that religion which would not uphold its belief by the hand of the executioner, nor inundate the earth with blood to support unintelligible sophisms; that religion in which an ambiguous expression, a play upon words, and two or three supported charters, would not suffice to make a sovereign and a god out of a priest who is often incestuous, murderous, and a poisoner; nor make kings subject to this priest; that which would teach only the adoration of one God, justice, tolerance, and humanity.

SIXTH QUESTION

It has been said, that the religion of the Gentiles was absurd in many points, contradictory, and pernicious; but has there not been imputed to it more harm than it ever did, and more absurdities than it ever preached?

For to see Jupiter as a bull,
Snake, swan or any other creature;
I hardly find appropriate,
Nor does it surprise me if people sometimes gossip about it.
(Prologue of Moliére's *Amphitrion*)

All this is of course highly impertinent, but can you show me in all antiquity a temple dedicated to Leda lying with a swan or Europa with a bull? Was there ever a sermon preached at Athens or at Rome, to persuade the young women to copulate with their poultry? Are the fables collected and adorned by Ovid a religion? Are they not like our Golden Legend, our Flower of the Saints? If some Brahmin or dervish were to come and object to our story of St. Mary the Egyptian, who, upon finding herself without any means to pay the sailors who conveyed her to Egypt, gave to each of them instead of money what are called "favors," we should say to the Brahmin: Reverend father, you are mistaken; our religion is not the Golden Legend.

We reproach the ancients for their oracles and prodigies; if they could return to this world, and the miracles of our Lady of Loretto and our Lady of Ephesus could be counted, in whose favor would be the balance on the account?

Human sacrifices were established among almost every people, but very rarely put in practice. Among the Jews, only Jephthah's daughter and King Agag were immolated; for Isaac and Jonathan were not. Among the Greeks, the story of "Iphigenia" is not well authenticated; and human sacrifices were very rare among the ancient Romans. In short, the religion of the Pagans caused very little blood to be shed, while ours has deluged the earth. Ours is doubtless the only good, the only true one; but we have done so much harm by its means that when we speak of others we should be modest.

Seventh Question

If a man would persuade foreigners, or his own countrymen, of the truth of his religion, should he not go about it with the most insinuating mildness and the most engaging moderation? If he begins with telling them that what he announces is demonstrated, he will find a multitude of incredulous persons; if he ventures to tell them that they reject his doctrine only inasmuch as it condemns their passions; that their hearts have corrupted their minds; that their reasoning is only false and proud, he disgusts them; he causes them to revolt, he incenses them against himself; he himself ruins what he seeks to establish.

If the religion he announces be true, will violence and insolence render it more so? Do you put yourself in a rage, when you say that it is necessary to be mild, patient, beneficent, just, and to fulfill all the duties of society? No; because everyone is of your own opinion. Why, then, do you insult your brother when preaching to him a mysterious system of metaphysics? Because his opinion irritates your self-love. You are so proud as to require your brother to submit his intelligence to yours; wrath comes from humbled pride wrath; it has no other source. A man who has received twenty wounds in a battle does not fly into a passion; but a divine, wounded by the refusal of your assent, at once becomes furious and implacable.

EIGHTH QUESTION

Must we not carefully distinguish the religion of the state from theological religion? The religion of the state requires that the imans keep registers of the circumcised, the vicars or pastors registers of the baptized; that there be mosques, churches, temples, days consecrated to rest and worship, rituals established by law; that the ministers of those rites enjoy consideration without power; that they teach good morals to the people, and that the ministers of the law watch over the morals of the ministers of the temples. This religion of the state cannot at any time cause any disturbance.

This is not the case with theological religion: which is rather the source of all imaginable follies and disturbances; it is the mother of fanaticism and civil discord; it is the enemy of mankind. A bonze asserts that Fo is a God, that he was foretold by fakirs, that he was born of a white elephant, and that every bonze can by certain grimaces make a *Fo*. A *talapoin* says, that Fo was a holy man, whose doctrine the bonzes have corrupted, and that *Sammonocodom* is the true God. After a thousand arguments and contradictions, the two factions agree to refer the question to the *dalai-lama*, who resides three hundred leagues away, and who is not only immortal but also infallible. The two factions send a solemn deputation to him; and the dalai-lama begins, according to his divine custom, by distributing among them the contents of his chamber pot.

The two rival sects at first receive these contents with equal reverence; have them dried in the sun, and encase them in little rosaries which they kiss devoutly. No sooner have the *dalai-lama* and his council pronounced in the name of *Fo*, however, but the condemned party throw their rosaries in the vice-god's face, and try to give him a hundred lashes. The other party defends their *lama*, from whom they have received good lands; both fight a long time; and when at last they are tired of mutual extermination, assassination, and poisoning, they curse and insult each other, while the *dalai-lama* laughs, and continues to distribute his excrement to whosoever is desirous of receiving the good father lama's precious favors.

RÉSURRECTION / RESURRECTION

FIRST SECTION

THEY say that the Egyptians built their pyramids for no other purpose than to make tombs of them, and that their bodies, embalmed within and without, waited there for their souls to come and reanimate them at the end of a thousand years. But if these bodies were to come to life again, why did the embalmers begin the operation by piercing the skull with a gimlet, and drawing out the brain? The idea of coming to life again without brains would make one suspect that—if the expression may be used—the Egyptians had not many while alive; but let us bear in mind that most of the ancients believed the soul to be in the breast. And why should the soul be in the breast rather than elsewhere? Because, when our feelings are at all violent, we do in reality feel a dilatation or compression about the region of the heart, which caused it to be thought that the soul was lodged there. This soul was something aerial; it was a slight figure that went about at random until it found its body again.

The belief in resurrection is much more ancient than historical times. Athalides, son of Mercury, could die and come to life again at will; Æsculapius restored Hippolytus to life, and Hercules, Alceste. Pelops, after being cut to pieces by his father, was resuscitated by the gods. Plato relates that Heres came to life again for fifteen days only.

Among the Jews, the Pharisees did not adopt the dogma of the resurrection until long after Plato's time.

In the Acts of the Apostles there is a very singular fact, and one well worthy of attention. St. James and several of his companions advise St. Paul to go into the temple of Jerusalem and, although he was a Christian, to observe all the ceremonies of the Old Law, in order— they say—" that all may know that all that is said of you is false, and that you continue to respect the law of Moses." This is clearly saying: "Go and lie; go and perjure yourself; go and publicly deny the religion which you teach."

St. Paul then went seven days into the temple; but on the seventh he was discovered. He was accused of having come into it with strangers, and of having profaned it. Let us see how he extricated himself from this situation

Knowing that part of those present were Sadducees and the other part Pharisees, Paul cried out in the council: "Men and brethren, I am a Pharisee, the son of a Pharisee; because of the hope of another life and the resurrection of the dead they seek to condemn me." (Acts 23:6–8) There had been no mention of resurrection of the dead in this affair; Paul only said this to incense the Pharisees and Sadducees against each other.

V. 7. And when he had so spoken there arose a dissension between the Pharisees and the Sadducees; and the multitude was divided.

V. 8. For the Sadducees say that there is no resurrection, neither angel nor spirit; but the Pharisees confess both, etc.

It has been asserted that Job, who is very ancient, was acquainted with the doctrine of resurrection; and these words are cited: "I know that my Redeemer lives, and that one day His redemption shall rise upon me; or that I shall rise again from the dust, that my skin shall return, and that in my flesh I shall again see God."

But many commentators understand by these words that Job hopes soon to recover from his malady, and that he shall not always remain lying on the ground, as he then was. The sequel sufficiently proves this explanation to be the true one; for he cries out the next moment to his false and hardhearted friends: "Why then do you say let us persecute Him?" Or: "For you shall say, because we persecuted Him." Does not this evidently mean—you will repent of having ill used me, when you shall see me again in my future state of health and opulence. When a sick man says: I shall rise again, he does not say: I shall come to life again. To give forced meanings to clear passages is the sure way never to understand one another; or rather, to be regarded by honest men as lacking sincerity.

St. Jerome dates the birth of the sect of the Pharisees but a very short time before Jesus Christ. The rabbi Hillel is considered to have been the founder of the Pharisaic sect; and this Hillel was contemporary with St. Paul's master, Gamaliel.

Many of these Pharisees believed that only the Jews were brought to life again, and that the rest of mankind was not worth the trouble. Others maintained that there would be no rising again but in Palestine; and that the bodies of such as were buried elsewhere would be secretly conveyed into the neighborhood of Jerusalem, there to rejoin their souls. But St. Paul, writing to the people of Thessalonica, says that, *as they will witness, the second coming of Jesus Christ is for him and for them.*

V. 16. For the Lord Himself shall descend from heaven with a shout, with the voice of the archangel, and with the trump of God; and the dead in Christ shall rise first.

V. 17. Then we which are alive and remain shall be caught up with them in the clouds to meet the Lord in the air; and so shall we ever be with the Lord. (1 Thess. 4)

Does not this important passage clearly prove that the first Christians counted on seeing the end of the world, foretold as it was by St. Luke to take place in his own lifetime? But if they did not see this end of the world, if no one rose again in their day, that which is deferred is not lost.

St. Augustine believed that children, and even still-born infants, would rise again as adults. Origen, Jerome, Athanasius, Basil, and others, did not believe that women would rise again with the marks of their sex.

In short, there have ever been disputes about what we have been, about what we are, and about what we shall be.

SECOND SECTION

Father Malebranche proves resurrection by the caterpillars becoming butterflies. This proof, as everyone may perceive, is no weightier than the wings of the insects from which he borrows it. Calculating thinkers bring forth arithmetical objections against this truth which he has so well proved. They say that men and other animals are really fed and derive their growth from the substance of their predecessors. The body of a man, reduced to ashes, scattered in the air, and falling on the surface of the earth, becomes corn or vegetable. So Cain ate a part of Adam; Enoch fed on Cain; Irad on Enoch; Mahalaleel on Irad; Methuselah on Mahalaleel; and thus we find that there is not one among us who has not swallowed some portion of our first parent. Hence it has been said that we have all been cannibals. This is the most clear after a battle; not only do we kill our brethren, but at the end of two or three years, when the harvests have been gathered from the field of battle, we have eaten them all; and we, in turn, shall be eaten with the greatest facility imaginable. Now, when we are to rise again, how shall we restore to each one the body that belongs to him, without losing something of our own?

So say those who trust not in resurrection; but the resurrectionists have answered them very pertinently.

A rabbi named Samaï proves resurrection by this passage of Exodus: "I appeared unto Abraham, Isaac, and Jacob, and swore to give unto them the land of Canaan." Now—says this great rabbi—notwithstanding this oath, God did not give them that land; therefore, they will rise again to enjoy it, in order that the oath be fulfilled.

The profound philosopher Calmet finds a much more conclusive proof in vampires. He saw vampires issuing from churchyards to go and suck the blood of good people in their sleep; it is clear that they could not suck the blood of the living if they themselves were still dead; therefore they had risen again; this is peremptory.

It is also certain that at the Day of Judgment all the dead will walk under ground, like moles—so says the Talmud—in order that they may appear in the valley of Jehoshaphat, which lies between the city of Jerusalem and the Mount of Olives. There will be a good deal of squeezing in this valley; but it will only be necessary to reduce the bodies proportionally, like Milton's devils in the hall of Pandemonium.

This resurrection will take place to the sound of the trumpet, according to St. Paul. There must, of course, be more trumpets than one; for thunder itself cannot be heard for more than three or four leagues round. Some people ask how many trumpets there will be—the theologians have not yet made the calculation, but they will.

The Jews say that Queen Cleopatra, who no doubt believed in the resurrection like all the ladies of that day, asked a Pharisee if we were to rise again quite naked. The doctor answered that we shall be very well dressed; for the same reason that the corn that has been sown and perished under ground rises again in ear with a robe and a beard. This rabbi was an excellent theologian; he reasoned like Dom Calmet.

SALOMON / SOLOMON

THE name of Solomon has always been revered in the East. The works believed to be his, the "Annals of the Jews," and the fables of the Arabs, have carried his renown as far as the Indies. His reign is the great epoch of the Hebrews.

He was the third king of Palestine. The First Book of Kings says that his mother, Bathsheba, obtained from David the promise that he should crown Solomon, her son, instead of Adonijah, his eldest. It is not surprising that a woman who was an accomplice in the death of her first husband would have had artifice enough to cause the inheritance to be given to the fruit of her adultery, and to cause the legitimate son (who was also the eldest) to be disinherited.

It is a very remarkable fact that the prophet Nathan, who reproached David with his adultery, the murder of Uriah, and the marriage which followed this murder, was the same who afterwards seconded Bathsheba in placing that Solomon on the throne, who was born of this bloody and infamous marriage. This conduct, if we reason only according to the flesh, would prove that the prophet Nathan had, according to circumstances, two weights and two measures. The book itself does not say that Nathan received a particular mission from God to disinherit Adonijah. If he had one, we must respect it; but we can only accept that which we find written.

Adonijah, excluded from the throne by Solomon, asked him but one favor—permission to marry Abishag, the young girl who had been given to David to warm him in his old age.

Scripture does not say whether Solomon argued with Adonijah over the concubine of his father; but it does say that Solomon, on the basis of this one request, had Adonijah assassinated. Apparently God, who gave him the spirit of wisdom, refused him that of justice and humanity, as he afterwards refused him the gift of continence.

It is said in the same Book of Kings that he was the master of a great kingdom which extended from the Euphrates to the Red Sea and the Mediterranean; but unfortunately it is said at the same time, that the king of Egypt conquered the country of Gezer, in Canaan, and that he gave the city of Gezer as a portion to his daughter, whom they claim Solomon married. It is also said that there was a king at Damascus; and the kingdoms of Tyre and Sidon flourished. Surrounded thus with powerful states, he doubtless manifested his wisdom in living in peace with them all. The extreme abundance which enriched his country could only be the fruit of this profound wisdom, since, as we have already remarked, in the time of Saul there was not a single ironworker in the whole country, and that only two swords could be found when it came time for Saul to go to war against the Philistines, to whom the Jews were subjugated at the time.

Saul, who started out with only two swords for his entire state, quickly amassed an army of three hundred and thirty thousand men. The sultan of Turkey never had such armies, large enough even to conquer the whole world. These contradictions seem to exclude all logical debate, but those who wish to reason find it problematic that David, the successor of Saul, so vanquished by the Philistines, could have established so vast an empire.

The riches which he left to Solomon are still more wonderful; he gave him in ready money one hundred and three thousand talents of gold, and one million thirteen thousand talents of silver. The Hebraic talent of gold is worth six thousand pounds sterling, the talent of silver, about five hundred pounds sterling.

The sum total of the legacy in ready money, without the jewels and other effects, and without the ordinary revenue—proportioned no doubt to this treasure—amounted, according to this calculation, to one billion, one hundred and nineteen million, five hundred thousand pounds sterling, or to five billion, five hundred and ninety-seven German crowns, or to twenty-five billion, forty-eight million francs. There was not then so much money circulating through the whole world.

In the face of all that we can't see why Solomon went to so much trouble to send his fleets to the land of Ophir to bring back gold. It is even harder to guess how this powerful monarch, in all his vast states, had not a single man who knew how to cut wood from the forest of Lebanon. He was obliged to beg Hiram, king of Tyre, to lend him woodcutters and laborers to work it. It must be confessed that these contradictions test the genius of commentators.

Every day, fifty oxen and one hundred sheep were served up for the dinner and supper of his houses, and poultry and game in proportion, which might be about sixty thousand pounds of meat per day. He kept a good house. They also say that he had forty thousand stables, and as many houses for his chariots of war, but only twelve thousand stables for his cavalry. That's a great many chariots for a mountainous country; and it was a great equipage for a king whose predecessor had had only a mule at his coronation, and for a territory which bred only donkeys.

It was not becoming a prince possessing so many chariots to be limited to only a few women; they say he therefore possessed seven hundred who bore the name of queen; what is strange, however, is that he had but three hundred concubines; contrary to the custom of kings, who have generally more mistresses than wives. He kept four hundred and twelve thousand horses, doubtless to take the air with them along the lake of Gennesaret, or that of Sodom, or in the neighborhood of the Brook of Kedron,

which would be one of the most delightful places upon earth—
if the brook was not dry nine months of the year and if the earth
was not a wee bit stony.

As to the temple which he built and which the Jews believed to
be the finest work of the universe, if the Bramantes, the
Michelangelos, and the Palladios, had seen this building, they
would not have admired it. It was a kind of small square fortress,
which enclosed a court; in this court was one edifice measuring
forty cubits long, and another measuring twenty; and it is said, that
this second edifice, which was properly the temple, the oracle, the
holy of holies, was only twenty cubits in length and breadth, and
twenty cubits high. There does not exist a European architect who
would not have considered such a building a barbarian monument.

The books attributed to Solomon have lasted longer than his
temple. It is perhaps one of the great proofs of the power of
prejudice and the weakness of the human spirit.

The name of the author alone has rendered these books
respectable. They have been believed to be good, because they
were believed to be written by a king, and this king passed for
the wisest of men.

The first work attributed to him is that of Proverbs. It is a collection of trifling, low, incoherent maxims, in bad taste, and
without meaning. How can one be persuaded that an enlightened king would have composed a collection of sentences in
which not one addresses the art of government, politics, manners of courtiers or the customs of a court?

Entire chapters talk about nothing but prostitutes, who invite
passersby in the streets to lie with them. Let us look at a few random examples of these proverbs.

"There are three things that are never satisfied, a fourth which
never says 'enough'; the grave; the barren womb; the earth that is
not filled with water, are the three; and the fourth is fire, which
never says 'enough.'

"There are three difficult things, and a fourth which I know not. The way of an eagle in the air, the way of a serpent upon a rock, the way of a ship in the midst of the sea, and the way of a man with a maid.

"There be four things which are the littlest upon the earth, but yet are wiser than the wise men; the ants, a little people who prepare their food during harvest; the hares, a feeble race, yet they make their houses in rocks; the locusts have no king, and so travel in bands; the lizard, who works with her hands, and lives in the palaces of kings."

How can we impute such absurdities to a great king, to the wisest of mortals? Those who name him the author of such childish platitudes, and who then admire them, are certainly not the wisest of men.

The Proverbs have been attributed to Isaiah, Elijah, Sobna, Eliakim, Joachim, and several others. But whoever it was that compiled this collection of Eastern sentences, it does not appear that it was a king who gave himself the trouble. Would he have said that the terror of the king is like the roaring of a lion? It is thus that a subject or a slave speaks, who trembles at the anger of his master. Would Solomon have spoken so much of unchaste women? Would he have said: "Look thou not upon the wine when it is red, when it gives its color in the glass?"

I doubt very much whether there were any drinking glasses in the time of Solomon; it is a very recent invention; all antiquity drank from cups of wood or metal; and this single passage perhaps indicates that this Jewish rhapsody was composed in Alexandria, just like so many other Jewish books.*

---

* A pedant asserts that he has found an error in this passage: he claims that the goblet, which was, he says, made of wood or metal, was incorrectly translated by the word *glass*. But how does he think the wine could have sparkled in a metal or wood goblet? And what does it matter!

The Book of Ecclesiastes, which is attributed to Solomon, is of quite a different order and taste. The speaker in this work is a man undeceived by visions of grandeur, tired of pleasures, and disgusted with science. He is an Epicurean philosopher who repeats on every page that the just and unjust are subject to the same accidents; that man has nothing more than the beasts; that it is better not to be born than to exist; that there is no other life; and that there is nothing good and reasonable but the peaceful enjoyment of the fruit of one's labor with the woman one loves.

The entire work is that of a materialist, who is simultaneously sensual and disgusted. It appears as though he stuck an edifying word or two on God in the last verse in order to diminish the scandal which such a book must necessarily create.

Critics will have difficulty persuading themselves that this book be Solomon's. It is not natural that he would say: "Woe to thee, O land, when thy king is a child!" The Jews had not yet had such kings.

It is not natural that he would say: "I observe the face of the king." It is much more likely, that the author wished to make Solomon speak in his text, and that by this alienation of mind that fills all the works of the Jews, he often forgot as he wrote that he was then supposed to be speaking as a king.

What is still surprising is that this impious work has been consecrated among the canonical books. If the canon of the Bible were to be established now, the Book of Ecclesiastes would certainly not be included; but it was inserted at a time when books were very rare, and more admired than read. All that can be done now is to mitigate as much as possible the Epicureanism which prevails in this work. The Book of Ecclesiastes has been treated like many other things which disgust in an entirely different manner. They were established in times of ignorance and we are forced, to the shame of reason, to maintain them in enlightened times and to disguise the either the absurdity or the horror of them by allegories.

The "Song of Songs" is still attributed to Solomon because the name of that king is found in two or three places; because the beloved is told that she is as beautiful as the curtains of Solomon; because she says that she is black, it was believed that Solomon referred to his Egyptian wife in this manner.

These three reasons are each equally ridiculous.

1. When the beloved, in speaking to her lover, says "The king hath brought me into his chamber," she is obviously speaking of someone besides her lover; therefore the king is not this lover; it is the king of the festival; it is the paranymph, the master of the house, whom she means; and this Jewess is so far from being the mistress of a king that throughout the work she is a shepherdess, a country girl who goes seeking her lover through the fields and in the streets of the town and who is stopped at the gates by guards who steal her dress.

2. "I am as beautiful as the curtains of Solomon," is the expression of a villager, who would say: I am as beautiful as the king's tapestries; and it is precisely because the name of Solomon is found in this work, that it cannot be his. What monarch could make so ridiculous a comparison? "Behold," says the beloved in the third chapter,? "behold King Solomon with the crown wherewith his mother crowned him in the day of his espousals!" Who doesn't recognize in these expressions the common comparisons which ordinary girls make in speaking of their lovers? They say: "He is as beautiful as a prince; he has the air of a king," etc.

It is true that the shepherdess who is made to speak in this amorous song says that she is tanned by the sun, that she is brown. Now if this was the daughter of the king of Egypt, she was certainly not so tanned. Women of rank in Egypt are fair. Cleopatra was so; and, in a word, this person could not be at once a peasant and a queen.

A monarch who had a thousand wives might have said to one of them: "Let her kiss me with the lips of her mouth; for thy breasts are better than wine." A king and a shepherd, when the subject is of kissing, might express themselves in the same manner. It is true that it is quite strange that some claim that it is the girl who speaks at this point, singing the praises of the tits of her lover.

Nor will I deny that a gallant knight might have made his mistress say: "A bundle of myrrh is my well beloved unto me; he shall lie all night between my breasts." And while I many not have a very good idea of what exactly a bundle of myrrh might be, when the beloved advises her lover to put his left hand around her neck and to embrace her with the right hand, I understand quite well.

Perhaps we could ask the author of the Song of Songs to elaborate when he says "Thy navel is like a round goblet in which there is always something to drink; thy belly is like a heap of wheat; thy two breasts are like twin fawns; and thy nose as the tower of Lebanon."

I confess that the *Eclogues* of Virgil are in a different style; but to each his own, and a Jew is not obliged to write like Virgil.

Here's yet another fine turn of Eastern eloquence: "Our sister is still very young, and she hath no breasts. What shall we do with our sister? If she be a wall, we will build upon her; and if she be a door, we will close it."

Solomon, the wisest of men, might have spoken thus when he was tipsy; but several rabbis have maintained, not only that this voluptuous eclogue was not King Solomon's, but that it is not authentic. Theodore of Mopsuestes was of this opinion, and the famous Grotius calls the "Song of Songs," a libertine flagitious work. However, it is consecrated, and we regard it as a perpetual allegory of the marriage of Jesus Christ with the Church. One must admit that the allegory is rather strong, and we see not what the Church might mean when the author says that his little sister has no breasts.

After all, this song is a precious relic of antiquity; it is the only book of love of the Hebrews which remains to us. True, it is a somewhat inept rhapsody, but there is a great deal of sensuality.

All it talks about is kissing on the mouth, breasts sweeter than wine, cheeks the color of turtledoves. Sexual pleasure is often mentioned. It is a Jewish eclogue. The style is like that of all the works of eloquence of the Hebrews, without connection, without order, full of repetition, confused, ridiculously metaphorical, but containing passages which breathe simplicity and love.

The "Book of Wisdom" is in a more serious taste; but it is no more Solomon's than the "Song of Songs." It is generally attributed to Jesus, the son of Sirac, and by some to Philo of Biblos; but whoever the author may be, it would seem that in his time the Pentateuch did not yet exist; for he says in chapter x., that Abraham was going to sacrifice Isaac at the time of the Deluge; and in another place he speaks of the patriarch Joseph as of a king of Egypt.

As for Ecclesiastes, which we already discussed, Grotius claims that it was written under Zorobabel. We have seen what liberties the author of Ecclesiastes takes in his expression; we know that he says that "men have nothing more than beasts; that it is better not to be born than to exist; that there is no other life, that there is nothing good but to take pleasure in one's works with the woman one loves."

It could have been that Solomon said such things to some of his wives; it is claimed that these are objections that he makes to himself; but these maxims with their air of libertinage don't resemble objections at all, and it's a mockery to claim that an author is saying the opposite of what he says.

Besides which, several church fathers have claimed that Solomon had made penitence, and that we could thus pardon him.

It is very likely that Solomon was rich and learned for his time and people. Exaggeration, the inseparable companion of vulgarity, attributes riches to him which he could not have possessed, and books which he could not have written. Respect for antiquity has since consecrated these errors.

But what does it matter to us, that these books were written by a Jew? Our Christian religion is founded on the Jewish, but not on all the books which the Jews have written. For instance, why should the "Song of Songs" be more sacred to us than the fables of Talmud? It is, say they, because we have included it in the canon of the Hebrews. And what is this canon? It is a collection of authentic works. Well, does being authentic necessarily make a work divine? A history of the little kingdoms of Judah and Sichem, for instance—is it anything but a history? This is a strange prejudice. We hold the Jews in horror, and we insist that all that which has been written by them, and collected by us bears the stamp of Divinity. There never was so palpable a contradiction.

SECTE / SECT

EVERY sect, of whatever sort it may be, is a rallying point for doubt and error. Scotists, Thomists, Realists, Nominalists, Papists, Calvinists, Molinists, and Jansenists, are only combative pseudonyms.

There is no sect in geometry; we never say: A Euclidian, an Archimedian.

When truth is evident, it is impossible to divide people into parties and factions. Nobody disputes that it is broad day at noon.

Ever since that part of astronomy which determines the course of the stars and the return of eclipses became known, there is no longer any dispute among astronomers.

No one says in England, "I am a Newtonian, I am a Lockian, Halleyan . . ." and why? Because whoever has read anything cannot refuse to acknowledge the truths taught by these three great men. The more Newton is revered, the less likely anyone is to call themselves a Newtonian; this mot presupposes the existence of anti-Newtonians in England. We may yet have a few Cartesians in France, but this is only because Descartes' system is a web of ridiculous and imaginative errors.

It is similar with a small number of well-established truths. The Acts of the Tower of London having truly been collected by Rymer, there are no Rymerians, because no one would think to argue with this archive. We find therein no contradictions, no absurdities, no prodigies, nothing contrary to reason—nothing, therefore, but sectarians striving to uphold or to reverse cases through absurd arguments. Everyone agrees therefore that the Acts of Rymer are trustworthy.

You are a Mohammedan, and therefore there are many people who are not Mohammedans, and therefore you could very well be in the wrong.

What would be the true religion, if Christianity did not exist? That one in which there would be no sects; that one in which all minds necessarily agreed.

Now, in what doctrine are all minds agreed? In the adoration of one God, and in integrity. All the philosophers on earth who have professed a religion have said in all eras: "There is a God, and we must be just." Behold then the universal religion, established throughout all time and among all men!

The point then upon which all agree is therefore true; the systems by which all differ are therefore false.

My sect is the best, says a Brahmin. But, my friend, if your sect is the best, it is necessary; for if it were not absolutely necessary, you must confess that it would be useless. If, on the contrary, it is necessary, it must be so to all men; how then is it that all men do not possess that which is absolutely necessary to them? How is it that the rest of the world laughs at you and your Brahma?

When Zoroaster, Hermes, Orpheus, Minos, and all the great men say: Let us worship God, and be just, no one laughs; but all the world sneers at him who pretends, that the only way to please God is to die holding a cow's tail or at him who claims we should cut off a particle of foreskin for the same purpose; or at him who consecrates crocodiles and onions; or at him who attaches eternal salvation to the bones of dead men carried underneath the shirt, or to a plenary indulgence purchased at Rome for two and a half sous.

Where does this universal convergence of laughing and hissing from one end of the universe to the other come from? Obviously things which all the world derides are not evident truths. What shall we say of a secretary of Sejanus, who dedicates a pompous book entitled *The Truth of the Sibylline Oracles, Proved from Facts* to Petronius?

This secretary at first proves to you, that it was necessary that God send many Sibyls down to earth, one after the other, because he had no other means of instructing men. It is proven that God communicated with these Sibyls, because the word "sibyl" means "Advice of God." They ought to live a long time, for this is the least of privileges for persons with whom God communicates. They numbered twelve, because this number is sacred. They certainly predicted all the events in the world, because Tarquin the Proud bought three of their books from an old woman for a hundred crowns. What unbeliever, exclaims the secretary, dare deny all these evident facts, which took place in one corner of the earth, in the face of all the world? Who can deny the accomplishment of their prophecies? Has not Virgil himself cited the predictions of the Sibyls? If we have not the first copies of the sibylline books, written at a time when no one could read and write, have we not authentic copies nonetheless. Impiety must be silent before such proofs. Thus spoke Houteville to Sejanus, in the hopes of obtaining the post of chief augur, with revenue of fifty thousand pounds; but he obtained nothing.

That which my sect teaches me is obscure, I confess it, exclaims a fanatic; and it is because of obscurity that I must believe it; for it says itself that it abounds in obscurities. My sect is extravagant, therefore it is divine; for how else could something so seemingly mad have been embraced by so many people? It is precisely like the Koran, which the Sonnites say presents at once the face of an angel and that of a beast. Be not scandalized at the muzzle of the beast and revere the face of the angel. Thus speaks this madman; but a fanatic of another sect replies to the first fanatic: It is you who is the beast, and I who am the angel.

Now who will judge this process, and decide between these two inspired personages? The reasonable and impartial man who is learned in a science which is not that of words; the man divested of prejudice, and a lover of truth and of justice; the man, in fine, who is not a beast, and who pretends not to be an angel.

SENS COMMUN / COMMON SENSE

THERE is sometimes in vulgar expressions an image of what passes in the heart of all men. *Sensus communis* signified among the Romans not only common sense, but also humanity and sensibility. As we are not equal to the Romans, this word with us conveys not half what it did with them. It signifies only good sense—plain, straight-forward reasoning—the first notion of ordinary things—midway between dullness and intellect. To say, "that man has no common sense," is a gross insult; while the expression, "that man has common sense," is also an affront; it implies that he is not entirely stupid, but that he lacks what we call intellect. But what is the meaning of common sense, if it be not the senses? Men, when they invented this term, supposed that nothing entered the mind except by the senses; otherwise would they have used the word "sense" to signify the result of the common faculty of reason?

They say sometimes, "Common sense is very rare." What does this expression mean? That, in many men, dawning reason is arrested in its progress by a few prejudices; that a man who judges quite reasonably in one situation will grossly deceive himself in another. The Arab, who, besides being a good calculator is a learned chemist and an exact astronomer; nevertheless believes that Mohammed put half of the moon into his sleeve.

How is it that he was so much above common sense in the three sciences above mentioned, and beneath it when he proceeded to the subject of half the moon? It is because, in the first case, he had seen with his own eyes, and perfected his own intelligence; and, in the second, he had used the eyes of others, by shutting his own, and perverting the common sense within him.

How could this strange perversion of mind operate? How could the ideas that marched with so regular and firm a step through his brain on many subjects, trip so miserably on another subject, a thousand times more palpable and easy to comprehend? This man has still the same principles of intelligence; he must have therefore possessed a polluted organ, as it sometimes happens that the most delicate epicure has a depraved taste in regard to a particular kind of nourishment.

How did the organ of this Arab, who saw half of the moon in Mohammed's sleeve, become disordered?—by fear. He was told that if he did not believe in this sleeve his soul, immediately after his death, in passing over the narrow bridge, would fall forever into the abyss. He was told much worse—if ever you doubt this sleeve, one dervish will call you an impious person; another will prove that you are mad, because, having every possible reason to believe, you will not submit your superb reason to evidence; a third will refer you to the insignificant divan of a small province, and you will be legally impaled.

All this produces a terrified panic in the good Arab, his wife, sister, and all his little family. They possess good sense in all the rest, but on this article their imagination is diseased like that of

Pascal, who continually saw a precipice at the edge of his chair. But does our Arab really believe in the sleeve of Mohammed? No; he tries to believe it; he says it is impossible, but it is true—I believe that which I do not credit. He forms a chaos of ideas in his head in regard to this sleeve, which he fears to disentangle, and that is truly to lack common sense.

Sensation / Sensation

OYSTERS, it is said, have two senses; moles four; all other animals five, like man. Some people contend for a sixth, but it is evident that the voluptuous sensation to which they allude is reducible to that of touch; and that five senses are our lot. It is impossible for us to imagine or desire anything beyond them.

It may be that in other globes the inhabitants possess sensations of which we can form no idea. It is possible that the number of senses augments from globe to globe, and that an existence with innumerable and perfect senses will be the final attainment of all being.[68]

But with respect to ourselves and our five senses, what is the extent of our capacity? We constantly feel in spite of ourselves, and never because we will it so: it is impossible for us to avoid having the sensation which our nature ordains when any object excites it. The sensation is within us, but does not depend on us. We receive it, but how do we receive it? It is evident that there is no connection between the stricken air, the words sung to me, and the impression which these words make upon my brain.

We are astonished at thought, but sensation is equally wonderful. A divine power is as manifest in the sensation of the least of insects as in the brain of Newton. In the meantime, if a thousand animals die before your eyes, you are not at all anxious to know what becomes of their faculty of sensation, though it be the work of the Supreme Being; you regard them as machines of nature, created to perish and give way to others.

For what purpose and in what manner might their sensations persist, when they exist no longer? What need has the author of all things to preserve the properties of a subject that no longer exists? It is as reasonable to assert that the power of the plant called "sensitive," to withdraw its leaves towards its branches, continues to exist when the plant is no more. You will doubtless ask how it is that the sensation of animals perishes with them while the mind of man perishes not? I cannot answer this question; I do not know enough to resolve it. The eternal author of mind and of sensation alone knows how he gives it, and how he preserves it.

All antiquity maintained that our understanding contains nothing which has not been received by our senses. Descartes claims in his fantasies that we have metaphysical ideas before we are acquainted with the nipple of our wet nurse. A faculty of theology proscribed this dogma, not because it was erroneous, but because it was new. Finally, however, it was adopted, because it had been destroyed by the English philosopher Locke, and an Englishman must necessarily be in the wrong. Finally, having so often changed opinion, the faculty once again proscribed the ancient opinion which declares that the senses are the inlets to the mind. In this it is acting like deeply indebted governments, who issue a currency on one day and deny it the next, but no one has honored the faculty of theology's currency in a long time.

All the academic faculties in the world will never prevent philosophers from seeing that we begin by sensation, and that our memory is nothing but a continued sensation. A man born without his five senses would be destitute of all ideas, supposing it possible for him to live. Metaphysical notions are obtained only through the senses; for how is a circle or a triangle to be measured, if a circle or a triangle has neither been touched nor seen? How can one form an imperfect notion of infinity, without a notion of limits? And how to redefine limits, without having either beheld or felt them?

Sensation encompasses all our faculties, says a great philosopher. (page 128, volume 2, *Traité des sensations*)[69]

What ought to be concluded from all this? You who read and think, conclude.

The Greeks had invented the faculty "*Psyche*" for sensation, and the faculty *Nous* for thought. We are, unhappily, ignorant of the nature of these two faculties: we possess them, but their origin is no more known to us than to the oyster, the sea-nettle, the polypus, worms, or plants. By what inconceivable mechanism is feeling diffused throughout my body, and thought in my head alone? If the head be cut off, it is highly unlikely that you will then be able to solve a problem in geometry. In the meantime, your pineal gland, your fleshly body, in which abides your soul, exists for a long time without alteration, while your separated head is so full of animal spirits that it frequently exhibits motion after having been separated from the trunk. It seems as if at this moment it must possess the liveliest ideas, resembling the head of Orpheus, which still uttered melodious song and chanted Eurydice when they cast it into the waters of the Hebrus.

If you think no longer, after losing our heads, how is it that the heart still feels when it is torn out?

You feel, you say, because all nerves have their origin in the brain; and yet if you are trepanned, and a portion of your brain is burned, you feel nothing. Men who know the reasons of all this are very clever.

SONGES / DREAMS

Somnia quæ mentes ludunt volitantibus umbris,
Non delumbra deum nec ab æthere numina mittunt,
Sed sibi quisque facit.

According to Petronius, dreams are not of divine origin, but self-formed.

But how, all the senses being defunct in sleep, does there remain an internal one which retains consciousness? How is it, that while your eyes see not, your ears hear not, you nonetheless see and hear in our dreams? The hound renews the chase in a dream: he barks, follows his prey, and is in at the death. The poet composes verses in his sleep; the mathematician examines his diagrams; and the metaphysician reasons well or poorly; of all of which there are striking examples.

Are these the only the organs of the machine which act? Is it the pure soul, submitted to the empire of the senses, enjoying its faculties at liberty?

If the organs alone produce dreams by night, why not produce ideas alone by day? If the soul, pure and tranquil, acting for itself during the repose of the senses, is the sole cause, the single subject of our ideas while we are sleeping, why are all these ideas usually irregular, unreasonable, and incoherent? What! It is at the time when the soul is least disturbed, that there is the most perturbation in its imagination? It is free, and it is crazy! If it was born with metaphysical ideas, as asserted by so many writers who dream with their eyes wide open, its correct and luminous ideas of being, of infinity, and of all the primary principles, ought to be revealed in the soul with the greatest energy when the body sleeps. We should then never be good philosophers except when dreaming.

Whatever system you embrace, whatever your vain endeavors to prove to yourself that memory impels the brain, and that the brain acts upon the soul, you must concede that your ideas come, in sleep, without you and in spite of you: your will plays no part in it. It is therefore certain that you can think seven or eight hours running without the least desire to do so, and even without being certain that you think. Weigh that, and endeavor to figure out how animals are constituted.

Dreams have always been an object of great superstition, and nothing is more natural. A man deeply affected by the sickness of his mistress dreams that he sees her dying; she dies the next day; therefore the gods have predicted her death to him.

The general of an army dreams that he wins a battle that he subsequently wins; the gods had decreed that he should be a conqueror.

We only keep track of those dreams which have come true. Dreams form a great part of ancient history, just as do oracles.

The "Vulgate" thus translates the end of Leviticus 19:26: "You shall not observe dreams." But the word "dream" exists not in the Hebrew; and it would be exceedingly strange if attention to dreams was reproved in the same book in which it is said that Joseph became the benefactor of Egypt and his family in consequence of his interpretation of three dreams.

The interpretation of dreams was a thing so common, that the supposed art had no limits, and the interpreter was sometimes called upon to guess what another man had dreamed. Nebuchadnezzar, having forgotten a dream he had, ordered his Magi to guess what it was he had dreamed, and threatened them with death if they failed; but the Jew Daniel from the school of the Magi saved their lives by divining at once what the king had dreamed, and interpreting it. This history, and many others, may serve to prove that the laws of the Jews did not forbid oneiromancy, that is to say, the science of dreams.

SUPERSTITION / SUPERSTITION

Chapter taken from Cicero, Seneca, and Plutarch

FIRST SECTION

Almost everything that goes beyond the adoration of a supreme being and the submission of the heart to his eternal orders is superstition. The forgiveness of crimes through certain ceremonies is a particularly dangerous one.

> *Et nigras mactant pecudes, et manibuu' divis,*
> *Inferias mittunt.*
> > —Lucretius, b. iii, 52–53.

> *O faciles nimium qui tristia crimina caedis,*
> *Fluminea tolli posse putatis aqua!*
> > —Ovid, *Fasti* ii, 45–46.

You think that God will forget your homicide, if you bathe in a river, if you sacrifice a black sheep and if a few words are pronounced over you. A second homicide then will be forgiven you at the same price, and so a third; and a hundred murders will cost you only a hundred black sheep and a hundred ablutions. Oh miserable mortals, you must do better—let there be no murders, and no offerings of black sheep.

What a contemptible idea, to imagine that a priest of Isis and Cybele will reconcile you to the Divinity by playing cymbals and castanets. And who then is this priest of Cybele, this wandering eunuch, who preys upon your weakness to set himself up as a mediator between you and heaven? What patent has he received from God? He receives money from you for muttering words; and you think that the Being of Beings ratifies the utterances of this charlatan?

There are innocent superstitions; you dance on festival days, in honor of Diana or Pomona, or one of the minor divinities that fill your calendar; so be it. Dancing is very agreeable; it is useful to the body; it exhilarates the mind; it does no harm to any one; but do not imagine that Pomona and Vertumnus are grateful that you have jumped in honor of them, and that they may punish you for having failed to jump. There are no Pomona and Vertumnus but the gardener's spade and hoe. Do not be so imbecile as to believe that your garden will be hailed upon if you have failed to dance the *pyrrhic* or the *cordax*.

There is one superstition which is perhaps pardonable, and even encouraging to virtue—that of placing among the gods great men who have been benefactors to mankind. It would doubtless be better to limit ourselves to regarding them simply as venerable men, and, above all, to try to imitate them. Venerate, without worshipping, a Solon, a Thales, a Pythagoras; but do not adore a Hercules for having cleansed the stables of Augeas, and for having lain with fifty girls in one night.

Above all, beware of establishing worship for rogues who have no merit but ignorance, enthusiasm, and filth; who have made idleness and beggary their duty and their glory. Do they who have been at best useless during their lives merit an apotheosis after their deaths?

Let it be noted that the most superstitious times have always been those of the most horrible crimes.

Second Section

The superstitious man is to the knave what the slave is to the tyrant; nay more—the superstitious man is governed by the fanatic, and becomes a fanatic himself. Superstition, born in Paganism, adopted by Judaism, infected the Church in the earliest ages. All the fathers of the Church, without exception, believed in the power of magic. The Church always condemned magic, but she nonetheless believed in it; she excommunicated sorcerers, not as mistaken madmen but as men who truly had dealings with the devils.

Nowadays, one half of Europe believes that the other half has long been and still is superstitious. The Protestants regard relics, indulgences, macerations, prayers for the dead, holy water, and almost all the rites of the Roman church as mad superstitions. According to them, superstition consists in mistaking useless practices for necessary ones. Among the Roman Catholics there are some, more enlightened than their forefathers, who have renounced many of these formerly sacred usages; and they defend their adherence to those which they have retained by saying they are indifferent, and what is merely indifferent cannot be an evil.

It is difficult to mark the limits of superstition. A Frenchman traveling in Italy finds almost everything superstitious; nor is he much mistaken. The archbishop of Canterbury asserts that the archbishop of Paris is superstitious; the Presbyterians cast the same reproach upon his grace of Canterbury, and are in turn called superstitious by the Quakers, who in the eyes of the rest of Christians are the most superstitious of all.

Among Christian societies, then, no one can agree upon what superstition is. The sect which appears to be the least violently attacked by this mental disease is the one which has the fewest rites. But if, with but few ceremonies, it is strongly attached to an absurd belief, that absurd belief is of itself equivalent to all the superstitious practices observed from the time of Simon the Magician, down to that of the curate Gaufredi.

It is therefore evident that what is the foundation of the religion of one sect is regarded by another sect as superstitious.

The Muslims accuse all Christian societies of superstition, and are in turn accused of it by them. Who shall decide this great debate? Shall not reason? But each sect declares that reason is on its side. Force then will decide, at least until such a time as reason shall have penetrated into a sufficient number of heads to disarm force.

For instance: there was a time in Christian Europe when newlyweds were not permitted to enjoy the nuptial rights until they had bought that privilege from the bishop and the curate.

Whosoever did not leave a part of his property to the Church in his will was excommunicated and deprived of burial. This was called dying unconfessed—i. e., not confessing the Christian religion. And when a Christian died intestate, the Church relieved the deceased from this excommunication by making a will for him, stipulating and enforcing the payment of the pious legacy which the defunct should have made.

That is why Pope Gregory IX and St. Louis ordained, after the Council of Nice in 1235, that every will not witnessed by a priest should be null; and the pope decreed that the testator and the notary would be excommunicated.

The tax on sins was, if possible, still more scandalous. The laws to which the superstition of nations submitted were upheld by force; and it was only in the course of time that reason caused these shameful vexations to be abolished, while at the same time allowing so many others to persist.

How far does policy permit superstition to be undermined? This is a very thorny question; it is like asking to what degree a man with dropsy should be punctured, given that he could die from the operation. This decision depends on the prudence of the physician.

Can there exist a people free from all superstitious prejudices? It is as if to ask if there can exist a people of philosophers? It is said that there is no superstition in the magistracy of China. It is likely that the magistracy of some towns in Europe will also be free from it.

These magistrates then will prevent the superstition of the people from being dangerous. Their example will not enlighten the mob; but the principal bourgeoiscitizens will restrain it. Formerly, there was perhaps not a single religious tumult, not a single violence, in which the bourgeois townspeople did not take part, because these townspeople were then part of the mob; but reason and time will have changed them. Their ameliorated manners will improve those of the lowest and most ferocious populace; we have striking examples of this in more than one country. In short, the fewer superstitions, the less fanaticism; and the less fanaticism, the fewer calamities.

THÉISTE / THEIST

THE theist is a man firmly persuaded of the existence of a Supreme Being as good as he is powerful, who has formed all extended, vegetating, sentient, and reflecting beings; who perpetuates their species, who punishes crimes without cruelty and rewards virtuous actions with kindness.

The theist does not know how God punishes, how He rewards, how He pardons; for he is not presumptuous enough to flatter himself that he understands how God acts; but he knows that God does act, and that He is just.[70] The difficulties opposed to a providence do not shake him in his faith because they are only great difficulties and not proofs; he is subject to that providence, although he only perceives some of its effects and appearances; and judging things he does not see according to those he does see, he thinks that this providence pervades all places and all ages.

United in this principle with the rest of the universe, he does not embrace any one of the sects, who all contradict themselves; his religion is the most ancient and the most widespread; for the simple adoration of a God has preceded all the systems in the world. He speaks a language which all nations understand, while they are unable to understand each other's. He has brethren from Peking to Cayenne, and he considers all wise men to be his brothers. He believes that religion consists neither in the opinions of incomprehensible metaphysics, nor in vain decorations, but in adoration and justice. His worship is to do good; his doctrine, to submit oneself to God. The Mohammedan cries out to him: "Beware, if you do not make the pilgrimage to Mecca." "Woe be to you," says a Franciscan, "if you do not make a journey to our Lady of Loretto." He laughs at Loretto and Mecca; but he succors the indigent and defends the oppressed.

THÉOLOGIEN / THEOLOGIAN

I knew a true theologian; he had mastered the languages of the East, and was as knowledgeable as one can be in the ancient rites of nations. The Brahmins, Chaldaeans, Fire-worshippers, Sabeans, Syrians, and Egyptians, were as well known to him as the Jews; the various lessons of the Bible were familiar to him; and for thirty years he had tried to reconcile the gospels to get the Church fathers to agree. He sought to establish the exact date of composition of the creed attributed to the apostles, as well as the so-called creed of Athanasius; to understand how the sacraments were instituted one after the other and specify the difference between synaxis and mass; to understand how the Christian Church has been divided since its origin into different parts, and how the predominating society categorized all others as heretics. He sounded the depth of the politics which always permeate these quarrels; and he distinguished between politics and wisdom, between the pride that would subjugate minds and the desire for self-enlightenment, between zeal and fanaticism.

The difficulty of arranging so many different things in his head, things whose very nature it is to be confounded, and of throwing a little light on so many clouds, often daunted him; but as these researches were the duty of his profession, he dedicated himself to them despite his distaste. He at length arrived at a level of knowledge unknown to the greater part of his brethren: but as he grew more learned he also grew more mistrustful of all that he knew. While he lived he was indulgent; and at his death he confessed that he had spent his life uselessly.

TOLÉRANCE / TOLERANCE [71]

FIRST SECTION

WHAT is tolerance? It is the prerogative of humanity. We are all full of weakness and error; let us mutually pardon each other our follies—it is the first law of nature.

When, on the floor of the stock exchange in Amsterdam, London, Surat, or Bassora, the Guebre, the Banian, the Jew, the Mohammedan, the Chinese Deist, the Brahmin, the Christian of the Greek Church, the Roman Catholic Christian, the Protestant Christian and the Quaker Christian traffic together, they do not draw daggers on each other in order to convert souls to their religion. Why then have we been cutting one another's throats almost without interruption since the first Council of Nice?

Constantine began by issuing an edict that allowed all religions, and yet in the end he persecuted them. Before him, people rose up against the Christians only because they were beginning to form a party in the state. The Romans permitted all kinds of worship, including that of the Jews and even of the Egyptians, for whom they had so much contempt. Why did Rome tolerate these religions? Because neither the Egyptians, nor even the Jews sought to question the ancient religion of the empire, or ranged through land and sea in search of converts; they thought only of making money; but it is undeniable that the Christians wished their own religion to be the dominant one. The Jews would not suffer the statue of Jupiter at Jerusalem, but the Christians didn't even want it to be in the capitol. St. Thomas had the candor to admit that if the Christians did not dethrone the emperors, it was only because they were not able to. Their opinion was that the whole earth ought to be Christian. They were therefore necessarily enemies of the whole earth, up until it was converted.

Among themselves, they were the enemies of each other on all their points of controversy. First of all, was it necessary to regard Jesus Christ as God? Those who deny it are anathematized under the name of Ebionites, who themselves anathematized the adorers of Jesus.

Do some of them wish all things to be held in common, as some claim they were in the time of the apostles? Their adversaries called them Nicolaites, and accused them of the most ignominious crimes. Others, professing a mystical devotion were termed Gnostics, and attacked with fury. Let Marcion quarrel on the Trinity and he is treated as an idolater.

Tertullian, Praxeas, Origen, Novatus, Novatian, Sabellius, Donatus, were all persecuted by their brethren, before Constantine; and scarcely had Constantine made the Christian religion the ruling one but the Athanasians and the Eusebians tore each other to pieces; and from that time to our own days the Christian Church has been deluged with blood.

The Jewish people were, I confess, a very barbarous nation. They mercilessly slaughtered all of the inhabitants of an unfortunate little country upon which they had no more claim than they had upon Paris or London. However, when Naaman was cured of the leprosy by being plunged seven times in the Jordan—when, in order to show his gratitude to Elisha, who had taught him the secret, he told him he would adore the god of the Jews out of gratitude, he reserved for himself the freedom to adore also the god of his own king. He asked Elisha's permission to do so, and the prophet did not hesitate to grant it. The Jews adored their god, but they were never astonished that every nation had its own. They considered it perfectly acceptable that Chemos give a certain district to the Moabites, provided their god would give them one also. Jacob did not hesitate to marry the daughters of an idolater. Laban had his god, as Jacob had his. Such are the examples of toleration among the most intolerant and cruel people of antiquity. We have imitated them in their absurd passions, and not in their indulgence.

It is clear that every private individual who persecutes a man, his brother, because he is not of the same opinion, is a monster. This presents no difficulty. But the government, the magistrates, the princes!—how do they conduct themselves towards those who have a faith different from their own? If they are powerful foreigners, it is certain that a prince will form an alliance with them. The Most Christian Francis I will join forces with the Muslims against the Most Catholic Charles V. Francis I will give money to the Lutherans in Germany to support them in their rebellion against their emperor; but he will begin, as per the usual custom, by having the Lutherans in his own country burned. He pays them in Saxony for political reasons; for political reasons he burns them in Paris. But what follows? Persecutions make proselytes. France will soon be filled with new Protestants. At first they will let themselves be hanged; afterwards they will hang in their turn. There will be civil wars; then the Saint Bartholomew's Day massacre will come; and this corner of the world will be worse than all that the ancients and moderns ever said of hell.

Imbeciles, who have never been able to render a pure worship to the God who made you! Wretches, whom the example of the Noachides, the Chinese literati, the Parsees, and all the wise men has never been able to guide! Monsters, who need superstitions like the gizzard of a raven needs carrion! You have already been told—and there is nothing else to say—if you have two religions among you, they will massacre each other; if you have thirty, they will live in peace. Look at the Grand Turk: he governs Guebres, Banians, Christians of the Greek Church, Nestorians, and Roman Catholics. The first who tries to cause an uproar is impaled; and all is tranquil.

SECOND SECTION

Of all religions, the Christian is the one that ought doubtless to inspire the most toleration, although so far the Christians have been the most intolerant of all men.

Jesus, having deigned to be born in poverty and lowliness like his brethren, never condescended to practice the art of writing. The Jews had a law written with the greatest detail, and we have not a single line from the hand of Jesus. The apostles were divided on several points. St. Peter and St. Barnabas ate forbidden meats with the new foreign Christians, and abstained from them with the Jewish Christians. St. Paul reproached them this conduct; and this same St. Paul, the Pharisee, disciple of the Pharisee Gamaliel—this same St. Paul, who had persecuted the Christians with fury, and who after breaking with Gamaliel, became a Christian himself—nevertheless went afterwards to sacrifice in the temple of Jerusalem during his apostolate. For eight days he observed publicly all the ceremonies of the Jewish law he had renounced; he even added excess devotions and purifications; he Judaized completely. The greatest apostle of the Christians spent eight days doing the very things for which men are condemned to the stake among a large portion of Christian nations.

Theudas and Judas called themselves Messiahs before Jesus: Dositheus, Simon, Menander, called themselves Messiahs after Jesus. From the first century of the Church onward, and before even the name of Christian was known, there were a score of sects in Judea.

The contemplative Gnostics, the Dositheans, the Cerintheins, existed before the disciples of Jesus had taken the name of Christians. There were soon thirty churches, each of which belonged to a different society; and by the close of the first century thirty sects of Christians might be reckoned in Asia Minor, in Syria, in Alexandria, and even in Rome.

All these sects, despised by the Roman government and concealed in their obscurity, nevertheless persecuted each other in the hiding holes where they lurked; that is to say, they insulted one another. This is all they could do in their abject condition: they were all almost wholly composed of the dregs of the people.

When at length some Christians had embraced the dogmas of Plato and mingled a little philosophy with their religion, which they separated from the Jewish, they gradually became more considerable, but were still divided into many sects without there ever having been a time when the Christian church was united together. It took root in the midst of the divisions of the Jews, the Samaritans, the Pharisees, the Sadducees, the Essenes, the Judaites, the disciples of John, and the Therapeutae. It was divided in its infancy; it was divided even amid the persecutions it sometimes endured under the first emperors. The martyr was often regarded by his brethren as an apostate; and the Carpocratian Christian expired under the sword of the Roman executioner who was excommunicated by the Ebionite Christian, which same Ebionite was anathematized by the Sabellian.

This horrible discord which has lasted for so many centuries is a very striking lesson that we must mutually forgive each other our errors: discord is the great evil of the human species, and tolerance is its only remedy.

There is nobody who does not assent to this truth, whether meditating coolly in his closet, or examining the truth peaceably with his friends. Why, then, do the same men who in private concede charity, beneficence, and justice, rise up so furiously against these virtues in public? Why!—it is because their motivation is their god; it is because they sacrifice all to this monster whom they adore.

I possess a dignity and power built upon ignorance and credulity. I trample on the heads of men prostrated at my feet; if they should rise and look me in the face, I am lost; they must, therefore, be kept bound down to the earth with chains of iron.

Thus have men reasoned, who were rendered powerful by ages of fanaticism. They have other persons in power under them, and these latter again have underlings, who all enrich themselves with the spoils of the poor man, fattening themselves with his blood and laughing at his imbecility. They all detest toleration, as contractors enriched at the expense of the public are afraid to render their accounts, and as tyrants dread the name of liberty. Finally, to crown it all off they encourage fanatics who cry aloud: "Respect the absurdities of my master; tremble, pay, and be silent."

Such was the practice for a long time in much of the world; but now, when so many sects attenuate the power of the others, what side must we take among them? Every sect, we know, is a mere title of error; there is no sect of geometricians, of algebraists, of arithmeticians because all the propositions of geometry, algebra, and arithmetic are true. In all the other sciences one may be mistaken. What Thomist or Scotist theologian would dare to assert seriously that he goes on sure grounds?

If there is any sect that reminds one of the time of the first Christians, it is undeniably that of the Quakers. Nothing more closely resembles the spirit of the apostles. The apostles received the spirit; Quakers receive the spirit. The apostles and disciples spoke three or four at once in an assembly on the third floor; the Quakers do as much on the ground floor. Women were permitted to preach, according to St. Paul, and according to the same St. Paul they were forbidden to do so. Female Quakers preach by virtue of the first permission.

The apostles and disciples swore by yea and nay; the Quakers will not swear in any other form.

There was no rank, no difference of dress among apostles and disciples; the Quakers have sleeves without buttons, and are all clothed alike.

Jesus Christ baptized none of his apostles; the Quakers are never baptized.

It would be easy to push the parallel farther; it would be still easier to demonstrate how much the Christian religion of our day differs from the religion which Jesus practiced. Jesus was a Jew, and we are not Jews. Jesus abstained from pork, because it is unclean, and from rabbit, because it ruminates and its foot is not cloven; we fearlessly eat pork, because it is not unclean for us, and we eat rabbit which has a cloven foot and does not ruminate.

Jesus was circumcised, and we retain our foreskin. Jesus ate the Paschal lamb with lettuce, He celebrated the feast of the tabernacles; and we do none of this. He observed the Sabbath, and we have changed it; He sacrificed, and we never sacrifice.

Jesus always concealed the mystery of His incarnation and His dignity; He never said He was equal to God. St. Paul says explicitly in his Epistle to the Hebrews that God created Jesus inferior to the angels; and despite all of St. Paul's words, Jesus was recognized as God at the Council of Nice.

Jesus has not given the pope either the march of Ancona or the duchy of Spoleto; and yet somehow the pope possesses them by divine right.

Jesus did not make a sacrament either of marriage or of deaconry; and for us marriage and deaconry are sacraments.

If we would only pay attention, the Catholic, apostolic and Roman religion is in all its ceremonies and in all its dogma the reverse of the religion of Jesus.

But what! Must we all Judaize, because Jesus Judaized all His life?

If it were allowed to reason logically in matters of religion, it is clear that we ought to all become Jews, since Jesus Christ, our Savior, was born a Jew, lived a Jew and died a Jew, and since He expressly said that He accomplished and fulfilled the Jewish religion. But it is still more clear that we ought mutually to tolerate one another, because we are all weak, irrational, and subject to change and error. Should a reed prostrated by the wind in the muck—say to a neighboring reed placed in the opposite direction: Creep after my fashion, wretch, or I will present a request for you to be seized and burned?

TORTURE / TORTURE[72]

THOUGH there be few articles of jurisprudence in these honest alphabetical reflections, a word or two must nonetheless be said on torture, otherwise called "the question." It is a strange manner of questioning men. It was not invented, however, by innocent curiosity—there is every evidence that this part of our legislation owes its origins to a highwayman. Most of these gentlemen are still in the habit of screwing thumbs, burning feet, and questioning by various torments those who refuse to tell them where they have put their money.

The conquerors who followed in the footsteps of these thieves found the invention very useful to their interests; they made use of it when they suspected that there were plots against them: as, for example, that of seeking freedom—a crime of high treason, human and divine. The accomplices had to be known; and to accomplish this those who were suspected were made to suffer a thousand deaths, because, according to the jurisprudence of these primitive heroes, whoever was suspected of merely having a disrespectful opinion of them was worthy of death. As soon as one has thus merited death, it hardly matters that several days or even weeks of horrifying suffering be added to the penalty; in some ill-defined way this practice even seems to be derived from the Divinity. Providence sometimes puts us to the torture by employing kidney stones, gravel, gout, scrofula, leprosy, smallpox; by tearing the entrails, by convulsions of the nerves, and other executors of the vengeance of Providence.

Now, as the first despots were, in the eyes of their courtiers, images of the Divinity, they imitated it as much as they could.

What is very singular is that the question, or torture, is never spoken of in Jewish books. It is a great pity that so mild, honest, and compassionate a nation knew not this method of discovering the truth. In my opinion, the reason is that they had no need of it. God always made the truth known to them as to His cherished people. Sometimes they played at dice to discover the truth, and the suspected culprit always had double sixes. Sometimes they went to the high priest, who immediately consulted God by the *urim* and *thummim*. Sometimes they addressed themselves to the seer and prophet; and you may well believe that the seer and the prophet discovered the most hidden things every bit as well as the *urim* and *thummim* of the high priest. The people of God were not reduced, like ourselves, to interrogation and conjecture; and therefore torture could not be the practice among them, which was the only thing wanting to complete the mores of that holy people. The Romans only inflicted torture on slaves, but slaves were not counted as men. Nor is there any evidence that a counselor of the criminal court regards a man who is brought to him wan, pale, distorted, with sunken eyes, long and dirty beard, covered with vermin which have gnawed at him in a dungeon as one of his fellow creatures. He gives himself the pleasure of putting him to the major and minor torture until he is in danger of death, in the presence of a surgeon who counts his pulse and after which they recommence; and as the comedy of the "Suitors" says so well, "it serves to pass away an hour or two."

The grave magistrate, who has bought the right of making these experiments on his neighbor for some small sum, tells his wife over dinner all that took place in the morning. The first time, madam was revolted by it; the second, she began to acquire a taste for it, because, after all, women are curious; and afterwards the first thing she says when he enters is: "Dear heart, have you tortured anybody today?" The French, who are considered, I know not why, a very humane people, are astonished that the English (who had the inhumanity to take all Canada from us) have renounced the pleasure of putting men to the question.

When the Chevalier de La Barre, grandson of a lieutenant-general of the army, a young man of much sense and great expectations, but possessing all the recklessness of unbridled youth, was convicted of having sung impious songs, and even of having dared to pass before a procession of Capuchins without taking his hat off, the judges of Abbeville, men comparable to Roman senators, ordered not only that his tongue should be torn out, that his hand should be cut off and his body burned over a slow fire, but they further tortured him in order to know precisely how many songs he had sung, and how many processions he had watched go by with his hat on his head.

It was not in the thirteenth or fourteenth century that this affair happened; it was in the eighteenth. Foreign nations judge France by its spectacles, novels, and pretty verses; by opera girls who have very sweet manners, by graceful opera dancers; by Mademoiselle Clairon, who recites verse delightfully. They do not know that there is no more fundamentally cruel nation than the French.

The Russians were considered barbarians in 1700; this is only the year 1769; yet an empress has just given to this great state laws which would do honor to Minos, Numa, or Solon, if they had the intelligence to invent them.[73] The most remarkable is universal tolerance; the second is the abolition of torture. Justice and humanity have guided her pen; she has reformed all. Woe to a nation, which though civilized for so very long, is still led by atrocious ancient customs! "Why should we change our jurisprudence?" she says. "All of Europe uses our cooks, tailors, and wig-makers; therefore, our laws are good."

TRANSUBSTANTIATION / TRANSUBSTANTIATION

PROTESTANTS, and above all, philosophical Protestants, regard transubstantiation as the ultimate proof of the impudence of monks and the imbecility of laymen. They do not hold back in the slightest with this belief, which they call monstrous, and assert that it is impossible for any man of good sense ever to have believed in it, having once given it serious reflection. It is, they say, so absurd, so contrary to every physical law, so contradictory that it would be a sort of annihilation of God, to suppose Him capable of such inconsistency. Not only a god in a wafer, but a god in the place of a wafer; a thousand crumbs of bread become in an instant so many gods, which same innumerable crowd of gods make only one god. Whiteness without a white substance; roundness without rotundity of body; wine changed into blood that retains the taste of wine; bread changed into flesh and into fibers, and yet preserving the taste of bread—all this inspires such a degree of horror and contempt in the enemies of the Catholic, apostolic, and Roman religion, that it sometimes verges insensibly on rage.

Their horror augments when they are told that, in Catholic countries, it is quite common to see monks who, rising from an incestuous bed, and without washing their hands soiled with impurity, go forth and make gods by hundreds; who eat and drink these gods, shit and piss their gods. But when they reflect that this superstition, a thousand times more absurd and sacrilegious than any of those of the Egyptians, produces a pension of fifteen to twenty million for an Italian priest, and the domination of a country a hundred thousand leagues square, they are ready to take arms and march to drive away this priest from the palace of Caesar. I know not if I shall join them, because I love peace; but when they are established at Rome, I will certainly pay them a visit.

(by M. Guillaume, a Protestant minister)

TYRANNIE / TYRANNY

THE tyrant is a sovereign who knows no laws but his caprice; who takes the property of his subjects, and afterwards enlists them to go and take that of his neighbors. We have none of these tyrants in Europe.

We distinguish the tyranny of one and that of many. The tyranny of many is that of a body which would invade the rights of other bodies, and which would exercise despotism by favor of laws which it corrupts. Neither are there any tyrannies of this kind in Europe.

Under what tyranny should you like best to live? Under none; but if I must choose, I should detest less the tyranny of a single one than that of many. A despot has always some good moments; an assemblage of despots never has any. If a tyrant does me an injustice, I can disarm him through his mistress, his confessor, or his page; but a company of tyrants is inaccessible to all seductions. When they are not unjust, they are at the very least harsh, and they never dispense favors.

If I have but one despot, I am can get by with flattening myself against a wall when I see him pass, or prostrating myself, or striking my forehead against the ground, according to the custom of the country; but if there is a company of a hundred tyrants I may have to repeat this ceremony a hundred times a day, which is very tiresome for those who do not have supple joints. If I have a farm in the neighborhood of one of our lords, I am crushed; if I complain against a relative of the relatives of any one of our lords, I am ruined. How must I act? I fear that in this world we are reduced to being either the anvil or the hammer; happy the man who escapes this alternative!

VERTU / VIRTUE[74]

WHAT is virtue? Beneficence towards one's neighbor. Can I call virtue anything but that which does me good? I am indigent, you are liberal. I am in danger, you save me. I am deceived, you tell me the truth. I am neglected, you console me. I am ignorant, you teach me. I can easily call thee virtuous, but what will become of the cardinal and theological virtues? Some will remain in the schools.

What does it matter to me whether or not you are temperate? It is a principle of health which you observe; you are the better for it and I congratulate you on it. You have faith and hope; I congratulate you even more; they will procure eternal life for you. Your theological virtues are celestial gifts; your cardinal ones are excellent qualities which serve to guide you; but they are not virtues in relationship to your neighbor. The prudent man does himself good; the virtuous one does good to other men. St. Paul was right to tell you that charity ranks above faith and hope.

But how! can we not admit other virtues than those which are useful to one's neighbor? How can I admit any others? We live in society; there is therefore nothing truly good for us but that which does good to society. A hermit will be sober, pious, and dressed in sackcloth: very well, he will be holy; but I will not call him virtuous until he shall have done some act of virtue by which men will have profited. While he is alone, he is neither beneficent nor the contrary; he is nothing to us. If St. Bruno had made peace in families, if he had assisted the indigent, he was virtuous; if he fasted and prayed in solitude, he is a saint. Virtue between men is a commerce of good actions: he who has no part in this commerce must not be included. If this saint were in the world, he would doubtless do good, but while he is not in the world, the world has no reason to call him virtuous: he will be good for himself, and not for us.

But, say you, if a hermit is gluttonous, drunken, given up to a secret debauch with himself, he is vicious; he is therefore virtuous if he has the contrary qualities. I cannot agree to this: he is a very vile man if he has the faults of which you speak; but he is not vicious, wicked, or punishable by society, to which his infamies do no harm. It may be presumed that if he re-enters society he will do evil to it; that he will be very vicious; and it is even more probable that he will be a wicked man than it is certain that the other temperate and chaste hermit will be a good man; for in society faults increase and good qualities diminish.

A much stronger objection is made: Nero, Pope Alexander VI, and other monsters of the kind performed good actions. I reply boldly that they were virtuous on that day.

Some theologians say that the divine Emperor Antoninus was not virtuous; that he was an obstinate Stoic, who, not content with commanding men, would further be esteemed by them; that he gave himself credit for the good which he did to mankind; that he was all his life just, laborious, beneficent, through vanity; and that he only deceived men by his virtues. To which I exclaim: My God! Send us such knaves more often!

→ APPENDIX ←

SELECTIONS FROM CHAUDON'S ANTI-PHILOSOPHICAL DICTIONARY

WITH THE *PHILOSOPHICAL DICTIONARY*, VOLTAIRE HIT A RAW nerve among contemporary orthodox thinkers, driving them to pen numerous refutations. Prominent among these, distinguished both by its bulk and the scope of its ambitions, the *Anti-philosophical Dictionary* vividly illustrates the strength of the sentiments engendered by Voltaire's work and the urgency with which his critics sought to counter his influence. First published in Avignon in 1767, this unsigned work by Louis Mayeul Chaudon went through at least six more printings by 1785.

Chaudon's text seethes with hatred for the Enlightenment drive to reform traditional ways of thinking and reigning political and religious hierarchies. At the same time, however, the author of the *Anti-philosophical Dictionary* is forced to admit reluctant admiration for Voltaire's brilliance as a polemicist. For this reason, Chaudon adopts many of his enemy's tactics in his attempt to repel these radical new ideas. In the article "Freedom of the Press" (see p. 422), for example, he imitates the dialogue form used to such great effect by Voltaire at various points in the *Philosophical Dictionary*. From this perspective, the *Anti-philosophical Dictionary* bears testimony to the power of Voltaire's nimble critique. The *philosophe* successfully redefined the rules of debate, forcing his adversaries to venture onto a new rhetorical ground where their arguments lost a significant portion of their force, dispersed and fragmented by the randomness of alphabetical order.

To strengthen his case, at the beginning and end of the *Anti-Philosophical Dictionary*, Chaudon transcribed a number of official documents intended to demonstrate that the influence of the *philosophes* was seriously undermining the foundations of French society. Specifically, he charged that, by encouraging free thought and the willingness to question traditional forms of authority, Voltaire authorized his readers to engage in anti-social and anti-religious behavior. As prime evidence, Chaudon referred to the infamous case of the Chevalier de La Barre, citing in its entirety the official decree (see p. 407) that enumerated the young man's blasphemous crimes (including the singing of "impious songs") and prescribed a regimen of public humiliation, torture, execution, and immolation. As shocking as this document seems today—Voltaire himself was quick to exploit it for his own purposes in combating intolerance—, Chaudon believed it simply confirmed his argument. In his mind, social stability could not withstand transgressions of this type. Further circulation of philosophical ideas could lead only to more executions, not broader religious tolerance or greater personal freedoms. His "Notice" at the very beginning of the first volume established this ominous theme. For Chaudon, liberal ideas and those who were propagating them were enemies of the State: "Their impious and satirical writings are currently the only reading of the young. They nourish themselves on these works, and their impetuous imagination, enflamed by this dangerous torch, unleashes itself in actions that can lead them to the ultimate punishment. This is precisely what we witnessed in Abbeville two years ago; this is what will perhaps happen again, for the shame of our century. Humanity, sensitivity and an interest in the honor of families and the tranquility of the State suffice to convince us that we must guide them away from this false light that could precipitate them into the chasm."

Preface.

In his preface, Chaudon perceptively identifies (and denounces) Voltaire's ideological goals and rhetorical strategies. In particular, he expresses alarm at the philosophe's *ability to camouflage his motives and to appeal to readers in terms that extend beyond the purely intellectual. In his eyes, the* Philosophical Dictionary *thus becomes a sort of insidious poison, penetrating the very fabric of eighteenth-century society.*

Error has been laid out in the form of a dictionary. We must do the same for truth. The apostles of impiety use all sorts of forms to propagate their poison. Won't the defenders of religion seek a way to make their antidotes more appealing? Alphabetical order is the flavor of the day, and we must adopt it if we wish to have readers.

Of all the works that the fury of irreligion has brought into the world, there is perhaps none marked by darker traits than the *Philosophical Dictionary*. It is an altar erected to libertinism and an open school of materialism. All the authorities[1] have taken up arms against this detestable work. . . .

This *Dictionary* is not a futile literary text that will eventually make its way from the dressing room of a fop to the grocer's store where it will be used as wrapping paper. Everyone is reading it; everyone is citing it—members of the military, magistrates, women, clergymen. It is a chalice from which people of all conditions and ages imbibe the poison of impiety. There have already been six editions, and our printers are so wise and disinterested that these will no doubt be followed by several others.

Based on what prestige has this dangerous work attained such broad and rapid diffusion? It is only too easy to ascertain. This book severs all the ties that bind individuals to virtue. It attacks religion, in its tenets, its morality and its laws. It scarcely acknowledges the existence of the Supreme Being, and this existence, insofar as it is acknowledged, has no bearing on man. God has no need of our tributes; we have nothing to expect from his mercy, nothing to fear from his justice. How would he reward or punish us? The soul dies with the body; man thinks with the same organs as animals, lives and dies like them, etc., etc.

Such principles would no doubt provoke disgust if they were presented openly. But the author makes them enter the mind with insidious skill. This is a corrupt essence that imperceptibly introduces itself into the bloodstream. Ingenious barbs, little jokes, titillating remarks, brilliant contradictions, striking contrasts, seductive descriptions, bold reflections, energetic expressions, all possible stylistic graces, all the accoutrements of wit abound in the text.

These characteristics clearly identify the author. Such a work can only come from the reckless and fertile pen that the demon of wit and irreligion created in the depths of hell. The creator of the *Maid of Orleans* has in vain denied responsibility for the *Philosophical Dictionary*; each line reveals its origins. When the work first appeared, everyone immediately recognized the father of this child of the shadows.

Everyone knows that Monsieur de V., the sharpest wit in Europe, the greatest poet of the century, having attained the highest degree of literary reputation, at an age when the passions disappear, is henceforth consumed exclusively by the furor of proselytism. But how absurd this proselytism is! and how horrible! It is unworthy of a philosopher who calls himself the benefactor of the human race. . . .

Decree of *Parlement*, condemning the *Portable Philosophical Dictionary* and the *Letters Written From the Mountain*, by Jean-Jacques Rousseau, . . . to be lacerated and burned by the Executioner of High Justice.

Immediately following his preface, and as a perfect complement to his own ideas, Chaudon inserted a decree issued by the Parisian Parlement *in March 1765, ordering that the* Philosophical Dictionary *be burned. As the following excerpt makes clear, the condemnation was based on the premise that the* Philosophical Dictionary, *like Rousseau's Letters* Written From the Mountain, *was an extremely dangerous work. Because it called into questions many points of Catholic orthodoxy, it was accused of destroying the basic fabric of civil society, which, the* Parlement *maintained, depended on a universal respect for Christianity. As the conclusion of the decree indicates, involvement in the sale or distribution of such banned works was a risky business, leading to frequent searches, interrogations and, in some cases, imprisonment.*

. . . If false philosophy, which so depraves our morals, is neither enlightened enough nor of sufficient good faith to forsake its errors, at the very least it should nurture its illusions and absurdities in silence. Initially, in its attempts to create disciples imperceptibly, it advanced by dark paths and used means that were not accessible to everyone. The *Parlement*, however, stopped it in its tracks; and its early efforts, though able to fool official vigilance momentarily, were unable to escape censorship indefinitely. It is strange that today, shaking off shamelessly the veil by which it had hitherto disguised its progress, false philosophy shows its face openly for what it is and loudly preaches iniquity, opens its mouth against heaven, and aspires to spread more readily the poisonous incredulity of its thoughts and the libertinage of its heart throughout the world. The scandalous publication of the *Portable Philosophical*

Dictionary has no other possible goal, and this offense has been committed under the reign of a king who, in his government of the people, seeks only to reinforce in the their hearts the truths of dogma and moral purity.

If the author were known, you would see that he is no less worthy than his work of the most rigorous punishment. What sort of frenetic fury possesses certain minds of our times? What profit do they hope to reap from their heretical and even inhuman doctrine? What do we find in this *Dictionary?*—the tenets of Christianity presented as innovations accrued over the course of time; mocking of the discipline and practices of the Church; annihilation of the holy Scriptures and of all revelation. The author attempts to undermine the foundations of the Christian religion; he denies the divinity of Jesus Christ; he neither fears nor blushes to treat as a fanciful tale the accounts of his life by the Evangelists; he pretends that the creed and discipline of the Church are a human invention; he dismisses the Sacraments and the cult of Saints as superstitions. He cites the allegories and metaphors found in the Holy Scriptures but hides from his readers the meaning of these allegories, the truths and facts contained in the metaphors, without which the pertinence and accuracy of these figures is absent. . . .

Such is the work that the Republic of Geneva has already condemned to the flames and that no well-administered State, even if it does not enjoy the advantage of being part of the Catholic Church, can avoid prohibiting. For there is no society whose interests are not attacked by licentiousness, independence, and irreligion. . . .

The Court orders that the two aforementioned books be lacerated and burned at the base of the grand staircase of the Hall of Justice by the Executioner. All those who are in possession of copies of these works are enjoined to bring them to the Clerk of the Court, so that they may be destroyed. All printers, booksellers, peddlers, or others are forbidden to print, sell, convey, or otherwise distribute these works, subject to all pertinent penalties. It is ordered that, on request of the General Prosecutor of the King, and in the presence of the Reporter named by the Court, that all those who have composed, printed, sold or otherwise distributed the two designated works be investigated, so that the information procured thereby can be communicated to the General Prosecutor of the King, and he shall demand such punishment as reason and the Court deem appropriate. It is, in addition, ordered that the present decree be printed, published, and posted wherever necessary. Established by the *Parlement*, all assembled chambers, March nineteenth, seventeen hundred sixty-five.

Persecution. Should impious dogmatists be punished?

Here Chaudon responds directly to an article from the Philosophical Dictionary *in which Voltaire argues that individuals should not be persecuted simply because they hold opinions that do not concur with those of powerful religious zealots. Chaudon explains, on the contrary, that the public expression of unorthodox opinions leads to the disintegration of society at large. In support of this argument, he cleverly focuses his discussion on radical atheism and draws on material generated from within the philosophical camp, quoting from both Diderot and d'Alembert's Encyclopedia (the article "Atheism," written by the abbé Yvon) and Rousseau. The most damning factor, in Chaudon's eyes, is the recent execution of the Chevalier de La Barre, condemned for blasphemy, which he mentions in the concluding paragraph. Heterodox ideas are indeed dangerous in a society that puts young men to death for singing impious songs!*

M. de Voltaire protests strongly, in his article Persecution, against those men whose injured pride and furious fanaticism harass the Prince or Magistrates and force these authorities to punish innocent individuals whose only crime is not thinking like them. But what men have ever sought to have the thoughts of others punished, when these thoughts have not been expressed in conversation or in published writings? Certain works can be just as dangerous for society as a theft or a murder. Such are works that preach materialism, that is, a sort of toned-down atheism. For if man is nothing but matter, and if his soul perishes along with his body, there is no connection between him and God, and it is therefore indifferent whether the Supreme Being exists or not.

We must ask therefore, whether it is permissible to repress with exemplary punishments the authors of works that disrupt society by destroying the fundamental moral principles of that society. It seems to me there can only be one response to this question. And although the sword, the stake, and the gallows appear to be rather violent punishments, nevertheless some steps must be taken-although less terrifying-to prevent such authors from dogmatic preaching. Let them be shut away and removed from the sight of the world they hope to overturn with their works. It is a peculiar contradiction that we condemn to be burned young libertines who, seduced by these impious texts, have publicly insulted Religion, whereas the authors of the offending texts remain free to produce new poisons that will per-haps fester in other weak minds. . . .

The author of the article *Atheism* in the *Encyclopedia* shares our way of thinking about the duty and obligation to repress atheists, materialists, and even those who, without denying the existence of a Divinity, render this existence useless by negating the idea of providence, etc. "Atheism," he says, "when it is professed publicly, is punishable, according to natural law. One must strongly oppose numerous barbarous procedures and inhuman executions that have arisen from simple suspicions or the pretext of atheism. But, on the other hand, the most tolerant individual will not deny that the authorities have the right to repress, and even to put to death, those who dare to profess atheism, if they are unable to rid society of them by other means."

In fact, the partisans of the broadest tolerance have always made an exception of declared atheists. "If the authorities," continues the author of the *Encyclopedia* article, "can punish all those who harm a single individual, they certainly have every bit as much right to punish those who harm a whole society by denying there is a God or that he intervenes in human conduct in order to reward those who work for the common good and punish those who attack it."

Let us listen to M. *Rousseau* of Geneva's reflections on Montesquieu's maxim, *We should honor the Divinity and never avenge it*: "He is right. Nevertheless, outrageous ridicule, vulgar impiety, and blasphemies against religion are punishable. Why? Because it is not simply religion that is attacked, but all those who profess that religion; they are insulted, they are offended in their worship; that which they respect and they themselves are treated with scorn. Such outrages should be punished by law because they implicate individuals who have every right to feel resentment." Thus, in adding M. *Rousseau's* arguments to those we presented above, we find that all factors should encourage the authorities to repress the voices of incredulity who insolently dogmatize and whose perverse lessons can eventually lead to the wheel or the pyre. This is what we saw in 1766 in Toulouse and Abbeville. Even if the incredulous had done some good—which we are far from believing—would this fleeting benefit offset the lasting shame that the deadly effects of their texts have cast on honest families and the terrible sorrows that have engulfed them?

Press. On the Freedom of the Press.

In this article, Chaudon adjusts slightly the terms of his exchange with Voltaire. Instead of addressing the question of "Freedom of Thought," as Voltaire had done, the author of the Anti-philosophical Dictionary *chooses to focus on the* publication *of free thoughts, which for him is quite a different matter. In this way, although he does not technically condemn creative thinking, Chaudon arrives at the menacing conclusion that the State should silence, even by violence, writers who express opinions that undermine respect for either the State or the Church. Here again, the specter of the Chevalier de La Barre looms large, proof (in Chaudon's opinion) that radical ideas really do corrupt innocent minds, leading youths to commit scandalous criminal acts and forcing the authorities to invoke the ultimate penalty.*

The Admirer: Why don't you want to allow others to write whatever they wish? The man you want to hinder helps make the book trade prosper. His in-octavo *Complete Works* consumed the product of four paper manufactories for a period of ten years. His in-quarto *General History* will give business to ten more. What would we do with our rags if there weren't good writers to turn them into something of value?[2]

The Censor: I proposed hindering only the enemies of religion and the State; let the others write in peace. Nothing is more just. But just because you don't know what to do with your rags, should it be allowed to publish with impunity anything at all?

The Admirer: And why not? The State would benefit. The ability to convert shreds of cotton into thick volumes of prose and verse causes foreign money to circulate in France. And along with a few ideas of little or no value, we also reap some solid thoughts.

The Censor: This is no doubt a great advantage; but you pay dearly for it! Morality is corrupted, integrity is compromised, and our modern skeptics have produced more than one highwayman.

The Admirer: If this is so, I have nothing to say. If a few writers ruin the mind and the heart, they should be repressed. But we should not prevent our pharmacists from selling real medicine just because some of their colleagues have sold poison.

The Censor: Nor do I desire anything else. Let the book trade flourish, that's fine by me. But it should not do so at the expense of morality. I know that there are hundreds of men employed making paper, marking it with black and white, transforming it into brochures. It is only right that they earn a living. If they were cultivating the earth, they would perhaps be more useful to the State; but since they have an honest profession, let them keep it. But will any of them die of hunger simply because the sale or printing of an impious hundred-page brochure has been prohibited? No, the typographical trade will continue all the same.

The Admirer: You want to restrict intellectual activity and the freedom to write exclusively to that which is useful and honest. That is a plan worthy of the first centuries of the Christian era; but it would constrict the genius of our modern writers.

The Censor: Not at all. Were *Fénelon, Bossuet, Boileau,* and many other writers from the last century less accomplished because they confined their talents precisely within these boundaries that look to you like a hindrance?

The Admirer: But if our contemporary poets had imitated them, would we have so many pretty bagatelles, like the *Maid of Orleans, the Holy Candle of Arras, the Tales of William Vadé,* and the *Philosophical Dictionary?*

The Censor: In truth, we would be less rich in such masterpieces. But wealth based on this kind of treasures is truly poverty. It would be better to have a solid fortune than to possess chimerical promissory notes that corrupt or lead to the hanging of those who possess them.

The Admirer: We haven't ever seen an author perform such a scene in the public square.

The Censor: But you have seen booksellers ruined because they printed or sold these infamies. You have seen a young gentleman, intoxicated with this wretched poison, die at the hand of the hangman in Abbeville. You have seen human authorities forced by the continuous excesses of our modern Diogenes to invoke this terrible sentence. After such an event, tell me as insistently as you wish that the freedom of the press provides food and drink for an author or a bookseller, I will tell you that it would be preferable that both of them eat nothing but dry bread and drink nothing but water, rather than produce such fatal catastrophes by the sale of their drugs. Believe me, when Heaven is attacked, the earth always suffers.

The Admirer: Most of our writers are far from having such ideas. They will tell you straight out that no book has ever done harm. If it's boring, there is no need to read it; if it's amusing, this diversion strikes them as necessary.

The Censor: We would doubtless allow them to provide amusement for their fellow citizens, if they weren't seeking to amuse them at the expense of the government and religion.

The Admirer: But ideas crop up; they have to be written down. Like an egg, they can't be prevented from hatching once the hen has been formed.

The Censor: We crush the egg when it holds a rotten seed. And if the rooster tires us with his singing, we put an end to his ability to sing.

The Admirer: Would you want to lock up all those who sing poorly?

The Censor: No, but certainly all who speak too loudly of things they should respect. Their lives should not be threatened; let us not embrace a sanguinary intolerance. But let us be guided by the wise tolerance that imprisons the corruptor in order to reduce corruption. In the prison where they are confined, they should be given good bouillon to ease their mind; but they should be deprived of ink because they only use it to write foolishness. This is the attitude, the way of thinking, of our wisest authorities. They favor liberty; they condemn licentiousness. They are not cruel; they are just. And you yourself would have to be intolerant to accuse them of intolerance.

The Admirer: The English are more indulgent.

The Censor: That is a misconception. They put to death in prison the detractor of the Miracles of J. C., the impious *Woolston.* And I hope with all my heart that those who copy him in France will not meet the same end.

Decree of the Parlement of Paris, condemning the young criminals of Abbeville.

In horrifying detail, couched in formal legalese, the Parisian Parlement *spelled out the crimes of the young Chevalier de La Barre and his three accomplices, condemning them all to public ceremonial execution. This appalling document was included by Chaudon in the* Anti-philosophical Dictionary *because it specifically mentioned the corrupting influence of certain "nefarious" books that La Barre owned and honored with a sort of mock religious cult. Chief among these works was Voltaire's* Philosophical Dictionary. *Indeed, the conclusion of the document specified "that the* Portable Philosophical Dictionary, *found among the books deposited with the Clerk of the Court, will be thrown by the Executioner of High Justice onto the same pyre along with the body of the selfsame Lefebvre de la Barre." In the eyes of Voltaire's adversary, nothing could be clearer: the forces of justice had acted appropriately to stamp out the unfortunate but inevitable effects of philosophical propaganda. For his part, Voltaire quickly incorporated the case in his own polemic writings, publicizing the disproportion between La Barre's petty crimes and the enormity of the punishment he received for them.*

. . . Concerning Jean-François Lefebvre Chevalier de la Barre, he has been declared duly tried and convicted of having walked past the Holy Host, during the most recent festival of Corpus Christi, with impiety and deliberate intent, at a distance of twenty-five paces, as it was carried in procession by the monks of Saint Peter in the selfsame town [Abbeville], without doffing the hat he had on his head and without falling to his knees; of having uttered horrible and execrable blasphemies against God, the Holy Host, the Holy Virgin, Religion and the Commandments both of God and the Church, as mentioned in the proceedings; of having sung publicly and on different occasions two impious songs filled with the most atrocious, abominable and execrable blasphemies against God, the Holy Host, the Holy Virgin, and the Saints, as mentioned in the proceedings; of having given signs of respect and adoration to the nefarious and impure books that were on a shelf in his room, kneeling while passing before them and saying that everyone must kneel when passing before the Tabernacle; of having desecrated the sign of the Cross, by making this sign and by kneeling and pronouncing the impure words mentioned in the proceedings; of having desecrated the Mystery of the blessing of the wine, making fun of it on several occasions by mumbling impure words over a glass of wine he held in his hand and then drinking this wine, as mentioned in the proceedings; of having profaned the blessings used by the Church and among Christians, by making the cross and blessing with his hand various objects, while uttering the impure words mentioned in the proceedings; finally, of having proposed to a fellow named Perignot who was serving mass, by approaching him near the altar, to bless the oil receptacles by uttering the impure words mentioned in the proceedings; in reparation of which, he is condemned to make honorable amends before the principal door of the Royal and Collegial Church of Saint Vulfranc in the selfsame town of Abbeville, where he will be led by the Executioner of High Justice in a tumbrel, and there, on his knees, bare-headed and bare-footed, with a rope around his neck, wearing a panel both front and back bearing these words: *Guilty of Impiety, Blasphemy and Abominable and Execrable Sacrilege*; and holding with both hands a burning torch of yellow wax weighing two pounds, to say and proclaim in a loud, intelligible voice, *that nastily and with impiety, he intentionally walked past the Holy Host, without doffing his hat and without falling to his knees, and uttered blasphemies against God, the Holy Host, the Holy Virgin, Religion and the Commandments of God and the Church, as mentioned in the proceedings; and sang two songs filled with execrable and abominable blasphemies against God, the Holy Host, the Holy Virgin and the Saints, as mentioned in the proceedings; and gave signs of respect and adoration to nefarious books and profaned the sign of the Cross, the Mystery of the blessing of the wine and the blessings used by the Church and among Christians, for which he repents and asks forgiveness from God, the King and Justice;* and on this selfsame spot to have his tongue cut out; this done, to be led in the same tumbrel to the primary public market square of the selfsame town in order to, on a platform erected there for this purpose, have his head cut off, his dead body and head thrown into the fire of a blazing pyre to be reduced to ash, and the ashes scattered in the wind; and, prior to the execution, the selfsame Lefebvre de la Barre will be tortured and put through ordinary and extraordinary interrogation, in order to learn from his mouth the truth concerning certain matters revealed during the trial and the revelation of his accomplices. . . .

ENDNOTES

PHILOSOPHICAL DICTIONARY

1 This preface was first inserted in the 1765 edition of the *Dictionary*. As indicated by its full title in the 1769 edition ("Preface to the edition immediately preceding this one"), it reflects the evolving character of the work, to which Voltaire regularly added new articles from 1764 to 1769. In addition, it sustains the fiction of a collective work—one of the strategies Voltaire used to help deflect censorship.

2 This line comes from a popular song of the period that teased the abbé about his amorous sorties. The allusion would have been immediately apparent to Voltaire's contemporaries and apt for introducing the dual themes of paternity and religious function.

3 Nicolas Fréret (1688–1789) had a reputation as an anti-Christian author, and after his death the *philosophes* frequently attributed radical works to him.

4 Voltaire's reference is to the article, "Amour Nommé Socratique / Love Called Socratic."

5 "Love is everywhere the same" (Vergil, *Georgics*, iii.244).

6 François Rabelais (c.1490–1553) had addressed the prologue of his *Gargantua* (1532) to "Illustrious drinkers and you, much cherished pox-bearers." The origins of syphillis are a frequent theme for Voltaire; see also *Candide*, chapter 4.

7 The footnote at the end of this article was an addition to the 1769 edition. Voltaire himself was among the "protectors" who saved the abbé Desfontaines from death in 1725, and Deschauffours was, in fact, burned alive for sodomy in 1726 in Paris. The seventeenth-century poet Despréaux (Boileau) dedicated his twelfth satire to the nefarious nature of equivocal statements.

8 This anecdote seems to be authentic; Voltaire related it on various occasions throughout his life.

9 Bragelogne, a member of the Academy of Sciences, had died in 1741. Voltaire knew that the real author of the article in the *Encyclopedia* was, in fact, Naigeon, a disciple of Diderot's.

10 Voltaire defended Vanini's innocence on many occasions. His execution had taken place more than a century earlier, in 1619.

11 Nicolas-Antoine Boulanger (1722–1759) was another radical thinker to whom the *philosophes* attributed various works after his death.

12 Gottfried Wilhelm von Leibniz's *Theodicy* was first published in 1710. Of course, the phrase, "the best of all possible worlds" had previously appeared prominently in *Candide*.

13 Voltaire was familiar with all three of these writers because of the time he had spent in England. He had previously taken exception to the idea of "all is well" in his "Poem on the Lisbon Disaster" (1756).

14 Michel de Montaigne (1533–1592), the author of the *Essais*, had adopted as his motto the phrase, "Que sais-je?" (II, 12).

15 It goes without saying that this text was actually written by Voltaire. But Father Fouquet (1655–1741) was a real Jesuit who had lived in China and written several works about Chinese philosophy. It is possible that Voltaire met Fouquet in Paris in 1722. Throughout this "catechism," Voltaire makes use of information gleaned from Jesuit writings, particularly the works of J.-B. Du Halde.

16 Voltaire added this note in 1765, in response to one of his early critics.

17 Here and in the "Japanese Catechism," Voltaire uses anagrams to thinly veil references to contemporary Europe. The abbé de Saint Pierre (1658–1743) was a prolific writer, well known for his idealist reform proposals. Voltaire cited him frequently, often ironically.

18 In eighteenth-century France, actors and actresses were officially subject to excommunication by the Church. For Voltaire, who believed in the pedagogical power of the theater and who vaunted the great literary achievements of French dramatists, this idea was preposterous. He here refers to two of the great masterworks of the previous century: Molière's *Misanthrope* (1666) and Jean Racine's *Athalie* (1691).

19 In this dialogue, Voltaire has the "Japanese" present the history of English clerical affairs. The astonished "Indian," naturally, represents French perplexity in the face of English religious tolerance.

20 Louis Racine (1692–1763), son of the great dramatist Jean Racine, published his *Poème sur la Grâce* in 1720.

21 The abbé de Prades' article had appeared in the second volume of the *Encyclopedia* in 1751. The victory at Fontenoy (1745) and Saxe's death (1750) were both recent events.

22 Voltaire continues to assert the superiority of Newton over Plato. In Greek Antiquity, the Cassiderides were mythic islands; the name was also applied to the British Isles.

23 These events date from 1710; the very direct causality outlined by Voltaire was lacking in Bolingbroke's account.

24 Fontenelle (1657–1757) was the author of *Conversations on the Plurality of Worlds* (1688), an extremely popular set of dialogues dealing with astronomy.

25 The miracles of Saint-Medard began with the death of the deacon Paris in 1727 (rather than 1724 as Voltaire states). The tomb became a gathering site for followers of austere Jansenism who were often seized by violent convulsions. As Voltaire notes further, the physical tests endured by the convulsionaries were taken to extreme lengths.

26 Despite differences of opinion on religious doctrine, Jansenist and Jesuit critics found themselves united in opposition to Montesquieu's *Spirit of the Laws* in 1748.

27 This abbé de Saint-Pierre is the same who is cited in the "Chinese Catechism." The Credo, of course, is Voltaire's own, although the final exclamation was a phrase favored by Saint-Pierre.

28 The whole of this article is taken up with a commentary on recent literary quarrels. Voltaire's self-interested argument is that critics are often motivated by jealousy and spite rather than true literary sensibility.

29 "The raucous temples of the underworld, / reverberating through the caves of hell, / causing the dark to quiver at the cry, / summon to the assembly all who dwell / in that eternal night. With such harsh roar / no thunderbolt from heaven ever fell, / nor have the winds that swell the womb of earth / with such terrific fury broken forth" (Torquato Tasso, *Jerusalem Delivered. Gerusalemme liberata,* trans. Anthony M. Esolen [Baltimore and London: The Johns Hopkins University Press, 2000], p. 72 [IV.3]).

30 Philippe Quinault (1635–1688) authored the libretto of Lully's opera, *Armide* (1686):

Sidonie: "Hatred is frightful and barbaric, / Love compels the hearts that it seizes / To suffer most rigorous pains. / If your destiny is in your hands, / Choose indifference, / Which assures you a happier fate."

Armide: "No, no, it is no longer possible for me / To pass from agitation to a more peaceful state of mind, / My heart can not be consoled; / Renaldo offends me too much, he is all too loveable, / For me it is henceforth imperative / Either to hate or to love him."

31 These stanzas are taken from the works of Antoine Houdar de La Motte (1672–1731).

"Sometimes a young beauty / Resists the flame that enchants her / And against herself she takes up the arms / Of a painful firmness of heart. / Alas, this extreme constraint / Deprives her of the weakness she loves, / In order to flee the shame she hates. / Her severity is only pomp, / And the distinction of appearing chaste, / Encourages her in her resolve."

"In vain this severe stoic, / Weighed down by thousands of faults, / Prides himself on his heroic soul / Entirely devoted to virtue; / But virtue is not at all what he loves, / Rather his heart, in love with itself, / Would like to claim the incense; / And with his foolish sobriety / He only wants to disguise the idol / He holds up for mortal admiration."

"The battlefields of Pharsalos and Arbela / Witnessed the triumph of two conquerors / Both models worthy / Of inspiring great hearts. / But success alone created their glory; / And if the seal of victory / Had not graced these two half-gods, / Alexander, in the eyes of the people, / Would only be a reckless man/ And Caesar nothing but a mutineer."

[32] These comments come from Jean-Baptiste Rousseau (1669–1741):

"A certain gosling, farmyard prey"

"The boring beauty of his words"

". . . I only perceive one weakness, / Which is that the author ought to have written in prose. / Those odes of his are reminiscent of Quinault."

[33] These stanzas, chosen by Voltaire for their ridiculous imagery and twisted syntax, are all drawn from various odes by J.-B. Rousseau:

"This sovereign influence / Is only an illustrious chain for him / That attaches him to the happiness of others; / All the brilliance that enhances him, / All the talents that ennoble him, / Are in him, but do not belong to him."

"There is nothing that time doesn't absorb and devour, / And things of which we are unaware / Are little different from things that never were."

"The goodness that sparkles in her / of her sweetest charms, / Is the image of the goodness / That she sees shining in you. / And enriched by you alone, / Her politeness freed / From the smallest shadows, / Is the reflected light / Of your supreme beams."

"They saw, by your good faith, / Of their terrified subjects / The fears happily deceived, / And uprooted forever / The hatred so often received / As the inheritance of peace."

"Unveil before my eager gaze / These adopted deities, / Synonyms of thought, / Symbols of abstraction."

"Is it not good fortune, / When a common charge / Is borne by two halves? / Let the lesser ask for it all; / And that the happiness of the soul / Be paid for by the body alone?"

[34] "The irritable race of poets" is taken from Horace's *Epistles.*

[35] Voltaire added this article in the 1767 edition. His interest in David and Saül dated back many years, however. He had completed a burlesque farce, entitled *Saül,* in 1762.

[36] Some editions spell out the name in full, "Calvin," and in the following paragraph, "Servet." Michel Servet was burned at the stake in Geneva in 1553 with Calvin's encouragement. Voltaire's interest in this case was a sore point with his Genevan neighbors.

37 This formula, as it is articulated at the very end of the article, generally accompanied royal edicts. The variation on this formula in the preceding paragraph is Voltaire's modified (and improved) version.

38 Voltaire had a long-standing interest in this text that was purported to be the political testament of Louis XIII's chief minister, Cardinal Richelieu. Modern scholars generally believe that Richelieu did actually play some role in its composition, but Voltaire insisted that it was a fabrication. He had explored these issues as greater length in a text entitle, *Des Mensonges imprimés* (*On Printed Lies*), in 1749.

39 Voltaire refers here to Montesquieu's *Considérations sur les causes de la grandeur des Romains et de leur décadence (Considerations on the Causes of the Grandeur and Decadence of the Romans)*, published in 1734. The following two paragraphs generally allude to ideas taken from the same author's Spirit of Laws.

40 This article on "Geneva" is not found in the *Philosophical Dictionary*. Rather, it was a contribution by Voltaire's friend d'Alembert to the *Encyclopédie* in 1757. It had stirred great controversy, both by questioning the faith of Genevan pastors and by suggesting that the town should establish a municipal theater. Jean-Jacques Rousseau responded in great length in his *Letter to d'Alembert.*

41 The infamous Saint Bartholomew's Day massacre began in Paris on August 24, 1572, when French Catholics tried to eliminate the Huguenot faction. Late in life, Voltaire reported that he was routinely taken with fever on the anniversary date of this event. In the following paragraph, Clément, Châtel, Ravaillac, and Damiens were all assassins of French kings. Most recently, Damiens had succeeded in injuring Louis XV on January 5, 1757.

42 This work was first published in 1674. In the French text, Voltaire plays with Esprit's name, which can be translated either as "spirit" or "wit."

43 Voltaire here rejects the kind of reductive causality that characterizes the Doctor Pangloss; see *Candide*, chapter 1.

44 Voltaire had previously referred to Rabelais at the end of the article "Amour / Love." Late in life, he developed new admiration for the caustic humor of the author of *Gargantua* and *Pantagruel.*

45 Erasmus first published his *Praise of Folly* in 1511.

46 Voltaire's interest in this question is evidenced by the fact that he had in 1756 published a text entitled, "To What Extent Should the People Be Deceived") and in the *Treatise on Tolerance* (1763), he included a chapter "Whether it is Useful to Maintain the People in Superstition?"

47 This was the motto of the Jesuit order; thus, the entire tale is colored by the inferred presence of this powerful Catholic order, which was finally expelled from France in 1764.

[48] Disputes over the question of grace were a subject of controversy throughout the Middle Ages. They reemerged with great vehemence in seventeenth-century France, sharply diving the Jansenists and the Jesuits. These disputes continued to engender persecution of the Jansenists throughout the eighteenth century.

[49] Eighteenth-century readers would have been all too familiar with the rituals of warfare, particularly in the wake of the Seven Years War (1756–1763). The song "composed in a language unknown to all who fought" was the *Te Deum*, performed, as Voltaire notes, in a variety of public ceremonies.

[50] As in the "Country-Priest's Catechism," Voltaire attacks the Catholic Church for its condemnation of the theater. *Polyeuctus* (1643), by Pierre Corneille and *Athalia* (1691), by Jean Racine, were both edifying dramas, based on religious subjects.

[51] Jean-Baptiste Massillon (1663–1742) and Louis Bourdaloue (1632–1704) were both famous orators who had preached at the court of Louis XIV.

[52] *The Universal French and Latin Dictionary* published by the Jesuits of Trevoux was a standard reference work in the eighteenth century. Voltaire, obviously, was not always in agreement with the opinions of its authors! At stake in this article is the legitimacy of non-Christian religions.

[53] Throughout this article, Voltaire stages a personal interaction with Job. On the basis of personal wealth and shared health problems, he feigns great sympathy for the Biblical character. The signature at the end of the article is a further reference to Voltaire himself.

[54] Voltaire later reprinted this article when he edited the *Discours de l'empereur Julien contre les chrétiens (Discourse of the Emperor Julian against the Christians)* in 1769.

[55] In his footnote, Voltaire responds to the criticism of J.-A. Rosset de Rochefort in his *Remarques sur un livre intitulé Dictionnaire philosophique portatif (Remarks on a Book Entitled Portable Philosophical Dictionary,* 1765). The exchange gives some idea of the tone adopted by Voltaire's critics. For an additional response, see the appendix to the present volume.

[56] In this dialogue, Voltaire plays with national stereotypes prevalent at the time. The English were generally admired for the boldness of their philosophical and political opinions, while the Mediterranean nations were seen as submissive, dominated by the tyranny of the Catholic Church and, in Portugal particularly, the Inquisition.

[57] The reference is to Montesquieu's *Spirit of Laws* (1748), a work with which Voltaire continued to maintain a dialog, well after the author's death in 1755.

[58] The "Poem on Natural Law" was written by Voltaire himself, published in 1752.

59 As in the article "De la Liberté / On Liberty," Voltaire is responding to Rosset de Rochefort.

60 "Know above all that luxury enriches / A large state, even as it impoverishes a small one." Voltaire quotes from his own work, the "Defense of the Worldling, or the Apology of Luxury" (1737).

61 Voltaire was quite proud of the work he had done to improve the living conditions for peasants around his manor house at Ferney.

62 Paul Lucas (1664–1737) was the author of several works chronicling his travels in the Middle East.

63 Voltaire has a very specific target in view in the conclusion of this article. Jean-Jacques Lefranc de Pompignan had been the object of a constant stream of Voltairean satires ever since giving an anti-philosophical speech at the French Academy in 1760.

64 Nicolas-Antoine Boulanger, one of the collaborators on the Encyclopédie, had died in 1759, and a number of radical texts had been attributed to him subsequently.

65 Pierre Bayle (1647–1706) was author of the *Dictionnaire historique et critique (Historical and Critical Dictionary*, 1695–1697), which was one of the principal models for Voltaire's *Dictionary*. Pierre Jurieu (1637–1711), a French Protestant leader, was one of Bayle's most persistent persecutors. Michel Le Tellier (1643–1719) was the confessor of Louis XIV; he was largely responsible for persecution of the Jansenists. All of these individuals have appeared previously in the *Dictionary*, notably in the article "Persecution."

66 Bernard le Bovier de Fontenelle (1657–1757) was the nephew of the great French dramatist, Pierre Corneille. He published the *Histoire des oracles (History of Oracles)*, to which Voltaire refers here, in 1687.

67 As King of the Franks, Clovis won the battle of Tolbiac in the year 496. As recorded by Gregory of Tours, his conversion to Christianity was the result of an oath made during this battle.

68 The idea that creatures from other planets might have a different number of senses than terrestrial beings had inspired Voltaire's philosophical tale, *Micromégas* (1752).

69 Etienne Bonnot de Condillac was the popularizer of Lockean sensationism in France. His *Traité des sensations (Treatise on the Senses)* was published in 1754.

70 The theist is thus devoid of the type of superstition Voltaire discusses in the previous article. The sequence of articles at the end of the *Dictionary* is characterized by a particularly strong sense of logical continuity as the argumentation carries over from one to the next. In this respect, the conclusion of the work is perhaps much more carefully structured than the middle portions.

71 The connections between this article and the *Traité sur la tolérance* (*Treatise on Tolerance*), published in 1763, are evident. As in the longer work, Voltaire here particularly condemns systematic intolerance exercised by the government. In the second section, as in the earlier work, he also argues that Christianity should, by nature, be a particularly tolerant faith.

72 As Voltaire specifies at the end of this text, this article was an addition to the edition of 1769. It responds particularly to the condemnation and torture of the chevalier de La Barre, as discussed in the introduction to this volume.

73 Voltaire maintained a personal correspondence with Catherine the Great of Russia for some fifteen years, beginning in 1763. Under her direction, an important proposal for Russian legal reform was formulated in 1767.

74 Apparently benign by modern standards, this article scandalized Voltaire's critics because it separated virtue from religion. Several of them were particularly offended by the final exclamatory request for more virtuous pagans.

APPENDIX

1 *Note by Chaudon:* The Parisian *Parlement* condemned this book to be burned in its decree of 19 March 1765 (which can be read in its entirety at the end of this preface) as a scandalous satire of Christian mysteries, morals and doctrine, as a thorough course in materialism, and as a collection of blasphemies that for eighteen centuries have been repeated a thousand times by the impious and refuted a thousand times. These illustrious magistrates made an even bolder statement in 1766, when the execution of the Chevalier de La Barre was carried out in Abbeville. They decreed that this sacrilegious work would be burned along with the body of the young criminal it had corrupted. . . .

2 *Editor's note:* In the eighteenth century, paper was made from cotton pulp, derived largely from old rags.